A STUDY IN BOSS POLITICS

TARR, Joel Arthur. **A study in boss politics; William Lorimer of Chicago. Illinois, 1971. 376p il tab bibl 72-133945. 12.50.** SBN 252-00139-7

CHOICE   APR. '72

Political Science

Tarr's study of William Lorimer makes a significant contribution to the growing body of literature on the boss in American politics. Following the trend set by Mandelbaum's *Boss Tweed's New York* (CHOICE, Nov. 1965), Z. L. Miller's *Boss Cox's Cincinnati; urban politics in the Progressive Era* (CHOICE, Feb. 1969), and Dorsett's *The Pendergast machine* (CHOICE, Sept. 1968), Tarr avoids moral judgment in favor of an analysis of Lorimer's role ordering in the chaotic political situation in Chicago. Lorimer's success in politics is traced from his organization of a Republican ward club in 1884 to his expulsion from the U.S. Senate in 1912. In the years between he influenced not only Chicago and Illinois politics but became a force three Presidents had to contend with. The central theme, and most important contribution of the volume, is the analysis of the ethno-cultural basis for the division between machine supporters and urban reformers. Though focused on Lorimer's activities in Chicago, this aspect of the study provides an excellent background for understanding the problems facing the American city at the beginning of the 20th century. A computer analysis of voting and demographic patterns, though limited by availability and reliability of data, tends to substantiate the author's conclusions. Students and teachers of urban politics will find this an interesting and rewarding book.

WILLIAM LORIMER

Courtesy of Felix Kucharski

A STUDY IN
BOSS POLITICS

★ ★ ★ ★ ★ ★ ★ ★ ★ ★ ★

William Lorimer of Chicago

JOEL ARTHUR TARR

University of Illinois Press
URBANA CHICAGO LONDON

To the memory of Arlene
and for our children
   Michael Jay
   Joanna Sue

Table of Contents

★ ★ ★ ★ ★ ★ ★ ★ ★ ★ ★

List of Illustrations

★ ★ ★ ★ ★ ★ ★ ★ ★ ★ ★

BETWEEN PAGES 184 AND 185

Victor Lawson

Herman H. Kohlsaat

Medill McCormick

Robert W. Patterson

Joseph Medill

Traction baron

Charles Tyson Yerkes

Banker John R. Walsh

Preface

CONGRESSMAN WILLIAM LORIMER, the Blond Boss of Chicago, controlled the Republican party in Cook County and the state of Illinois for over a decade at the turn of the century. Himself an English immigrant, his power base was on Chicago's West Side in one of the city's heaviest concentrations of foreign-born residents. The city's reformers considered him a dangerous man, but Lorimer was a hero to many of his constituents. They admired him for his exemplary family life, for his loyalty to friends, and for his reputation for truthfulness. They were grateful for favors given them by Lorimer's machine. They shared his antipathy to the Chicago reform newspapers and delighted in his attacks upon the so-called "trust press."

In 1909 a bipartisan majority of the Illinois General Assembly elected Lorimer to the U.S. Senate. Approximately one year later, the Chicago *Tribune* published the confession of Assemblyman Charles A. White that he had been paid $1,000 for his Lorimer vote. The White confession began a series of events that resulted in Lorimer's ouster from the Senate in 1912, even though two Senate investigations and a 1911 Senate vote upheld his title to his seat. The Lorimer case, which has previously escaped close scrutiny, was one of the most important events splitting the Republican party in the 1910–12 period.

Although this work focuses upon the life of one man, it is intended more as a study of political behavior and of a political system than as a traditional biography. The emergence of a system of boss and machine politics in Chicago, as in other American cities in the late nineteenth century, caused a conflict between professional politicians coming from immigrant backgrounds, like William Lorimer, and elite native-American reformers. These reformers reflected a more "cosmopolitan" attitude toward the city and were influenced by corporate ideas of decision-making, expertise, and efficiency. Professional politicians who controlled political machines that rested upon ward and precinct foundations favored a concept of "personal liberty," allowing autonomy to local areas and to different ethnic and religious elements.

Distrust of the boss and of the immigrant groups from whom he usually derived his power were an important element in the progressive movement of the first part of the twentieth century. These attitudes played a key role in the campaign that eventually ousted William Lorimer from the U.S. Senate.

I began this study of the career of William Lorimer in 1960 at Northwestern University at the suggestion of Professor Arthur S. Link. After Professor Link's departure for Princeton University, Professors Ray Allen Billington and Robert H. Wiebe directed the completion of the dissertation. I have benefited from their continued encouragement and support in regard to its extension and publication.

Many colleagues aided me with criticism and comments. Both Otis L. Graham, Jr., of the University of California at Santa Barbara, and Paul J. Kleppner, of Northern Illinois University, read the entire manuscript at different stages of its preparation and greatly affected its direction. Mark Haller of Temple University, Claude Barfield of Yale University, and Irving Bartlett, Edwin Fenton, Eugene Levy, and Richard Schoenwald of Carnegie-Mellon University read and improved parts of the manuscript. Robert Ciaburri, then of Carnegie-Mellon University, helped with the computer analysis, and a number of student assistants, at both California State College at Long Beach and Carnegie-Mellon University, aided in gathering data. Miss Linda Little did a careful job of typing the final revision.

I am grateful to William T. Hutchinson of the University of Chicago for supplying copies of letters between Lorimer and Frank O. Lowden, to John Braeman of the University of Nebraska for calling my attention to materials in the George W. Perkins Papers, to Jerome Sternstein of Columbia University for supplying me with copies of letters from the Nelson Aldrich Papers, to Wayne C. Temple for providing material from the Illinois State Archives, to Robert A. Waller of the University of Illinois for material on the Lakes-to-the-Gulf Deep Waterway, to John Crane for permitting me access to the Charles R. Crane Papers, and to James S. Copley for permission to use the Ira C. Copley Papers. Mr. Walter L. M. Lorimer of Beverly Hills,

California, supplied valuable information about his family, as did his mother, Mrs. William Healy Lorimer of Chicago. A number of other individuals furnished insights into Chicago and Illinois politics through interviews and letters. The editors of *The Business History Review,* the *Journal of the Illinois State Historical Society,* and *Mid-America* kindly gave me permission to use material from articles I had previously published in their journals. A number of librarians at various institutions were extremely helpful, with special thanks being owed to Archie Motley, manuscript librarian at the Chicago Historical Society, and Margaret A. Flint, of the Illinois State Historical Library. Grants from California State College at Long Beach, the American Philosophical Society, and Carnegie-Mellon University made possible free summers for research and writing and covered most of the cost of preparing the manuscript for publication.

A STUDY IN BOSS POLITICS

CHAPTER **1**

★ ★ ★ ★ ★ ★ ★ ★ ★ ★ ★

The Making of a Political Boss

I T WAS A HOT, humid July day in Washington in the summer of 1912. Throughout the country men spoke of the recent national political conventions and speculated about the impact upon the presidential election of Theodore Roosevelt's bolt from the Republican party and his formation of the Progressive party. But in the Senate chamber a more immediate personal drama was occurring.

For three days a short, stocky, blond-headed man, who looked more like a schoolteacher or a minister than a politician, stamped up and down the chamber's center aisle, defending his right to his Senate seat and casting barbed challenges at his enemies. The man was William Lorimer of Illinois. The charge was that his seat had been purchased. His foes included the nation's most prominent politicians: President William Howard Taft, ex-President Theodore Roosevelt, and Senator Robert M. La Follette.

The final decision was the Senate's. Lorimer expected no mercy, and none was given. "Oh, Senators," he cried, "you may vote to turn me out," but such a decision would be "the crime of the Senate" rather than a judgment based on evidence. "I am ready," said Lorimer. And, while the packed galleries waited breathlessly, the Senate voted 55 to 28 to oust him from his seat.[1]

The Senate ejected Lorimer because a majority of its members believed, or at least voted as if they believed, that his seat had been acquired through corrupt means. In alienating senatorial and public opinion, however, Lorimer's identification as a political "boss" was perhaps as crucial as the specific charges levied against him. In the

[1] *Congressional Record* (hereafter cited as *CR*), 62nd Cong., 2nd Sess., XLVII, 8986.

vocabulary of American political reform a boss was a dictator who represented special and corrupt interests and who violated the rights of "the people." Since the progressive period was an age ostensibly committed to the extension of popular control and of democratic procedures, bosses were especially reprehensible. In addition, the term "boss" conjured up images of saloons and smoky back rooms, of unassimilable immigrants and city slums. The boss and his machine represented the worst aspects of the city to a generation of Americans predisposed to distrust the metropolis.

Lorimer was a boss. He used political power to influence party nominations and legislation. He had, however, neither absolute power nor power divorced from the interests of the voters in his district. Seven terms in Congress testified to his popularity. While Lorimer's organization gave him influence over the choice of Republican candidates for city, county, state, and federal offices, it satisfied more than his own ambitions. The organization was broadly based on a series of ward and precinct clubs and it supplied its members and the voters in Lorimer's district with governmental jobs and services. It represented several different immigrant groups and provided them with a vehicle to achieve political prominence.

Since Lorimer's organization represented a variety of separate interests rather than a single one, his power was never absolute but rested upon a "diffusion of power prerogatives and power exercise." Political scientist Samuel J. Eldersveld notes that a political party is a "reciprocal deference structure" rather than a "precisely ordered system of authority and influence from the top down. . . ." [2] Rapport between the various levels of party leadership and the voters rather than any authoritarian direction binds the organization. Lorimer maintained this rapport over a period of years and satisfied the aspirations of the separate groups that composed his organization. He thus remained in power in spite of reformers' attacks. It is upon William Lorimer—a politician who sprang from the urban masses and maintained his political machine for a decade, who dealt with businessmen and fought with reformers, and who established himself as a force with which three Republican presidents had to reckon—that this study focuses.

---

[2] Samuel J. Eldersveld, *Political Parties: A Behavioral Analysis* (Chicago, 1964), 9–10.

William Lorimer was born in Manchester, England, on April 27, 1861, the son of William Lorimer, Sr., a Scotch Presbyterian minister, and Sarah Harley Lorimer, also of Scottish descent. He was the first of six children, two boys and four girls. In 1865 a depression in Manchester persuaded the Lorimers to emigrate to the United States. They joined millions of other Europeans who had made, and would make, the same decision. The Lorimers first settled in Michigan and then in Ohio, where the elder Lorimer provided for his family by farming on weekdays and preaching on the Sabbath. Young William often accompanied his father on his Sunday church visits, carrying his Bible and hymnal. He later remembered that his father talked about "goodness" and was a "consistent Christian." But the combination of farming and preaching did not bring the expected prosperity, and in 1870 the family, hoping to improve their condition, moved to Chicago.[3]

Chicago in 1870 was a dynamic city. The English traveler George W. Steevens called it a "lodestone," attracting the "enterprise and commercial talent of two hemispheres."[4] Favorably located on the flat prairie land near the southern tip of Lake Michigan, and cut by river and railroad track, Chicago was the Midwest's economic hub. By 1870 it held the nation's leadership in the grain and lumber trades, in livestock processing, and in meat-packing. The Great Fire of 1871 briefly slowed its expansion, but the city rapidly recovered, and its land area increased more than fivefold from 1871 to 1893. During the same period Chicago's manufacturing industries also flourished; by 1890 it held second place in the country in the value of its products.[5]

The lumberyards, stockyards, grain mills, breweries, iron and steel mills, woodworking establishments, and clothing industries that con-

[3] The best source to reconstruct Lorimer's early life is U.S., Senate, *Election of William Lorimer: Hearings before a Committee of the Senate . . . , Senate Doc. 484*, 62nd Cong., 2nd Sess. (9 vols., Washington, 1912), VIII, 7653, 7664–67, hereafter cited as *Dillingham Committee Hearings*. Unless otherwise noted, all citations are to Lorimer's testimony. See also Lorimer's comments in *CR*, 61st Cong., 2nd Sess., XLV, 7064; "Senator Lorimer: A Veritable 'Ragged Dick' Hero," *Current Literature* (July, 1910), XLIX, 33–37; Edward G. Lowry, "Lorimer: The Career and Qualities of the Much-Discussed Junior Senator from Illinois," *Harper's Weekly* (Jan. 7, 1911), LV, 20.

[4] Bessie Louise Pierce, ed., *As Others See Chicago: Impressions of Visitors 1673–1933* (Chicago, 1933), 400.

[5] Bessie Louise Pierce, *A History of Chicago*, Vol. III: *The Rise of a Modern City 1871–1893* (Chicago, 1957), 20–49, 64–191.

stituted the heart of Chicago's economic empire were omnivorous in their demands for labor. Into the city flowed streams of migrants, drawn by hopes of improving their economic status. In 1870 Chicago held approximately 300,000 people, in 1880, 500,000, and in 1890, over a million. Twenty years later, in 1910, it passed the two million mark, a more than sixfold increase in a forty-year period.

Most of Chicago's newcomers were European immigrants. In 1890, 78.5 percent of the city's population was either foreign-born (41 percent) or had foreign-born parents (37.5 percent) of mainly German, Irish, Scandinavian, or English origin. During the 1890–1910 period, Chicago added to its immigrant base, the greatest number of new arrivals coming from eastern, southern, and central Europe. While the Germans still constituted the largest foreign-born group in 1910, their percentage of population had slipped by approximately a third. The Russian group (largely Jews) now occupied second place, followed by Scandinavians, Irishmen, Poles, Italians, and Bohemians.[6]

Immigrants lived in all sections of the city, especially near industry and where land was cheap. Constant change and flux characterized the residential situation, as individuals who improved their economic position moved out of the city's poorer sections and into areas offering better housing and more amenities. In turn, the newest immigrant arrivals took their place in Chicago's slums and tenement-house areas. While slum conditions existed in each geographical subdivision of the city, they were especially prevalent in the wards on Chicago's West Side, in the area adjoining the central business district, and along the banks of the Chicago River and its branches. These were the sections where industry was concentrated, and the availability of jobs and cheap housing attracted large numbers of immigrants.

The West Side presented a range of environments rather than a single homogeneous pattern of living. The most congested wards with inferior housing lay close to the central business district and along the rivers in an area where commercial and industrial needs constantly encroached upon residences. The characteristic Chicago working-

---

6 In 1890 Germans constituted 35.7, Scandinavians, 15.9, Irishmen, 15.5, and Englishmen, 6.3 percent of the Chicagoans who were foreign-born or had foreign-born parents; in 1910 the totals were Germans, 23.3 percent, Russians, 15.7, Scandinavians, 10.7, Irishmen, 8.4, Poles, 6.7, Italians, 5.8, and Bohemians, 4.5. U.S., *Eleventh Census, 1890,* "Population," I, 670–673, and *Thirteenth Census, 1910,* "Population," II, 512–514; Chicago Board of Education, *Annual Report* (Chicago, 1908), 12–19.

man's house was a one- or two-story frame building, sometimes at the rear of a lot and fronting on an alley, and often occupied by several families. Thousands of these frame buildings were erected on the West Side after the fire in 1871 and eventually created some of Chicago's worst housing problems. During the 1880's and 1890's, the Germans and Irishmen who lived in the close-in wards were gradually displaced by Russian Jews, Poles, Bohemians, and other eastern and central European peoples. To the west of the area adjoining the central business district stood Pilsen, a large Bohemian settlement, while to the southwest, at Thirty-ninth and Halsted, was the stockyards area, along with the crowded and largely Irish settlement known as "back of the Yards." The better-built homes of skilled workingmen and the "flats" and brownstone town houses of the largely native-American middle class tended to cluster in the outlying wards and away from industry, while the spacious mansions of the rich centered on Washington and Jackson boulevards.[7]

In the 1880's and 1890's, because of growing industrialization and increasing immigrant population, the West Side lost favor as a middle- and upper-class residential area. It had fewer paved streets, poorer transportation, and less amenities than the rest of the city. Criticism of Chicago slums by housing reformers concentrated on conditions in the near West Side and the river wards. An 1895 report from Hull House, for instance, commented on the near West Side's "filthy and rotten tenements, the dingy courts and tumble-down sheds, the foul stables and dilapidated outhouses, the broken sewer pipes [and] the piles of garbage fairly alive with diseased odors. . . ."[8] And yet, even though the poverty of Chicago's immigrant and working-class areas contrasted with the affluence of the city's elite sections, the immigrants who lived there did not necessarily use the normative terms of the housing reformers to describe their neighborhood. For them the area provided work and livelihood, and a place to raise their families

[7] This description of the West Side is drawn from Pierce, *Chicago*, III, 20–63; Edith Abbott, *The Tenements of Chicago 1908–1935* (Chicago, 1936), 8–33, 77– 106, 130–139, 170–204; Homer Hoyt, *One Hundred Years of Land Values in Chicago* (Chicago, 1933), 95–116, 311–320. Hoyt notes that both "high-class" and "cheap" residential areas in Chicago tended to grow in belts or sectors moving in progression from the downtown areas rather than in a series of concentric circles around the central business district.

[8] Jane Addams, comp., *Hull House Maps and Papers: A Presentation of Nationalities and Wages in a Congested District of Chicago* (New York, 1895), 5; Pierce, *Chicago*, III, 57–62; Hoyt, *One Hundred Years of Land Values in Chicago*, 132–137.

and build their schools and churches. While they planned to and often did move to better sections, their present neighborhoods provided them with the opportunity to make their adjustment to the city.[9]

When the Lorimer family moved to Chicago in 1870, it settled in a West Side "river ward," the Sixth, at North Ashland Avenue and Indiana Street. This choice of residence began a lifelong relationship between William Lorimer and Chicago's West Side. Shortly after the move to Chicago, Lorimer's father died, leaving his widow and six children without income or savings. Young Lorimer, the eldest boy, became family provider, and abandoned any chance to obtain an education.[10] From the ages of approximately ten to twenty-one, he pursued a number of jobs in his attempt to earn a living for his mother and brothers and sisters. For three years he delivered papers in the early morning and shined shoes for the rest of the day, picking up customers from gambling houses, saloons, business offices, and restaurants. Later he worked as a department-store cash boy, as a laundry solicitor, and as a laborer hauling coal. At the age of fifteen, like many other immigrants, he began work in the stockyards, and was employed at different times by the Wilson Packing Company, Nelson Morris & Company, and Armour & Company. In Lorimer's words, he "learned the meat-canning business in all its branches." [11]

In 1880 Lorimer exchanged his packinghouse job for one as a conductor on a Twelfth Street streetcar. A friendly alderman obtained the position for him. As a streetcar worker, Lorimer demonstrated his organizational abilities by forming a local chapter of the Street Railway Employees' Benevolent Association. During his five years on the cars, union members knew him as a firm friend in time of need. Lorimer's work experience on the streetcars, in the packinghouses, and in other West Side businesses gave him an intimate acquaintance with his section's people and industries. This proved extremely useful in later years, when he appealed to West Side voters for support or

9 See the editorial in the Bohemian newspaper *Denni Hlasatel,* May 31, 1902, which complains of the unfairly bleak picture that housing reformers painted of conditions in the immigrant sections. All foreign-language newspapers cited are in the Chicago Foreign Language Press Survey compiled by the Works Projects Administration. Microfilm copies of the translations made by the survey are in the Chicago Public Library. See *The Chicago Foreign Press Survey: A General Description of Its Contents* (Chicago, 1942).

10 Of the twenty bosses examined by Harold Zink in his book on city bosses, ten had lost their fathers when they were children. See Harold Zink, *City Bosses in the United States* (Durham, 1930), 7–8.

11 *Dillingham Committee Hearings,* VIII, 7664.

when he represented local industries, such as the meat-packers, in Congress.[12]

A number of Lorimer's youthful friendships also proved politically helpful. Although Lorimer was the son of a Presbyterian minister, many of his acquaintances were boys of Irish descent. Lorimer established close relations with the Irish community; he eventually married an Irish Catholic girl and converted to Roman Catholicism. Among his close early friends were "Hinky Dink" Kenna and "Bathhouse" John Coughlin, both First Ward aldermen for many years, and John R. Walsh, who became, through Lorimer's help, the city's leading political banker. Some of these friends belonged to a gang led by Lorimer, and it can be surmised that this formed an early training ground for machine politics.[13] On his trips downtown Lorimer often visited the travel agency of Andrew J. Graham, later a banker and an important Democratic politician. One of Lorimer's daughters would marry his son. And, while working in the stockyards, Lorimer lived in the home of two of his future political and business lieutenants, John and "Billy" Cooke. A network developed that was of significance for Chicago political history. In the words of one writer, Lorimer was "of the very soil of the city . . . a boy among boys who formed early and enduring friendships, expressed in joint business ventures and political schemes." [14]

According to Lorimer's recollection, he initially became interested in politics during the election of 1884, the first in which he could vote. As the son of a Scotch Presbyterian, he naturally became a Republican and a strong devotee of James G. Blaine, the "Plumed Knight" of that party. The election was a heated one. Both Democrats and Republicans held their conventions in Chicago, and the excitement generated there continued throughout the campaign. The Democrats

12 *Ibid.*, 7646, 7648, 7664.

13 In his work on Chicago gangs, Frederic Thrasher notes that the "political boss has usually received valuable training for politics in a street gang from which he has ultimately been graduated. . . ." The gang, like the political machine, had a hierarchical organization and its members were connected by mutual obligations. Frederic M. Thrasher, *The Gang* (Phoenix abr. ed., Chicago, 1963), 313, 320–322; William F. Whyte, *Street Corner Society* (Chicago, 1943), 12, 203–207; Lloyd Wendt and Herman Kogan, *Lords of the Levee: The Story of Bathhouse John and Hinky Dink* (New York, 1943), 15.

14 Lloyd Lewis and Henry J. Smith, *Chicago: The History of Its Reputation* (New York, 1929), 355; Chicago *Daily Tribune* (hereafter cited as *Tribune*), Feb. 27, 1902, May 3, 1918, Mar. 15, June 22, 1919; Chicago *Record-Herald* (hereafter cited as *Record-Herald*), May 27, 1909.

nominated the stolid New York governor, Grover Cleveland, while Lorimer's hero, Blaine, was the Republican candidate.[15]

An incident during the 1884 election convinced Lorimer to pursue politics as a full-time vocation rather than as an occasional activity. On election day he discovered that there was no one at the polls to supply him with a Republican ballot. Finding a Republican "ticket-peddler" at a polling place several blocks distant, he grasped a handful of ballots and returned to cast his own vote. He then distributed the extra ballots to other Republicans.[16]

Blaine carried Chicago in 1884, but he lost the election by a narrow margin. Lorimer thought that there was no man "more downcast, sorrowful, and dejected" at Blaine's defeat than he. But more significant than this disappointment was Lorimer's conviction that a lack of "perfect organization" had caused Blaine's defeat. "I determined," Lorimer later said, "that the precinct in which I lived should ever afterwards be organized and the party's interests cared for at the polling place in all future elections." [17]

That winter Lorimer organized a Republican club in his precinct. The club, composed largely of Lorimer's neighborhood friends, met first in his mother's kitchen. Its members were not Republicans; there were few Republicans in the Sixth Ward. They were Democrats "who had never affiliated with their party, but who thought they were Democrats because their good fathers were Democrats." [18] Lorimer probably explained to his friends the benefits in the form of political patronage and jobs that could be obtained from the Republican county leadership if the club became successful.

From this time forward politics became for Lorimer a full-time enterprise with commensurate economic rewards, not the voluntary giving of a few hours of conscientious party effort at election time. Lorimer's politicization had not derived from devotion to pure Republicanism; it grew out of expectation of material return. Lorimer's attitude was not unusual. The typical urban political boss or machine politician regarded politics as a business and used his power for per-

[15] Allan Nevins, *Grover Cleveland: A Study in Courage* (New York, 1932), 156–182.

[16] *Dillingham Committee Hearings*, VIII, 7851; *CR*, 61st Cong., 2nd Sess., XLV, 7064. Before the introduction of the Australian ballot, ballots were furnished by each party at the polls.

[17] *Ibid.*

[18] *CR*, 61st Cong., 2nd Sess., XLV, 7064, 61st Cong., 3rd Sess., XLVI, 3123.

sonal gain. He was a businessman who had as his chief stock in trade the goods of the political world—votes, influence, laws, and government grants—which he utilized to make a private profit. In short, he was a "political entrepreneur." As boss Richard Crocker of Tammany Hall admitted, "Like a businessman in business, I work for my own pocket all the time." [19]

This attitude toward politics stemmed to a large extent from the lower-class immigrant backgrounds of most machine politicians. Harold Zink's study of twenty bosses reveals that fifteen were raised in the city slums; fifteen also were either first- or second-generation immigrants. The studies of Sonya Forthal and Harold Gosnell show a similar type of background for Chicago precinct captains. The lower-class immigrant who entered politics could not afford an ideologically pure orientation. "Ideals" were the luxury of the well-to-do. The immigrant needed a material return.[20]

Politics furnished a ladder of mobility, a vehicle of self-advancement for the immigrant at a time when other doors to success were closed to him. In politics an ethnic background often became an asset, as support came from national loyalty and rising group self-consciousness. Thus, *Dziennik Zwiazkowy Zgoda* could appeal for the election of Polish candidates because "duty and national feeling impel us to do so," while the *Jewish Daily Courier* intoned that on "every Jew, lies the duty of electing a Jew. . . ." Any number of urban politicians rose to positions of status and power as their ethnic groups came to dominate the city.[21]

The politicians par excellence of the American city were the Irish, with whom Lorimer had close connections. A number of factors account for Irish success in capturing urban politics. They had a knowledge of the English language and a familiarity with Anglo-American

[19] Lincoln Steffens, *Autobiography* (New York, 1931), 238; Edward C. Banfield and James Q. Wilson, *City Politics* (Cambridge, 1963), 115–116; Joel A. Tarr, "The Urban Politician as Entrepreneur," *Mid-America* (Jan., 1967), XLIX, 55–67.

[20] Zink, *City Bosses*, 3–12; Harold F. Gosnell, *Machine Politics: Chicago Model* (Chicago, 1937), 51–68; Sonya Forthal, "Six Hundred Precinct Captains in the Chicago Party System 1926–1928" (unpublished Ph.D. dissertation, American University, 1938), 89–114; Oscar Handlin, *The Uprooted* (New York, 1951), 201–226.

[21] *Dziennik Zwiazkowy Zgoda*, Sept. 10, 1910; *Jewish Daily Courier*, Apr. 3, 1910. For discussions of how politics served as a vehicle of social mobility for ethnic minorities see Robert K. Merton, *Social Theory and Social Structure* (rev. ed., Glencoe, 1957), 71–72; Eric L. McKitrick, "The Study of Corruption," *Political Science Quarterly* (Dec., 1957), LXXII, 505–506. A penetrating study of how "crime" served a similar function is Daniel Bell, "Crime as an American Way of Life," in *The End of Ideology* (rev. ed., New York, 1961), 127–150.

culture, as well as a tight-knit family and neighborhood structure which provided a ready-made base for their organizations. And, unlike the native-American reformer, they understood that the immigrant voter was interested in a positive return for his vote, not abstractions about government.[22]

While Lorimer shared many Irish traits and attitudes, he was still not an Irishman. He was Scottish, a background which often proved beneficial. For while he spoke English and understood the Anglo-American culture, he did not rouse the animosity of other nationalities as the Irish did. As Germans and Bohemians, for instance, came into political consciousness, they resented the Irish political monopoly. *Die Abendpost* called on German voters to "emancipate themselves from their Irish bosses," while the Bohemians "reserved their bitterest contempt and hatred" for the Irish.[23] Lorimer carefully avoided stirring up ethnic animosity. When he moved into a ward of a different composition, or when the makeup of his district shifted, he gave recognition to the leading ethnic groups. Bohemian, Jewish, Polish, and German names, as well as Irish, appeared on the various "Lorimer" tickets. Lorimer communicated across ethnic barriers.

Most lower-class immigrants shared the Irish vocational attitude toward politics. "Politics," said *Die Abendpost,* "is a business which must be learned and mastered." Government was useless unless it furnished material aid. As Herbert Gans notes in his study of the Italian community in Boston's West End, "West Enders think of government primarily as an agency that should be an arm of the peer group society to satisfy their needs." [24] The same might be said of the ethnic groups in Lorimer's West Side district. They wanted personalized services and they wanted political recognition. As Lorimer rose to power and influence, he supplied these wants in increasing quantities.

The composition of Chicago's population and the immigrant's attitude toward government, then, explain much of Lorimer's political success. Immigrants generally settled in wards where they found other

[22] William V. Shannon, *The American Irish* (New York, 1963), 60–67; Edward M. Levine, *The Irish and Irish Politicians* (Notre Dame, 1966), 112–117.

[23] *Die Abendpost,* Jan. 21, 1895; *Denni Hlasatel,* Apr. 3, 1914; Alex Gottfried, *Boss Cermak of Chicago* (Seattle, 1962), 38, 40. The concept of "negative reference groups" is useful in understanding animosity between immigrant groups. See Merton, *Social Theory and Social Structure,* 225–386.

[24] *Die Abendpost,* Feb. 15, 1896; Herbert J. Gans, *The Urban Villagers* (Glencoe, 1962), 164.

people of their own nationality, language, and customs. A self-imposed "ghettoization" occurred, creating problems of acculturation, assimilation, and, above all, communication. In addition, immigrants were often desperately poor and unaccustomed to the workings of an impersonal capitalistic system. They frequently needed material help: access to jobs, a bucket of coal in winter, and food when cash was short. Machine politicians like Lorimer mediated between the immigrants and their new environment and aided them in times of need.[25] The politician from immigrant areas fulfilled the role of "ambassador to the outside world" for his constituency. He secured government favors for his voters, made government personally relevant to them, and represented "their point of view in the legislative and executive chambers." Simultaneously, he avoided imposing outside standards on the immigrants in the way that social workers, teachers, and native reform politicians often tried to do.[26]

Lorimer fulfilled the role of mediator for a number of separate ethnic groups in the West Side. Such was his relationship, for instance, with the Russian Jews who crowded into Chicago's Seventh, Eighth and Nineteenth wards in the late 1880's and 1890's. In the four years from 1888 to 1892, the percentage of registered voters in the wards who were Russians increased from 5 to 20 percent.[27] They constituted an opportunity for an aspiring politician such as Lorimer.

The newly arrived Russsian Jews were constantly harassed. "Street thugs" stoned them and pulled their beards. When the Jews attempted to vote, Lorimer noted, "they were insulted, abused, assaulted, and knocked down . . . [and] driven from the polls." [28] Lorimer did not share this common anti-Jewish feeling. As a young paper boy he had often lit Sabbath fires for the Orthodox Jews on his route. Later, when he worked on the streetcars, he was one of the few conductors who let Jewish peddlers carry their large bundles on the cars. When he discovered that prejudice extended into politics, Lorimer organized the

---

[25] Banfield and Wilson, *City Politics*, 117–125; Handlin, *The Uprooted*, 212–213; Elmer E. Cornwell, Jr., "Bosses, Machines and Ethnic Groups," *Annals of the American Academy of Political and Social Science* (May, 1964), CCCLIII, 27–31.

[26] The concept of "ambassador to the outside world" is that of Gans, *Urban Villagers*, 142–162, 170–177.

[27] Ward breakdowns of Chicago's registered voters in 1888 and 1892 by ethnic group are in *Daily News Almanac and Political Register for 1889*, 158, and *for 1894*, 318.

[28] *CR*, 61st Cong., 3rd Sess., XLVI, 3122.

Jewish precincts and offered the Jews protection at the polls. He even formed a Hebrew Republican club, and through its work added control of the Seventh Ward to the Sixth.[29]

But Lorimer's role as mediator between the unfamiliar environment and the immigrant Jew was not confined to election time. He acted as their advisor on many matters. "It got so," he later recollected, "they came to my home at night and talked over their little troubles . . . I helped them always." One of the problems faced by the newly arrived immigrants was their lack of cash to secure peddlers' licenses: Lorimer secured temporary permits by the hundreds. When Lorimer received patronage from the city, county, and state governments, Seventh Ward residents got positions. It was no wonder that he boasted that "no man can go among those people . . . as my enemy and live politically."[30]

Lorimer's personal qualities, as well as the services he performed, added to his popularity. Some of his characteristics were not those that one would expect from a successful politician. He was not a dynamic man. Unassuming in appearance, except for his reddish-blond hair and bushy moustache, he was somewhat small and heavy. Generally, he kept quiet until asked his opinion. "I think there is a time and a place to talk," said Lorimer; "that has been my policy all my life."[31]

Many of Lorimer's characteristics struck observers as "moralistic," and this helped in building his following. Possibly as a result of his father's influence, he neither drank nor smoked and dressed conservatively. Lorimer was a devoted family man, a trait common among political bosses, and he found his pleasures in the home. "I don't go to theatres and I don't go out to dinners, with anybody," he once said. He eventually sired eight children, two boys and six girls, all of whom were raised as Catholics.[32]

Perhaps Lorimer's reputation for keeping his word was the most important personal trait related to his political success. Politicians

---

[29] *Ibid.;* Louis Wirth, *The Ghetto* (Phoenix ed., Chicago, 1956), 180–181.

[30] *CR,* 61st Cong., 3rd Sess., XLVI, 3122; *Dillingham Committee Hearings,* VI, 6068–69 (Emanuel M. Abrahams testifying), VIII, 7607.

[31] See *Tribune,* May 4, 1916, for a summary of Lorimer's personal philosophy.

[32] For Lorimer's personal qualities see "Senator Lorimer: A . . . Hero," 33–37; Lowry, "Lorimer," 20; C. S. Raymond, "The Lorimer Scandal: Turning on the Light in Illinois," *The American Magazine* (Sept., 1910), LXX, 571–584. Raymond, a *Tribune* reporter, noted that "Sunday-school superintendents might—and sometimes do—point to his [Lorimer's] life as one to shed a peaceful and beneficent light over the young aspirations of their charges."

mentioned this quality repeatedly in explaining their devotion to him.[33] Thus, among his followers and his constituents, Lorimer built a reputation for trustworthiness. Since a "rapport system" between party elite and cadres is necessary for a functioning organization, trust in leadership is important, and especially so in ward politics, where most of the relationships consisted of face-to-face contacts and personal obligations. Once a politician lost his reputation for fidelity, his fortunes rapidly declined.[34]

The qualities of personal morality, devotion to family, and trustworthiness were admired in the immigrant communities. In his study of Irish politicians, Edward M. Levine notes that these were the standards by which Irish voters judged their politicians.[35] The same factors were important in the Bohemian, Jewish, Italian, and Polish groups. Lorimer always followed a strict code in regard to his personal relationships. His attitude toward the external world of government, however, varied from his standard of personal conduct. Government was meant to be exploited, to be used to advance the individual and the group. Moralistic standards did not apply. Thus Lorimer, like many other politicians and businessmen, maintained a "segmented morality that divided a man's life into compartments and judged each part by a separate standard." [36]

The combination of the needs of Chicago's large immigrant population and Lorimer's politically appealing personal qualities contributed to his political rise. The peculiar nature of Chicago's governmental structure also facilitated the development of a system of boss and machine politics. The Chicago metropolitan area contained hundreds of governmental bodies, each with a measure of legal authority, but none having enough of it to pursue a course which the others opposed. In 1890 the city had eleven major governments, each with independent taxing powers and their own set of officers and regulations, plus many minor governments. During the 1887–93 period, Chicago annexed a number of surrounding towns, increasing its area from 35 to 185 square miles and requiring a redistricting of ward and legislative

[33] See testimony in *Dillingham Committee Hearings,* speeches made in the Illinois General Assembly upon Lorimer's Senate election, cited in *Tribune,* May 27, 1909, and Harry B. Ward to Frank O. Lowden, Sept. 6, 1909, Frank O. Lowden Papers, University of Chicago.

[34] Eldersveld, *Political Parties,* 10; Whyte, *Street Corner Society,* 240–245.

[35] Levine, *The Irish,* 152–153.

[36] Robert H. Wiebe, *The Search for Order 1877–1920* (New York, 1967), 40; Gans, *Urban Villagers,* 175–177; Gottfried, *Cermak,* 32–47.

district boundaries, extension of city services, and adjustment of taxation.[37]

Among Chicago's most bothersome problems was the city's lack of home rule in regard to certain types of franchises and appointments, the absence of a municipal court, and overlapping city, county, and township taxation jurisdictions. The state held some of these powers and a constant struggle existed between the municipality and the state government for control over city affairs. But taxation remained the most vexing problem, since Chicago did not have the right to tax its own property or to collect its own funds except by special assessment. The townships assessed and taxed property and then surrendered the money to the county. The city depended upon the county for funds for its everyday needs. Even after the townships were abolished in 1899, the county retained direct control over city funds through two boards of review and assessment.[38]

The situation could have been simplified if city and county had been controlled by the same political party, but this did not often happen. From 1879 to 1915 the Democrats elected thirteen Chicago mayors, the Republicans only four. At the same time, the Republicans often controlled the county government when the Democrats controlled the city, and they used their power over taxation to harass the municipal offices.

Even the process of elections was confusing. In a given four-year period Chicago citizens voted for more than a hundred different local offices, ranging from constable and alderman to city mayor, county officials, sanitary board officers, and circuit, superior, and county judges. Ballots were long and elections were constant. Half of the city council was elected each spring, municipal officials in the spring of odd-numbered years, some county and state officials and legislators in the fall of even-numbered years, and other state officials every fourth year with national office-holders. Understanding the operation of government required a person's full-time attention.

[37] Edward C. Banfield, *Political Influence* (New York, 1961), 235; Pierce, *Chicago*, III, 331–339; Charles E. Merriam, *Chicago: A More Intimate View of Urban Politics* (New York, 1929), 90–91; Samuel Edwin Sparling, *Municipal History and Present Organization of the City of Chicago* (Madison, 1898), 158–159.

[38] Ellen J. Beckman, "The Relationship of the Government of the City of Chicago to Cook County from 1893 to 1916" (unpublished M.A. thesis, University of Chicago, 1940), 6–24; William Booth Philip, "Chicago and the Down State: A Study of Their Conflicts, 1870–1934" (unpublished Ph.D. dissertation, University of Chicago, 1940); Merriam, *Chicago*, 90–92.

The chaotic nature of Chicago government created problems not only for the voters but also for businessmen interested in expanding their operations. The confusion produced by overlapping city, county, and state jurisdictions, the lack of a central decision-making body, and the inexperience of government in dealing with urban conditions produced frustration among businessmen.[39] They discovered that when they wanted something from the city, e.g., a franchise or a license, they often had to deal with a panoply of agencies, any of which might block their request or demand payment for passing it on to the next authority. The situation desperately called for some central decision-making body or person.

Theoretically the political parties could overcome the disorganization of urban and metropolitan government and furnish some sort of centralization. But neither of the major parties, Democrat or Republican, was unified. Each party resembled a "conflict system," with various subgroups vying for power and recognition.[40] In addition, Chicago's variegated social and economic composition prevented either party from attracting a large enough clientele to sweep both city and county governments.

The major factors determining the nature of each party's following were ethnicity, religion, and socioeconomic class. In their treatment of these elements, however, historians have often combined the effect of immigrant derivation and religion, and then overemphasized the role of class. They portray the Democratic party in the cities as the party of immigrant working strata, and the Republican party as that of middle- and upper-class native Americans. Recent research has shown, however, that no party had a monopoly on the immigrant or native vote, and that ethnocultural factors were as important, if not more important, than class in deciding party preference.[41] Each party

[39] Richard Hofstadter, *The Age of Reform from Bryan to F.D.R.* (New York, 1955), 174–175; Forrest McDonald, *Insull* (Chicago, 1962), 82–89.

[40] Merriam, *Chicago*, 94–100; Eldersveld, *Political Parties*, 6–8.

[41] For elaboration of this point see the following studies: Lee Benson, *The Concept of Jacksonian Democracy: New York as a Test Case* (Atheneum ed., New York, 1964), 123–207; Gerhard Lenski, *The Religious Factor: A Sociologist's Inquiry* (Anchor ed., Garden City, 1962); Lawrence H. Fuchs, ed., *American Ethnic Politics* (New York, 1968); Paul J. Kleppner, "The Politics of Change in the Midwest: The 1890's in Historical and Behavioral Perspective" (unpublished Ph.D. dissertation, University of Pittsburgh, 1967), now published as *The Cross of Culture: A Social Analysis of Midwestern Politics, 1850–1900* (New York, 1970) (footnote references are to the Kleppner dissertation); Kleppner, "Lincoln and the Immigrant Vote: A Case of Religious Polarization," *Mid-America* (July, 1966),

therefore served as a vehicle for the cultural values of different ethnic and religious groups.

While ethnicity or national identity is a crucial element in understanding group voting behavior, it fails to explain why members of differing ethnic groups, such as the Irishmen and the Poles, usually voted in the same manner, or why members of other groups, such as the Swedes and the Bohemians, usually voted differently.[42] The crucial modifier in the voting pattern of immigrants as well as native Americans was the religious factor. Many nineteenth-century observers noted the pervasive influence of religion in American society. Studies by historians, political scientists, and sociologists have demonstrated that this influence extended to politics. The most significant religious question that affected politics concerned the split between revivalists or pietists and anti-revivalists or ritualists.[43] The ritualistic outlook emphasized the institutionalized formalities and historical teachings of the established Calvinist, Catholic, Lutheran, and Anglican churches of Europe. Salvation depended upon obedience to their

XLVIII, 176–195; Kleppner, "The Political Revolution of the 1890's: A Behavioral Interpretation" (unpublished paper, 1968 Midwest Political Science Association Convention); Richard Jensen, "The Winning of the Midwest: A Social History of Midwestern Elections, 1888–1896" (unpublished Ph.D. dissertation, Yale University, 1967), to be published as *The Winning of the Midwest: 1888–1896* (Chicago, 1971); Jensen, "The Historical Roots of Party Identification" (unpublished paper, 1969 American Political Science Association Convention); Ronald Formisano, "The Social Bases of American Voting Behavior, Wayne County, Michigan, 1837–1852, as a Test Case" (unpublished Ph.D. dissertation, Wayne State University, 1966); Formisano, "Analyzing American Voting, 1830–1860: Methods," *Historical Methods Newsletter* (Mar., 1969), II, 2–11; Samuel T. McSeveney, "The Politics of Depression: Voting Behavior in Connecticut, New York, and New Jersey, 1893–1896" (unpublished Ph.D. dissertation, University of Iowa, 1965); McSeveney, "The Political Realignment of the 1890's: Observations on the Northeast" (unpublished paper, American Political Behavior Conference, State University of New York at Cortland, 1968); John M. Allswang, "The Political Behavior of Chicago's Ethnic Groups, 1918–1932" (unpublished Ph.D. dissertation, University of Pittsburgh, 1967), now published as *A House for All Peoples: Ethnic Politics in Chicago, 1890–1936* (Lexington, 1971); Samuel P. Hays, "The Social Analysis of American Political History, 1880–1920," *Political Science Quarterly* (Sept., 1965), LXXX, 373–394; Walter Dean Burnham, "The Changing Shape of the American Political Universe," *American Political Science Review* (Mar., 1965), LIX, 7–28; Raymond E. Wolfinger, "The Development and Persistence of Ethnic Voting," *ibid.* (Dec., 1965), LIX, 896–908; Scott Greer, "Catholic Voters and the Democratic Party," *Public Opinion Quarterly* (Winter, 1961), XXV, 611–625.

[42] Kleppner, "Politics of Change in the Midwest," 56–105; Benson, *Concept of Jacksonian Democracy,* 165–207.

[43] See Winthrop S. Hudson, *Religion in America* (New York, 1965); Timothy L. Smith, *Revivalism & Social Reform: American Protestantism on the Eve of the Civil War* (New York, 1957).

doctrine, liturgy, sacraments, and hierarchy. By contrast, the pietists rejected liturgicalism and ritual and insisted that men could be saved by confronting Christ through the experience of conversion.[44]

Conflicts between ritualists and pietists shattered every major denomination in the nineteenth century, as a tide of evangelical religion swept through American and European Protestant churches. By the 1860's most Congregationalists, Disciples of Christ, Methodists, Quakers, and Unitarians were pietistic, while Catholics, Episcopalians, and Mormons remained ritualistic. Presbyterians and Baptists were split between pietists and ritualists. Lutherans divided into ritualists (especially the midwestern Missouri Synod Germans), pietists (the Scandinavians and native Americans), and a middle-of-the-road group of mixed membership.[45]

Linking religion and politics was the pietists' demand that government advance the cause of Christianity by opposing "sinful" institutions such as slavery and the saloon, and by halting the flow of "pernicious" Catholic immigrants. The evangelical Protestant sought "to use the secular power of the state to transform culture so that the community of the faithful might be kept pure and the work of saving the unregenerate might be made easier." [46] Ritualists, on the other hand, opposed the intrusion of the state into areas of morality, insisting that the realm of morality belonged to the church. "It is the duty of the secular government to prevent vice with lawful means," resolved the Missouri Synod, "but it is the duty of the church to save men by faith in Christ from committing sin." [47] Ritualists opposed the attempts of the pietists to use the state to forward their moralistic crusades. The struggle that had begun in the churches thus intruded into politics, and the issues that split the parties in the 1850's, anti-slavery, anti-liquor, and nativism, also divided pietistic and ritualistic groups.[48]

One scholar has hypothesized that when party lines re-formed after

[44] Jensen, "Historical Roots of Party Identification," 6–7. Jensen uses a "liturgical" rather than a ritualistic outlook.

[45] *Ibid.*, 7–8; Hudson, *Religion in America,* 131–203.

[46] Jensen, "Historical Roots of Party Identification," 8; Kleppner, "Politics of Change in the Midwest," 112–115; James H. Timberlake, *Prohibition and the Progressive Movement 1900–1920* (Cambridge, 1963), 5, 7.

[47] *Illinois Staats-Zeitung,* June 21, 1888.

[48] Jensen, "Historical Roots of Party Identification," 8; Joel Silbey, *The Transformation of American Politics, 1840–1860* (Englewood Cliffs, 1967), 28–34; Clifford S. Griffin, *Their Brothers' Keepers: Moral Stewardship in the United States, 1800–1865* (New Brunswick, 1960); Smith, *Revivalism & Social Reform.*

the Civil War, the large majority of midwestern pietists became Republicans while the ritualists became Democrats. This division remained until at least the 1890's, as cultural issues such as prohibition, Sunday blue laws, and the teaching of foreign languages in the schools continued to divide the parties.[49] New immigrants to this country often made their party choices according to their religious orientation, with most Catholics joining the Democratic party and a majority of Protestants the Republican party. The Catholic Democrats included Germans, Irishmen, Poles, Bohemians, and French Canadians, while Scandinavians, Englishmen, Northern Irishmen, and English Canadians fell into the Protestant Republican group. The leading exception among the Protestants were the German Lutherans of the Missouri Synod, who were ritualistic and who split between the two parties, but who moved into the Democratic party whenever temperance became an issue.[50] While there were sharp conflicts between the differing ethnic groups that adhered to one party or the other,

[49] Jensen, "Historical Roots of Party Identification," 9.

[50] *Ibid.*, 3–16; Kleppner, "Politics of Change in the Midwest," 56–105; Benson, *Concept of Jacksonian Democracy,* 165–207. The following chart was designed by Kleppner ("Politics of Change in the Midwest") to illustrate the *relative* allegiance of religious groups to the two parties.

ESTIMATED PARTY PERCENTAGES, ETHNOCULTURAL GROUPS

	"IMMIGRANTS" Dem. %	Rep. %		"NATIVES" Dem. %	Rep. %
Irish Catholics	95.0	5.0	Free Will Baptists	5.0	95.0
Polish Catholics	95.0	5.0	NY Methodists	10.0	90.0
German Catholics	85.0	15.0	Congregationalists	10.0	90.0
Dutch Catholics	85.0	15.0	Quakers	15.0	85.0
Bohemian Catholics	80.0	20.0	Presbyterians	30.0	70.0
French Canadians	75.0	25.0	NY Baptists	45.0	55.0
Old French	70.0	30.0			
German Lutherans	55.0	45.0			
German Reformed	55.0	45.0			
Danish Lutherans	45.0	55.0	Southern Presbyterians	55.0	45.0
Dutch True Reformed	45.0	55.0	Southern Baptists	60.0	40.0
German Sectarians	35.0	65.0	Disciples	60.0	40.0
Dutch Reformed	30.0	70.0			
Norwegian Lutherans	30.0	70.0			
Cornish Methodists	25.0	75.0			
English Canadians	15.0	85.0			
Swedish Lutherans	10.0	90.0			
Irish Protestants	5.0	95.0			
Welsh Methodists	5.0	95.0			
Haugean Norwegians	5.0	95.0			

Jewish voting was relatively unimportant until the large eastern European migrations that began after 1880. The literature suggests that German Jews, who made up the bulk of the Jewish community before 1880, bore some similarity in their religious beliefs or perspectives (American Reform Judaism) to native-American

these differences were overshadowed by a common religious perspective that produced a common political allegiance.

In Chicago, as in other parts of the Midwest, political preference followed ethnocultural lines, as the two parties cast, respectively, pietistic and ritualistic images. For many ritualistic immigrants, the local Republican party represented the anti-immigrant "know-nothings," desiring to close parks and saloons on Sunday, prevent gambling, and keep immigrants from the public payrolls. They remembered that Mayor Joseph Medill had enforced the Sunday closing law in 1873, that the "Law and Order League," formed to back Medill's order, had shut the famous Exposition Hall on the Sabbath, and that in 1889 the Republicans enacted the Edwards School Law, providing for the compulsory use of English in public and private schools.[51] These were typical evangelical Protestant measures. They combined a desire to restrain evil with the need "to educate and uplift." Ritualists, with a more lenient and forgiving attitude "in matters of private morality," rejected such enactments along with their sponsor, the Republican party, because they found the Democratic party more in accord with their beliefs.

The local Democratic party projected an image appealing to ritualistic groups.[52] Generally it favored a "wide-open" town, allowing saloons and parks to remain open on Sunday, tolerating pros-

Protestants of the upper and upper-middle classes. While many of the Russian Jewish immigrants of the late nineteenth century were Socialists, the majority seem to have had voting habits similar to those of ritualistic immigrants. See Nathan Glazer, *American Judaism* (Chicago, 1957), 22–78; Moses Rischin, *The Promised City: New York's Jews, 1870–1914* (Cambridge, 1962), 221–235; Charles S. Bernheimer, ed., *The Russian Jew in the United States* (Philadelphia, 1905), 273, 278.

Although the Irish emigration was divided between Catholic Irish and Protestant Irish, it was not possible to separate the two for Chicago. Scholars who have studied the question of the Irish emigration suggest that while many Protestant Irish came to the United States before 1831, the overwhelming number of Irish who came after that date were Roman Catholic. See William Forbes Adams, *Ireland and Irish Emigration to the New World from 1815 to the Famine* (New Haven, 1932), 190–191, 222–223, 396; Arnold Schrier, *Ireland and the American Emigration 1850–1900* (Minneapolis, 1958), 4–5; Gerald Shaughnessy, *Has the Immigrant Kept the Faith?* (New York, 1969), 108–111, 169. Negro voting in the late nineteenth and early twentieth centuries was overwhelmingly Republican. See, for instance, Allan H. Spear, *Black Chicago: The Making of a Negro Ghetto 1890–1920* (Chicago, 1967), 118–126.

[51] Pierce, *Chicago*, III, 341, 343, 367–369; *Svornost,* Sept. 17, 1884, June 22, 1892; *Die Abendpost,* Feb. 23, Sept. 26, 1892.

[52] Russian Jews were also more attracted to the local Democratic party than the Republican. "The Russian Jews," says one source, "are for personal liberty in the fullest sense of the word. Believing that the Democratic party can be more trusted in safeguarding the personal liberty of the people, and fearing a revival of

titution, and permitting the use of foreign languages in parochial schools. From 1879 to 1893, the flamboyant and charismatic Democratic leader, Carter H. Harrison ("our Carter"), held the mayoralty five times. An aristocratic ex-Confederate renowned for his white horse and black slouch hat, he shrewdly identified himself as of Irish, German, and Swedish descent. When he spoke to Chicago's large German population he addressed them in their native tongue. And, most important, he ran a wide-open town; he accepted drinking, gambling, and prostitution as ancient, ineradicable sins.[53]

Thus the Democratic party won the allegiance of ritualistic religious groups. The *Illinois Staats-Zeitung,* for instance, appealed to its readers to vote Democratic—for "those candidates who have inscribed true liberty upon their banners. Show the narrow-minded Puritans that you are in earnest in the question of personal liberty." [54] The ritualistic-minded Bohemian *Svornost* editorialized that "we are convinced that the Republican party is taking pains, with every effort, to yoke us under tyrannic laws, originated by the fanatic Puritans a century ago. . . . We ourselves denounce with fullest determination any law that limits personal liberty." [55] And *Die Abendpost* noted "that though the Democrats have their faults and are not all angels, they at least are no fanatics, hating foreigners. . . ." [56]

The religious and ethnic factors that largely influenced whether a man voted Democratic or Republican complicated life for an aspiring Republican politician such as Lorimer, for the West Side areas in which he attempted to build his organization were largely ritualistic Irish and German. New immigrant groups, such as the Bohemians and Poles, were also ritualistic, and generally voted Democratic. And yet, because of the elements mentioned earlier, Lorimer overcame some of the cultural factors that helped determine a man's political preference. Although he was the son of a Presbyterian minister, he had an Irish Catholic wife. Among his friends and political as-

---

the Blue Laws in Chicago, they generally vote the Democratic ticket." See Bernheimer, ed., *The Russian Jew in the United States,* 278.

[53] Claudius O. Johnson, *Carter Henry Harrison I: Political Leader* (Chicago, 1928), 185–199; Lewis and Smith, *Chicago,* 158–159; Carter H. Harrison, *Stormy Years: The Autobiography of Carter H. Harrison, Five Times Mayor of Chicago* (Indianapolis, 1935), 36–37.

[54] Quoted in Andrew J. Townsend, *The Germans of Chicago* (Chicago, 1927), 60; *Die Abendpost,* Feb. 23, Sept. 26, 1892.

[55] *Svornost,* Sept. 17, 1884, June 22, 1892.

[56] *Die Abendpost,* Sept. 26, 1892.

sociates he numbered Irishmen, Germans, Poles, Bohemians, and Russian Jews. He did not drink or smoke, but he did not attempt to impose his morality on others. Lorimer did not discuss divisive cultural questions; almost the sole topic of his speeches was the bland argument for the necessity of organizing politically. Unlike most members of evangelical Protestant religious groups, Lorimer did not regard politics as a forum for moral questions.

With these elements in his favor, Lorimer advanced quickly within the West Side Republican ranks. In 1885 local party members elected him Republican county committeeman from the largely Irish and German Sixth Ward. In 1886 he allied with the George R. Davis–George B. Swift "machine," and helped nominate Davis for county treasurer. In 1887 he supported the Davis-Swift candidate for mayor, John A. Roche. Roche won and appointed Lorimer assistant superintendent of the Department of Water-Main Extension. Lorimer used his office's patronage to strengthen his organization. Thus, in 1888, when he moved to the Seventh Ward, he became its county committeeman while continuing to control the party structure in the Sixth. Lorimer was becoming a power on the West Side.[57]

Yet how far could Lorimer, the immigrant ex-stockyards worker, the ex-streetcar conductor, who was married to an Irish Catholic wife, and who had his political base on the largely Democratic West Side, expect to rise in the Republican party—a party catering to pietistic Protestant voters that was led by men who considered themselves, if not among the city's elite, at least superior to the immigrants who lived in Lorimer's wards? Lorimer's future appeared limited. But there was a redeeming fact. The Republican party was not unified. It was split into a number of warring factions, each anxious for power and spoils. If one man could dominate more wards than any other factional head, he might attract enough allies to enable him to grasp party control. Such a leader, by unifying his party, could furnish the "informal centralization" needed to overcome the "formal decentralization" of Chicago's government.

By the beginning of the 1890's, Lorimer was an important Chicago politician. Whether he could overcome the limitations of his background and constituency and exploit his party's disorganization and Chicago's peculiar political conformation remained to be seen.

[57] *Dillingham Committee Hearings,* VIII, 7552, 7665, 7851–52; *Daily News Almanac for 1888,* 113; Pierce, *Chicago,* III, 362–363.

CHAPTER **2**

★ ★ ★ ★ ★ ★ ★ ★ ★ ★ ★

Victory through Organization

THE TWO-PARTY system dominated Chicago politics in the 1890's as it did politics in other large American cities. Third parties, although not unusual, were generally unsuccessful in polling a winning percentage of the vote. The "competing political parties . . . with the consent of voters secured by competitive election" largely governed the city.[1] But who ran and dominated the political parties? That is, who furnished political leadership in Chicago?

As previously noted, Mayor Carter H. Harrison ruled the Democratic party. Native-American "silk-stocking" Democrats, men "high in the professional, the social and business world," challenged his leadership and objected to his catering to the immigrant vote, but without success.[2] The Catholic Irish, German, Bohemian, and Polish wards and the German Lutheran wards provided the voting strength of the Democratic party, and Harrison appealed to them by championing "personal liberty," opposing Sunday closing, and defending the teaching of German and other languages in the public schools.

Republican leadership in the 1880's also reflected the social composition of the Republican areas of the city. The party was strongest in the Protestant sections, especially among the native Americans, British, Scandinavians, and English Canadians. In their Chicago campaigns, the Republicans promised to achieve economy and efficiency in government, suppress gambling, and maintain law and order. These planks were often summarized under a "good-government" label.

[1] Robert A. Dahl, *Who Governs? Democracy and Power in an American City* (New Haven, 1961), 5.
[2] Harrison, *Stormy Years,* 37.

24

Occasionally a specific anti-immigrant item appeared, such as a promise to enforce the Sunday closing law or a demand that only "citizens" be employed on the public payroll.[3]

Newspaper publishers and editors and the politicians who followed their advice shared party leadership. The heads of Chicago's great industries, department stores, and banks became involved in politics only sporadically, as "businessmen" candidates for mayor, as part of some "reform" crusade, or when their specific interests were affected.[4] George R. Davis, who controlled the Twelfth Ward, and George B. Swift, who ran the Eleventh, were the most powerful office-holders. Both wards were largely composed of middle-class native Americans. Davis served as congressman from the Third Illinois District from 1877 to 1884, and as county treasurer from 1886 to 1888. Swift was an alderman from 1877 to 1885, special treasury agent 1885–87, and Chicago public works commissioner 1887–89. From 1895 to 1897 he was mayor of Chicago.[5]

The key newspapermen with influence in the Republican party were Joseph Medill, publisher of the *Tribune;* Robert W. Patterson, Medill's son-in-law and *Tribune* managing editor; and Herman H. Kohlsaat, publisher at various times of the *Inter-Ocean,* the *Times-Herald,* and the *Record-Herald.* Medill and Patterson seldom varied in their support of both local and national Republican candidates, while Kohlsaat, although always supporting the Republican national ticket, was nonpartisan on the local level.[6]

Medill of the *Tribune* was most influential during the beginning

---

[3] *Tribune,* Mar. 15, 1891; Pierce, *Chicago,* III, 340–380; Merriam, *Chicago,* 134–148.

[4] Donald S. Bradley and Mayer N. Zald, "From Commercial Elite to Political Administrator: The Recruitment of the Mayors of Chicago," *American Journal of Sociology* (Sept., 1965), LXXI, 153–167. For the participation by businessmen in Chicago reform crusades during the late nineteenth century see Sidney I. Roberts, "Businessmen in Revolt: Chicago, 1874–1900" (unpublished Ph.D. dissertation, Northwestern University, 1960).

[5] *Tribune,* Apr. 9, 1895, Nov. 26, 1899; Pierce, *Chicago,* III, 363, 365.

[6] Pierce, *Chicago,* III, 408–419; Charles H. Dennis, *Victor Lawson: His Time and His Work* (Chicago, 1935); John Tebbel, *An American Dynasty: The Story of the McCormicks, Medills, and Pattersons* (Garden City, 1947); Frederick L. Paxson, "Herman Henry Kohlsaat," in Dumas Malone, ed., *Dictionary of American Biography* (New York, 1933), X, 489–490, hereafter cited as *DAB;* Royal J. Schmidt, "The Chicago *Daily News* and Illinois Politics, 1876–1923" (unpublished Ph.D. dissertation, University of Chicago, 1954). William Penn Nixon, publisher of the stalwart Republican paper *Inter-Ocean* from 1890 to 1897, appeared to have little impact upon party policies. Victor Lawson, publisher of the independent *Daily News,* was influential after 1904.

of Lorimer's career. Born in 1823 on a farm in St. John, New Bruns-wick, Canada, of Presbyterian Scotch-Irish parents, he migrated to the United States in 1832. Medill practiced law in the 1840's and then entered the newspaper field, acquiring in 1855, with Charles Ray, the Chicago *Tribune.* He was an early supporter of the Republican party and regarded it "as the product . . . of his own efforts." [7] In 1871 he made his only venture into active politics when, in the aftermath of the Great Fire, the voters elected him Chicago mayor on the "Union-Fireproof" ticket. Perhaps his most notable act during his one term was to enforce the Sunday closing law, a move which guar-anteed him the antagonism of Chicago's Irish and German popula-tion.[8]

The *Illinois Staats-Zeitung* noted that the *Tribune* and Medill allowed themselves to "be made a tool of the haters of foreigners," a generally accurate description.[9] Medill referred to the German fol-lowers of editor and Democratic politician A. C. Hesing as a "scaly crew" from the slums. After the Haymarket "riot," the *Tribune* observed that Chicago had "become the rendezvous of the worst ele-ments of the socialistic, atheistic, alcoholic European classes." Medill combined anti-immigrant feelings with a lack of sympathy for the jobless; in 1884 the *Tribune* suggested that the best way to deal with tramps was to "put arsenic" in their food. Medill felt that native Americans who comprised "the intelligent and educated classes, of moral worth and business enterprise, as well as . . . the patriotic elements, of the nation" should run the Republican party.[10]

Robert W. Patterson was less vehement on these matters than his father-in-law. As Medill aged, control of the *Tribune* in the 1890's gravitated to Patterson and the paper became more a disseminator of news than a personal organ. But Patterson came from the same type of evangelical religious background as Medill—he was the son of a prominent Scotch Presbyterian minister—and he too preferred to see power in the Republican party kept in the hands of native Americans

---

[7] Tebbel, *An American Dynasty,* 19; Tracy E. Strevey, "Joseph Medill," *DAB,* XII, 491–492.

[8] See, for instance, *Illinois Staats-Zeitung,* Jan. 31, 1872, Jan. 3, May 2, 1873; Pierce, *Chicago,* III, 341–343.

[9] *Illinois Staats-Zeitung,* Jan. 3, 1873.

[10] Philip Kinsley, *The Chicago Tribune: Its First Hundred Years* (3 vols., Chi-cago, 1943–46), II, 210, 227; Harry Barnard, *"Eagle Forgotten": The Life of John Peter Altgeld* (New York, 1938), 132–134; Tebbel, *An American Dynasty,* 54; Wayne Andrews, *Battle for Chicago* (New York, 1946), 48–49.

and immigrants of pietistic leanings, preferably of the proper social standing.[11]

Kohlsaat was the third of the newspapermen to wield influence in Republican party politics in the late 1880's and early 1890's. The son of a Norwegian Baptist minister who migrated to the United States in 1825, Kohlsaat grew up in Galena, Illinois. There he numbered among his boyhood friends George B. Swift and Hempstead Washburne, both future Chicago mayors. Kohlsaat was a self-made man. He moved to Chicago in 1865 at the age of twelve and worked into the ranks of Chicago's wealthy through a chain of low-cost lunchrooms, a wholesale bakery, and real-estate speculation. His acceptance into the Chicago elite was signaled by his marriage, in 1880, to Mabel Blake, the daughter of the president of the Board of Trade, and his entrance into the Episcopal Church.[12]

Kohlsaat, like Medill, was a strong egotist. According to Charles G. Dawes, Kohlsaat was "very arrogant and domineering in his positions" and constantly interfered in matters of Republican policy and patronage.[13] Kohlsaat thought of himself as a "reformer," and while he did back many noteworthy causes, reform to him often meant the support of men of social status similar to his rather than of a "lesser" type.

An attitude toward their papers that had little to do with the profit motive united the three newspapermen. As Edward C. Banfield and James Q. Wilson note, newspaper owners want nonmonetary as well as monetary returns. They seek power, prestige, and the opportunity to shape public events and governmental policies according to their value systems. In their own view, they serve their community; they hold what Banfield and Wilson call a "public-regarding" political philosophy. The programs of the Chicago publishers called for honesty, efficiency, impartiality, and businesslike methods in politics, an approach that often stemmed from their pietistic Protestant backgrounds.[14]

[11] Tebbel, *An American Dynasty*, 14–16, 56–57; Kinsley, *Chicago Tribune*, III, 224.

[12] *Tribune*, April 9, 1895; New York *Times*, Oct. 18, 1924; Paxson, "Herman Henry Kohlsaat," 489–490.

[13] Charles G. Dawes, *A Journal of the McKinley Years, 1893–1913*, ed. Bascom N. Timmons (Chicago, 1950), 367, hereafter cited as *Dawes Journal*. Kohlsaat's memoirs, *From McKinley to Harding: Personal Recollections of Our Presidents* (New York, 1923), reflect his egoism.

[14] Banfield and Wilson, *City Politics*, 41, 313–321.

In later years Lorimer consistently referred to those nominally Republican papers that criticized him from a reform perspective as the "trust press." The papers usually included in this group were the *Tribune,* the *Daily News,* the *Record-Herald,* and whatever paper Herman H. Kohlsaat happened to be publishing at the time. These were the papers that Lorimer viewed as trying to oust him from party leadership so they themselves could determine GOP policy. Lorimer's most spirited political battles throughout the years were between him and his machine followers and the "trust press" and its political followers.

Part of the conflict stemmed from the fact that while the newspaper publishers held a "public-regarding" political philosophy, machine politicians like Lorimer held a "private-regarding" attitude. That is, Lorimer entered politics mainly for material gain, not to force his value system on the voters. His constituents looked to him for services that were "both *specific* and *material.*" They, like Lorimer, were not interested in the pietistic and "public-regarding" philosophy of the newspaper publishers.[15]

Lorimer clashed early with the press lords, especially Medill. In 1885 Medill opposed Lorimer's aldermanic candidate in the Sixth Ward and then, in 1888, blocked the nomination of a Lorimer ally for circuit court clerk. Lorimer later bitterly reflected that during Medill's lifetime "no man could secure a nomination for any office . . . unless he had first climbed the steps of the *Tribune* office and begged its editor . . . for his permission to become a candidate." [16] But in the 1880's Lorimer could do little; Medill held too much power in the party.

By the end of the 1880's, however, a group of professional politicians appeared in the Chicago Republican party who were "chafing under the yoke of dictatorship" and who were also free of the reform and social prejudices of the publishers. They viewed government and

---

15 *Ibid.,* 41, 115–116, 234–235, 313–321.
16 Lorimer's comment is in *CR,* 61st Cong., 2nd Sess., XLV, 7065. J. Frank Aldrich, a Chicago congressman, noted in his memoirs that "there was seldom a time when he [Medill] didn't take a hand in Republican party nominations in Cook County." J. Frank Aldrich, "Note on Medill," in J. Frank Aldrich Papers, Chicago Historical Society. For other examples of *Tribune* interference in the appointment process and legislative matters see Robert W. Patterson to Governor Joseph W. Fifer, Jan. 13, July 2, 1890, Joseph W. Fifer Papers, and Joseph Medill to Governor John R. Tanner, June 8, 1897, John R. Tanner Papers, both collections in the Illinois State Historical Library, Springfield.

party as a means to satisfy their own and their constituents' material ends rather than for any abstract governmental purpose or cultural goal. In the words of Banfield and Wilson, the "machine . . . is apolitical; it is interested only in making and distributing income— mainly money—to those who run it and work for it. Political principle is foreign to it, and represents a danger and a threat to it." Or, as Lord Bryce put it, the machine's "cohesive force is the desire for office and office as a means of gain." [17]

In 1889 Lorimer allied with three upcoming politicians from different sections of the city. All shared his attitude toward politics as a business—as nonpietistic and culturally neutral. The alliance lasted for ten years and achieved complete domination over the Republican party in city, county, and state. The influence of the newspaper publishers was nearly eliminated.

The three politicians were Thomas N. ("Doc") Jamieson, James Pease, and Henry L. Hertz. Together with Lorimer they represented the four sections of Chicago. Jamieson, a handsome druggist with a curly moustache and cultured manner, was of Scotch Canadian background. He controlled the wealthy, native-American section on Chicago's South Side. In later years he became Lorimer's right-hand man.[18] Henry L. Hertz, a short, dark-haired Dane with only one foot, lived on the northwest side and shepherded its large Scandinavian population.[19] Jim Pease was born in Wisconsin, although, like Lorimer and Jamieson, he derived from a Scottish background. He held power on the North Side, in an area with a large native-American population and a mixture of Swedes and German Lutherans.[20]

At the end of the 1880's and the beginning of the 1890's, the Lorimer-Jamieson-Hertz-Pease faction, although powerful in the party, did not dominate. In 1889 Chicago reverted to its normal Democratic voting pattern in local elections and chose DeWitt Cregier as mayor,

[17] James Bryce, *The American Commonwealth* (2 vols., New York, 1909), II, 111; Banfield and Wilson, *City Politics*, 116.

[18] *Tribune*, Oct. 16, 1895; Chicago *Times-Herald* (hereafter cited as *Times-Herald*), Mar. 2, 1896; William T. Hutchinson, *Lowden of Illinois* (2 vols., Chicago, 1957), I, 80. Jamieson later served as Illinois Republican national committeeman, chairman of the Republican state central committee, criminal court clerk, and naval officer for the port of Chicago.

[19] Albert N. Marquis, ed., *Who's Who in Chicago, 1926* (Chicago, 1926), 408. Hertz was county coroner in 1889 and later became state treasurer and U.S. internal revenue collector.

[20] *Tribune*, Apr. 12, 1917. Pease was assessor of the town of Lake View for nine years and then Cook County sheriff for two terms.

depriving Lorimer of his city job. In 1890 Lorimer made a premature try for the nomination for county clerk but failed by a narrow margin.[21] Unable to control a majority of the wards, in 1891 the Lorimer group joined with Medill and Kohlsaat to nominate the socially prominent Hempstead Washburne, son of Elihu B. Washburne, minister to France during the Grant administration, as Republican candidate for mayor.[22]

Normally the Republicans would have had little chance for success. Elmer Washburn, a former Republican superintendent of police, was running on a Citizen's reform ticket and threatened to cut into the normal Republican vote.[23] The identification of the Republican party with the controversial Edwards School Law of 1889 requiring the use of English in both public and private schools, however, primarily militated against a Washburne victory.[24] The Edwards Law caused a large migration of ethnic voters, especially German Lutherans, from the Republican to the Democratic party. In the elections of 1890, for the first time in many years, the Democrats carried both the Cook County and state tickets.

But the Republicans benefited from a split in the opposing party. When the Cregier forces denied Carter H. Harrison the mayoralty nomination, he bolted the party, carrying with him a large number of Germans, Bohemians, and Poles. In the election that followed, although Washburne only secured 29.5 percent of the vote, it gave him the victory. Harrison and Cregier divided the normal Democratic majority, with Cregier winning 29.2 percent and Harrison 26.5, while Elmer Washburn finished last with 14.8 percent.[25]

The Lorimer faction was important in both Washburne's nomination and election, and the new mayor rewarded its members with key positions. Washburne appointed Lorimer superintendent of the patronage-rich water office and Jamieson City Sealer of Weights and Mea-

21 *Ibid.;* Chicago *Inter-Ocean* (hereafter cited as *Inter-Ocean*), Sept. 14, 1890.

22 *Tribune,* Mar. 14, 17, Apr. 4, 1891; Chicago *Daily News* (hereafter cited as *News*), Mar. 17, 1891.

23 *Ibid.,* Apr. 3, 6, 1891; *Tribune,* Mar. 11, 1891. Washington Hesing, editor of the *Illinois Staats-Zeitung,* claimed that Washburn was supported by a group of "know-nothings." In 1873 Washburn had tried to close the saloons on Sunday. See *Illinois Staats-Zeitung,* Feb. 4, Oct. 16, 1873.

24 *Illinois Staats-Zeitung,* Nov. 4, 1892; Pierce, *Chicago,* III, 367–369; D. C. Smith to Joseph W. Fifer, Aug. 11, 1892, Fifer Papers.

25 *Tribune,* Mar. 21–23, Apr. 7, 1891; Harrison, *Stormy Years,* 35–36; Pierce, *Chicago,* III, 369–371. Lorimer was West Side representative on the Republican campaign executive committee.

sures. Lorimer immediately applied that old adage, "to the victor belong the spoils," and on his first day in office discharged twenty-five Democrats and replaced them with his own followers. He carefully recognized the leading ethnic groups in his district, so Irish, Bohemian, Polish, and Jewish names appeared among his appointees.[26]

The beginning of the Washburne administration thus marked the rise of the "machine" element in the Republican party. Men like Lorimer and Jamieson, who regarded politics from a vocational rather than a "good-government" standpoint, assumed power, and because of their strength in the wards and on the county central committee were able to pressure Mayor Washburne to do their bidding. Chicago's decentralized governmental system and the Mayor's lack of executive strength meant that he needed the cooperation of the ward bosses. In the middle of his administration, the Lorimer group pressed Washburne for more voice over appointments. Washburne capitulated and made Jamieson chief patronage dispenser of his administration. "In laying off any surplus of help in any office departments," wrote Washburne to his department heads, "I will indicate to Dr. Jamieson the *number* in each department and Dr. Jamieson will select the parties to lay off, or in case of increase the Dr. will supply the names of [replacements]. . . ."[27]

The elite Republican newspaper "bosses" were outraged, and J. Frank Aldrich, public works commissioner who had been appointed through Medill's influence, resigned.[28] Their anger was also reflected in their newspapers, especially in Kohlsaat's *Inter-Ocean*. Kohlsaat believed Lorimer primarily responsible for the increased "machine" influence in the Republican party—for its abandoning of its "reform" role—and attacked Lorimer in the news columns and editorials of his paper in an attempt to discredit him. This antagonism between Lorimer and Kohlsaat continued throughout Lorimer's carreer and played a key role in his expulsion from the Senate in 1912.

Kohlsaat viewed Lorimer as a "renegade Republican"—not the "type" of man who belonged in the Republican party. His charges

[26] *Tribune,* Apr. 26, 1891, May 1, 1892; *News,* Apr. 29, 1892.

[27] Hempstead Washburne to J. Frank Aldrich, Nov. 14, 1892, Aldrich Papers, Chicago Historical Society.

[28] Hempstead Washburne to J. Frank Aldrich, Dec. 20, 1892, J. Frank Aldrich, "Public Works," undated manuscript, Aldrich Papers, Chicago Union League Club. These papers were made available to the author through the courtesy of the Board of Directors of the Chicago Union League Club.

against him had three themes: Lorimer supported bad men (saloon-keepers) for Republican nominations; he made deals with the "worst" elements in the Democratic party; and it was implied that he profited from his political endeavors.[29] These charges were valid, but from Lorimer's viewpoint there was nothing wrong with his activities. Saloon-keepers were just as good as anyone else, and, in addition, had considerable political influence. Deals with Democrats? All West Side machine politicians made "arrangements" to split patronage and to support each other's nominees. Politics was a business, not an ideological contest; one had to live and let live. Profit from one's position? So did most machine politicians. George Washington Plunkitt of Tammany Hall called it "honest graft." Lorimer had been doing it since his entry into politics and continued it throughout his career.[30] Events at the 1892 Republican national convention, at the county convention, and in the campaign created further antagonism between Lorimer and Kohlsaat. The first incident involved the national convention.

By 1892 Lorimer controlled the Republican organizations in the newly created Seventh, Eighth, Ninth, and Tenth wards. This gave him influence over the choice of national convention delegates from his district. In March Lorimer himself became a delegate and pledged to support President Benjamin Harrison for renomination. By the time of the national convention at Minneapolis, however, considerable sentiment existed in Chicago for Secretary of State James G. Blaine. Lorimer now discovered that Harrison was his district's "second choice" and Blaine the "unanimous and enthusiastic first choice." He attempted to win votes for Blaine, and by the eve of the convention had secured one-third of the delegation. Lorimer's efforts, however, were wasted when the convention nominated Harrison on the first ballot by a considerable margin over Blaine. Illinois gave a majority of her votes to the victor, with thirteen delegates joining Lorimer to vote for the "Plumed Knight." [31]

29 *Inter-Ocean*, Oct. 2, 13, 16, 1891, Mar. 29, 30, Nov. 4, 5, 1892.

30 William L. Riordan, *Plunkitt of Tammany Hall* (New York, 1948), 3–8. Under the Roche administration Lorimer held a city teaming contract; he later owned coal, brick, and contracting companies which held public contracts. See *Dillingham Committee Hearings*, VIII, 7665, 7853.

31 Illinois politicians did a good deal of shifting in the pre-convention period. U.S. Senator Shelby M. Cullom, who was originally a favorite-son candidate, declared for Harrison while Governor Joseph W. Fifer shifted from Harrison to Blaine. Lorimer, at the time, was in the Fifer faction. In June, an "unofficial"

Kohlsaat was infuriated by Lorimer's work for Blaine. A Harrison supporter, he viewed Blaine as the "tattooed man," the archetype of the corrupt spoils politician. During the convention Kohlsaat attacked Lorimer in the *Inter-Ocean* for his Blaine efforts and had one of his reporters warn Lorimer that unless he stopped trying to split the Illinois delegation he would drive him from the Republican party.[32] Now, although Blaine was defeated, Kohlsaat determined to punish Lorimer.

Kohlsaat saw his opportunity during the 1892 county campaign. In August Lorimer resigned from the Washburne administration in order to seek the Republican nomination for clerk of the superior court, an important office both for its patronage and its fees. Kohlsaat vigorously opposed the nomination in his paper's columns, but was unable to sway the convention. The delegates enthusiastically nominated Lorimer on September 7 by a large majority.[33] Not to be dissuaded, Kohlsaat went to Mayor Washburne to enlist his aid in blocking Lorimer.

Kohlsaat tried to convince Washburne that unless Lorimer was stopped, control of the party would pass into the hands of "disreputable" Republicans. Washburne was persuaded. On November 4, only four days before the election, he announced that irregularities had appeared in the water department books necessitating an investigation. The irregularities had occurred during Lorimer's tenure as commissioner.[34] The power play was obvious. The elite "good-government" newspaper publisher wrestled with the professional politician for party control. The day after Washburne announced the investigation, Lorimer and his allies visited the Mayor in his office. Although there is no record of the proceedings, Lorimer countered Kohlsaat's influence. For on the next day Washburne canceled the investigation, cleared

convention in Lorimer's district rescinded the Harrison instructions and announced for Blaine. See Shelby M. Cullom to John A. Roche, Mar. 28, 1892, Lorin C. Collins to Cullom, Apr. 1, 1892, John R. Tanner to Cullom, Mar. 21, May 8, 1892, Shelby M. Cullom Papers, Illinois State Historical Library, Springfield; J. W. Fifer to Benjamin Harrison, Mar. 14, 1892, Fifer Papers; *Tribune,* Mar. 25, Apr. 1, June 1, 5, 8, 1892; Donald M. Dozer, "Benjamin Harrison and the Presidential Campaign of 1892," *American Historical Review* (Oct., 1948), LIV, 49–69.

[32] *Dillingham Committee Hearings,* I, 460 (Herman H. Kohlsaat testifying), VIII, 7545–47. Kohlsaat threatened to attack Sheriff James Gilbert in the *Inter-Ocean* unless he was made a convention delegate. See E. R. Brainerd to Cullom, Apr. 27, 1892, Cullom Papers.

[33] *Inter-Ocean,* Aug. 24, Sept. 1, 8, 9, 1892; *Tribune,* Aug. 24, Sept. 8, 1892.

[34] *Tribune, Inter-Ocean,* and *News,* Nov. 4, 1892

Lorimer of all charges, and reiterated his friendship toward his candidacy.[35] Lorimer had demonstrated to the newspaper publishers that he could be a tenacious foe.

But whatever action Kohlsaat or Lorimer might take in the fall of 1892, they could do little to alter the election's outcome. Many of the voters who had left the Republican party in 1890 in protest over the Edwards School Law were not ready to return. They joined with the Democratic Irish, German Catholic, Polish, and Bohemian voters to produce a Democratic sweep of the city, county, and state. Lorimer lost with the rest of the ticket. For the first time since before the Civil War, Illinois elected a Democratic governor, the German John Peter Altgeld, and Chicago gave both him and President-elect Grover Cleveland substantial majorities.[36]

Some Chicago Republicans recognized the importance of cultural issues and ethnic factors in the city's politics. Lorimer, for instance, attempted to disassociate the Republican party from the Edwards Law.[37] More specifically, in March of 1893, when the question of a mayoralty nominee arose, he, Hertz, and Jamieson tried to persuade the party to nominate a West Side man, preferably the influential Irish Catholic businessman John M. Smyth, as its candidate. But Smyth, not relishing the idea of running against the popular Carter H. Harrison, the Democratic nominee, refused. The nomination went, practically by default, to the millionaire meat-packer Samuel Allerton, supported by a combination of Medill, Patterson, Kohlsaat, and a group of independent Republicans with strong temperance and Sabbatarian learnings.[38]

[35] *News*, Nov. 4–7, 1892; *Tribune*, Nov. 4–6, 1892; *Dillingham Committee Hearings*, VIII, 7549.

[36] *Die Abendpost*, Sept. 26, 1892; *Illinois Staats-Zeitung*, Oct. 28, 1892; *Svornost*, June 22, 1892; *Tribune*, Nov. 9–11, 1892. Cleveland secured 56.4 percent of the Chicago vote and Altgeld 55.9 percent. *Daily News Almanac for 1893*, 338–342. Kleppner finds that there was a +.897 correlation between percent Catholic and percent Democratic in all thirty-four Chicago wards. For lower-class wards the correlation was +.883; for upper-class wards it was +.904. Kleppner, "Politics of Change in the Midwest," 33–34. My calculations show a correlation of +.893 between percent Protestant and percent Republican and of +.758 between percent Republican and the vote of native-American wards. This was the highest correlation between these two variables for any election during the 1890's aside from the 1892 gubernatorial contest, suggesting that the 1892 election reduced the Republican party to a base of its most committed voters. (For an explanation of the statistical method of correlation used in this volume, see Appendix A.)

[37] *Tribune*, Apr. 7, 1891. Lorimer commented that the Republican party should disassociate itself from the "red school-house" voters.

[38] *Ibid.*, Mar. 1, 4, 7, 9, 12, 16, 1893; *Chicago Times*, Mar. 16, 17, 1893.

The result was practically foregone. Harrison won with over 54 percent of the vote. German, Irish, Bohemian, and Polish Catholics, as well as German Lutherans, alienated by the Republican candidate and the influences behind him, gave Harrison their votes.[39] Democratic control seemed fastened on the city.

The 1892 and 1893 debacles forcefully indicated to Lorimer that the Republican party needed to be reorganized. And restructuring should start at the bottom rather than the top; the party needed to rest upon the "social and economic institutions in the wards themselves." [40] Power would then flow upward from the precinct and ward levels. Decisions as to policy and nominations would represent the will of the majority of the county central committee rather than the wishes of a few socially elite newspaper publishers.

Lorimer invited key members of the Republican county central committee to a conference on the future of the party. As he later related, he "urged upon them the necessity of a precinct and ward organization in every ward and precinct in Chicago and every election district in Cook County. . . ." Organization, not issues, held Lorimer, was the most important factor in elections.[41]

The county committee accepted Lorimer's suggestion, and the chairman appointed a committee to formulate his proposals. Early in October of 1893 it presented a report reflecting Lorimer's influence, which recommended a hierarchical party structure composed of precinct and ward clubs topped by a central committee. The precinct clubs would elect their own officers and nominate men for ward committeemen. All party members could vote for the ward committeeman, who would represent the ward on the county committee. Theoretically there would be a direct line from the voters to the party command. The central committee would control all patronage and channel it to the ward clubs, which would then distribute it on the precinct level. The precinct clubs were responsible for canvassing, registration, naturalization, and other political duties in their own areas.[42]

Late in October the county judicial convention unanimously

---

[39] *Daily News Almanac for 1894*, 319–322. In this election percent Catholic correlated at +.788 with percent Democratic, while percent Protestant correlated with percent Republican at +.798.

[40] Samuel P. Hays, "The Politics of Reform in Municipal Government in the Progressive Era," *Pacific Northwest Quarterly* (Oct., 1964), LV, 163.

[41] *CR*, 61st Cong., 2nd Sess., XLV, 7065; *Dillingham Committee Hearings*, VIII, 7686.

[42] *Tribune*, Oct. 4, 1893.

adopted the report as the new party constitution. Lorimer was appointed chairman of the reorganization committee. During the following months, while Chicagoans and thousands of visitors gaped at the Great White City on the South Side, Lorimer labored at erecting ward and precinct clubs throughout the county. No doubt he placed his friends in important positions whenever possible.[43] Down at the grass roots, overlooked by reform crusades and elite newspaper publishers, Lorimer developed a machine to make democratic politics work as a source of livelihood and power to himself and his followers. At the end of a year of "constant effort," every precinct in the county had a Republican club, and Lorimer had laid the foundations for the first "permanent, cohesive organization of the party in Cook County."[44] Against such tireless effort, the episodic campaigns of reformers were to be futile.

But while reoganization might offer the means by which the party could be strengthened and leadership changed, it might not necessarily shift voter sentiment. Fortunately for Lorimer, forces that would affect the voter were already at work in the city. By May, 1893, the first shocks of the panic and depression of 1893 hit Chicago. In that month the Chemical National Bank, the Columbia National Bank, and the United States Loan and Trust Company failed. During the first eight months of 1893, twenty-four private banks also closed their doors. Many industries and retail and commercial establishments experienced a drastic decline in sales. During 1893 there were 566 business failures in Illinois, a 50 percent increase over 1892; in 1894 the number increased to 717.[45]

Business curtailment and failure caused widespread unemployment. Chicago's situation was particularly acute because the building of the World's Fair had added thousands of additional workers to the city's labor force. With the end of the fair and the onset of the depression, many of these men were destitute, and wages were severely cut for those who continued to work. In the month of August, 1893, thou-

---

[43] *Ibid.*, Oct. 7–8, 13 ,19, 1893.

[44] *CR*, 61st Cong., 2nd Sess., XLV, 7065.

[45] Charles Hoffman, "The Depression of the Nineties," *Journal of Economic History* (June, 1956), XVI, 137–164; F. Cyril James, *The Growth of Chicago Banks* (2 vols., New York, 1938), I, 580–582; Ernest Ludlow Bogart and John Mabry Mathews, *The Modern Commonwealth: 1893–1918*, Vol. V of *The Centennial History of Illinois*, ed. Clarence W. Alvord (Springfield, 1920), 400.

sands of the unemployed demonstrated on the lake front and in the Loop, and passed resolutions attacking "wage-slavery." [46]

The impact of the depression had an immediate effect upon Chicago politics, as all urban social groups shifted away from the Democrats. In December, 1893, the assassination of Carter H. Harrison by a demented office-seeker led to a special mayoralty election. Although this election, which was marked by a high voter turnout, resulted in a Democratic victory by a slight margin, the Republicans still secured substantial gains: 5.1 percentage points over the previous April and 7.5 points compared with the 1892 presidential vote. The Democrats lost voters in thirty-two of the city's thirty-four wards, while the Republicans gained strength among German Catholics, Lutherans, Bohemians, and Poles. Only the Irish Catholic wards, loyal to the candidacy of their fellow religionist and countryman John P. Hopkins, stayed with the Democratic party.[47]

This large increase in the Republican vote offered a tempting prize to rival Republican party managers who anticipated controlling the 1894 ticket. Two Republican factions developed, one composed of Lorimer and his allies, the other led by George B. Swift and backed by Kohlsaat, Medill, Patterson, and their newspapers. The first factional test came in the spring of 1894 in the party primaries held to select delegates to the county convention. The Swift faction had the backing of most of the ward committeemen from the native-American wards and of the influential *Tribune,* but the Lorimer group controlled the newly created organization in most of the remainder of the city. This proved the decisive factor. On primary day the Lorimer faction elected a majority of its delegates.[48]

The next day at the convention the delegates approved what Lorimer called the "first county ticket that was nominated by the Republicans without first submitting to the dictation of the *Tribune.* . . ." [49]

[46] Bogart and Mathews, *The Modern Commonwealth,* 400; Chester MacArthur Destler, *American Radicalism, 1865–1900* (Quadrangle ed., Chicago, 1966), 165–177.

[47] Election results are in *Daily News Almanac for 1894,* 326–330; Kleppner, "Politics of Change in the Midwest," 343. Hopkins had 112,969 votes or 49.71 percent and George B. Swift, the Republican candidate, had 111,669 votes or 49.14 percent. The Republicans contested the election; in 1896 the Illinois Supreme Court ruled that there had been no error in the count. See Pierce, *Chicago,* III, 379.

[48] John R. Tanner to Joseph W. Fifer, June 11, 1894, Fifer Papers; *Tribune,* June 8, 15, 18, 22, 23, 26, July 4, 1894.

[49] *CR,* 61st Cong., 2nd Sess., XLV, 7065.

Among others from the Lorimer faction, the convention nominated Pease for sheriff and Ernest J. Magerstadt, Lorimer's German ally from the Fifth Ward, for criminal court clerk. The county committee appointed Lorimer chairman of the important registration committee in recognition of his organizational ability and attractiveness to normally non-Republican groups. He was also appointed to the county executive committee, the ruling clique within the central committee.[50] The professional politicians had taken a large step in freeing the party from press dictation.

While Lorimer undoubtedly could have secured a county nomination, he had decided to seek the position of congressman from the Illinois Second District. If he won the congressional seat, he could add congressional patronage to his county and state patronage, as well as the increased status of a national office. The Tenth, Twenty-eighth, Twenty-ninth, and Thirtieth Chicago wards, and a number of county towns, the largest of which was Cicero, composed the Second District. Although Lorimer controlled the Tenth by virtue of being its ward committeeman, he was weaker in the other wards.

The district contained more industrial workers than any other district in the United States. Its large proletarian population labored in the packinghouses, railroad yards, and factories within its borders. The entire district, however, was not working-class; a number of middle-class citizens lived in the Tenth and Thirtieth wards and in the suburban towns. In 1892 the district contained approximately 47,000 voters, of whom 32,914 lived in Chicago. Of the latter, 54 percent were naturalized citizens and 46 percent native-born. Germans were the largest ethnic group, composing 17.7 percent of the voting population, closely followed by the Irish with 15 percent. Scandinavians, Poles, Bohemians, and Scotch-English each constituted about 5 percent.[51] The suburban towns had a higher percentage of native voters than did the Chicago wards.

Reflecting its preponderance of German, Irish, Polish, and Bohemian groups, the Second District usually voted Democratic. In the 1892 presidential election, the Democrats secured 54.6 percent of the vote, the Republicans 41.2 percent. In the county towns, however,

---

50 *Tribune,* June 22, 23, 26, July 4, 1894; *News,* June 5, 15, 23, 1894.

51 Inter-Ocean, *A History of the City of Chicago* (Chicago, 1901), 477; U.S., *Eleventh Census, 1890,* "Population," I, 161–182 (this volume of the census includes a description of each Chicago ward); *Daily News Almanac for 1894,* 318.

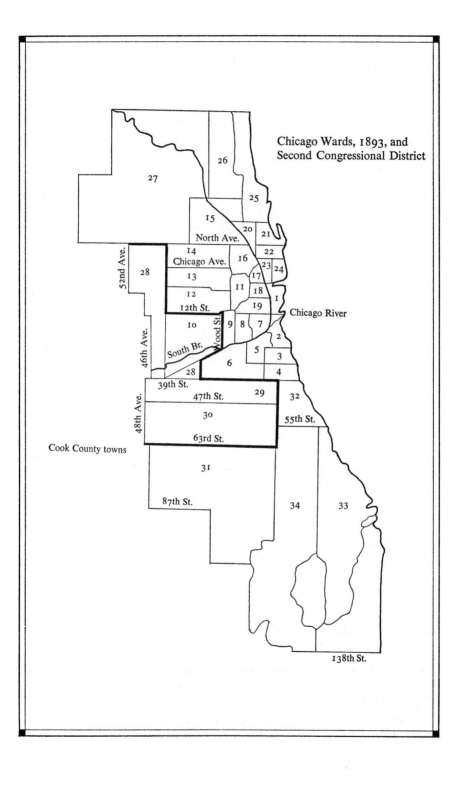

Chicago Wards, 1893, and
Second Congressional District

26

27

25

15

20

21

North Ave.

14

Chicago Ave.

16

22

52nd Ave.

28

13

23 24

17

12

11

18

I

12th St.

19

Chicago River

10

Wood St.

9 8

7

46th Ave.

South Br.

5

2

6

3

28

4

39th St.

47th St.

29

32

48th Ave.

30

55th St.

63rd St.

Cook County towns

31

87th St.

34

33

138th St.

representing about 20 percent of the district vote, the totals were nearly reversed, with the Republicans winning 54.3 percent, the Democrats 39.3 percent, and the Prohibitionists 5.2 percent.[52]

In the summer of 1894, while Lorimer built his organization and consolidated his hold over the party, the Second Congressional District experienced explosive labor conflicts. In May, 1894, after management reduced wages for the fifth time without a compensatory lowering of rents in company houses, the workers at the Pullman Palace Car works just south of Chicago struck. In late June the American Railroad Union, led by Eugene V. Debs, declared a sympathetic boycott of Pullman cars on all railroads. By early July, fear of rioting and the anti-union sentiments of the Cleveland administration brought federal troops into the city. Chicago assumed the appearance of an armed camp.[53]

The worst rioting occurred after the arrival of the federal troops. Several disturbances took place within the Second Congressional District, especially near the stockyards area. On July 7 an angry mob attacked a company of militia near the Grand Trunk line at Forty-ninth and Loomis streets. After the crowd pelted them with stones and fired upon them, the soldiers returned the fire. Four rioters were killed and twenty wounded. Between July 4 and 10, mobs prevented the movement of meat and livestock from the Union Stock Yards. By July 13 all rioting had ceased and the city returned to normal.[54]

The disastrous impact of the panic of 1893 and the chaos caused by the Pullman strike posed opportunities to two widely differing political groups. Because of its large working-class population and the heritage of bitterness left by the repression of the Pullman strike, labor union men, single-taxers, Populists, and other radicals considered the Second District a likely place to elect a congressman. In an attempt to replace the Democrats as the majority party in the district, on August 2 a unique labor-Populist coalition nominated John Z. White, a leading single-taxer, as the Populist party candidate on a platform containing single-tax and Socialist planks.[55]

[52] *Daily News Almanac for 1893*, 338–342.
[53] Almont Lindsey, *The Pullman Strike* (Chicago, 1942), 1–175; Ray Ginger, *Altgeld's America: The Lincoln Ideal versus Changing Realities* (Quadrangle ed., Chicago, 1965), 143–163.
[54] Lindsey, *Pullman Strike*, 203–238.
[55] Destler, *American Radicalism*, 181; Chicago *Times*, Aug. 3, 1894. In the December, 1893, mayoralty election, the Socialists won .85 percent of the vote in

The Republicans also saw an opportunity to capture the Second District. To those normal Democratic voters adversely affected by the depression and alienated from the Cleveland administration they could promise the return of the "full dinner pail." In addition, the presence of a vigorous Populist candidate would probably split the normal Democratic vote. There were three candidates for the Republican nomination: Lorimer from the Tenth Ward, Henry C. Darlington from the Thirtieth, and Charles E. Piper, a temperance man from the county towns. Lorimer and Piper were the chief contenders, although Piper, because of his temperance views, was probably the weakest of the candidates. After twelve close ballots, Lorimer won the nomination when Charles S. Deneen, Thirtieth Ward committeeman, switched his votes from Darlington.[56] This marked the beginning of an erratic alliance that was to prove of great importance to the careers of both men.

The campaign was vigorously fought. The Democrats had nominated John J. Hannahan of the Brotherhood of Locomotive Firemen in an attempt to hold the working-class and Irish vote. Hannahan emphasized his life-long work for "organized labor" and disassociated himself from the national administration.[57]

White ran on an anti-monopoly platform calling for public ownership of utilities, free silver, and the single tax. Noted radicals Henry D. Lloyd, Eugene V. Debs, Ignatius Donnelly, and Clarence S. Darrow spoke for him, and Populist tracts such as *Coin's Financial School* and *The Story of the Commonwealth* were distributed in the district. White, generally ignoring the Lorimer candidacy, concentrated his attacks upon the Cleveland Democrats, emphasizing that the Populists would help the working masses.[58]

Lorimer played a neutral role in this three-cornered contest; he neither attacked nor defended. He made few speeches and confined those to organizational matters and promises that the Republicans would bring the return of good times: "It is no use to shout about the grand old party on election day if you are not registered you can't vote, and wind work never won a campaign and never will. Someone

the Chicago wards of the Second Congressional District and the Populists won .27 percent.

56 *Tribune, Record,* and *Inter-Ocean,* Aug. 9, 1894.

57 Chicago *Herald* and *Tribune,* Sept. 26, 1894. The Chicago *Herald* was a Democratic paper reflecting the point of view of the national administration.

58 *Herald,* Sept. 12, 1894; Destler, *American Radicalism,* 193–205.

has got to do hard work and if the Republicans want a return of better times you must do your duty from now on . . . if idle men of the city want to see better days for themselves and families it behooves everyone of them, regardless of former party affiliations, to deposit a Republican ballot in November." [59] If he could hold and perhaps increase the normal Republican vote, Lorimer might win, since Hannahan and White stood to split the usual Democratic majority.

The election followed this pattern: Lorimer secured 45.5 percent of the vote, Hannahan had 36.2 percent, and White a disappointing—at least to Chicago radicals—18.2 percent. Lorimer increased the Republican vote by about 4 percentage points over 1892 and 1893 and won a majority of the votes in the Tenth and Twenty-eighth wards and in the county towns. In contrast, the Democrats lost heavily throughout the district in both numerical and percentage terms. The majority of Democrats who defected voted for the Populist White, although ironically he pulled his lowest percentage in the heaviest working-class ward of the district, the Twenty-ninth. [60]

Party lines, based primarily upon cultural factors, shattered under the impact of economic adversity. The Republican party's largest numerical and percentage gains were in Lorimer's home Tenth Ward, where large numbers of normally Democratic Germans, Poles, and Bohemians shifted to the GOP. While many Irish Catholics stuck by Hannahan, some defected to the Populists. Few, however, because of cultural identifications, were willing to support the Republicans. The Populist party became "a refuge for those voters who were dissatisfied with the Democrats, but were not willing to go to the extreme of casting a Republican ballot." [61] The Democratic party, the party of "hard times," was thus rejected by many formerly loyal social and religious groups, and Lorimer benefited.

Most Republicans did well in the 1894 election as masses of voters defected from the Democrats, some to vote Populist, others to join the Republican party. The Republican gains were part of a nationwide trend that made the GOP the majority party in the nation. Republicans swept the Cook County offices, elected twenty out of

[59] *Tribune*, Sept., 19, 30, Oct. 26, 1894; Chicago *Herald*, Sept. 26, 1894.

[60] Manuscript Election Returns, Second Congressional District, 1894, Board of Election Commissioners, Chicago.

[61] Kleppner, "Politics of Change in the Midwest," 346. The Populist vote for state treasurer in 1895 correlated at +.433 with the 1892 Democratic presidential vote. German Lutherans especially seemed attracted to the Populist party and the group's percentage strength correlated at +.657 with the 1894 Populist vote.

twenty-two Illinois congressmen, and took control of the General Assembly.[62] With renewed confidence, the party looked forward to capturing the mayoralty from the Democrats in 1895.

Lorimer, as one of Chicago's most powerful Republican politicians, stood to benefit greatly from the Republican successes. He now had the prestige of a congressman-elect and through his personal organization manipulated the vote of a number of West Side wards. In addition, his entente with Jamieson, Hertz, and Pease dominated the county committee and the major Cook County offices and patronage resources. Because he controlled the most ward committeemen, Lorimer was the most influential member and the spokesman of the group.

Lorimer's new prominence and power drew other politicians to his side. Among the most important were Daniel D. Healy, John M. Smyth, David Shanahan, and Gus Nohe. Healy was the president of the county board and lived in Lorimer's home ward. Smyth was a close friend of Healy. He owned the West Side's largest retail furniture store and had substantial interests in public utilities. Smyth was politically active and controlled several wards; he later served as chairman of the county central committee. Shanahan and Nohe were influential members of the Illinois General Assembly from Lorimer's district. All these men had originally opposed Lorimer, but by 1895 were his allies.[63]

The immediate prize the Republicans sought was the city government. Maneuvering for the mayoralty nomination began before the end of 1894. The Lorimer faction supported South Side alderman Martin B. Madden, chairman of the city central committee. The English-born Madden, however, had supported several questionable franchises while on the city council and proved unacceptable to the Kohlsaat-Medill-Patterson triumvirate. Their candidate was George B. Swift, who had been narrowly defeated in the special mayoralty election in 1893.

Swift was a popular favorite among Republicans, and the Lorimer faction decided to compromise rather than fight his nomination. In re-

[62] *Tribune,* Nov. 7–9, 1894; Charles A. Church, *History of the Republican Party in Illinois 1854–1912* (Rockford, 1912), 176–177. For a discussion of the nationwide significance of the 1894 election see Lee Benson, "Research Problems in American Political Historiography," in Mirra Komarovsky, ed., *Common Frontiers of the Social Sciences* (Glencoe, 1957), 166–171.

[63] Interviews with Mrs. William Healy Lorimer, Aug. 20, 1964, Chicago, and Walter L. M. Lorimer, Apr. 23, 1964, Beverly Hills; *Tribune,* Feb. 27, 1902. One of Lorimer's sons later married Healy's daughter.

turn for not opposing Swift, they named the candidates for city clerk, treasurer, and attorney. Swift also promised to recognize the Lorimer faction and the county organization in his distribution of patronage. The ticket, observed the *Tribune,* represented the Lorimer-Jamieson-Hertz combination "applying the screws." [64]

The city election of 1895 involved not only the election of municipal officers, but also a referendum on a civil service bill applying the merit system to city government. The bill was the result of a drive by a Joint Civil Service Committee, representing such civic organizations as the Union League Club and the Civic Federation, to eliminate the abuses of the spoils system. Its advocates believed that civil service, by elevating men of ability to city office, would achieve the reformation of urban government. Under the press of public opinion, both parties endorsed the bill, although without enthusiasm. As one Republican said, "While as Republicans we all believe in civil service reform we also believe there are enough good Republicans to comply with the best civil service rules ever devised." [65]

Lorimer campaigned for the ticket, particularly among Bohemian and Polish groups. He emphasized that the Democrats could not be trusted to restore "good times." In an obvious attempt to capture some of the votes that had gone to the Populists in 1894, he pictured Frank Wenter, the Democratic candidate, as the enemy of labor and of "all the reforms advocated by union associations"; he alleged that a Democratic victory in Chicago might mean a return of the Democrats in the 1896 presidential election.[66]

The continuance of bad times and the Republican strategy of linking these to the Democrats proved beneficial to the GOP. Swift was elected by the largest total ever given a Chicago mayor, receiving 55 percent of the vote. Wenter, although defeated, increased his party's totals by about 4 percent over 1894, while the Populists dropped to just under 5 percent of the vote. Apparently, a majority of those voters who had voted Populist in 1894 had shifted to the Republican

[64] *Tribune,* Dec. 21, 1894, Feb. 22, 1895; *Dillingham Committee Hearings,* I, 467 (Kohlsaat testifying), VIII, 7531–35; Lewis Ethan Ellis, "Martin Barnaby Madden," *DAB,* XII, 180–181.

[65] *Tribune,* Mar. 23–25, Apr. 1, 1895. For the fight for civil service in Chicago see Roberts, "Businessmen in Revolt," Chap. IV, "Civil Service and the Civic Federation."

[66] *Tribune,* Mar. 24, 25, 27, Apr. 1, 1895.

party.[67] An even larger majority, an astounding 65 percent, approved the civil service bill.[68]

While some optimists forecast a "new era in government" because of the passage of civil service, Swift dampened their expectations. A ninety-day period existed before the new statute took effect, and Swift used this opportunity to remove thouands of Democrats from city offices and replace them with Republicans. These came under the category of "hold-overs" and were not subject to the merit system. Furthermore, Swift's new appointees came entirely from his own faction. Probably moved by the urging of Kohlsaat, Swift broke his promise to Lorimer and largely ignored Lorimer's followers.[69]

Indignantly Lorimer accused Swift of building a personal machine. "Never was a political party so wantonly divided as has been the Republican of Cook County. . . . In fighting the men who had made him mayor Mr. Swift has not only weakened himself politically, but as an official." [70] Lorimer and his county followers quickly retaliated. Although a limited county civil service bill sponsored by Lorimer as a sop to public opinion covered some employees, there were still 1,440 county patronage positions. Lorimer, Jamieson, and county board president Dan Healy removed all Swift men from the appointment list and replaced them with Lorimer followers. It was "the most desperate patronage fight recorded in the history of [Chicago] local politics." [71]

Each faction sought a majority on the county central committee. Ostensibly at stake was control of the party during the crucial 1896 election year, but beneath the surface there were also social and cultural issues. The key question was whether the Cook County Republican party should be directed and controlled by a group of professional politicians coming mainly from Catholic, Jewish, and German Lutheran immigrant working-class wards or by socially elite newspaper

[67] *Daily News Almanac for 1896*, 375–382; Kleppner, "Politics of Change in the Midwest," 491.

[68] *Tribune*, Apr. 3–5, 1895.

[69] *Ibid.*, Apr. 10, 24, 1895; *News*, Apr. 12, May 15, 1895; Joseph Bush Kingsbury, "Municipal Personnel Policy in Chicago, 1895–1915" (unpublished Ph.D. dissertation, University of Chicago, 1923), 53.

[70] *Record*, June 24, 1895.

[71] *Ibid.*, Sept. 28, 1895; *Tribune*, July 3, 1895. For the origin and criticisms of the county civil service law see *Tribune*, May 27, 30, June 8, Sept. 17, 1895; *Times-Herald*, Apr. 7, 11, May 21, 28, June 7, 10, 1895; Citizen's Association of Chicago, *Bulletin No. 2* (Chicago, 1900).

publishers and politicians representing middle- and upper-class Protestant native-American wards.

This question could be answered only in the party primaries, and each faction used its fullest resources to achieve victory. Wards were gerrymandered, election officials bribed, and "sluggers," "thugs," and "crooks" enlisted to terrorize the opposition. Although the Swift or city forces had the larger amount of patronage, the Lorimer forces had the organization. This proved crucial, for on primary day the county forces prevailed by a large margin.[72] An analysis of the primary returns reveals the social and cultural issues involved in the contest. The county forces won eighteen wards, the city twelve, with four wards more or less evenly divided. The wards won by the city faction had more native Americans and Protestants than the county wards and represented a higher economic class. The wards won by the county faction, on the other hand, tended to be lower-class and Catholic. In addition, the county wards contained most of the city's Bohemians and Poles and a majority of the Germans, including most of the Catholic Germans. Well might Kohlsaat's newly acquired paper, the *Times-Herald,* lament: "In four years . . . [Lorimer] has transferred the seat of power in the party from the banner republican wards like the fourth, twelfth and thirty-second to the democratic wards of the old second congressional district. The stockyards, the Black road and Bridgeport rule the organization which but yesterday took the direction from neighborhoods less remote from the English-speaking centers." [73]

At the county convention the Lorimer forces further entrenched themselves in the central committee by deciding all contests in their own favor, as well as nominating their slate of candidates for drainage board trustees. Several days after the convention, the ward committeemen recognized Lorimer's preeminence by electing him chairman of the county central committee, as well as of its executive committee.[74]

---

[72] *News,* Sept. 15, 19, Oct. 2, 1895; *Tribune,* Sept. 18, 19, 21, 22, 24, 25, 29, Oct. 3, 1895. Lorimer claimed that Medill tried to persuade him to postpone the primaries and was "very much put out about it" when he refused. See *CR,* 61st Cong., 2nd Sess., XLV, 7066; *Dillingham Committee Hearings,* VIII, 7536.

[73] *Times-Herald,* Feb. 18, 1896. 43.9 percent of the voters in the county wards were native and 56.1 percent naturalized; 60.5 percent of the voters in the city wards were native and 39.5 percent naturalized. In the tightly contested mayoralty election of December, 1893, seven of the county wards voted Republican and eleven Democratic; in the same election, eight city wards voted Republican and four Democratic.

[74] *Tribune,* Oct. 3, 9, 1895; *Times Herald,* Oct. 4, 1895.

Lorimer's hard work and attention to detail in developing the organization had been successful. He carefully built his machine from the precinct level upward; he rewarded his political followers and aided his constituents; and he extended his alliances throughout the city. In the showdown battle with Swift and his newspaper allies, victory went to the superior organization.

Lorimer had become the most powerful Republican in Cook County, if not in the state. He was the "boss" of his party, with far-reaching influence over the operation of government, party nominations, and legislation. For nearly the next two decades, he was the most controversial figure in Illinois politics. More immediately, however, the important political events of 1896 were approaching and the eyes of the Cook County Republicans focused upon him for leadership.

★ ★ ★ ★ ★ ★ ★ ★ ★ ★ ★

CHAPTER 3

Reaching beyond Cook County: The Election of 1896

THE COUNTY CENTRAL COMMITTEE'S ELECTION of Lorimer as chairman in the spring of 1895 signified his arrival as the most powerful factor in Cook County Republican politics. But in order to maintain and solidify his position, Lorimer had to participate actively in all levels of politics. The revolution in voter preference that had occurred since 1893—revealed in the striking Republican victories of 1894 and 1895—offered a tempting set of prizes to whomever controlled the party machinery. Lorimer had temporarily vanquished his rivals, but they would lose no opportunity to contest his leadership. In this regard, the elections of 1896 loomed up with particular significance.

For Lorimer, the 1896 contests furnished an opportunity to strengthen his hold over the Cook County Republican party and to extend his influence to the state level. He was primarily concerned with the county and state tickets and only interested in the presidential contest as a means to further his local power. But the national race also held certain dangers. His party rivals, by endorsing a popular presidential candidate, could sweep control out of his hands. Thus, although Lorimer did not and could not see himself as a "president-maker," he had to become involved in the presidential contest in order to protect his local interests.

Of first moment for Lorimer was the state ticket, and here the choices were clear-cut. Henry L. Hertz wanted to be state treasurer and he could count upon the support of the Cook County organization.[1] For governor, Lorimer favored the tall, raw-boned, and rough-

---

[1] The state treasurer was elected for a two-year term. The office was considered

spoken John R. Tanner, the most powerful politician in the state outside of Cook County. Tanner, who managed U.S. Senator Shelby M. Cullom's extensive organization, had served as state senator, state treasurer, and in various federal posts. In 1895 the state committeemen elected him chairman of the Republican state central committee. As early as 1889 he had met Lorimer and recognized his potential. In the crucial fight between the county and city factions in 1895, Tanner stood with the Lorimer group. In return, Lorimer now guaranteed Tanner his help in Tanner's quest for the gubernatorial nomination.[2]

The presidential nomination was more complicated. By the fall of 1895 there were three leading candidates: Senator William B. Allison of Iowa; Speaker of the House Thomas B. Reed of Maine; and ex-Governor William McKinley of Ohio. Allison was a cautious, smooth politician who had substantial Senate power and prestige. A bimetallist, his record appealed particularly to the West and Midwest.[3] Reed was a giant of a man who stood six feet three inches and weighed nearly 300 pounds. He had revolutionized the speaker's role and vastly increased the influence of the lower house. Renowned for his caustic wit and keen intelligence, Reed had strong support in his home section of New England.[4] McKinley, however, was considered the favorite. As a congressman, he had become closely identified with the tariff issue. A quiet and astute manager of men, he represented "the dominant taste and morality of his time." As his recent biographer notes, McKinley favored the protective tariff and the Republican party because "he believed both promoted national rather than sectional interests or class development." McKinley's rhetoric echoed these beliefs and made him extremely popular among the mass of Republican voters.[5]

lucrative because of the treasurer's control over state funds. See Bogart and Mathews, *The Modern Commonwealth,* 242.

[2] *Tribune,* Sept. 15, Oct. 12, Nov. 23, 1895, May 24, 1901. For evidence of Tanner's early friendship with Lorimer see Tanner to J. W. Fifer, Nov. 12, 1889, Fifer Papers.

[3] Leland L. Sage, *William Boyd Allison: A Study in Practical Politics* (Iowa City, 1956), 248–264; H. Wayne Morgan, *William McKinley and His America* (Syracuse, 1963), 196; Stanley L. Jones, *The Presidential Election of 1896* (Madison, 1964), 100.

[4] Jones, *Election of 1896,* 100–102; William A. Robinson, *Thomas B. Reed: Parliamentarian* (New York, 1930); Morgan, *McKinley,* 197–199.

[5] H. Wayne Morgan, "William McKinley as a Political Leader," *Review of Politics* (Oct., 1966), XXVIII, 418; Jones, *Election of 1896,* 187–208.

An experienced businessman-politician who had hopes of becoming a "president-maker" managed each of the three leading candidates. Allison's manager was James S. Clarkson, the Iowa representative on the Republican national committee, who had extensive eastern contacts. Reed's manager was Joseph H. Manley, who was chairman of the Republican executive committee. And McKinley's associate was Marcus Alonzo Hanna, a Cleveland industrialist who entered politics for the purpose of making his close friend McKinley president. In retrospect, while all three were astute politicians, Hanna's ability as a party organizer, his efficiency, and his large financial resources elevated him above his rivals.[6]

The de-centralized structure of American politics complicated the game of president-making. Political power rested with the state and local organizations rather than with any national body. The professionals were the state and local politicians; their organizations were the repositories of power. Thus, as Robert D. Marcus observes, although the president-maker with a strong candidate could make life uncomfortable for the local bosses, he "could not afford to exercise any positive power in the state or the state leader could make life not just difficult but impossible for him."[7] Most desirable for the state or local leader was to trade his influence over the determination of a national candidate for solidification of his state power. In this regard, he would avoid commitment to a candidate as long as possible.

Neither Manley nor Clarkson planned to contest actively for their candidates. Clarkson's strategy was to secure second-vote commitments for Allison from delegates who were pledged to state favorite sons on the first ballot. Manley planned to exploit Reed's strength among eastern business interests, as well as to use Reed's influence in Congress to win support.[8] Each manager hoped that the powerful New York and Pennsylvania bosses Thomas C. Platt and Matthew Quay, both of whom wanted to block McKinley, would support their candidate in the convention. Meanwhile, Platt and Quay, what Hanna

[6] Jones, *Election of 1896,* 187–208; Morgan, *McKinley,* 185–187; Sage, *Allison,* 263.

[7] Robert D. Marcus, "Republican National Party Organization, 1880–1896" (unpublished Ph.D. dissertation, Northwestern University, 1967), vii, 493–496, now published as *Grand Old Party: Political Structure in the Gilded Age, 1880–1896* (New York, 1971); V. O. Key, Jr., *State Politics: An Introduction* (New York, 1956), 38–39; Jones, *Election of 1896,* 100–101.

[8] Sage, *Allison,* 263; Morgan, *McKinley,* 197–198.

called "the combine," encouraged the emergence of favorite-son candidates to impede the McKinley boom.[9]

McKinley had to be stopped if the other hopefuls were to stand a chance in the convention. While he and Hanna effectively utilized a small group of friends such as Ohioans Joseph P. Smith and Charles H. Grosvenor and McKinley cousins William M. ("Will") Osborne and Abner McKinley as nationwide liaisons, they had no real national organization. The McKinley forces depended upon their success in winning separate state groups to capture the nomination. In most states, Hanna supplied money and coordination to whomever was willing to support McKinley. Since most state leaders were determined to hold out for "terms," Hanna often worked with independent forces unattached to the ruling state organization.[10]

In Illinois, for instance, Hanna placed Charles G. Dawes, a young Nebraska lawyer who had moved to Chicago in 1895, in charge of the state campaign. Dawes had met McKinley through his father, a former Ohio congressman, and had developed a vast admiration for him. Hanna probably chose him as McKinley's Illinois manager because of his freedom from factional associations which could have complicated the McKinley movement.[11] Tall and thin, with a big nose and handlebar moustache, Dawes did not look impressive, but he convinced Hanna of his ability. Also supporting the McKinley cause in Chicago was Herman H. Kohlsaat, a long-time McKinley admirer, whose *Times-Herald* was the only Chicago newspaper backing the Ohioan.[12]

Lorimer and Tanner played the typical game of state leaders in regard to the presidential race; that is, they held out for terms from the various candidates. They presented Senator Cullom as favorite-son candidate,[13] but his candidacy did not preclude "working" the other hopefuls. In November, for instance, Lorimer went to Washing-

[9] James S. Clarkson to William B. Allison, Aug. 25, 31, Dec. 14, 1895, William B. Allison Papers, Iowa State Department of History and Archives, Des Moines; Jones, *Election of 1896*, 100–104.

[10] Jones, *Election of 1896*, 110–111; Marcus, "Republican National Party Organization," 443, 451.

[11] John C. McNulta to William McKinley, Apr. 9, 1896, William McKinley Papers, Library of Congress.

[12] *Dawes Journal*, 51; Kohlsaat, *McKinley to Harding*, 21; Jones, *Election of 1896*, 119.

[13] John W. Gates to William B. Allison, Feb. 17, 1896, Allison Papers; William Talley to William McKinley, Feb. 5, 1896, Charles G. Dawes Papers, Northwestern University Library, Evanston; Charles H. Grosvenor to Richard J. Oglesby, Mar. 16, 1896, Richard J. Oglesby Papers, Illinois State Historical Library, Springfield.

CORONATION OF KING WILLIAM I

Chicago *Times-Herald*, Nov. 26, 1895

ton with Tanner and Jamieson and held several conferences with Reed and his midwestern representative, former Chicago congressman J. Frank Aldrich. Doubtless the presidential contest was the topic of conversation. Evidence of Reed's attempts to woo Illinois came in late December when the state delegation was given five committee chairmanships, including the important appropriations, and was represented on every leading House committee. As the *Tribune* noted, Reed had a "warm spot" in his heart for Illinois.[14] Tanner also received substantial financial aid from the Allison forces, who hoped to win the state.[15]

The McKinley organization was not averse to making a deal with Lorimer and Tanner, but negotiations proved exceedingly difficult. Hanna approached Tanner in May, 1895, and later in the year talked to Jamieson, who had succeeded Tanner as state central committee chairman, but the Illinois politicians preferred to stay officially uncommitted.[16] The attitude of Herman H. Kohlsaat, who was attempting to serve his own interests in the campaign, further complicated the position of the McKinley forces. On the one hand, Kohlsaat was "merciless in his attack on the 'bosses,' " especially Lorimer and Tanner. Naturally, this journalistic criticism hampered McKinley's dealings with the machine leaders and made "a combination with the County organization impossible. . . ."[17] On the other hand, Kohlsaat refused to allow Swift and the city faction to fight for McKinley because he was unwilling to risk a further political defeat at the hands of the Lorimer organization.[18]

Since he depended upon the *Times-Herald* as McKinley's only Chicago newspaper support, Dawes reluctantly went along with Kohlsaat. He erected McKinley clubs throughout the city and planned to turn the annual Republican "love feast" into a McKinley rally.[19]

Cullom denied that he was a front for another candidate. See Shelby M. Cullom, *Fifty Years of Public Service* (Chicago, 1911), 273.

[14] James S. Clarkson to William B. Allison, Dec. 23, 1895, Allison Papers; *Times-Herald,* Oct. 28, Dec. 2, 14, 1895; *Tribune,* Dec. 22, 1895.

[15] J. E. Blythe to William B. Allison, Oct. 6, Nov. 15, 1895, G. B. Pray to Allison, Oct. 12, 1895, James S. Clarkson to Allison, Feb. 10, 1896, John W. Gates to Allison, Feb. 17, 1896, Allison Papers; Jones, *Election of 1896,* 151.

[16] Mark A. Hanna to C. A. Vaughan, Jan. 13, 1896, Dawes Papers; *Dawes Journal,* 54.

[17] Charles G. Dawes to Joseph P. Smith, Dec. 11, 1895, Dawes Papers.

[18] *Dawes Journal,* 66–67.

[19] Joseph P. Smith to Dawes, Dec. 20, 1895, Dawes Papers; *Dawes Journal,* 67–68.

When these plans leaked out, Lorimer and Cullom protested at turning such a sacred occasion into a partisan gathering. Cullom, who had just announced his own candidacy, bitterly complained at McKinley's "invasion" of the state and insisted that as favorite son his claim to the state delegation should not be contested.[20] The McKinley organization, believing that the Cullom delegation "in the end would have been under the control of the 'combine' . . . to be transferred at their dictation," would not agree.[21]

The love feast caused no surprises. Both sides saw in it what they wished to see. For Dawes "the overwhelming McKinley sentiment" dominated, while Lorimer noted Cullom's strength among the politicians.[22] Whatever the actual situation, the love feast did temporarily alter Lorimer's plans. On January 27 he, Jamieson, and Madden telegraphed Mark Hanna that they wished to have "an important interview" with him on the 29th. When Hanna and Osborne appeared in Chicago, however, Lorimer and his allies did not keep their appointment. According to the anti-McKinley *Tribune,* they notified Hanna that "we are taking care of Illinois politics and are not friendly to outside interference."[23] Evidently Cullom's decision to become an active candidate had caused a further change in Lorimer's plans. Dawes viewed Lorimer's and Jamieson's failure to meet with Hanna as a declaration of war, and noted in his diary that the fight was now between "McKinley and the people against the 'County' machine and its state branches."[24]

The campaign cry of "the people against the bosses," while probably believed by Dawes, was also a useful technique for a popular candidate to use against an entrenched political organization. Many of the rank and file who objected to Lorimer's control of the party machinery found in the McKinley campaign a rallying point. In addition, defeated factional leaders like Mayor George B. Swift saw in the McKinley organization a vehicle to restore their damaged fortunes. Thus, although McKinley's "popularity became a test of whether or not the newly powerful state and local leaders would be

20 Shelby M. Cullom to Peter S. Grosscup, Apr. 4, 1896, McKinley Papers; *Dawes Journal,* 65–66.
21 Peter S. Grosscup to William McKinley, Apr. 4, 1896, McKinley Papers; Charles H. Grosvenor to Richard J. Oglesby, Mar. 16, 1896, Oglesby Papers.
22 *Dawes Journal,* 66; *Tribune,* Jan. 29, 1896.
23 *Tribune,* Jan. 31, 1896; Joseph P. Smith to Charles G. Dawes, Jan. 27, 1896, Dawes Papers.
24 *Dawes Journal,* 66.

responsive to the 'will of the people,' " it was also a test as to whether they could maintain control over their organizations.[25]

Lorimer perceived McKinley's strength among the party rank and file and the necessity to capture the delegates before the McKinley forces did. Accordingly, early in February, the county central committee announced that the county convention and all but two of the congressional conventions would be held on February 25, several months sooner than usual. Lorimer justified these "snap" conventions by claiming that the McKinley backers used cash to get votes.[26] When Dawes heard of the early conventions, he protested that the organization was "not fighting fair," and arranged a protest rally. But only 300 persons attended and the convention plans went ahead as scheduled.[27]

The most crucial of the "snap" conventions was the county, and here Lorimer had other concerns besides the presidential race. The key local office at stake was that of Cook County state's attorney, for which Lorimer had slated his friend and ally Charles S. Deneen. Deneen was a short and stocky individual with the determined look of a bulldog. A skilled and intelligent politician, he controlled several wards in the Englewood area on Chicago's southwest side, part of Lorimer's congressional district. Deneen was a lawyer, and in 1895 Lorimer secured his appointment as attorney to the Chicago Sanitary District. Now, in regard for his political services, he was due for promotion.[28]

Deneen's nomination, however, became the basis of a challenge to Lorimer's control by Alderman Martin B. Madden, who had aspirations toward heading the county machine. After a stormy debate, Lorimer fought off the challenge, as Jamieson, Hertz, Pease, and John M. Smyth rallied to aid the nomination of Deneen and the rest of Lorimer's county slate.[29] On the same day as this victory, the Second District congressional convention unanimously renominated Lorimer for Congress and named him as delegate to the national convention. These victories established Lorimer's dominance, and the *Record*

[25] Marcus, "Republican National Party Organization," 420, 444.
[26] *Dawes Journal*, 67; *Tribune*, Feb. 4, 1896; *Record*, Feb. 8, 1896.
[27] *Dawes Journal*, 67–68; *Record* and *Inter-Ocean*, Feb. 11, 1896.
[28] There is a good sketch of Deneen in Carroll Hill Wooddy, *The Case of Frank L. Smith: A Study in Representative Government* (Chicago, 1931), 184–197; also see Merriam, *Chicago*, 180–182.
[29] *Tribune* and *Inter-Ocean*, Feb. 15, 1896.

acknowledged him as "Czar," while the *Times-Herald* crowned him "Lorimer, Rex," and lamented that "no Chicago politician has ever enjoyed so much power. . . ."[30]

The action of the county convention on the state and national offices further affirmed Lorimer's control. While the convention adopted instructions for Tanner and Hertz, it left the two presidential delegates uninstructed and available for bargaining, in spite of the widespread McKinley sentiment among the rank and file. Industrialist John W. Gates, a McKinley opponent, wrote Senator Allison that "the Cook County delegates were practically stolen from McKinley. The sentiment in Chicago had been worked up to such an extent by the *Times-Herald,* Mark Hanna and his money, that if a popular vote had been taken thirty days ago McKinley would have had more votes in Cook County than all other candidates put together."[31] Lorimer had skillfully stifled the McKinley feeling and maintained an uncommitted delegation. His argument was that an endorsement would so commit the state that if the McKinley campaign collapsed, "Illinois would be left in the lurch."[32]

During the next few weeks, the Lorimer and Tanner forces held their own against the rising McKinley tide. The inability of Dawes to break the Lorimer organization caused the McKinley forces to make another attempt to negotiate an agreement. Whether they succeeded is not clear. Dawes and William Osborne seemed to think that the machine had "unconditionally surrendered" and that it would help secure McKinley instructions.[33] More likely, whatever agreement was made was either limited or disregarded by the machine forces. Lorimer and Tanner continued to work for a delegation either pledged to Cullom or uninstructed. Several times at the end of March and the beginning of April Lorimer gave out statements that the McKinley strength was at its crest and that the Illinois delegation would be uninstructed. After one of these interviews, Hanna wrote to Dawes that "we must keep up our fight, and make them [Lorimer and Tanner] eat their words."[34] In disgust over the seeming worthlessness of their

---

[30] *Record,* Feb. 17, 1896; *Times-Herald,* Feb. 24, 1896; *Tribune,* Feb. 16, 1896.
[31] Gates to Allison, Feb. 17, 1896, Allison Papers.
[32] William G. Edens to Charles G. Dawes, Feb. 20, 1896, Dawes Papers.
[33] Dawes to McKinley and to John Thurston, Mar. 13, 1896, Osborne to Dawes, Feb. 26, 1896, Dawes Papers; *Dawes Journal,* 72; *Tribune,* Feb. 29, 1896.
[34] Hanna to Dawes, Apr. 3, 1896, William W. Tracy to McKinley, Mar. 16, 1896, Dawes Papers; *Tribune,* Mar. 25, Apr. 2, 8, 1896.

agreement with the machine, Joseph Smith complained to Dawes that "Illinois has some of the most adroit and cunning political schemers on this continent. Next to the fellows in Louisiana and Texas I have never seen their equals in duplicity and scoundrelism." [35]

Negotiations between the Lorimer-Tanner organization and the McKinley forces proceeded up to the state convention. The "desideratum" for state politicians in such a contest was, as Robert D. Marcus observes, "to lose with profit, to trade potential national power for real state control. . . ." [36] In late March Cullom offered to withdraw from the race in return for concessions to the regular organization, but McKinley, finding the price too high, rejected the offer.[37] This decision disturbed a number of experienced McKinley men. General John C. McNulta, Dawes's leading lieutenant, wrote to McKinley that "many delegates who are for us have some favorable candidates for State offices whose interests they hold paramount to ours. . . ." He warned that "the skillful political leaders and the party organization" would pressure these delegates to abandon McKinley.[38]

Aware of the dangers McNulta cited, Dawes attempted to insure that state issues did not confuse the vote for McKinley instructions. At a pre-convention caucus of the McKinley forces, he proposed that no contest be made on Lorimer's and Tanner's control of the organization of the convention or upon the selection of state officers and delegates-at-large. The vote on instructions had to "be entirely unconnected with the plans and ambitions of individuals." [39] Dawes's plans were attacked by Mayor Swift, who wanted to use the McKinley campaign to bolster his and his faction's political fortunes, but Dawes deflected Swift's challenge. Dawes communicated his position to Tanner and Jamieson and they agreed to let the vote on instructions be held after the nomination of state officers but before the nomination of delegates-at-large.[40]

On Wednesday, April 29, amid the waving of flags and the blaring

[35] Smith to Dawes, Apr. 3, 1896, Osborne to Dawes, Apr. 6, 1896, Dawes Papers.
[36] Marcus, "Republican National Party Organization," 495.
[37] Cullom to Peter S. Grosscup and Grosscup to McKinley, Apr. 4, 1896, McKinley Papers; *Dawes Journal*, 74; Jones, *Election of 1896*, 124.
[38] McNulta to McKinley, Apr. 9, 1896, McKinley Papers; Andrew J. Lester to McKinley, Moses P. Handy to Mark Hanna, C. W. Pavey to Dawes, all Apr. 22, 1896, Dawes Papers.
[39] *Dawes Journal*, 77.
[40] *Ibid.*, 77–79; George B. Swift to Richard J. Oglesby, Apr. 27, 1896, Oglesby Papers; Dawes to William M. Osborne, May 4, 1896, Dawes Papers.

of bands, the convention began. The Lorimer-Tanner forces quickly demonstrated their control over the convention in regard to state issues. They elected their candidates for temporary and permanent chairmen with little challenge, and nominated Tanner for governor and William A. Northcott for lieutenant governor by an overwhelming vote. They again showed their power when, after the news arrived that the Vermont convention had instructed for McKinley, Lorimer forced a recess that forestalled a McKinley rally.[41]

The following day the convention completed the state nominations and reached the question of instructions. Four resolutions followed in quick order. The first, by a Cullom man, called for instructions for his candidate; the next, by William J. Calhoun, the McKinley floor leader, substituted McKinley's name for Cullom's. The third was by Martin B. Madden, who proposed endorsements of Reed and Allison if McKinley's nomination failed at the national convention. And a Lorimer man made the fourth, moving that all previous resolutions be tabled and the delegates left unpledged. Calhoun protested that the regular order called for a vote on instructions, but the convention chairman overruled him and called for a vote on the last resolution. McKinley's delegates, however, surprised the opposition by defeating the motion to table 832 to 503. Conceding defeat, the Lorimer-Tanner forces presented a McKinley resolution. With its passage the Ohio man won the most "signal and significant" victory of the nominating campaign.[42]

Lorimer, while disappointed at McKinley's victory, took it philosophically. He attributed the endorsement to the work of Calhoun, "a shrewd, smart and practical" tactician.[43] And well might Lorimer be generous, because he had lost little by the McKinley triumph. Rather, he and Tanner had maintained their control of the state organization and nominated their full list of candidates for state and local posts. Dawes, in order to insure the voting of instructions, had sacrificed all

[41] *Times-Herald*, Apr. 30, 1896; *Dawes Journal*, 79–80; John E. Pixton, "The Early Career of Charles G. Dawes" (unpublished Ph.D. dissertation, University of Chicago, 1952), 106–107. Dawes claimed that Lorimer's motion to adjourn had been defeated by voice vote, although the chairman ruled that it had carried.

[42] *Tribune* and *Times-Herald*, May 1, 1896; *Dawes Journal*, 80; Pixton, "Early Career of Charles G. Dawes," 106–107; Frederick E. Coyne, *In Reminiscence: Highlights of Men and Events in the Life of Chicago* (Chicago, 1941), 117-118; Jones, *Election of 1896*, 123–124; Morgan, *McKinley*, 205–206.

[43] *Tribune*, May 2, 1896.

the local ambitions, such as Swift's, that went into the McKinley campaign. Lorimer was now without challenge in Chicago politics.[44]

Lorimer demonstrated his power and independence at the Republican national convention at St. Louis. There, at a meeting of the Illinois delegation, he helped elect Jamieson to the Republican national committee—this over the objection of Hanna, who preferred Dawes or Calhoun.[45] Although the McKinley nomination was practically a certainty, Lorimer held that the Illinois delegation should remain uncommitted. While the state gave 46 out of 48 votes to McKinley on the first and decisive ballot, Lorimer and his ally John M. Smyth voted for Reed. The man "of the people" had conquered, but Lorimer would not be a party to his triumph.[46]

A crucial problem for Republican leaders as they faced the election of 1896 was how to avoid the mistakes made in 1892 and hold the gains the party had made in the elections of 1894 and 1895. Some believed working-class and ethnic voters in the cities to be the critical element. In 1892, for instance, Joseph H. Manley wrote that he was humiliated that "the slums of Chicago, Brooklyn, and New York should settle the destinies of this country for four years," while Cullom complained to Benjamin Harrison that "we lost Illinois by the tremendous democratic vote of Chicago." [47] How to hold their recent gains among urban social groups was a vital question for Republicans, and in its determination urban politicians such as William Lorimer were key.

Lorimer's congressional district, containing as it did great numbers of industrial workers of various ethnic groups, was a test for the Republicans. If they could triumph in such districts, they would have little trouble in winning the cities. While there is not a great amount of material on Lorimer's election activities, there is enough to indicate

[44] Marcus, "Republican National Party Organization," 450.

[45] *Tribune*, June 10, 11, 1896. After Jamieson had been elected Illinois national committeeman, he supported Dawes for membership on the Republican executive committee in order to block William Kerr of the Swift faction, whom Swift had been pushing for the executive post. See *Dawes Journal*, 87–88; Dawes to Hanna, July 1, 1896, Dawes Papers; Dawes to McKinley, July 3, 1896, McKinley Papers; Marcus, "Republican National Party Organization," 466.

[46] At the convention Lorimer voted for the resolution calling for a gold plank in the platform. See *Tribune*, June 15, 1896; *Inter-Ocean* and *Times-Herald*, June 16, 1896.

[47] Quoted in Marcus, "Republican National Party Organization," 378.

his awareness of the necessity of holding the new voters attracted to the party in 1894. This could best be done, he believed, by convincing workingmen "that the republican platform . . . is in the interest of prosperity." [48] Since the Democrats claimed that the free and unlimited coinage of silver would bring prosperity, their argument had to be countered. Lorimer proposed that districts be canvassed by "sound and able speakers, who will show the voters that the republican platform is right on this currency question" and that the Republicans were in favor of "honest money" that would maintain wages and supply jobs for workingmen.[49] The sound-money argument, however, was insufficient. The deceptive simplicity of the free-silver issue as a means to increase the supply of money in the hands of workers and to eliminate debts was attractive; the argument for gold and the "honest dollar" had limitations. More related to the worker's experience, however, was the link between the Democratic low-tariff policy and the depression of 1893.

The Republicans claimed that protectionism equaled prosperity, and McKinley's advocates pictured him as "the advance agent of prosperity" and the guardian of "the full dinner pail." [50] The Republican tariff argument offered an explanation for the hard times caused by the depression of 1893 and a promise of future security, and appealed directly to urban workers. The *Tribune* reflected this sentiment among the party managers by devoting more space in its editorials to advocating tariff ideology than to condemning free silver.[51]

Lorimer widely utilized this theme. In speaking to working-class groups, he referred to his own background as a stockyards worker, and reminded his listeners how plentiful jobs had been under Republican protectionist policies and how scarce they became after 1892 and the passage of the "Gorman Wilson free trade bill"; how wages had gone up during Republican administrations, but down after 1892. Free silver, maintained Lorimer, was merely a "dickey" or "false front" to cover up Democratic free-trade policies.[52]

[48] Chicago *Evening Post* (hereafter cited as *Post*) and *Times-Herald*, July 15, 1896.

[49] *Ibid.*

[50] Jones, *Election of 1896*, 287–288.

[51] Kleppner, "Politics of Change in the Midwest," 471–472. Analyzing what he calls "symbol space" in the *Tribune* editorials, Kleppner finds that the paper devoted 42.5 percent of its editorial space to condemning free silver and 57.5 to tariff ideology.

[52] *Tribune*, Oct. 4, 20, 1896.

Late in the summer, as the election drew closer, Lorimer held Republican campaign rallies in a mammoth movable circus tent which held over 10,000 people. He used the tent in the working-class areas of the West Side and near the stockyards. Parades involving thousands of workingmen culminated in the tent, where the audiences were alternately harangued by orators and soothed by entertainers. Speakers such as Joseph B. Foraker, Mark Hanna, Robert G. Ingersoll, and Thomas B. Reed, in addition to Lorimer, attacked Democratic heresies. Between speeches, voters were entertained with band concerts, popular singers, and fireworks.[53] When Democrats like Governor John Peter Altgeld claimed that the workers were coerced into attending the rallies, Lorimer jibed that the only case of coercion he had heard of was "that of an old woman I know who told her husband he could pack up and go if he didn't vote for McKinley." [54]

In essence, each of the major parties chose "candidates for the presidency whose ideologies and images were consonant with the party's view of the depression and its cures." [55] William Jennings Bryan, through his free-silver ideology, tried to mobilize the working masses, both rural and urban, and restore the Democratic voting levels of 1892. Republican strategists, on the other hand, sought to hold the voters that they had won in 1894 and 1895. They attacked free silver, warned of low-tariff heresies and a return to the horrors of 1893, and derided Bryan, trying to convince normally Democratic voters that he was not really a Democrat.[56] In this endeavor, in Chicago as in the rest of the nation, the Republicans were successful.

In Chicago on election day the Republican party won a sweeping victory. McKinley took the city with 57.3 percent of the popular vote to 41.3 percent for Bryan. Tanner ran considerably behind with 53.2 percent, as Altgeld did well among German voters.[57] The GOP swept the Cook County offices, increased their representation in the Illinois General Assembly, and elected six of seven congressmen from the Chicago area. As for Lorimer, his vote in the Chicago wards of his district was actually higher than that of McKinley's, as he won the

[53] *Ibid.,* Sept. 23, 29, Oct. 2–6, 9, 20, 25, 1896; *Inter-Ocean,* Oct. 25, 1896.

[54] *Tribune,* Oct. 20, 23, 25, 1896.

[55] Kleppner, "Politics of Change in the Midwest," 459.

[56] *Ibid.,* 459, 575; Paolo E. Coletta, *William Jennings Bryan I. Political Evangelist, 1860–1908* (Lincoln, 1964), 170–172.

[57] Altgeld had 44.8 percent of the Chicago vote. His vote correlated at +.363 with the percent German population while Bryan's vote correlated at +.275. For the election returns see *Daily News Almanac for 1897,* 384–391.

election over Democratic candidate John Z. White with 55.3 percent of the total.[58]

Lorimer's victory in his working-class industrial district symbolized Bryan's failure to mobilize the laboring class. Although the Democratic percentage of the vote rose in twenty-one wards as compared with 1895, and in twenty-nine wards as compared with 1894, in no case did it equal Democratic strength in 1892. The average Democratic vote in the ten poorest wards in the city in 1896 was 51.5 percent; this was an improvement over 1894, when the percentage in those wards was 45.4, but a large decrease over 1892, when the percentage was 66 percent. The Republican vote, on the other hand, was up in twenty-one wards as compared with 1895 and in thirty-two wards as compared with 1894. The Republican average percentage in the ten poorest wards was 47.5 percent in 1896, as compared with 49.3 in 1895, 41.3 in 1894, and 33.9 in 1892. McKinley and the Republicans had made large inroads into the normally Democratic working class.[59]

Part of the Republican majority undoubtedly came from voters who had voted Democratic in 1892 but Populist in 1894. The Populists had captured 12 percent of the Chicago vote in 1894 to the Democrats' 35.3. Two years later, in 1896, the Democrats had only increased their percentage 6 points even though the Populists were no longer on the ticket, while the Republicans increased their percentage over 1894 by 5.8. The much larger vote in 1896 than in 1894 or 1892 reduces the significance of these figures, but it does appear that the Populist party had served as a temporary way station for Chicago voters dissatisfied with the Democrats. Once the Populists had disappeared from the ballot, voters moved back into the two major parties.[60]

In addition to the division of the Populist vote and the decline in Democratic strength among the working class, there were also

[58] In the Chicago wards in his district Lorimer had a mean of 49.4 percent of the vote and McKinley 48.4. Lorimer had a total of 35,045 votes, John Z. White 28,309. See Manuscript Election Returns, Second Congressional District, 1896, Board of Election Commissioners, Chicago.

[59] Kleppner calculated the Democratic mean percents by class for Chicago; his figures for the lower class are within 3 percentage points of mine. Kleppner, "Politics of Change in the Midwest," 446–447; Jones, *Election of 1896,* 345–346.

[60] Jones, *Election of 1896,* 344; Kleppner, "Politics of Change in the Midwest," 491.

cultural dimensions to the political changes of the 1890's. The 1896 figures suggest that Germans, both Lutheran and Roman Catholic, and Catholic Bohemians and Poles objected to Bryan more than did pietistic native Protestants and Swedes and Norwegians. The Catholic Irish, long the most loyal unit in the Chicago Democratic party, showed less variation than other groups.[61] Paul J. Kleppner has observed that ritualistic German Lutherans and Roman Catholics were "repelled by the evangelical fervor of the Bryan crusade," while pietists, such as Swedish and Norwegian Lutherans, were attracted by his morality. Republican party managers de-emphasized cultural factors in their appeal, making it easier for formerly Democratic ritualistic voters to enter their party.[62]

The political realignment of the 1890's reversed the Democratic victories of 1892 and made the Republican party dominant in much of the nation. Because McKinley carried seventy of the eighty-two cities with a population of 45,000 or more, Carl Degler has concluded that the elections of 1894 and 1896 "mark the emergence of the Republican party as the party of the rising cities." [63] Actually, as studies by V. O. Key, Jr., Duncan Macrae, Jr., and James A. Neldrum Paul J. Kleppner, and Samuel T. McSeveney show, the Republican resurgence bore little relation to an independent variable called "urbanism." Rather, the Republicans had "succeeded in drawing new support, in about the same degree, from all sorts of economic and social classes" in both city and county.[64] The GOP had ceased to

[61] The Democratic party lost 19.8 percent from 1892 to 1896 in the largest German ward, 19.7 in the largest Bohemian ward, 14.2 in the largest Swedish ward, and 13.3 in the heaviest native-American ward. See also Kleppner, "Politics of Change in the Midwest," 504–532; McSeveney, "Political Realignment of the 1890's," 11–12; Jones, *Election of 1896,* 345–346. The Democratic party only lost 9.7 percent from 1892 to 1896 in the leading Irish ward.

[62] Kleppner, "Politics of Change in the Midwest," 486–487, 532–533, 576–577; McSeveney, "Voting in the Northeastern States during the Late Nineteenth Century" (unpublished paper delivered at the University of Wisconsin Political and Social History Conference, 1968), 12.

[63] Carl N. Degler, "American Political Parties and the Rise of the City: An Interpretation," *Journal of American History* (June, 1964), LI, 48; Jones, *Election of 1896,* 344–348.

[64] Kleppner, "Politics of Change in the Midwest," 147–150; V. O. Key, Jr., "A Theory of Critical Elections," *Journal of Politics* (Feb., 1955), XVII, 12–13; Duncan Macrae, Jr., and James A. Neldrum, "Critical Elections in Illinois: 1888–1958," *American Political Science Review* (Sept., 1960), LIV, 678–681; Benson, "Research Problems in American Political Historiography," 113–183; McSeveney, "Political Realignment of the 1890's," 11–13.

be "a narrowly based social vehicle in the hands of evangelical crusaders." It had become "a functioning integrative mechanism with a
much broadened social base of support." [65]

Lorimer now faced the post-1896 period with a strengthened
position. His allies held the key Cook County and state offices;
Jamieson was Illinois national committeeman; and Lorimer had won
re-election to Congress. In achieving these gains, Lorimer astutely
used the national contest to further his local political goals, as he
compelled the McKinley forces to keep hands off the contests for
Illinois and Cook County offices. Lorimer had enhanced the power of
his organization even though his presidential choice was not nominated. If he could secure control of the city government, he could
become one of the nation's most powerful politicians. For this even-
tuality to occur, however, the Chicago Republican party would have
to further its role as an "integrative mechanism." But while Lorimer
was willing to advance such a change, the elite newspaper publishers
who had formerly dominated the GOP, and many of their followers,
were prepared to contest his program and his leadership.

[65] Kleppner, "Politics of Change in the Midwest," 589.

CHAPTER **4**

★ ★ ★ ★ ★ ★ ★ ★ ★ ★ ★

The Political Machine as Public Servant

O PPOSING AND CONTRADICTORY FORCES—some integrating and centralizing, others distintegrative and fragmenting—beset the American industrial city at the end of the nineteenth century and affected its march toward modernization and development. On the one hand were the disintegrative and decentralizing forces: localism and provisionalism, tension between immigrant and native and immigrant and immigrant, and religious and class antagonisms. The lack of centralization characterized politics and government, where party factions and the town and ward system allowed "local and particularistic interests to dominate." [1] The concerns of their localities rather than the city as a whole dominated the activities of the city's political representatives.

On the other hand were the forces of centralization. Many of these derived from the structural and technological transformation reshaping American urban life. The streetcar line, the telephone, and the mass-circulation newspaper were part of a communications revolution that knit the city closer together. Other forces of centralization reflected the corporate thrust toward systematization, rationalization, and efficiency. Many enlightened business leaders believed that these tendencies should be applied to the public as well as the private sector

---

[1] Hays, "Politics of Reform," 161; Hays, "Political Parties and the Community-Society Continuum," in William Nisbet Chambers and Walter Dean Burnham, eds., *The American Party Systems: Stages of Political Development* (New York, 1967), 164–165; Wiebe, *Search for Order*, 44–75, 164–195; Seymour J. Mandelbaum, *Boss Tweed's New York* (New York, 1965), 1–45. See also Frederic C. Howe, *The City: The Hope of Democracy* (New York, 1905), and *The Modern City and Its Problems* (New York, 1915).

and used to improve the total quality of city life. The growing body of urban professionals in fields such as medicine, law, and engineering also held these attitudes. These professionals, as Samuel P. Hayes notes, were concerned with questions of education, health, and public welfare from a "universal rather than parochial perspective." [2] They liked corporate systems of decision-making because of their pervasive scope and their "coercive potential." They offered the opportunity for the professionals to carry their "standards of life" to the population at large and to compel it to abandon its parochialism.

The political machine occupied a halfway position between the forces of centralization and those of decentralization. Rooted in the wards and precincts, of necessity it gave recognition and political power to local and particularistic interests. But the machine also had an important integrating and centralizing function. It mediated between the immigrant poor and the unfamiliar environment; through favors it eased the impact of hard conditions. It supplied a ladder of upward mobility for the immigrant and, through its control of government, an opportunity for its members to profit through forms of graft, honest and otherwise. And, perhaps most important, the machine replaced the city's legalized political disorder with an informal centralization focusing in the boss.[3]

This consolidation of political power proved particularly useful to powerful business interests, especially those involved in activities requiring public franchises. Since franchises were "a privilege, a thing of value," [4] great controversy existed over their longevity and the compensation to be paid to the city. In an attempt to escape these uncertainties, as well as the hold-up attempts of individual legislators, businessmen turned to the political bosses. During the 1890's in Chicago, a series of accommodations developed between the bosses and utilities and traction companies in quest of extended franchises.

This set of accommodations, while serving a centralizing function, proved increasingly "burdensome and unsatisfactory" to many in the

[2] Hays, "Political Parties," 154–157, 165–167, 169–173; Wiebe, *Search for Order*, 111–132.

[3] Banfield and Wilson, *City Politics*, 115–127; Merton, *Social Theory and Social Structure*, 71–82; Tarr, "The Urban Politician as Entrepreneur," 56–60.

[4] Edward C. Kirkland, *Industry Comes of Age: Business, Labor, and Public Policy 1860–1897*, Vol. VI of *The Economic History of the United States* (New York, 1961), 251.

business and professional community. Efficiency-minded businessmen and professionals from the middle and upper classes were especially dissatisfied.[5] Holding a "cosmopolitan" rather than a restricted view of the possibilities of urban life and embracing corporate concepts of vertical decision-making, they found the arrangements between businesses and the machine to be expensive, wasteful, and uncertain. And, even more pertinent, they found that these arrangements strengthened the existence of a political system which was rooted on the local level and denied political power to groups at the top of the emerging socioeconomic structure. If their goal of centralizing the city and applying corporate concepts of systematization, rationalization, and efficiency to city life was to succeed, the political machine and its arrangements with public-service corporations had to be destroyed.

In pursuit of this aim, in the late 1890's in Chicago, a number of these upper-level cosmopolitan professionals and businessmen joined in organizations or pressure groups to challenge the machine and to effect the distribution of political power in the city. These men are often collectively grouped under the heading "municipal reformers." While they bore some resemblance to earlier "reformers," they differed in the scope of their vision, the content of their appeal, and their involvement in the political process. Where earlier reformers were content to pass resolutions calling for "good government," press for civil service, and call for the prosecution of grafters, the new reformers envisioned the eventual total restructuring of urban government. Their model was the systematized and rationalized bureaucratic organization. Their ideal was a nonpartisan city government staffed by experts and directed by a city manager.[6]

But Chicago reformers also realized that their ideal could not be immediately accomplished. They therefore concentrated their efforts upon the election of "honest" men to the city council and, when they grasped how closely city affairs were connected to state, to the General Assembly. The two most important organizations were the Municipal Voters' League, founded in 1896, and the Legislative Voters' League, founded in 1901. Both groups used a similar technique: the investiga-

---

[5] Hays, "Political Parties," 176–181; Hays, "Politics of Reform," 161–163.
[6] Hays, "Politics of Reform," 159–161, 163–165; James Weinstein, "Organized Business and the City Commission and Manager Movements," *Journal of Southern History* (May, 1962), XXVIII, 166–182; Chicago Bureau of Public Efficiency, *The City Manager Plan for Chicago* (Chicago, 1917).

tion and publication of the backgrounds and records of candidates. The Municipal Voters' League and the Legislative Voters' League issued reports and recommendations before each primary and general election and these were publicized in the newspapers most sympathetic to their cause: Victor Lawson's *Daily News* and *Record,* Kohlsaat's *Times-Herald* and *Evening Post,* and the *Tribune.* On occasion the reform groups entered directly into ward politics in order to insure the nomination of a desired candidate. If necessary, they would make a deal or compromise with one of the parties.[7]

Aside from their more systematic approach to political change, the new breed of municipal reformers differed in another significant regard from their predecessors. They held that they represented "the people"; that they were advancing the cause of democracy. The machine had led the people astray; the reformers would restore them to the right course.[8] Oddly enough, however, there was little in the affiliations or origins of these reformers to identify them with the "people." They were largely wealthy businessmen and professionals of considerable education who belonged to the best clubs—the Union League, the Chicago, the Iroquois, the Commercial, and the Merchants—and whose names were found in Chicago's *Blue Book,* the register of the city's elite.

One of these reform groups, the Municipal Voters' League, has been analyzed by Joan S. Miller, who found that out of a sample of fifty leaders of the Municipal Voters' League in the period from 1896 to 1920, thirty were professionals, with lawyers predominating, while the remaining twenty were businessmen. There were no "blue- or white-collar workers" among the group. Almost all were wealthy or near-wealthy, or, if of the social worker–minister type, such as Graham R. Taylor of the Chicago settlement or Jenkin Lloyd Jones of the Abraham Lincoln Center, they mingled with the rich. Over 80 percent of the sample were native-born Protestants with a college education or better. There were no Catholics in the group and, al-

---

[7] Sidney I. Roberts, "The Municipal Voters' League and Chicago's Boodlers," *Journal of the Illinois State Historical Society* (Summer, 1960), LIII, 131–148; Hoyt King, *Citizen Cole of Chicago* (Chicago, 1931), 1–141; Merriam, *Chicago,* 104–108.

[8] Hays, "Politics of Reform," 160; Joan S. Miller, "The Politics of Municipal Reform in Chicago during the Progressive Era: The Municipal Voters' League as a Test Case, 1896–1920" (unpublished M.A. Thesis, Roosevelt University, 1966), 37–43.

though there were five Jews, none were of eastern European origin. As for political affiliation, 70 percent were identified as Republicans, even though "non-partisanship" in civic affairs was their announced aim.[9]

Walter L. Fisher, the traction expert and president of the Municipal Voters' League in 1906, typified such reformers. A lawyer and a graduate of Hanover College in Indiana, Fisher was a member of the Episcopal Church and belonged to the Chicago, Commercial, and Union League clubs. Although he supported both Democrats and Republicans for mayor and city council, his usual affiliation was Republican. President William Howard Taft appointed him Secretary of the Interior in 1911. Fisher supposedly strongly believed in popular government, but many of the comments made about him by his reform colleagues cast doubt on his democratic credentials. William Kent, for instance, boasted about Fisher's willingness to take "the whole responsibility of the city government on his shoulders" and his ability in "running the city." Charles H. Dennis, editor of the Chicago *Daily News* and a strong supporter of the Municipal Voters' League, noted that Fisher's faith in the people involved a "confidence in being able to steer them into right courses on policies that he advocated." And Lincoln Steffens, in his article on Chicago in *Shame of the Cities,* referred to Fisher as a "reform boss." [10]

Reformers such as Fisher wished not only to centralize decision-making in the city through such measures as charter reform, the elimination of townships, and a city manager system, but also to alter the "occupational and class origins of decision makers." The Municipal Voters' League and the Legislative Voters' League supported well-educated professionals and businessmen for office and opposed poorly educated workingmen and small businessmen. Saloon-keepers were especially anathema to the reform organizations. In addition, in their recommendations to voters, the Municipal Voters' League and the Legislative Voters' League consistently supported native-born Prot-

---

[9] Miller, "Politics of Municipal Reform in Chicago," 23–25. In his study of Chicago big businessmen engaged in civic reform in the 1950's, Peter Clark found that most civic leaders were Protestants interested in improving the public morality. Cited in Banfield and Wilson, *City Politics,* 249.

[10] Joel A. Tarr, "William Kent to Lincoln Steffens: Origins of Progressive Reform in Chicago," *Mid-America* (January, 1965), XLVII, 55; Miller, "Politics of Municipal Reform in Chicago," 38; Lincoln Steffens, *The Shame of the Cities* (New York, 1960), 184.

estants over foreign-born Catholics, especially Irishmen and Bohemians.[11]

In pursuit of their objective of centralizing decision-making power in their own hands or the hands of people with similar social backgrounds, the reformers often found the bosses, especially William Lorimer, blocking their way. The reformers resented Lorimer's control of the Republican party and his support of men they considered unfit for public office. Lawyer William C. Boyden, an active member of the Municipal Voters' League, wrote that Lorimer represented the "cheap and nasty elements of the community." [12] In part, their resentment represented an intra-city regional conflict. Reformers lived in elite areas of the North and South sides of Chicago or in affluent suburbs such as Evanston. Lorimer represented the West Side and sought to secure for his area some of the governmental "largesse" that had, for many years, gravitated to the city's elite sections. Under Lorimer's leadership, the West Side wards, which often voted Democratic, dominated the Republican party on the city and county level, further embittering Republican "reformers" who considered the Republican party as the proper vehicle for municipal "improvement." [13]

But in a deeper sense, the reformers objected most to the fact that the West Side, with its particular social composition of Catholic and Jewish immigrants, wielded political power. In their opinion the people of the West Side would not be competent to govern until the proper values had been "hammered and drilled into them," and until they had learned to accept the proper leadership.[14] And this leadership was not that of William Lorimer. In the words of Henry Smith, Lorimer always stood outside of the more elite Chicago business and social relationships: "The Chicago was not Mr. Lorimer's club." [15]

[11] Miller, "Politics of Muncipal Reform in Chicago," 31–36; Hays, "Politics of Reform," 163; Hays, "Political Parties," 175–178. Miller restricts her examination to the MVL recommendations; I conducted my own analysis of the LVL recommendations.

[12] William C. Boyden to William Kent, June 7, 1909, William Kent, "The Republican Party in Illinois," unpublished manuscript dated Nov. 22, 1901, William Kent Papers, Yale University Library, New Haven; Walter L. Fisher to Theodore Roosevelt, Feb. 19, 1904, Theodore Roosevelt Papers, Library of Congress.

[13] See *Tribune* editorial, Apr. 3, 1901; Carter H. Harrison, *Growing up with Chicago: Sequel to "Stormy Years"* (Chicago, 1944), 209–211; Richard C. Wade, "Urbanization," in C. Vann Woodward, ed., *The Comparative Approach to American History* (New York, 1968), 197–199.

[14] See Tarr, "William Kent to Lincoln Steffens," 55; Kent, "The Republican Party in Illinois."

[15] Lewis and Smith, *Chicago*, 358. Edgar Lee Masters noted that "Lorimer . . . despite his regularity as a party man, and all that he did to enrich the pockets

If the reformers disliked Lorimer and the machine, he and his followers, in fact all Chicago professional politicians, reciprocated in full. While the reformers disapproved of their values, they found the reform impulse incomprehensible. What were the reformers after? Honesty? Good government? These were abstractions that had no meaning in a concrete world—mere words used to mislead the voters and to cause them to shift their allegiance. Lorimer called the reformers "four-flushers," out for personal glorification and booty.[16] They had merely chosen a different and more hypocritical method of gaining power. This attitude toward reform was common in the immigrant community, where the machine was at its strongest. There was "No Place for Reformers Among Bohemians," editorialized *Denni Hlasatel.* "We have with us many reformers, but their work does not meet with much success. The reason for this is that people do not take much stock in the sincerity of their uplifting exhortations. Their activities comprise the suppression of 'boodle,' the exposure of scandals, and crusades against 'grafters.' They conduct this agitation to satisfy their own political ambitions. . . ."[17]

The machine's approach to dealing with the problems of urban life rested upon a different value system than that of the reformers. The machine offered the American materialistic "Gospel of Success" without an insistence upon middle-class morality and ethics. It supplied an organizational answer to the problems of adjustment to and exploitation of the urban environment but based upon local customs and institutions. It accepted the immigrant as he was, asking only that, in return for material aid, he surrender his vote (which essentially had little meaning to the immigrant) to the machine at election time.[18]

Machine politicians seldom responded to the attacks of the reformers or tried to counter their arguments, but Lorimer was an exception. He specifically offered his "organization" to the voters as an alternative to the reformers' program. The "organization," he held, would furnish the means by which men could deal with the problems and take advantage of the opportunities created by Chicago's growing

of those whose activities constituted the power and the wealth of Chicago magnates, was regarded as a low fellow. . . . The truth is he did not belong to the best set. . . ." *The Tale of Chicago* (New York, 1933), 294–295.

16 *Tribune,* Apr. 5, 1902.

17 *Denni Hlasatel,* June 27, 1905; *Narod Polski,* Dec. 24, 1902; *Die Abendpost,* Feb. 4, 1911.

18 Banfield and Wilson, *City Politics,* 115–118; Hofstadter, *Age of Reform,* 176–184.

pains. The reformers tried to present the machine as evil, but only those who did not understand its function would accept this argument. "They think that the organization means a few men who control it," asserted Lorimer, but if they would join it these "erroneous impressions" would be removed. They would discover that the machine rested upon the grass roots in the wards and precincts and that through it they would not only help themselves but their neighborhoods as well.[19]

Although Lorimer and the other leaders of the machine probably never saw the irony of it, they, like the reformers who opposed them, were attempting to deal with the same essential problem—the need to integrate the city and to enable men to fulfill themselves within the complex urban environment. The Lorimer organization, like most city political machines, actually operated on three different levels in its integrating function: service to the voter, service to the members of the machine, and service to certain business elements in the city. These functions were not performed altruistically, but rather because they helped to perpetuate the machine. However, in the process of helping itself, the machine aided others in dealing with the city environment.

The service that the Lorimer organization supplied to the voters might be called its social welfare function. In addition to the usual handouts of food and coal, Lorimer secured jobs on county and state payrolls, as well as with public-utility companies, for numerous individuals. In November, 1901, alone, for instance, Lorimer placed 868 men on the West Park payrolls.[20] Lorimer also intervened a number of times with the city, county, state, and federal governments to secure help for individuals who were in trouble with the law or who had some small favor to ask of government. "Have been requested by strong friends to secure pardon for Earl Platt, who was sent to house of correction [sic] on charge obtaining money by false pretenses," wrote Lorimer to Governor Tanner; "would deem it a personal favor if you can assist him." On other occasions, Lorimer secured scholarships, pensions, and licenses for residents of his district.[21] Favors such

[19] See Lorimer's speeches quoted in *Tribune,* Apr. 20, July 2, Aug. 9, Sept. 3, 1902.
[20] *Ibid.,* Nov. 14, 1901.
[21] See Lorimer to Tanner, Apr. 24 (two telegrams), Sept. 12, 1900, John R. Tanner Papers, Illinois State Archives, Springfield. For other favors see Charles S. Deneen to Lorimer, Jan. 8, 1900, Lorimer to Tanner, Jan. 12, 1900, *ibid.;* Lorimer

as these, given without obligation, won Lorimer and his machine voter loyalty.

The second area of service, that of the machine to its own members, involved several levels of operation. The first was the government jobs that the organization secured for its minor functionaries, the precinct and ward workers. In 1900, in a single primary district of Lorimer's home ward, the Tenth, forty-five Republicans held governmental posts. This patronage was the lifeblood of the organization and held its members' loyalty. Lorimer controlled thousands of patronage positions from the city, state, and federal governments.[22] As he later described the process, he was "advised with by the county committeemen for all the wards in [his] neighborhood": "At their request I practically took charge of all the patronage for those wards. I got that patronage from the sheriff, the county clerk, the county treasurer, all the clerks of the different courts, the state administration, that is, through the governor, the park commissioners, the mayor, the city clerk, the city attorney, and all the different elected officials; and . . . it rarely happened . . . that any appointments of any kind, big or little, were made in the section of the city in which I lived without my recommendation." [23] And, of course, Lorimer also had a dominant voice over the nominations of many of these major government officers.

Significant also were the opportunities for profit that the organization's more influential members secured from their political power. The machine's philosophy in this regard was well expressed by Tammany Hall's George Washington Plunkitt when he said that all professional politicians agreed on "the main proposition that when a man works in politics, he should get something out of it." Thus the machine politician often became a "political entrepreneur" who used the goods of the political world—influence, laws, government grants—to make a private profit.[24]

There were many ways in which the urban politician could profit. Especially common was so-called "honest graft": involvement in

---

to Governor Richard Yates, Jan. 13, 15, 17, June 5, 1902, Richard Yates Papers, Illinois State Archives.

[22] *Tribune*, Apr. 24, 1900; *Dillingham Committee Hearings*, VIII, 7854; James Q. Wilson, "The Political Economy of Patronage," *Journal of Political Economy* (Aug., 1961), LIX, 369–380.

[23] *Dillingham Committee Hearings*, VIII, 7854.

[24] Riordon, *Plunkitt of Tammany*, 3–8; Wilson, "Political Economy of Patronage," 380; Tarr, "The Urban Politician as Entrepreneur," 55–56.

companies that would benefit from the politician's inside influence. Another frequent practice was that of "boodling," where the legislator or councilman sold his vote. Oftentimes businessmen would be forced to pay as much to prevent adverse legislation as to obtain it. Public funds were frequently deposited in banks that made "loans" to politicians or in which politicians held stock. Tax assessments were raised or lowered depending upon the generosity of the person or corporation being taxed. And politicians often pocketed large sums secured through the holding of fee offices or the retaining of bank interest upon public deposits.[25]

Lorimer himself specialized in "honest graft." During his career he had interests in several firms that benefited from his political position. As early as 1888, for instance, he employed fifty teams of horses and men to fulfill a hauling contract obtained from the Roche administration. The Murphy-Lorimer Brick Company (Murphy was Seventh Ward Democratic alderman), organized in 1895, the O'Gara King Coal Company, in which Lorimer served as a silent partner, the Lorimer & Gallagher Construction Company, and Lorimer's Federal Improvement Company all received extensive public contracts. In addition, in 1909 Lorimer founded the La Salle Street National Bank, which held substantial city and county deposits.[26] By the turn of the century, through his many "political businesses," Lorimer was on his way to becoming a wealthy man.

So were many other Chicago machine politicians, both Republican and Democratic, who engaged in "honest graft." Coal companies and bonding and construction firms were especially popular among the politicians, while Martin B. Madden owned a stone company which held government contracts. The Lorimer & Gallagher Construction Company, the Chicago and Great Lakes Dredging and Dock Company controlled by Democratic bosses Roger C. Sullivan and John P. Hopkins, and a firm in which Thomas Gahan, Democratic county chair-

25 Tarr, "The Urban Politician as Entrepreneur," 61–67; Merriam, *Chicago,* 25–69.

26 Lorimer lists his businesses in *Dillingham Committee Hearings,* VIII, 7665. For Lorimer's coal companies and their public contracts see *Tribune,* June 24, 1899, Sept. 6, 1901; for the brick company, Chicago West Park Commissioners, *Annual Reports* (Chicago, 1897–1903); for construction contracts, see Index to Contracts Listed in the Proceedings of the Chicago Sanitary District, 1892–1914, manuscript volume, Chicago Historical Society; for his bank see James, *Growth of Chicago Banks,* II, 830–837.

man in the 1890's, was a partner, did much of the building and maintenance on Chicago's drainage canal.[27]

In addition to offering its members the opportunity to profit through their political positions, the machine also provided a mobility vehicle. A poor immigrant, for instance, through hard work and determination, could rise in the organization to a position of power and influence. His particular ethnic background, which might be a hindrance to success in the larger society, often became of positive benefit in politics, as votes came from ethnic loyalty.[28] Thus the machine had positive value for its own members in a manner that enabled them to cope better with and succeed in the urban environment.

The third area of service provided by the machine was to business interests anxious to exploit the economic opportunities presented by the growing city.[29] Most of these businesses were dependent upon governmental action or franchises for their continued existence. For this reason, they benefited from arrangements or accommodations with the political machine. The machines eased the process by which corporations secured their grants or franchises, and in return received a direct money payment as well as jobs on traction or utility company projects.[30]

In Chicago at the turn of the century, an interlocking agreement between the political machines and traction, gas, and banking interests overshadowed all minor business-political deals. The specific groups involved were the Lorimer Republican machine, the Sullivan-Hopkins Democratic machine, the Charles Tyson Yerkes traction companies, the People's Gas Light & Coke Company, the Ogden Gas Company, and the John R. Walsh banks. This "combine," which controlled two newspapers, marshaled great economic and political power. It had a far-reaching effect upon the character of Chicago, Cook County, and Illinois government, upon the disposal of public funds held by these governments, and upon the involved problem of granting public franchises.

The municipal reformers objected to the businessmen involved in

[27] *Inter-Ocean*, May 25, 1910; Marquis, ed., *Who's Who in Chicago, 1926*, 88, 554–555; Index to . . . Proceedings of the Chicago Sanitary District; Lincoln Steffens, *The Struggle for Self-Government* (New York, 1906), 49–50.

[28] Cornwell, "Bosses, Machines and Ethnic Groups," 31–34; Handlin, *The Uprooted*, 209–212.

[29] Wiebe, *Search for Order*, 167.

[30] Merriam, *Chicago*, 112–114.

the combine not only because of their activities but also because of their social backgrounds. Two of the men, banker John R. Walsh and merchant John M. Smyth, for instance, were Irish Catholic immigrants. Walter L. Fisher referred to the pair as the "most dangerous and demoralizing political influences in this community. . . ." [31] William Kent accused them of being "at the bottom of most of the devilment in local government," and called Smyth, in an obvious anti-Catholic reference, "father confessor to the county machine." [32] Yerkes, who according to Fisher had come to Chicago directly "from his Pennsylvania Penitentiary," had antagonized a number of Chicago investors by his shady methods and financial dealings. Chicago merchant prince Marshall Field expressed the opinion that "Mr. Yerkes is not a safe man." [33]

The business members of the combine were chiefly interested in control over deposits of public funds and the passage of gas and traction franchise legislation. The link between the two areas was banker John R. Walsh. Walsh was an Irish immigrant who had made a fortune through the distribution of newspapers and periodicals. From 1895 to 1905 he ran the Chicago *Chronicle* and used its pages to protect his political and financial interests from adverse criticism.[34] In 1881 Walsh entered the financial field and by 1893 controlled three banks—the Chicago National, the Home Savings, and the Equitable Trust Company—which depended upon public funds for a large part of their total deposits. During the 1890's and through 1905, they held a sizable percentage of the public deposits of the city of Chicago, Cook County, the Chicago Sanitary District, and the West and South Park boards, as well as sharing in the state deposits with several downstate banks.[35]

[31] Fisher to Theodore Roosevelt, Feb. 19, 1904, Roosevelt Papers.

[32] Kent, "The Republican Party in Illinois."

[33] Fisher to Theodore Roosevelt, Feb. 19, 1904, Roosevelt Papers; Sidney I. Roberts, "Portrait of a Robber Baron: Charles T. Yerkes," *Business History Review* (Autumn, 1961), XXXV, 349–354.

[34] For a study of Walsh's career see Joel A. Tarr, "John R. Walsh of Chicago: A Case Study in Banking and Politics, 1881–1905," *Business History Review* (Winter, 1966), XL, 451–466.

[35] In 1905 the Walsh banks held over $4,500,000 of the West Park Board, South Park Board, and Sanitary District funds, $3,761,000 of county funds, and $2,490,000 of city funds. See National Bank Examiner's Reports for the Chicago National Bank, June 22, Dec. 9, 1905, Records of the Office of the Comptroller of the Currency (Record Group 101), National Archives; Charles E. Merriam, *Report on the Municipal Revenues of Chicago* (Chicago, 1906), 108. These funds were deposited by government officials with no competitive bidding or security requirements. The

Although he called himself a Democrat, Walsh secured the public deposits through close alliance with the Lorimer Republican and the Sullivan-Hopkins Democratic machines. Lorimer had known Walsh since the days when he had been a newsboy, when Walsh owned a downtown newsstand. The connections between the Lorimer organization and the Walsh banks were Lorimer allies John M. Smyth and Fred M. Blount. Blount was cashier and then vice-president of the Chicago National and a director of the Home Savings and the Equitable Trust. Smyth was a director and a heavy stockholder of the three banks. Democrats Sullivan and Hopkins held stock in the Chicago National, as did banker-politician Andrew J. Graham, who was allied to their faction.[36] Sullivan, Hopkins, and Graham were close Lorimer friends.

Through his political allies, and especially Lorimer in the 1896–1905 period, Walsh controlled appointments to positions with power over public funds. He, fellow Chicago National Bank director William Best, and Vice-President Lyman C. Walton of the Equitable Trust Company composed the Chicago South Park Board, Walsh serving as treasurer from 1888 to 1905. Blount was treasurer of the West Park Board from 1888 to 1894 and 1897 to 1905, and of the Chicago Sanitary District from 1896 to 1906. Andrew J. Graham was also a member of the West Park Board. In 1905, Walsh's last active year as a financier, his three banks held over $4,500,000 of the West Park Board, South Park Board, and Sanitary District funds. No other Chicago bank held deposits from these government bodies.[37]

---

only requirement was that the disbursing official be bonded; it was customary for officials to deposit funds in the banks supplying their bond and Walsh did most of the Cook County bonding. In 1905 he endorsed the bonds of the city treasurer for $500,000, and of the several park board treasurers for an aggregate of $1,500,000. See *Record-Herald*, Mar. 3, 1906.

[36] National Bank Examiner's Report, June 11, 1913. This report includes a list of Chicago National stockholders in December, 1905.

[37] *Tribune*, June 5, 1904, Dec. 19, 1905; Chicago South Park Commissioners, *Annual Reports* (Chicago, 1888–1905); Chicago West Park Commissioners, *Annual Reports* (Chicago, 1888–1905); Chicago Sanitary District, *Proceedings of the Board of Trustees* (Chicago, 1896–1906). Loans to politicians seem to have furnished one *quid pro quo* for the deposit of public funds. In 1905 loans to politicians and their enterprises from the Chicago National amounted to over $1,000,000. Some of the larger sums involved were Smyth, $475,000 ($375,000 over the legal limit for the Chicago National); John P. Hopkins, $50,000; Roger Sullivan, $80,000; Andrew Graham, $145,000 ($30,000 from the Equitable Trust); Fred Blount, $40,000 (Equitable Trust); and $72,000 to the O'Gara King Coal Company, in which Lorimer was a silent partner. Other Lorimerites who held loans were Judge

Reformers knew of the connections between the Walsh banks and the two political machines, but saw little they could do about them. As Walter L. Fisher wrote, these activities were "not of the character necessary to prove in court a violation of the criminal code." [38] Neither were they the type of issue that could be used to rouse public opinion against the politicians and their business allies. The situation differed, however, in regard to public franchises.

During the 1890's in Chicago and other large American cities, municipal reformers demanded either the strict regulation of public-service franchises or the institution of municipal ownership. Usually they made these demands in the name of "the people" as against streetcar and gas monopolists. But, as was often common when the reformers spoke of "the people," they actually referred to the middle and upper classes rather than the lower or working class. The case of traction is an issue in point, since to a large extent it was not the working classes that used the streetcar lines.

During the decade from 1880 to 1890 a large number of suburban towns and villages had developed outside the then Chicago city limits. The city annexed these areas in the late 1880's and the early 1890's and they continued to increase in population; other suburban areas developed beyond the new city limits. This suburban growth depended upon the development of transit facilities. Because it had superior transportation to the downtown business district, the South Side suburbs underwent the most rapid growth in population and land values. By the late 1890's, comparable facilities were in existence on the North and West sides, and the underdeveloped areas of these sections also underwent a housing boom.[39]

Most available evidence suggests that predominantly middle- and upper-class people who lived in the outlying parts of the city but who worked and shopped in the downtown section used the streetcar lines. Usually only middle- and upper-income groups could afford the time and money required to commute to work. At a time when the average work week for semi-skilled and unskilled labor extended from forty-

---

Elbridge Hanecy, Lorimer's candidate for governor in 1900 and mayor in 1901, $46,000; Joseph C. Braden, Sanitary District trustee, $19,000; Daniel D. Healy, $7,445; and James P. Gallagher, Lorimer's business partner, $20,000. See National Bank Examiner's Reports, Dec. 9, 1905, July 3, 1906.

[38] Fisher to Theodore Roosevelt, Feb. 19, 1904, Roosevelt Papers.

[39] Hoyt, *One Hundred Years of Land Values In Chicago,* 134–195; Pierce, *Chicago,* III, 327–333.

eight to seventy-two hours a week and the average wage was $1 to $3 a day, few workers were willing to spend precious leisure time or a substantial percentage of their daily wages on transportation. Workingmen, therefore, tried to live within walking distance of their place of employ, and such sites were usually "poorly provided with street improvements and with surface-car transportation." [40]

Commuters were not the only ones interested in cheap and efficient traction service. Businessmen also, especially downtown retail merchants, desired high-quality transportation so customers could have easy access to the downtown shopping centers. Real-estate brokers too understood that land values depended upon adequate transit facilities, while industrialists knew that available and cheap street transportation helped insure a labor supply. The same point applies to other municipal services. Businessmen were large consumers of municipal services such as gas, water, and electricity. Again, cheapness and efficiency was their aim. As a result, as Edward C. Kirkland notes, "even the apostles of laissez faire were willing to grant to municipalities a range of activities vouchsafed to few forms of government." [41]

A major clash over the issue of municipal services occurred in Chicago in the first half of 1897. The municipal reformers and their elite and business supporters ranged on one side, while on the other side stood businessmen directly involved in traction and gas and their political allies. The intensity of that year's struggle permanently marked the character of Illinois and Chicago politics and also the political career of a number of important Illinois politicians, especially William Lorimer.

The focal point of the conflict, because of Chicago's lack of complete control over public franchises, was the Illinois General Assembly. All of the business members of the "combine" mentioned earlier had important legislation pending. The key items concerned gas and traction. The gas legislation provided for a consolidation between the Ogden Gas Company and the People's Gas Light & Coke Company. John R. Walsh, whom Walter L. Fisher called the "financial and

---

[40] Hoyt, *One Hundred Years of Land Values in Chicago*, 311; Sam B. Warner, Jr., *Streetcar Suburbs: The Process of Growth in Boston, 1870–1900* (Cambridge, 1962), 52–66, 154–166; Warner, *The Private City: Philadelphia in Three Periods of Its Growth* (Philadelphia, 1968), 191–194; George Rogers Taylor, "The Beginnings of Mass Transportation in Urban America, Part II," *Smithsonian Journal of History* (Autumn, 1966), I, 50–52.

[41] Kirkland, *Industry Comes of Age*, 250–251.

political agent" of the "gas trust," was a director of both companies, as well as the Northwestern Gas Light and Coke Company.[42] The Chicago National Bank held large investments in gas stocks and bonds, as well as those of electric and traction companies. C. K. G. Billings, president of the People's Gas, was a director and stockholder of the three Walsh banks.[43]

The Ogden Gas Company, which sought to combine with the People's, was not an ordinary utility. Its president was Roger C. Sullivan, Democratic political boss, and its principal stockholders were politicians from both parties. Democratic machine politicians formed it in 1895 for the purpose of blackmailing People's Gas into buying its franchise at a large profit to its founders. But the price was too high, and Ogden Gas actually began to produce gas and engage in intermittent price competition with People's Gas.[44] By 1897, however, largely through Walsh's mediation, the two companies reached an amiable agreement. Accordingly, their political allies introduced merger legislation in the Illinois Senate in April of 1897.[45]

The other key legislation concerned Charles Tyson Yerkes, the chief *bête noir* of Chicago's reformers. Yerkes had come to the city in 1881 from Philadelphia, where he combined a brilliant financial career with a short term in the Pennsylvania penitentiary for embezzlement. In the 1880's, with the aid of Philadelphians Peter A. B. Widener and William Elkins, he acquired the traction lines on the North and West sides.[46] Yerkes made a number of spectacular improvements in urban transportation, electrifying and unifying the system, but he was still extremely unpopular among the users of his system as well as among Chicago business leaders and reformers.

Chicago's commuters complained constantly about the service Yerkes provided. His cars, they said, were crowded, unventilated, dirty, and poorly heated and lighted. To this Yerkes frankly answered that it is "the strap-hangers who pay the dividends." Yerkes also re-

---

[42] *Tribune*, Nov. 9, Dec. 9, 1905. There is a list of Walsh's directorships in James, *Growth of Chicago Banks*, II, 715.

[43] In 1905 the People's Gas Company had $784,000 in deposits in the Walsh banks. In 1898 Yerkes had loans totaling $953,400 from the Walsh banks.

[44] For the complicated story of Ogden Gas see Harrison, *Stormy Years*, 192–199; Sidney C. Eastman, "Corruption in Illinois," undated typewritten manuscript, Sidney C. Eastman Papers, Chicago Historical Society; *Tribune*, Feb. 26, 1895, Feb. 26–28, Mar. 1, 3–6, May 7, 1897.

[45] *Senate Journal, Fortieth General Assembly* (Springfield, 1897), 932; *Tribune*, May 7, 1897.

[46] See Roberts, "Portrait of a Robber Baron," 344–371.

sisted the city's attempts to compel him to use adequate safety devices on his cars, and he outraged property owners on the streets along which he extended his tracks by his high-handed methods in obtaining frontage consents.[47]

Because of his "failure to observe the normal amenities of business life," Yerkes had few friends among Chicago's business elite. He "double-crossed" his partners and investors in his companies and was ruthless in his financial dealings. His association with eastern financiers alienated many Chicago businessmen. And he antagonized most of Chicago's influential editors and publishers by refusing to talk with reporters, banning newsboys from his cars, and filing libel suits at the slightest provocation.[48]

Chicago reformers found Yerkes' purchase of franchises from the city council especially reprehensible. Because his system consisted of a number of smaller companies, Yerkes constantly sought franchise extensions from the council. This placed him at the mercy of the politicians and, for purposes of self-defense, the financier became "a master of the arts of political bribery and legislative manipulation." Whether or not Yerkes was the "wellspring of political corruption in Chicago," or "its principal victim," as Forrest McDonald maintains, was irrelevant to the reformers. To them the financier was responsible for organizing "sporadic graft." [49]

But spend as he might, Yerkes could not force the council to extend his franchises for more than twenty years, the limit set by state law. This greatly complicated the problem of long-term financing and Yerkes was forced to turn to the General Assembly for suitable franchise extensions.[50] In February, 1897, Lorimer man John ("Farmer") Humphrey introduced the Yerkes bills into the Illinois Senate. They provided for a forty-year extension of all existing street railway franchises and regulation by an appointed state commission. The traction companies were to pay an annual sliding fee starting at 3

[47] *Ibid.*, 352–354.

[48] *Ibid.*, 352.

[49] Max Lerner and Mary F. Holter, "Charles Tyson Yerkes," *DAB*, XX, 609–611; McDonald, *Insull*, 84–85; Walter L. Fisher to Ida Tarbell, Aug. 25, 1908, Walter L. Fisher Papers, Library of Congress.

[50] In 1895 Yerkes attempted to secure a ninety-nine-year franchise extension from the state. Governor John Peter Altgeld vetoed the so-called "eternal-monopoly bills," supposedly refusing a $500,000 bribe from Yerkes. See Barnard, *"Eagle Forgotten,"* 404; Ray Ginger, *Altgeld's America: The Lincoln Ideal versus Changing Realities* (New York, 1958), 173.

percent to the state in lieu of other taxes.[51] In April the Yerkes bills were joined by the measures providing for a consolidation of the Ogden Gas Company with People's Gas. These also included a frontage provision to block the formation of new competitors.

Chicago reformers opposed the two sets of bills on the grounds that they violated the principle of home rule and paid inadequate compensation to the city.[52] The reformers sensed, moreover, that they had in the Yerkes and the gas bills issues which could rally public opinion against the business-political combine. The reformers organized a Citizens' Committee of One Hundred against the traction legislation led by George E. Cole, president of the Municipal Voters' League (the "human buzz saw of reform"), John H. Hamline, president of the elite Union League Club, and several other prominent business and civic leaders. The committee began an intensive anti–Humphrey bill campaign, holding daily "mass" meetings in downtown Chicago, pouring out pamphlets, and attacking legislators who supported the measures. The newspapers controlled by Victor Lawson, Herman H. Kohlsaat, and Joseph Medill gave the campaign strong press support. When the gas bills were introduced in mid-April, the reformers used the same organization and techniques against them.[53]

Initially the leaders of the business-political combine were not particularly concerned by the attack. They too had their press outlets in John R. Walsh's *Chronicle* and in Yerkes' newly purchased *Inter-Ocean,* edited by George W. Hinman.[54] Most important, Lorimer appeared to be in complete control of the General Assembly. In the Senate a faction headed by Lorimer lieutenant "Eddie" Dwyer controlled the organization, while in the House Lorimer's personal representative, "Fire Escape" Gus Nohe, chaired the party caucus. Edward C. Curtis, Lorimer's personal choice, was speaker of the House. Machine men were in charge of all important House committees, especially the critical Corporations and Railroads. In mid-April, under

[51] *Senate Journal, Fortieth General Assembly,* 272; *Tribune,* Feb. 19, 1897.

[52] *Senate Journal, Fortieth General Assembly,* 932; *Tribune,* May 7, 1897; Eastman, "Corruption."

[53] Roberts, "Portrait of a Robber Baron," 356. The key papers were Lawson's *Daily News* and *Record,* Kohlsaat's *Times-Herald* and *Evening Post,* and the *Tribune.* See the scrapbooks for 1897 in the Civic Association Scrapbook collection (John C. Ambler, comp.), Chicago Historical Society.

[54] Tarr, "John R. Walsh," 457–458. Yerkes had brought Hinman to Chicago in 1897 from the New York *Sun.* See Charles M. Faye to Victor Lawson, Sept. 25, Nov. 27, 1897, Victor Lawson Papers, Newberry Library, Chicago; Elbert J. Benton, "George Wheeler Hinman," *DAB,* IX, 65.

the leadership of the Lorimer representatives, the Humphrey bills passed the Senate by a vote of 29 to 16.[55]

By this time, however, the outcry of the reformers against the Yerkes bills and the politicians who supported them began to have an impact. The first sign that Lorimer's help for Yerkes would be politically damaging came in the 1897 mayoralty election. On February 26 at the Republican city convention, Lorimer dictated the nomination of Judge Nathaniel C. Sears of the Cook County Supreme Court as the Republican candidate for mayor.[56] Sears was a personable young man with a good judicial record, but to many he seemed a machine tool. Kohlsaat's *Evening Post* held that Sears was nominated "simply and only because it suited the game of machine politics, as manipulated by William Lorimer, Henry L. Hertz, and Sheriff Pease, to tempt him with the offer: 'We will make you Mayor of Chicago if you will worship us and do our bidding.'" Also damaging was the charge that Sears favored the Yerkes traction interests. No matter how often he denied it, the fact that Lorimer was his chief backer seemed to confirm the charge.[57]

The obvious discontent of much of the Republican press and many Republicans with Sears brought another Republican, John Maynard Harlan, ex-Princeton football player and now reform alderman, into the race as an independent. Harlan was an ambitious, egotistical man who specialized in verbal assault. "He led on the Council floor," noted William Kent, "and his splendid powers as a speaker gave the papers a chance to print interesting stuff and give publicity to our fight. . . ."[58] Harlan coordinated his campaign with the Citizens' Committee

---

[55] For Lorimer's control see *House Journal, Fortieth General Assembly*, 10–11; Charles S. Deneen to Lawrence Y. Sherman, Jan. 8, 1897, Lawrence Y. Sherman Papers, Illinois State Historical Library, Springfield; *Tribune*, Jan. 6, Feb. 6, 1897; *Times-Herald*, Jan. 6, 23, Feb. 5–6, 1897. For passage of the Humphrey bills see *Senate Journal, Fortieth General Assembly*, 580–581; Roberts, "Portrait of a Robber Baron," 357.

[56] *Tribune*, Feb. 27, 1897. Lorimer said, "I was completely swept off my feet by Sears' nomination." See *News*, Feb. 27, 1897.

[57] *Post*, Feb. 27, 1897. General John C. McNulta wrote that by accepting the nomination Sears had "besmirched the robes of the Judge to become the tool of machine politicians. . . ." McNulta to Charles G. Dawes, Feb. 2, 1899, Dawes Papers. Roy O. West, then a member of the Lorimer machine and later Secretary of the Interior under President Coolidge, wrote, "We think we have nominated a winning ticket . . . we expect to roll up a handsome majority and give the Republican party and, incidentally, the machine, a quiet boost." West to Lawrence Y. Sherman, Feb. 27, 1897, Sherman Papers.

[58] Tarr, "Kent to Steffens," 54.

of One Hundred and concentrated on the traction issue. He abused Sears as the creature of Lorimer and Yerkes and warned that a Republican victory would be a disaster. "The time has come," said Harlan, "when we want to stop talking and thinking about what the railroad companies will allow us to do and begin to talk and think about what we will allow them to do." [59]

As the campaign progressed, Harlan's vigorous stand against Yerkes and Lorimer attracted a great number of normally Republican voters. But whether Harlan was in the race or not, it was doubtful if the Republican ticket had much chance of victory. For the Democrats had nominated Carter H. Harrison, son of the former five-time mayor. Harrison astutely capitalized on his father's popularity and followed his father's formula of emphasizing the need for "the fullest measure of personal liberty consistent with the maintenance of public order." "Judge Sears stands for a puritanical government of this municipality," charged Harrison, "while we Democrats believe in liberty of individual action. This is a fight between the people and the puritanical classes." [60] As for traction, Harrison ignored the issue, allowing Harlan to lead the attack on Sears. Harrison understood that "personal liberty," a cultural issue, mattered more to the mass of Chicago Democratic voters than the traction question, and on election day they swept him into office.[61]

An analysis of the election returns reveals the correctness of Harrison's prognosis for his campaign. The Democratic candidate secured 50.2 percent of the vote, Harlan 23.5 percent, and Sears finished a poor third with 20.08 percent. Even a combination of the Harlan and Sears votes left Harrison a winner. The Democrats secured their largest gains over 1896 in the Bohemian, German, and Irish Catholic working-class wards, where voters who had left the party in 1894 and stayed out in 1896 returned in large numbers to vote for a man who reflected their cultural values. The pattern of Harrison's victory in 1897 was very similar to that of his father in 1893, as Chicago returned to its normal voting tendencies. Harrison's vote correlated at +.955 with his father's 1893 totals, the highest correlation between

[59] *Tribune,* Mar. 21, 1897; "Non-Partisan Voters' Bulletin," Doc. 14, Bull. 5, April, 1897, Graham Taylor Papers, Newberry Library, Chicago; Harold L. Ickes, *The Autobiography of a Curmudgeon* (New York, 1943), 86–87.

[60] Quoted in Weston A. Goodspeed and Daniel D. Healy, *History of Cook County, Illinois* (2 vols., Chicago, 1909), II, 644.

[61] Harrison, *Stormy Years,* 114.

two Democratic votes in the decade. Harlan, in contrast to Harrison, did extremely well in native upper-class Protestant wards and in Scandinavian areas. Harlan's vote correlated at $+.735$ with McKinley's 1896 totals, showing how largely he drew from the Republican party. Sears did not win a plurality in any single ward, as the Republican party sustained its greatest percentage drops in the areas where Harlan scored heavily.[62]

The Republican press blamed Sears's crushing defeat upon Lorimer. If Lorimer had not associated with Yerkes and if he had left the convention free to make its own choice, said the newspapers, the GOP would have kept the voters gained in the two previous elections.[63] Actually, while Lorimer's control of the convention probably played a role in the loss of the native-American and Scandinavian vote to Harlan, no Republican could have won unless he matched Harrison's cultural appeal. The voters who had left the Democrats in 1896 to vote for McKinley could not be retained on the local level with a reform candidate. Their chief interest was in protecting their cultural norms and life-styles, and Harrison promised better than any other candidate to do this.

While the reform press gloated over the blow dealt Lorimer in the election and predicted his ouster and the defeat of the Yerkes bills, neither prediction came true. The outcry over the traction issue, however, did cause both men to alter their positions. Yerkes, for instance, had his political allies replace the Humphrey bills with the so-called Allen bill. This new traction measure dropped the state commission and authorized the city council to extend existing franchises for fifty years.[64] Reformers protested over the inequity of these bills as they had over the Humphrey bills, but this time in vain. With Lorimer using political methods of persuasion and Yerkes supplying cash, the Allen bill passed the General Assembly and Governor Tanner signed it in early June. Simultaneously, Tanner approved the gas bills, which

---

[62] Harrison had 148,880 votes, Harlan 69,730, and Sears 59,542. See *Daily News Almanac for 1898,* 349. The Harrison vote correlated at $+.791$ with percent Catholic while the Harlan vote correlated at $+.787$ with percent Protestant. The Sears vote correlated at $+.549$ with percent Protestant. The Harrison vote correlated at $-.735$ with a rank-ordering of wards by class, while the Harlan correlation was $+.595$.

[63] See *Tribune* and *Times-Herald,* April 7, 1897. John Peter Altgeld regarded Harrison's victory as one for free silver. See Altgeld to Lambert Tree, May 11, 1897, Lambert Tree Papers, Newberry Library, Chicago.

[64] *House Journal, Fortieth General Assembly,* 951–952; Roberts, "Portrait of a Robber Baron," 360.

had swept through the legislature in late May. By this act, Tanner convinced many Chicagoans that "the stream of corruption that rolled through senate and house did not stop at the door of the executive mansion." [65]

During the next two years the agitation over the Yerkes bills continued unabated. In the April, 1898, city election, the voters elected enough anti-Yerkes aldermen to the city council to sustain a possible veto of franchise legislation by Mayor Harrison. And at the 1898 Republican legislative nominating convention, the delegates denied renomination to eighteen of the twenty-four Republican Cook County assemblymen who had voted for the Allen bill. [66] But throughout this period, Lorimer continued to defend the Allen Law in spite of the obvious political cost.

On June 8, for instance, at the Republican county convention, Hertz and Pease sponsored an anti–Allen Law resolution that declared the measure to be "in opposition to the interests of the people" and recommended its prompt repeal. The two machine leaders, both of whose bailiwicks had lost a large percentage of Republican votes in 1897, gambled for a political advantage over their former ally. But Lorimer did not take the challenge quiescently; springing to his feet, he defended the Yerkes measures. "Any person knows," said Lorimer, "that a corporation can afford to pay more in the way of compensation for a fifty-year franchise than it can for a twenty-year franchise." He criticized the newspapers for attacking the Allen Law without "argument or reason" and praised Tanner for signing such a worthwhile measure. When Lorimer moved to table the Hertz-Pease resolution, however, the delegates defeated his motion 870 to 246. [67]

In the months that followed, the hostility against the Allen Law increased as reformers and their press drummed up public opinion, and

[65] *House Journal, Fortieth General Assembly,* 1145–48; *Senate Journal, Fortieth General Assembly,* 1096–97; *Tribune,* May 8–10, 24, 27, 31, June 5, 6, 1897; *Times-Herald,* June 4, 5, 1897; Roberts, "Portrait of a Robber Baron," 360–362. Joseph Medill warned Governor Tanner that if he signed the Allen bill he would "part from the confidence of your friends and of the people of Chicago irrespective of party, during the rest of your life. Think the mater [*sic*] over seriously before committing so destructive an error [*sic*]." Medill to Tanner (telegram), June 8, 1897, Tanner Papers, Illinois State Historical Library.

[66] *Tribune,* Apr. 6, May 6, June 2, 9–10, 1898; Harrison, *Stormy Years,* 151–152.

[67] *Tribune,* June 9, 1898. Several days later, however, at the Republican state convention, Lorimer and Tanner blocked the passage of resolutions condemning the Allen Law. See *ibid.,* June 15, 16, 1898; Church, *History of the Republican Party,* 187–188.

Lorimer could do little about it. In December, 1898, Yerkes failed to get a franchise extension under the Allen Law through the city council. Mayor Harrison, who had formerly ignored the traction question, now realized its political potential and became a leading Yerkes foe. The following March, by a nearly unanimous vote, the Illinois General Assembly erased the Allen Law from the statute books. It had failed to serve its purpose and the politicians could no longer afford to carry its political liability. Yerkes himself disposed of practically all his traction holdings in 1899 to a syndicate controlled by Peter A. B. Widener and William Elkins and left for Europe, never again to be active in Chicago traction.[68]

As for the gas legislation, while Mayor Harrison temporarily blocked its implementation, the merger was finally completed in 1906, after Harrison had left office. The politicians who controlled Ogden Gas found it to their benefit to wait until the public had lost interest in the issue: the settlement was worth two-thirds of a million dollars to each of the eleven stockholders in the company.[69]

The struggle over the traction legislation in 1897–98 furnishes an interesting case study of the methods and motives of both reformers and machine politicians. Reformers opposed the Yerkes bills because they violated rights of local self-government and established long-term franchises with insufficient compensation to the city. They believed that they themselves would eventually assume control of the city government and enact the proper laws. In the meantime, however, having no plan ready to substitute for the Yerkes measures, they "perpetuated the law of the jungle" for Chicago utilities.[70] For the reformers had underestimated the difficulties they would have in changing Chicago government, just as they had not appreciated the improvements Yerkes had made in Chicago traction or the reforms he had sought through the Humphrey traction legislation.

Because Yerkes was openly contemptuous of not only his customers and stockholders, but also the city's reformers and business elite, most Chicagoans overlooked the fact that he gave them the best transportation system of any large American city. In the Humphrey bills, with

[68] Chicago City Council, *Proceedings, 1898–99* (Chicago, 1899), 1197–98; *Senate Journal, Forty-first General Assembly* (Springfield, 1899), 205–206, 221, 236; Roberts, "Portrait of a Robber Baron," 365–371.

[69] Harrison, *Stormy Years*, 197–199; McDonald, Insull, 82–83.

[70] McDonald, *Insull*, 88.

their regulatory commission and long-term franchise and compensation provisions, Yerkes sought to free himself from the hold of the "gray wolves" on the city council, establish a basis for adequate long-term financing, and satisfy the demands of city and state for adequate compensation.[71] Reformers and their press, however, ignored the benefits of the legislation and, because of their dislike for Yerkes and his political allies, launched a campaign that defeated the measures without providing an adequate replacement. The traction issue was back in the hands of the partially reformed but still disunited city council.

The reformers made the same miscalculation in their attack upon William Lorimer. Because many citizens attended their mass protest rallies and voted for Harlan, they believed that the "people" were with them and against the bosses. Because Lorimer could not prevent the county central committee from condemning the traction laws, they believed him a "dethroned sovereign."[72] And because they opposed the traction and gas legislation and Lorimer supported it, they chose to believe that they were honorable men and Lorimer corrupt. But they were incorrect in all three assumptions.

The "people" who supported Harlan and opposed Sears because of his connections with Lorimer and Yerkes were members of the middle and upper classes who did not reside in Lorimer's district. Although these groups could prevent Lorimer's candidates from winning citywide elections, they could not disturb his power base in the lower-class immigrant areas. While Lorimer and his machine probably did benefit from connections with various business interests, only those with the same standards of honesty as the reformers found this reprehensible. Most of those who resided in Lorimer's district and who benefited from the ministrations of his machine saw nothing wrong with his receiving compensation for his services. They continued to support him, and Lorimer continued to perform the services for business interests that brought him condemnation in 1897 and 1898. As a result, the heated battles between Lorimer and the reformers that had marked those years continued throughout his career.

[71] *Ibid.,* 84–88. See Charles Tyson Yerkes to Carter H. Harrison, Apr. 22, 1897, Carter H. Harrison Papers, Newberry Library, Chicago, in which Yerkes complains that "I have yet to find a single person in this city who is acquainted with their [the Humphrey bills] true purport and meaning. . . . The mass meetings . . . have tended to mislead the people rather than enlighten them."

[72] *Times-Herald,* June 9, 1898.

★ ★ ★ ★ ★ ★ ★ ★ ★ ★ ★

CHAPTER 5

The Federal Faction versus the State Faction, 1896-1902

WHILE WILLIAM LORIMER'S POSITION as party boss and his alliances with traction and gas interests subjected him to severe attack from municipal reformers, these critics never posed a serious threat to his base of political power. The voters who elected him to Congress for seven terms looked to the positive benefits they received from Lorimer and his organization and rejected the criticisms as unimportant.

More threatening to Lorimer than the vocal but often powerless reformers were his factional party rivals, especially the politicians who had formed the McKinley organization in the 1896 nominating campaign. If McKinley had lost in 1896, his Illinois supporters would have had no rationale for their continued existence as a separate entity and no patronage to make such existence possible. But McKinley was elected, and his backers had to be rewarded. Two Republican organizations thus appeared in Illinois—the first tied to the state administration which had opposed McKinley's nomination and the second to the federal. On one side were Lorimer, Tanner, and their followers; on the other Charles G. Dawes and "original McKinley men" like William J. Calhoun, Charles U. Gordon, and General John C. McNulta. Eventually, the two U.S. senators from Illinois, Shelby M. Cullom and William E. Mason, also stood with the federal faction.

Structural factors partially accounted for this intra-party struggle. Because of the country's federal form of government and the absence of a strong national organization, political power rested with the state or local party. Major political parties represented little more than an amalgamation of state organizations that united every four years to nominate and elect a president.[1] While the parties became more organized during the 1890's, this was predominantly on the state rather than the national level. In most states the party leaders or bosses were U.S. senators who cooperated with federal administrations to secure patronage.[2] In some states, however, such as Illinois, state politicians controlled the organization, causing friction with politicians tied to either the national administration or the senators.

The presence in the federal group of old foes of the state organization such as George B. Swift and newspaper publisher Herman H. Kohlsaat intensified the Illinois situation. Other antagonisms stemmed from the nominating campaign and the determination of some McKinleyites to punish the men who had tried "to pervert the will of the people in the hope of selling out the presidency to the best bidder. . . ."[3] And finally, the President's supporters felt that unless they thrust Lorimer and Tanner from power, the Republicans would have difficulty in carrying the state in the next presidential election.[4]

Because the McKinleyites believed that Lorimer and Tanner hindered the party, the federal-state factional battle pervaded almost every aspect of Illinois politics during the McKinley administration. This conflict first appeared at the beginning of 1897 during the contest for the U.S. Senate seat vacated by John M. Palmer. The federal faction spokesmen demanded that the nominee be "loyal" to McKinley, thus eliminating, in their opinion, any candidate of the state faction. So they opposed Martin B. Madden, the choice of Lorimer and the Cook County organization, because he would be "disloyal" to the President.[5] More acceptable to the McKinleyites was William J. Calhoun or William E. Mason, a flamboyant ex-congressman from Chicago who had done good work for McKinley in the campaign.[6]

In addition to the McKinleyites, Chicago reformers and Republi-

---

1 V. O. Key, Jr., *Politics, Parties, and Pressure Groups* (4th ed., New York, 1958), 310–312; Marcus, "Republican National Party Organization," vii, 493–497.

2 David J. Rothman, *Politics and Power: The United States Senate, 1869–1901* (Cambridge, 1966), 159–178.

3 William F. Calhoun to Charles G. Dawes, Dec. 22, 1896, Dawes Papers.

4 *Ibid.;* John C. McNulta to Dawes, Feb. 22, 1898, Jan. 16, 1899, Jesse W. Tull to Dawes, Mar. 6, 1899, Dawes Papers.

5 William J. Calhoun to Dawes, Jan. 26, 1898, Dawes Papers; *Times-Herald*, Jan. 12–14, 1897; *Tribune*, Jan. 10, 1897; *Record*, Jan. 12, 1897.

6 W. R. Jewell to Joseph G. Cannon, Jan. 20, 1897, Joseph G. Cannon Papers, Illinois State Historical Library, Springfield; *Times-Herald*, Jan. 11, 1897; Coyne, *In Reminiscence*, 131–134.

can newspapers such as the *Evening Post,* the *Tribune,* and the *Times-Herald* also opposed Madden. Lorimer knew of the uncertainties in Madden's election and proposed that Cullom be appointed to a cabinet post, thus providing two senatorial vacancies. The organization could then pair Madden with a downstate candidate more acceptable to the McKinleyites. The plan failed, however, when Dawes and the other McKinley leaders refused to endorse Cullom.[7] Lorimer and the other Cook County organization heads concluded that Madden could not be elected, and on January 14 Lorimer asked him to withdraw. Madden reluctantly consented.[8] That evening, at a caucus of the Cook County Republican assemblymen, to the surprise of the politicians and of the press, Lorimer presented himself as the new organization candidate.[9]

Lorimer's reasons for entering the race are difficult to assess. Seemingly the same factors that had blocked Madden would work against him. The *Times-Herald* warned that "no friend of President-elect McKinley can vote for William Lorimer," Joseph Medill telegraphed legislators that Lorimer was a "preposterous candidate," and George E. Cole of the Municipal Voters' League added that "Lorimer is not a fit man to represent Illinois in the United States Senate. . . ."[10]

Madden had been seriously hurt by the reluctance of downstate legislators to support a senatorial candidate who supposedly would not cooperate with the administration and now Lorimer confronted the same problem. Lorimer and Jamieson hoped Governor Tanner could overcome this opposition, but Tanner would not expend his influence in a doubtful and controversial cause. Lorimer left the executive mansion with "thunder clouds" on his brow, faced by the end of his senatorial bid.[11] That evening, after he had failed to arrange any deals

[7] Dawes to Joseph Smith, Nov. 14, 1896, Dawes Papers; *Dawes Journal,* 112; Morgan, *McKinley,* 258–259.

[8] There was a great deal of Chicago opposition to Madden because of his supposedly corrupt activities on the city council. William Kent called him the most "sinister and disreputable element" in the council. See Kent, "The Republican Party in Illinois"; Victor Lawson to Hon. Fred Busse, Jan. 13, 1897, Lawson Papers; *Tribune,* Nov. 28, Dec. 23, 1896; *News,* Dec. 24, 1896. For the feelings of the downstate politicians see G. Young to Lawrence Y. Sherman, Jan. 12, 1897, J. H. Atterbury to Sherman, Jan. 16, 1897, Sherman Papers.

[9] *News, Times-Herald,* and *Tribune,* Jan. 15, 1897.

[10] *Times-Herald* and *Tribune,* Jan. 15–17, 1897.

[11] W. R. Jewell to Joseph G. Cannon, Jan. 20, 1897, Cannon Papers.

with the other candidates, Lorimer threw his votes to Mason. He thus salvaged "the glory of nominating Mason" and perhaps gained some political capital for the future.[12]

Although political factors primarily caused Lorimer's defeat, other considerations were also involved. Many Illinois Republicans resented the idea of being represented in Washington by the boss of Chicago's West Side immigrant wards. As one Republican said, Lorimer did not represent "the brains of the party and . . . would in no wise reflect honor upon the party or upon the State. . . ." [13] The *Tribune* called him "a common ward machine politician" whose "puerile" speeches were filled with ungrammatical sentences.[14] In short, Lorimer was unacceptable as much for his low social origins as for his political associations.

The defeat of Lorimer's Senate candidacy in 1897 marked the beginning of the conflict between the state and the federal factions— a conflict which extended next to the question of patronage. During 1897 and 1898, Dawes, the two U.S. senators, and key McKinley men, but no members of the state faction, drew up a federal appointment slate for Illinois. Some recommendations, such as that of Charles U. Gordon for Chicago postmaster, were made over Lorimer's objections. Other important appointments included Dawes as comptroller of the currency, and a number of McKinley campaign workers, as well as followers of Senators Cullom and Mason, for key Illinois federal posts.[15] No member of the state faction obtained a federal position. McKinley, who did not usually hold grudges, agreed with this policy of depriving the state organization of federal patronage because of his bitterness over Lorimer's and Tanner's tactics in the 1896 nominating campaign.[16]

The state leaders reacted quickly to the slights of the federal forces.

[12] *Ibid.; Tribune* and *Times-Herald,* Jan. 20, 1897.

[13] J. H. Atterbury to Lawrence Y. Sherman, Jan. 16, 1897, W. H. Hainline to Sherman, Feb. 6, 1897, Sherman Papers.

[14] *Tribune,* Jan. 17, 1897; *Times-Herald,* Jan. 20, 24, 1897.

[15] Frederick E. Coyne, Mason's campaign manager, was appointed Chicago collector of internal revenue; John C. Ames and Charles P. Hitch, both Cullom lieutenants, U.S. marshals; Solomon H. Bethea, federal district attorney; Richard Yates, Springfield collector of internal revenue; and General John C. McNulta and George B. Swift, national bank receivers. See *Dawes Journal,* 117, 120, 130; Shelby M. Cullom to Herman H. Kohlsaat, Mar. 13, 1897, Kohlsaat to William McKinley, May 15, 1897, McKinley Papers; Dawes to George B. Swift, Apr. 27, 1898, Dawes Papers; *Tribune,* June 20, Oct. 14, Dec. 19, 1897.

[16] James R. Mann to J. Frank Aldrich, Apr. 17, 1897, Aldrich Papers.

On the day of his inauguration, Tanner excluded all original Mc-Kinley men from the ceremony. McKinleyites were not considered for state or county patronage posts, and Tanner and Lorimer used their Washington influence to attempt to block the appointments recommended by the Dawes group. "I think I can safely defy Governor Tanner to show that he has made a single appointment in this State to an original McKinley man," complained a collector of internal revenue to Dawes. Tanner seems "out to punish every McKinley man who aspires to a position under him or under the President." [17]

Events during the remainder of Tanner's gubernatorial term, such as Lorimer's and Tanner's support of the Yerkes traction measures, Tanner's obvious preparations to capture Cullom's senatorial seat, and the exposure of state corruption and salary assessments on state employees, aggravated the hostile relations between the two groups. Tanner received much of the criticism, and many Republicans opposed his renomination.[18] "Why," asked one Republican federal office-holder, "should the republicans of this state bow before a threat of a governor who has tarnished the good name of the party, even though he is backed by a political machine bent upon perpetuating itself in power? . . . the renomination of Tanner means our defeat in this state, and it might mean the loss of the state on the national ticket." [19]

The 1898 state, county, and congressional elections and the 1899 Chicago mayoralty election convinced many McKinleyites that Lorimer and Tanner indeed endangered the ticket in 1900. In the 1898 state and county elections the Republican vote markedly declined as compared with the 1896 election. Republican candidates lost the city of Chicago, although they carried the county and state. In addition, the Republicans lost several assemblymen and three Cook County congressional seats, although Lorimer was easily re-elected. While these were normal off-year election results, the federal faction blamed them on "Tannerism." [20]

The McKinleyites similarly interpreted the results of the 1899

[17] Richard Yates to Dawes, Dec. 17, 1896, A. J. Dougherty to Dawes, Aug. 2, 1899, Dawes Papers.

[18] Charles M. Faye to Victor Lawson, Sept. 25, 1897, Lawson Papers; Harrison, *Growing up with Chicago,* 152.

[19] Henry B. Dement to Dawes, Nov. 27, 1898, A. J. Dougherty to Dawes, Aug. 2, 1899, Dawes Papers.

[20] *Tribune,* Nov. 9–12, 1898; *Times-Herald,* Nov. 9, 1898; Church, *History of the Republican Party,* 188–189. The Republican candidate for state treasurer secured 47.9 percent of the Chicago vote. *Daily News Almanac for 1899,* 405–410.

mayoralty election. Lorimer's hand-picked mayoralty candidate was his close friend and neighbor Zina R. Carter.[21] Carter, a typical Republican businessman-politician, had been president of the Board of Trade, alderman, and commissioner of the Sanitary District.[22] Carter's Democratic opponent was Carter H. Harrison, who, fresh from his victory over Yerkes, posed as the only candidate who could safeguard the city's streets against the raids of the traction baron. Former Governor John Peter Altgeld also appeared in the race. Altgeld contested Harrison's anti-traction credentials and ran on a platform calling for municipal ownership of streetcar lines.[23]

Carter suffered from his Lorimer attachment, for in the eyes of many voters this connected him to Yerkes. His platform advocated a twenty-year restriction on franchises and "adequate compensation" to the city, but this could not remove the Lorimer-Yerkes taint. Of the nine Chicago English-language newspapers, only two, the *Tribune* and the *Inter-Ocean*, supported the Republican candidate. Apathy marked the Carter campaign. The Republican national committee refused to help finance it, and many Republicans calmly accepted Dawes's belief that "success was not to be with us this year."[24]

On election day Carter received only 35 percent of the vote, a loss of 12 percentage points for the Republicans over the state elections of the previous year. Harrison won 48.5 percent, a slight drop from his 1897 total, while John Peter Altgeld, running on a municipal-ownership ticket, gathered 15.5 percent. Altgeld probably hurt the Republicans more than the Democrats, although he drew from both parties. He ran the strongest with German voters, especially German Lutherans, suggesting that there was more than municipal-ownership sentiment to his support. The Altgeld candidacy also provided a resting point for voters who had moved into the Republican column in national and state contests, but who were not prepared to do so on the local level. Lorimer's control of the convention alienated some

[21] *Tribune* and *Times-Herald*, Mar. 5, 1899; *Chronicle*, Mar. 6, 1899.

[22] *Tribune*, Mar. 5–6, 1899.

[23] *Times-Herald*, Apr. 3, 1899; Harrison, *Growing up with Chicago*, 284; Barnard, "*Eagle Forgotten*," 420–421.

[24] *Tribune*, Mar. 8, 11, 18, 1899; Victor Lawson to Charles Snapp, Mar. 28, 1899, Lawson Papers; Dawes to Alexander H. Revell, Mar. 31, 1899, to Zina R. Carter, Apr. 7, 1899, to Bernard A. Eckhart, Apr. 7, 1899, Dawes Papers.

THE MACHINE IN DISTRESS

WANTED—A VOLUNTEER JONAH.

Chicago *Tribune*, Apr. 7, 1899

voters, but it seems more likely that the local cultural image of the Republican party and Harrison's personal-liberty appeal primarily accounted for the Democratic victory.[25]

Operating on the assumption that the "election of Carter H. Harrison makes it very plain that the renomination of Tanner for Governor would be a fatal mistake," the federal faction planned to nominate William J. Calhoun, then serving on the Interstate Commerce Commission.[26] McKinleyites were pleased when the "better element of the party" received the Calhoun candidacy with "avidity," and interpreted this to mean that Lorimer was "losing ground, and . . . will not be able to control very many delegates from Cook County." [27]

The defection of Hertz and Pease from the Cook County organization further convinced the federal faction that Lorimer's power was declining. The two machine men had chafed at Lorimer's and Tanner's leadership since the fight over the anti–Allen Law resolutions in 1898, and Republican vote losses in their wards in 1898 and 1899 made them believe that their political survival necessitated a break with Lorimer. Shortly after the mayoralty election a "Cook County machine leader," probably Hertz, called on General John C. McNulta to propose "cooperation," and claimed his "ability and willingness to secure a solid delegation from County to next state convention for satisfactory candidate for Governor." [28]

The press speculated that Tanner's unpopularity might cause Lorimer to abandon the Governor, but on July 12 Lorimer announced that if Tanner ran, he would support him. "Illinois never had a better Governor than John R. Tanner," declared the Blond Boss.[29] Lorimer's proclamation, however, did not halt the rumors that he would spring another gubernatorial candidate. The federal faction worried

[25] *Daily News Almanac for 1900,* 379, 382. The Altgeld vote correlated at +.789 with the percent German population; at −.452 with the Democratic vote; and at −.170 with the Republican vote. The Democratic vote correlated at +.573 with Catholic strength and at −.485 with class ranking, while the Republican vote correlated at +.663 with Protestant strength and at +.563 with class.

[26] Charles U. Gordon to Dawes, Apr. 8, 1899, Dawes Papers; *Tribune,* Apr. 5, 1899.

[27] John C. McNulta to Dawes, Jan. 16, Apr. 28, 1899, Charles U. Gordon to Dawes, Apr. 15, 1899, Dawes Papers.

[28] John C. McNulta to Dawes, Apr. 6, 1899, Henry L. Hertz to Dawes, Jan. 8, 1899, Dawes Papers. Hertz suggested to Dawes that John M. Smyth be won away from the Lorimer faction by appointing him to a federal post.

[29] *Tribune,* July 12, 1899.

that Lorimer would "pull . . . [Tanner] off at the last minute, and rush in a new man." [30]

In the meantime, the Calhoun boom proceeded. A number of federal officials actively pushed his candidacy. An assorted group of U.S. marshals, postmasters, and internal revenue collectors so dominated a Calhoun organizational meeting held in Chicago in July that Calhoun protested that it had the wrong "tone." [31] Actually, Calhoun was probably concerned that he might lose the nomination unless Lorimer was in his camp. Dawes asked Lorimer to back Calhoun and wipe out "factional differences" within the state, but Lorimer refused.[32] He still hoped to nominate his own man as governor.

Lorimer's refusal of support, as well as his own financial difficulties, forced Calhoun to withdraw from the contest. The federal faction lacked a candidate and several men entered the race hoping to win its backing. Richard Yates of Jacksonville, son of the Illinois Civil War governor and collector of internal revenue at Springfield, came first. A vigorous campaigner with an illustrious family name, Yates collected a number of downstate delegates. A Cullom follower, Congressman Walter Reeves of Streator, a "run-of-the-mill politician with a decent but colorless record," also announced his candidacy.[33] Late in November still a third entry, Judge Elbridge Hanecy, a tough, hard-boiled political judge from Chicago, entered the competition. Hanecy claimed to be an independent, although the press speculated that he was Lorimer's substitute for Tanner.[34]

The most important political event before the state convention was the annual "love feast," held in Springfield on December 29, 1899. Here Tanner combined an announcement that he would not be a candidate for renomination with a bitter attack on Cullom. With Tanner out of the picture, Lorimer declared for Hanecy, and called upon Hertz and Pease to support the Cook County candidate. Either

[30] William J. Calhoun to Dawes, July 31, 1899, John C. McNulta to Dawes, July 24, 28, 1899, Dawes Papers.

[31] William J. Calhoun to Dawes, July 31, 1899, A. J. Dougherty to Dawes, July 31, 1899, Dawes Papers.

[32] John C. McNulta to Dawes, Aug. 3, 1899, A. J. Dougherty to Dawes, Aug. 2, 1899, Dawes Papers.

[33] Two undated letters, but probably Sept., 1899, from William J. Calhoun to Dawes, Dawes Papers; *Tribune*, Sept. 3, 7, 1899; Josiah M. Clokey to Dawes, Apr. 16, 1900, Dawes Papers; Ickes, *Autobiography*, 39–40.

[34] Ickes, *Autobiography*, 39; *Tribune*, Nov. 12, 26, Dec. 20, 1899.

because of Lorimer's threat to deprive them of county patronage, or because they were buying time, Hertz and Pease consented.[35]

They did not remain with Hanecy for very long. Late in January, a number of North Side Chicagoans submitted Judge Orin N. Carter as the candidate of those who resented "the attempt of four or five men to deliver them . . . at the polls." [36] The Carter movement furnished a rallying point for Chicago members of the federal faction who wanted a governor from Cook County but would not support Hanecy. Four Chicago newspapers, the *Tribune,* the *Daily News,* the *Record,* and the *Times-Herald,* supported the "reform" candidate.[37] Hertz and Pease also adopted the "reform" guise and declared for Carter, claiming that Hanecy had become "affected with Tannerism." [38]

The crucial test for the Cook County candidates as well as for their sponsors were the Cook County primaries for state and county convention delegates. According to the *Tribune,* the primaries would determine "whether Lorimerism is to die or live in Illinois." [39] Defeat for Lorimer could mean the end of his county and state influence, the loss of patronage, and the destruction of his organization. "I am in a struggle for my very political existence," telegraphed Lorimer to James W. Wadsworth, chairman of the House Committee on Agriculture, to explain his absence from committee hearings. "A day's absence might mean my defeat." [40]

Whatever his fears, the primaries revealed that Lorimer, even without the support of Hertz and Pease, still dominated the Cook County GOP. Hanecy emerged with approximately 338 delegates, while Carter won 222, almost all from the North and northwest side bailiwicks of Hertz, Pease, and Illinois Senator Fred Busse. The Lorimer strength was in his own West Side wards, the West Side wards run by John M. Smyth, the downtown wards controlled by Sheriff Magerstadt, and the Deneen territory on the southwest side.[41] Lorimer's organization had again demonstrated its superiority over newspaper influence.

[35] *Tribune,* Dec. 29–31, 1899, Jan. 1, 1900; *Times-Herald,* Dec. 29, 1899.

[36] Graeme Stewart to Dawes, Jan. 15, 1900, Dawes to Mark Hanna, June 23, 1899, Dawes Papers; *Tribune,* Jan. 1, 20, 22, 25, Feb. 3, 1900.

[37] *Tribune,* Mar. 4, 1900; *Times-Herald,* Apr. 11, 15, 1900; *Record,* Mar. 2, 1900; *News,* Mar. 2, 1900.

[38] Dawes to Henry L. Hertz, Feb. 28, 1900, Dawes Papers; *Tribune,* Apr. 21, 24, 1900; *Times-Herald,* Apr. 20–21, 24, 1900.

[39] *Tribune,* May 1–3, 1900.

[40] Printed in *Times-Herald,* May 3, 1900.

[41] *Tribune,* May 3, 4, 1900.

Lorimer's primary victory gave him the power to punish Hertz, Pease, and Busse. Astutely, however, he postponed all county nominations until after the state convention. At the county convention on May 3, after a test vote showed that Lorimer controlled 729 of 1,114 delegates, he halted the proceedings until May 12, three days after the state convention. County officials and those hopeful for office would now reconsider throwing their votes against Hanecy. Lorimer made no secret of the reason for the delay: "The feeling against some of the men who have been prominent factors for many years was so intensely bitter it could not have been controlled had we gone ahead with the nomination of candidates. It will be different," he added, "one week hence. Everyone will know then the result of the fight for governor." [42]

The postponement of the county convention strengthened Lorimer's position at the state convention in Peoria. Lorimer confidently forecast Hanecy's nomination on the first ballot with 400 votes from Cook County and 483 from the rest of the state. His and Tanner's apparent control of the convention left the "anti-machine element" in a "demoralized and disintegrated" state.[43]

On the morning of May 7, Charles G. Dawes arrived in Peoria from Washington. He had not intended to interfere in the convention; he felt that as a federal official "it would be unwise as well as improper for me to become identified with a state contest for state positions." [44] Now, however, Dawes decided that his intervention was necessary to prevent "the demoralization of the Republican party in Illinois and the continuance in power indefinitely of the old and discredited Tanner regime." [45] Confronted by the possibility of the defeat of his allies and thus also the disruption of his political ambitions, Dawes decided to contest the Lorimer-Tanner control of the convention. The *Tribune* interpreted his action as pitting the McKinley administration against the Blond Boss and the Governor.[46]

Dawes proposed to the Carter and Reeves leaders that he make his "test for control" of the convention over the office of temporary chairman, a position that for twenty years had been filled by the state committee. A steering committee composed of Dawes, former governor

---

[42] *Post,* May 4, 1900; *Tribune,* May 5, 1900.
[43] *Dawes Journal,* 224–225; *Tribune* and *Times-Herald,* May 6, 7, 1900.
[44] Dawes to William J. Calhoun, July 6, 1899, to James N. Brady, Apr. 30, 1900, Dawes Papers.
[45] *Dawes Journal,* 224.
[46] *Tribune,* May 8, 1900.

and now Interstate Commerce Commissioner Joseph W. Fifer, Federal District Attorney Solomon H. Bethea, and Robert W. Patterson, editor of the *Tribune,* demanded that Charles B. Rannels, chairman of the state central committee, allow the delegates to choose the temporary chairman. When Rannels protested that the state committee customarily named this official and refused to say whether he would recognize a motion to substitute another name, Dawes made his request public.[47]

Lorimer moved to counteract the Dawes threat. Believing that Dawes could be halted by embarrassing the national administration, he announced that unless Dawes withdrew his candidacy for temporary chairman, he would present a resolution to the delegates condemning the controversial Puerto Rican tariff. Simultaneously, he had the state committee send the President a telegram of protest: "The regular republican organization of Illinois will consider the candidacy of Mr. Dawes, your comptroller of the currency for temporary chairman of the state convention as a direct interference in our state policies by the national administration. . . . Your friends here doubt the wisdom of this move. It will connect your administration with a local contest in the party among your friends. It will certainly endanger republican success at the polls in November." [48]

McKinley placed this telegram before his cabinet. Several members remembered Lorimer's and Tanner's opposition in 1896 and recommended that McKinley allow Dawes to proceed. The President agreed, and had his secretary, George B. Cortelyou, send the following answer to the state committee: "I am instructed by the President to say that your telegram received at eleven o'clock to-day was his first intimation that any officer of the Government was taking part in any controversy in the Illinois convention. He has not been consulted or informed on the subject." [49] This innocuous response suggested administration approval of Dawes's action. Many downstate delegates to the state convention heard of the exchange of telegrams and resolved not to be caught on the side opposed to McKinley.[50]

The next day on the convention floor the Reeves, Carter, and

[47] *Dawes Journal,* 224–225; *Tribune* and *Record,* May 8, 1900.

[48] Charles B. Rannels and Charles R. B. Van Cleave to the President, May 7, 1900, Dawes Papers; also printed in *Dawes Journal,* 227.

[49] George B. Cortelyou to Charles B. Rannels and R. B. Van Cleave, May 7, 1900, Dawes Papers; also printed in *Dawes Journal,* 227.

[50] *Record,* May 8, 1900.

Yates forces combined to substitute Dawes's name for the choice of the central committee as temporary chairman. On the roll call Lorimer mustered 316 out of 560 Cook County votes for the organization candidate, but it was not enough to overcome Dawes's lead among the downstate delegates. In addition, the federal forces gained control of the credentials committee and took 42 of 65 contested delegates from Hanecy.[51] Hanecy still possessed more votes than any other candidate, but remained short of a majority.

Under these circumstances, combinations were inevitable. The federal forces, believing that Congressman Reeves had the best chance of success, arranged to give him the Carter votes. Lorimer still hoped for a Hanecy nomination, but he agreed to transfer his delegates to Yates if Hanecy had not won by the third ballot. Tanner approved of the plan when Yates agreed to the renomination of Tanner's executive officers.[52]

The convention voted on May 9. As expected, Hanecy led on the first ballot by over 200 votes, followed by Reeves, Carter, and Yates. On the second ballot, however, Hanecy's total fell, while on the third Reeves moved to the front. The key roll call was the fourth—the ballot chosen by the federal forces to change the Carter votes to Reeves and by Lorimer to transfer the Hanecy delegates to Yates.

Pandemonium resulted from the attempted dual shift and the convention lapsed into disorder. Lorimer kept his head in the midst of the uproar, and grasping a large Yates banner, he raced with it to the front of the convention hall and planted it by his home ward delegation, thus indicating the shift of Hanecy to Yates. The Reeves forces held a counter-demonstration and it was followed by yet another demonstration for Yates by the Lorimer forces. At the end of an hour of frenzied activity, enough order had returned to take the final ballot, as Hanecy and Carter withdrew. A narrow Yates victory resulted. Because of Lorimer's dramatic act, the delegates nominated the candidate who had entered the convention with the least support.[53]

Opinion varied among politicians and in the press as to whether Yates's nomination was a Lorimer victory. Yates, denying that he had made any agreement with Lorimer beyond the renomination of the

[51] *Dawes Journal*, 224–226; *Tribune, Times-Herald*, and *Chronicle*, May 9, 1900.
[52] Charles U. Gordon to Dawes, Apr. 26, 1900, Dawes Papers; *Tribune* and *Record*, May 10, 1900.
[53] The best description of the events of the convention is in *Tribune*, May 10, 1900; see also *Record*, May 10, 1900.

Tanner officers, claimed he was "the freest man in Illinois." [54] Dawes, for his part, regarded Yates's selection as a triumph for the anti-Lorimer forces. Reeves had been defeated but the state faction no longer dominated the state central committee, thereby "reclaiming for the majority of the party in the State an organization which belonged to it, but which had been for some time used for personal and individual purposes." [55]

Cullom and his lieutenants wanted to purge the committee of all Lorimer and Tanner men and put it in control of Yates and the federal forces, but Dawes objected. To follow this policy, he wrote, would be "to encourage the policy of vindictiveness which had so much to do with wrecking the old organization. Let every leader and member of the party have that recognition from the organization that his usefulness merits." [56] Yates chose the chairman and secretary, Fred Rowe and Walter Fieldhouse, and they were acceptable to Lorimer as well as to Cullom and Dawes. The state committee thus consisted of three factions: the Yates faction, the Dawes-Cullom federal faction, and the Lorimer-Tanner group, with the last two vying for the support of the first. Although the federal faction believed that Yates would aid them in controlling the committee, the Governor's feelings in this regard were not as fixed as Dawes believed.[57]

Lorimer dismissed his loss of state committee control as "of no particular consequence . . . when compared with the position in which Henry L. Hertz and James Pease now find themselves with the Cook County organization." [58] For even though Lorimer had not nominated his man for governor, neither had his two former allies. The reckoning came at the county convention. For the first time in years, Hertz and Pease were excluded from the slate-making caucus. Lorimer deprived Hertz of all county patronage, while Pease was only left the recorder's office, held by his assistant Robert Simon. The convention lasted forty minutes and was "merely a ratification meeting

54 *Tribune,* May 10, 1900.
55 Dawes to Albert J. Beveridge, May 21, 1900, to Major B. B. Ray, May 22, 1900, to Dan Campbell, May 22, 1900, Dawes Papers; Volney Foster to William McKinley, May 10, 1900, McKinley Papers.
56 John Ames to Dawes, May 19, 22, 1900, Dawes to Richard Yates, May 21, 1900, to Walter Fieldhouse, May 23, 1900, to Graeme Stewart, July 23, 1900, Dawes Papers; *Dawes Journal,* 227–228.
57 *Dawes Journal,* 227–228; John L. Stevens to Dawes, May 28, June 5, 1900, Walter Fieldhouse to Dawes, May 25, July 14, 1900, Dawes to Richard Yates, May 28, 1900, to John L. Stevens, June 8, 1900, Dawes Papers.
58 *Tribune,* May 11, 1900.

for the Lorimer-Smyth caucus." "We have selected the best ticket the Republicans ever presented to the people of the county," Lorimer said. "It is a ticket of clean, decent, honorable men, and one which all good citizens can support." [59] Lorimer remained in control of Cook County Republican politics.

Remaining boss, however, required winning elections as well as intra-party battles. Most crucial for Lorimer was his own congressional seat and the county offices. Still acting on the assumption that organization brought success, Lorimer restructured the county central committee. He took over the chairmanship from John M. Smyth and placed his lieutenants in the executive positions. To arouse those Republicans who had not voted in the 1899 mayoralty contest, Lorimer established a "Republican Legion" with regiments from each congressional district and companies representing different nationalities. In addition, Lorimer began a "young voters' league" to enlist new voters into the Republican party.[60]

Lorimer used the "Legion" companies, along with bands and singers, to entertain voters in his own district. His political rallies resembled carnival shows. Lorimer's speeches were, as usual, short and devoid of excess verbiage; they stressed the good times brought by the Republican administration and the disasters that would befall the nation if the Democrats secured control of the government. The Republican party, said Lorimer, stands "for progress, while the Democracy stands for negation, obstruction, and stagnation. . . ." [61]

In spite of Lorimer's campaign tactics, the Republicans did poorly in Chicago as compared with 1896. McKinley won the city over Bryan, but with a greatly reduced margin as compared with 1896. McKinley's percentage of 49.6 represented a loss of 7.7 points, while Bryan's 47.6 percent was a gain of 6.3. These totals are surprising, since nationwide McKinley increased his percentage over 1896.[62] The Republicans lost most heavily in German, Bohemian, and Polish wards, the areas where McKinley had made his largest relative gains in the previous election. Losses in native, Irish, and Swedish wards were approximately equal to the citywide changes. It is difficult

59 *Ibid.,* May 12–14, 1900; *Times-Herald,* May 12–13, 1900.

60 *Tribune,* June 29, July 1, 12, 14, 24, 25, 1900.

61 *Ibid.,* Sept. 20, 22, Oct. 9, 1900.

62 In 1896 McKinley secured 51.07 percent of the nationwide vote and 55.8 percent of the Illinois vote; in 1900 the percentages were 51.7 and 53. See Edgar Eugene Robinson, *The Presidential Vote 1896–1932* (Stanford, 1947).

to explain these voting shifts, except to suggest that perhaps some of
Carter H. Harrison's popularity as well as the appeal of the German
Jewish Democratic gubernatorial candidate, Samuel Alschuler, transferred to Bryan. Although Alschuler lost the election to Yates, he won
a majority of the Chicago vote.[63] The Democrats also secured control
of the drainage board, the office of county coroner, and three county
commissionerships from the Republicans.

The greatest blow to the GOP was the loss of five congressmen
from Cook County. And among these was William Lorimer, defeated
by a young Irish lawyer, John J. Feeley. Lorimer's unseating was a
shock to Chicagoans. Newspapers ran such headlines as "LORI-
MER'S FALL EPOCH MAKING." [64] The *Tribune* viewed his defeat
as a "rebuke administered by Republican voters of the district to his
dictatorship" while the *Inter-Ocean* blamed the administration for
Lorimer's downfall and said that the federal forces had withheld their
support to punish him for his opposition to McKinley. Lorimer explained that it "was simply a Democratic vote in a district normally
Democratic," and demanded a reapportionment to prevent future
losses.[65]

Lorimer's analysis was substantially correct. Any explanation of
his defeat must take into account the decline in the Chicago Republican vote since 1896 and the other Republican losses in the city in
1900. Lorimer actually ran ahead of McKinley and Yates in the
Chicago wards in his district, and while his suburban vote declined as
compared with 1898, so did McKinley's. Lorimer's defeat did not result from any widespread anti-boss feeling, but rather from a general
decline in Republican Cook County strength.[66]

The press's tendency to proclaim that Lorimer's defeat meant "his
passing" showed a misunderstanding of his base of power. While
Lorimer's prestige was diminished and his position weakened, he still
had control of the Cook County Republican organization and contacts

[63] Alschuler had 50.9 percent of the Chicago vote and Yates 46.5 percent. See
Daily News Almanac for 1901, 391.

[64] *Tribune*, Nov. 7, 8, 1900.

[65] *Ibid.*, Nov. 8, 1900; *Inter-Ocean*, Nov. 8, 1900.

[66] Lorimer had 25,425 votes in the Chicago wards of his district while McKinley
had 23,550. Lorimer had 47.69 percent of the district vote and Feeley 50.63 percent.
The voter turnout was 14.16 percent larger than in 1898. See Manuscript Election Returns, Second Congressional District, 1900, Board of Election Commissioners, Chicago. There may also have been cultural factors involved in Lorimer's defeat.
Feeley was aided by several priests, and one Lorimer lieutenant told a *Tribune* reporter that "religious lines figured in the campaign." See *Tribune*, Nov. 8, 1900.

with politicians throughout the state. But if Lorimer was to recapture his former influence, new allies were needed. In this regard, the governor-elect, Richard Yates, was the most logical target.

Yates was a handsome, ambitious man with limited ability. Harold Ickes called him "a weak, easy-going nonentity with few ideas, no real purpose, and little character." [67] Always seeking to advance his political interests, he too sought political allies. He had primarily two options: he could turn either toward the Dawes-Cullom federal faction or toward Lorimer and the remains of Tanner's organization. During his first half-year in office, Yates wavered between these two groups.

Yates's unsteadiness disturbed the federal faction. During the summer of 1900, Dawes, Graeme Stewart, James Pease, U.S. Marshal John C. Ames, Illinois Senator Fred A. Busse, and Speaker Lawrence Y. Sherman of the Illinois General Assembly held several important political meetings. They agreed to cooperate in Illinois politics in regard to four goals: control of the organization of the General Assembly; the re-election of Senator Cullom in 1901; the election of Dawes as senator in 1903 as a replacement for Mason; and the removal of Lorimer from control of Cook County Republican politics. [68] The accomplishment of these goals, however, depended largely upon Yates's sympathy or at least neutrality.

Lorimer sought to win Yates away from the federal faction. On November 10 and again several times in December, Lorimer conferred with Yates and sought to convince him that the Dawes group was organizing the General Assembly against his "wishes and welfare." By mid-December Lorimer had succeeded, and the Governor's closest legislative allies declared for David Shanahan, Lorimer's candidate for speaker of the House. [69] Yates denied that he had instructed them or that he had combined with Lorimer, but one of his lieutenants commented that "Lorimer stood by us at Peoria and we must stand by him now." [70]

Lorimer also worked to block another part of the federal faction's program—the re-election of Senator Cullom. On November 17, 1900,

[67] Ickes, *Autobiography*, 41–42.

[68] Graeme Stewart to Dawes, July 19, 1900, Dawes to Stewart, July 23, 1900, Dawes Papers; *Dawes Journal*, 243–244.

[69] Graeme Stewart to Dawes, Nov. 14, 1900, Dawes Papers; *Tribune*, Nov. 11, 13, 19, Dec. 15, 23, 1900.

[70] *Tribune*, Dec. 24, 25, 30, 1900; J. L. Pickering to Lawerence Y. Sherman, Dec. 27, 1900, R. D. Robinson to Sherman, Jan. 4, 1901, Sherman Papers.

he met in Chicago with Tanner and three other senatorial hopefuls. Lorimer proposed that the four join to halt Cullom and then decide among themselves who would take his seat. The news of this meeting, and Representative Robert R. Hitt's announcement of his candidacy, so dismayed Cullom that he wanted to leave the race and let Dawes take his place.[71]

These developments alarmed Dawes, and on December 28 he met with Yates to dissuade him from joining with Lorimer. Dawes warned the Governor that his interference in the General Assembly would "accomplish nothing and only make him unpopular." [72] Yates, torn between the alternatives, moved back toward the federal faction. He pulled his friends out of the Shanahan camp and early in January Shanahan withdrew as a candidate for speaker.[73] On January 8 the Republican caucus unanimously chose Sherman. One week later, in spite of further attempts by Lorimer to persuade Yates to interfere, the Republican caucus nominated Cullom by acclamation.[74]

Lorimer's defeats by the federal faction occurred mainly because Yates had withdrawn his support. If the Governor continued to ally with the federal faction and if Lorimer found it impossible to attract new allies, his position in the party would further disintegrate. His opponents threatened him not only on the state level, but also in Chicago, where for the first time in years there was a serious challenge to Lorimer's control of the city convention. Graeme Stewart, representing the federal faction, and John Maynard Harlan, supported by Victor Lawson and municipal reformers William Kent and Walter L. Fisher, led the opposition.[75]

In order to fragment the opposition, Lorimer brought out five candidates, most prominent of whom was Judge Hanecy. By the time of the convention, Stewart decided that no Republican could win against

[71] Graeme Stewart to Dawes, Nov. 14, 1900, Dawes Papers; *Dawes Journal,* 253; Cullom, *Fifty Years of Public Service,* 445–446; *Tribune,* Nov. 8, 10, 15, 17, 19, 1900.

[72] Stewart to Dawes, Jan. 12, 1901, Dawes Papers; *Dawes Journal,* 257; *Tribune,* Dec. 29, 1900.

[73] Stewart to Dawes, Jan. 6, 11, 1900, Dawes Papers; *Tribune,* Jan. 6, 9, 1901.

[74] Lorimer, Tanner, and Congressmen Robert R. Hitt and George W. Prince held several meetings with Yates to try to persuade him to support either Tanner or Frank O. Lowden, a Chicago lawyer. See Stewart to Dawes, Jan. 12, 17, 18, 1901, Dawes Papers; *Tribune,* Jan. 12, 14–17, 1901; Cullom, *Fifty Years of Public Service,* 447–449.

[75] *Tribune,* Nov. 25, 28, 1900, Feb. 8, 10, 25, 27, Mar. 1, 2, 1901; Victor Lawson to Frank O. Lowden, Feb. 11, 1901, to Robert W. Patterson Mar. 1, 1901, Lawson Papers.

Mayor Carter H. Harrison and left the contest.[76] Harlan remained as the only anti-boss candidate but he could not unite the forces opposed to Lorimer. Politicians such as Pease and Busse preferred a Lorimer man to reformer Harlan, and on the eighth ballot the delegates nominated Judge Hanecy as the Republican mayoralty candidate.[77]

Hanecy was the third consecutive Lorimer man to win the mayoralty nomination and he encountered the same difficulties that had plagued the Lorimer candidates in 1897 and 1899. The independent press and Republican voters from elite and native-American wards would not support him. They objected to the West Side boss's control of the convention, and they did not believe that Hanecy could give "as strong an assurance to the people of a courageous safeguarding of the public's rights in the matter of the renewal of the street railroad franchises as Mayor Harrison. . . ." [78] Harrison emphasized Lorimer's ties to Yerkes and Hanecy's ties to Lorimer in his campaign literature. "Judge Hanecy is Lorimer's nominee," read a public Harrison letter. "When Chicago as a matter of popular right and justice was demanding the repeal of the Allen law, 'Billy' Lorimer, alone in this great city . . . commended that infamous measure as a good thing for Chicago. . . ." [79]

Hanecy denied the validity of the charges. He insisted that he would make the traction companies pay "full and fair compensation," and he attacked Harrison for crime in the streets and violations of civil service. He appealed to the personal-liberty immigrant vote and to the working-class vote in an unusual manner for a Republican candidate by announcing that he opposed "blue laws" and supported labor unions.[80] But whatever his appeal, Hanecy had little chance of success. Normally Republican reform-oriented native Americans viewed him as the prisoner of Boss Lorimer, while Democratic groups interested in personal liberty saw little reason to choose Hanecy over Harrison. Harrison won a third term with 52.7 percent of the vote to Hanecy's 43.1. These results represented a gain of 5.1 points for the Democrats

[76] Dawes to Stewart, Nov. 17, 1900, Stewart to Dawes, Dec. 8, 1900, Dawes Papers; *Tribune*, Jan. 22, 1901.

[77] *Tribune*, Mar. 1, 2, 1901; *News*, Mar. 1, 1901.

[78] Victor Lawson to Frank O. Lowden, Feb. 11, 1901, to Editor, *Record-Herald* [Frank B. Noyes], May 27, 1903, Lawson Papers. Lawson claimed that Hanecy asked him for his support.

[79] Carter H. Harrison to ———, Mar. 29, 1901, Harrison Papers; Harrison, *Stormy Years*, 204–206; *Tribune*, Mar. 7, 9, 15, 20, 23, 24, 1901.

[80] *Tribune*, Mar. 8, 21, 23, 1901.

over 1900 and a Republican loss of 6.5. As compared with the 1899 mayoralty election, the Republicans increased their total by 7.8 points, while Harrison gained 3.9 percent. The Republicans lost in German, Bohemian, Polish, and especially native-American areas, while gaining in Irish wards.[81] Large numbers of Republicans did not bother to vote, and several newspaper editorials expressed the opinion that Lorimer was a "millstone about the neck of the Republican party in Chicago," and that the GOP would not elect a mayor until he was displaced from power.[82]

But while some Republicans considered Lorimer a "millstone," Governor Yates did not. After much hesitation, he decided to cement his relations with the boss.[83] Yates's action was largely the result of Dawes's unusually ethical if not naive approach to politics. Yates actually preferred Dawes to Lorimer as his ally, and had offered to support him for both Cullom's senatorial seat and Mason's seat, but Dawes had refused. Dawes held that he only desired Yates's impartiality, and insisted that the party should act without interference from elected office-holders.[84] Yates, however, did not want to be neutral. He wanted to strengthen himself to insure renomination for governor in 1904 and nomination for senator in 1906. If Dawes would not become his ally, he would turn to Lorimer.[85]

The first clear evidence of the Yates-Lorimer combination came in the spring, when Yates chose a Lorimer lieutenant as Chicago state grain inspector, another as West Park superintendent, and appointed Lorimer's slate of candidates to the West Park Board.[86] It was evident, Stewart wrote Dawes, that Yates and Lorimer had "joined issue," and

[81] Because of a 1900 ward reapportionment, it is difficult to make comparisons between this election and previous elections. The correlation between the Republican vote and percent native American was +.536, the weakest for any election in the 1900–1912 period except for the 1908 gubernatorial election. Because of data limitations, it was difficult to obtain significant or accurate correlations between religious composition and voting percentages, although correlations between percent Catholic and percent Democrat remained high throughout the period. For complete voting figures see *Daily News Almanac for 1902*, 285–293.

[82] See *Tribune*, Apr. 3, 1901, and the survey of editorial opinion in *ibid.*, Apr. 4, 1901; Stewart to Dawes, Apr. 11, 1901, Dawes Papers.

[83] Sol H. Bethea to Dawes, Feb. 6, 1901, Dawes Papers.

[84] *Dawes Journal*, 257; Dawes to Graeme Stewart, Jan. 21, 1901, Dawes Papers.

[85] St. Louis *Globe Democrat*, Oct. 18, 1901, clipping in Charles G. Dawes Scrapbooks, Northwestern University Library, Evanston; Pixton, "Early Career of Charles G. Dawes," 212–213.

[86] *Tribune*, Apr. 18, June 15, 26, 1901; Stewart to Dawes, Mar. 16, 1901, Dawes Papers.

that Yates's path would "not be strewn with roses for a long time to come." [87] The same comment might have been made about Dawes's political future.

In addition to Lorimer's alliance with Yates, there were other signs of the boss's resiliency during the first half of 1901. Lieutenant Governor William A. Northcott, a powerful downstate politician, joined with the Yates-Lorimer alliance because Lorimer could "deliver more than any other man in Cook County" and because he objected to Dawes's attempt to "dictate the election of a United States Senator and governor." [88] Lorimer also blocked reapportionment of the Cook County General Assembly districts until there was a division favorable to his control. The same apportionment also provided Lorimer with a safe congressional district.[89]

These developments, however, did not halt Dawes. He formally entered the Senate race on May 19 and resigned as comptroller two weeks later. Confident of his election, Dawes wrote in his diary that the "fight will be cleancut and either Lorimer or I must be counted out when it is over. Unless my opponents buy it, I think I will certainly win." [90]

Dawes based his confidence on the expectation that the McKinley administration and its Illinois appointees would aid him in his campaign.[91] Lorimer, however, sought to offset the federal influence by promoting Vice-President Theodore Roosevelt's presidential aspirations. He formed a "Roosevelt-for-President-in-1904" organization and he and Yates emphasized their roles as "original" Roosevelt men.[92] Lorimer's activities distressed the federal faction and several of its members warned Dawes that if Lorimer and Yates controlled

[87] Stewart to Dawes, Mar. 16, May 1, 1901, Dawes Papers.

[88] Malcolm McDowell to Dawes, June 24, July 1, 1901, Dawes Papers.

[89] Lorimer blocked the reapportionment through his control of the lower house; the federal forces controlled the Senate. The dispute dragged on from February through May, and Dawes tried to arrange for Mark Hanna, chairman of the Republican national committee, to mediate the dispute. Lorimer, however, refused. See George W. Stubblefield to Dawes, Jan. 24, Feb. 7, 1901, U. C. Hinman to Dawes, Apr. 8, 1901, Lawrence Y. Sherman to Dawes, Apr. 10, 1901, Graeme Stewart to Dawes, Feb. 5, May 1, 1901, Dawes to Stewart, Apr. 10, 1901, to George W. Perkins, Apr. 15, 1901, Dawes Papers; *Tribune*, Feb. 8, 10, 13, 15, 19, 20, Mar. 13, 14, Apr. 5, May 1, 5, 1901.

[90] *Dawes Journal*, 269–272, 288; *Tribune*, July 6, 1901.

[91] *Dawes Journal*, 310–311.

[92] Graeme Stewart to Dawes, July 11, 1901, Dawes Papers; L. White Busby, ed., *Uncle Joe Cannon: The Story of a Pioneer American* (New York, 1927), 203.

the Roosevelt boom, Dawes's senatorial chances would be badly damaged.[93]

To counteract Lorimer's influence with Roosevelt, Dawes visited him at his Oyster Bay, Long Island, home and assured him of his support for the presidential nomination.[94] Sol H. Bethea and Graeme Stewart of the federal faction took similar steps in August when the Vice-President stopped in Illinois. Roosevelt "will be grateful for all favors . . . from Yates, Lorimer and others," wrote Bethea to Dawes after his meeting, "but will depend upon you and will work through you Senator Cullom and his friends. . . ." [95] Roosevelt, who was anxious not to become identified with either faction, wrote that "the Illinois people are openly for me." [96]

If President McKinley had completed his second term and Roosevelt had succeeded him in 1904, his campaign for the nomination would probably have little affected Illinois politics. Both factions had assured him of their loyalty and neither could monopolize him. But the death of McKinley on September 14, 1901, and Roosevelt's assumption of the presidency altered the situation. Dawes lost a supporter in the White House and Lorimer no longer had to be concerned with a hostile national administration. Moreover, Dawes stood close to Senator Marcus A. Hanna, whom Roosevelt feared as his chief potential rival for the nomination. Although Dawes had assured Roosevelt of his support, he added the proviso that he would have to reconsider his position if public sentiment shifted.[97] These considerations made it doubtful that Roosevelt would openly side with Dawes.

Would he, however, help Lorimer and Yates in their opposition to Dawes and aid their Senate choice, Congressman Albert J. Hopkins? The support of most of the Illinois congressional delegation for Hopkins was an important consideration. Backing Hopkins were Joseph G. Cannon, chairman of the Committee on Appropriations and

[93] Sol H. Bethea to Dawes, Aug. 1, 1901, John L. Stevens to Dawes, Sept. 2, 1901, Dawes Papers.

[94] *Dawes Journal,* 272–273.

[95] Sol H. Bethea to Dawes, Sept. 2, 1901, Dawes Papers.

[96] Roosevelt to Dawes, Aug. 27, 1901, to Sol H. Bethea, Sept. 10, 1901, to William Allen White, Sept. 3, 1901, in Elting E. Morison, ed., *The Letters of Theodore Roosevelt* (8 vols., Cambridge, 1951–54), III, 138, 139, 144, 145, hereafter cited as *Roosevelt Letters;* Abel L. Allen and Luther L. Smith to Roosevelt, n.d. [probably 1901], Roosevelt Papers.

[97] *Dawes Journal,* 273.

after 1903 speaker of the House; Robert R. Hitt, chairman of the House Committee on Foreign Affairs; and Vespasian Warner, George W. Prince, and George W. Smith.[98]

Lorimer's welcome at the White House reflected the contrast between Roosevelt's positive and McKinley's negative attitude toward him. On October 4, 1901, Lorimer lunched with the President and spent several hours with him reportedly comparing "family notes." [99] On November 15 Lorimer presented Congressman Hopkins to Roosevelt as the man to unite the Illinois Republican party and make the state safe for the President.[100] Reports of Roosevelt's reception of Lorimer alarmed Dawes's supporters, one of whom wrote from Washington "that I very much fear that the President will take some action in Illinois matters which will have a tendency to help Lorimer-Hopkins-Yates . . . in their ambition to 'put you on the shelf.' " [101]

Lorimer also protested to Roosevelt about the activities of federal officials and comptroller's office appointees for Dawes. He arranged for scores of protest letters to be sent to the White House and complained personally to the President.[102] In early February, 1902, in the House of Representatives, Hopkins and Cannon sponsored an amendment to an executive department appropriations bill that required the listing of all comptroller's office employees in the government "Blue Book." Comptroller William B. Ridgely, Dawes's successor and Cullom's son-in-law, was ordered to furnish the Committee on Appropriations with a list of his office personnel for the previous five years.[103]

The list revealed that Dawes's and Ridgely's appointments were confined to the Dawes-Cullom faction. Prodded by Lorimer and Cannon, Roosevelt required his approval of future appointments and warned Comptroller Ridgely to keep his men out of the Illinois senatorial fight. In addition, he instructed federal officials not to inter-

[98] W. F. Albertson to Dawes, Dec. 28, 1901, Malcolm McDowell to Dawes, July 1, 1901, George Eells to Dawes, Dec. 8, 1901, Shelby M. Cullom to Dawes, May 9, 1902, Dawes Papers; *Tribune*, Nov. 29, Dec. 8, 1901.

[99] *Tribune*, Oct. 5, 1901.

[100] *Ibid.*, Nov. 16, 17, 1901.

[101] W. F. Albertson to Dawes, Nov. 16, 1901, W. A. Rodenberg to Dawes, Dec. 9, 1901, Dawes Papers.

[102] W. A. Rodenberg to Dawes, Dec. 9, 1901, Henry C. Payne to Dawes, Apr. 10, 1902, Dawes Papers.

[103] *CR*, 57th Cong., 1st Sess., XXXV, 1474–75; Pixton, "Early Career of Charles G. Dawes," 216; William B. Ridgely to Dawes, Feb. 1, 1902, Dawes Papers; *Dawes Journal*, 295–296.

fere in state politics.[104] While these were ostensibly neutral gestures, they could only hurt Dawes.

Further evidence of Roosevelt's partiality toward the Lorimer faction came when he appointed a Lorimer-Yates follower as collector of internal revenue for the Southern District of Illinois. Roosevelt explained that most of his other appointments had favored the Dawes group, and that he wanted to show the voters he was " 'toting fair' and not trying to interfere one way or the other in the factions in Illinois." [105] However, since this position normally belonged to the senators, the President's move was interpreted as evidence of his preference for Hopkins. The incident disquieted Dawes, who wrote in his journal that although Roosevelt probably wanted to be impartial, he had "created the impression that he is against me in the fight." [106]

Dawes knew he had to take some action to shift his campaign from the "defensive to the aggressive," and to unite Lorimer's enemies. Dawes, Cullom, and Mason issued a public letter to Speaker Lawrence Y. Sherman describing certain improper actions taken by the state organization for Hopkins and asking Sherman to lead the fight against the Lorimer-Hopkins-Yates combine.[107] Cullom explained that his signature on the "round robin" meant that he was "against Lorimer's definition of the party machine. Lorimer's influence in politics is hurtful to the party and he must be set aside." [108] Rather than responding to the attack, Lorimer shrugged it off as a dispute between "down-the-state" Republicans.[109]

Lorimer could afford to be casual, for he controlled the situation. On May 5, in the primary for delegates to the county convention, Lorimer's organization, working with an efficiency reminiscent of past years, defeated the federal faction. Dawes only did well in the North

104 *Record-Herald* and *Inter-Ocean*, Mar. 4, 1902; Julian P. Lippincott to Dawes, Apr. 10, 1902, Dawes Papers. For evidence of Dawes's use of the patronage to aid his own faction see Dawes to D. G. Tunnecliffe, Feb. 13, 1901, to Lawrence Y. Sherman, Mar. 22, Apr. 3, 16, June 11, Aug. 10, 1901, Sherman Papers.

105 Roosevelt to William J. Calhoun, Feb. 19, 1902, *Roosevelt Letters*, III, 234; *Tribune* and *Inter-Ocean*, Feb. 23, 1902.

106 *Dawes Journal*, 301; Dawes to Henry C. Payne, Mar. 31, 1902, Dawes Papers.

107 State office-holders had to contribute time and money to the Hopkins campaign; Fred Rowe, state central chairman, used his office to solicit support for Hopkins. See Dawes to John L. Stevens, Sept. 5, 1901, to Henry C. Payne, Mar. 31, 1902, to John J. McCook, Feb. 21, 1902, Julian P. Lippincott to Dawes, Mar. 21, 1902, Dawes Papers; *Dawes Journal*, 296–299; *Tribune*, Feb. 5, 12, 13, 1902.

108 *Post*, Feb. 13, 1902; Lawrence Y. Sherman to Cad Allard, Apr. 9, 1902, Sherman Papers.

109 *Tribune* and *Chronicle*, Feb. 19, 1902.

Side German wards controlled by Busse, the Hertz and Pease territory, and upper-class Hyde Park and Evanston, Dawes's home town.[110] At the county convention "William Lorimer was the chauffeur of the band wagon from first to last," as the delegates approved his county and state slates by acclamation. Lorimer ignored Hertz and Pease in the allocation of offices, but as a conciliatory gesture, Lorimer had the convention endorse Busse for state treasurer. Lorimer confidently told newspaper reporters that Cook County would supply over 400 votes for an endorsement of Hopkins at the state convention. [111]

This was a characteristic overstatement—the actual figure was 365 Cook County votes for Hopkins out of 519, but it easily won Hopkins the state convention's approval. In addition, Lorimer and Yates secured their slate for state offices and tightened their control over the state central committee.[112] With his senatorial hopes dashed, Dawes announced his withdrawal from the contest and also from politics. He would now turn his attentions, he wrote in his journal, "to business . . . where promises are redeemed and faith is kept." [113]

Dawes's defeat and Hopkins' endorsement represented the culmination of Lorimer's efforts to return to power after his losses in 1900. Undoubtedly, without McKinley's death, which elevated Roosevelt to the presidency, Lorimer's course would have been more difficult. Senator Cullom, for instance, although admittably not an unbiased source, blamed the new President for Dawes's defeat. Roosevelt, he complained, had revived "Lorimer into life again by coddling him around the White House"; had given Lorimer and his allies an appointment which "under the rule" belonged to the senators; and had kept federal officials out of the campaign.[114] Dawes believed that the President had "greatly injured" him, but he also criticized Yates for being "led away by his vanity and being used by stronger and abler men." [115]

Illinois politics from 1896 through 1902, therefore, was marked by strife between two Republican factions, one representing Lorimer and his Cook County machine in alliance with the state forces of

110 *Tribune,* May 6, 1902; *News,* May 5, 1902.
111 *Tribune* and *Chronicle,* May 7, 1902.
112 *Tribune,* May 7, 1902; *Chronicle* and *Inter-Ocean,* May 8, 1902.
113 *Dawes Journal,* 311.
114 Cullom to Dawes, May 9, 1902, Dawes Papers.
115 *Dawes Journal,* 310–311.

Governors Tanner and Yates, and the other tied to the McKinley administration and composed of Dawes, the U.S. senators, and Illinois federal office-holders. By 1900 the federal forces had Lorimer on the defensive. Tanner was forced to step down as governor, Lorimer's choice, Elbridge Hanecy, was blocked as a substitute, rebellion threatened the Cook County organization, and Lorimer had lost his congressional seat. By 1902, however, Lorimer had regained the initiative. The new Governor was his ally; he had strengthened his hold on the county organization; he had a safe congressional district; and his candidate for senator was victorious. The coincidence between Lorimer's and Roosevelt's political interests was important in his revival, but Lorimer's own political astuteness enabled him to capitalize on this fact. He was chief among those "stronger and abler men" that Dawes had blamed for his senatorial defeat.

CHAPTER **6**

★ ★ ★ ★ ★ ★ ★ ★ ★ ★ ★

A Boss No Longer

WILLIAM LORIMER FOUND THE years from 1902 to 1904 a time of testing. He entered the period with his fortunes on the upswing. The state convention had endorsed Hopkins for senator, Dawes had retired from politics, and Governor Yates was Lorimer's ally. The period ended, however, with much of Lorimer's power dissipated. He had lost control over the Cook County committee, and a former ally, now turned enemy, occupied the governor's chair.

The explanation for Lorimer's decline lay in the nature of party organization. The Cook County organization, like most such bodies, rested upon subgroups that remained loyal to the boss in return for "side payments," usually in the form of patronage.[1] Various factors, however, could result in the "spin-off" of a subgroup: the ambition of a factional head, for instance, who believed that his fortunes could be improved elsewhere, or the failure of the party to win elections while under a particular leader. In addition, the organization had alliances with business interests that supplied financial aid in return for legislation. At times, however, the needs of the political and economic proups conflicted. Support by the organization for certain legislation alienated voters, forcing subgroup leaders to break with the organization rather than risk defeat at the polls. These factors contributed to Lorimer's decline. One of his key allies, Charles S. Deneen, broke with the organization to run for governor, Lorimer's candidates lost important elections, and Lorimer again became involved in controversial traction legislation.

Also important was the resistance of Republican politicians and voters to boss leadership, a resistance accentuated because Lorimer

[1] Eldersveld, *Political Parties,* 6–8.

115

came from and represented an area of the city that had a different cultural and ethnic composition than most Republican sections. The *Tribune* editorialized after the 1901 mayoralty election that if Democratic wards dominated Republican conventions, Republican voters could not be expected to support the party's nominees.[2] The *Tribune*'s comment implied that Republicans would not allow their party to be controlled by wards inhabited primarily by Catholic and Jewish new immigrants.

Lorimer knew he had to strengthen his organization both citywide and in his new congressional district. The Sixth District consisted of the Thirteenth, Twentieth, and Thirty-fourth Chicago wards and several Cook County towns. Its composition resembled that of Lorimer's old district, although it was somewhat more prosperous.[3] Two-thirds of the population of the Chicago wards was either foreign-born or native-born of foreign-born parents, the largest groups being Irish and German. In addition, there was a large bloc of Russians in the Twentieth Ward and of Bohemians in the Thirty-fourth. The three Chicago wards were supposedly safely Republican, but, as might be expected by their majority of ritualistic ethnic groups, they voted Democratic in the 1901 mayoralty election.

During the 1902 congressional campaign, in order to attract voters into his organization and to counteract press criticism, Lorimer conducted a membership drive. He stressed that the organization was an open body "in which every member has a voice and a remedy if they do not like the leaders." He held lawn parties in his district at which he explained how the organization benefited its workers and also gave them the chance to help their neighborhoods. He mingled with his guests and sought to erase the negative image given him by the press.[4]

On election day the voters gave Lorimer a narrow victory over his Democratic opponent, Allan C. Durborow, elected Republicans to most of the Cook County offices, and chose Lorimer's slate of candidates to the General Assembly.[5] The boss was restored to a

---

[2] *Tribune*, Apr. 3, 1901.

[3] U.S., *Thirteenth Census, 1910*, "Population," I, 512–514; Chicago Board of Education, "School Census of Minors taken as of May 9, 1906," *Annual Report* (Chicago, 1906), 217–218.

[4] *Inter-Ocean*, June 28, Aug. 19, 22, 27, 1902; *Tribune*, June 21, July 2, 28, 1902.

[5] Lorimer received 16,540 votes or 49.7 percent of the district vote; he had 50.1 percent of the Chicago vote and 47.9 percent of the suburban vote. Durborow received 15,555 votes or 46.7 percent; he had 46.5 percent of the Chicago vote and

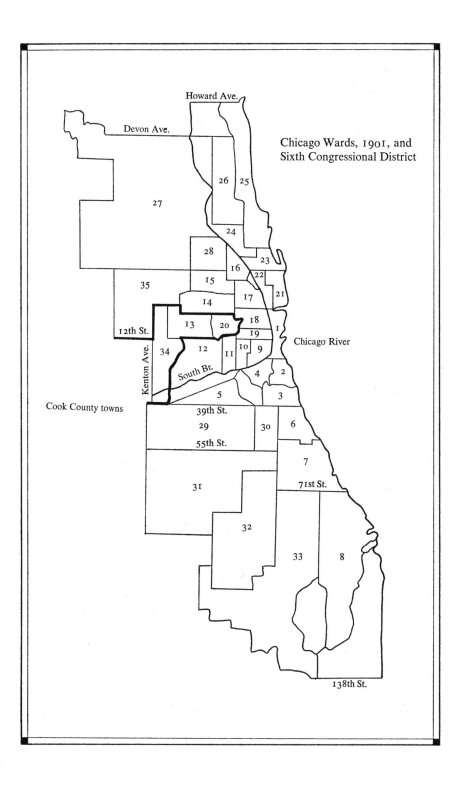

Chicago Wards, 1901, and
Sixth Congressional District

position of party strength, although a more tenuous one than appeared to the casual observer. Dangerous contests lay ahead which could quickly erode Lorimer's hold on the organization.

The first challenge to Lorimer came in the 1903 mayoralty race. The candidates for the Republican nomination were John M. Harlan, who was backed by a group of municipal reformers, and Graeme Stewart, supported by members of the old federal faction and powerful North Side politicians. Both men had opposed Lorimer in the past. Rather than risk a Harlan nomination, Lorimer made a deal with Stewart, from his point of view the more acceptable candidate. In exchange for a share of city patronage, Lorimer threw his organization's support behind Stewart. Stewart won the mayoralty primary with 54 percent of the vote and the Republican city convention nominated him on the first ballot. The Republican platform attacked the Harrison administration, called for the "best street car service attainable," and promised to restrict traction franchises to twenty years.[6]

The campaign revolved primarily around the issues of streetcar franchises and the extent to which Stewart was beholden to Boss Lorimer. Reformers presented as their solution to the traction problem the Mueller bill, an enabling act written by Walter L. Fisher, which permitted municipal ownership and operation of street railways. Both Stewart and Harrison approved the measure and each appointed a committee of twenty-five to work for its passage. Harrison, however, who posed as the city's defender against the traction interests, accused Stewart of secretly being in league with the streetcar companies. He charged that Stewart's committee of twenty-five looked like a directory of the Union Traction Company and that the streets would be unsafe with the Republicans in office.[7]

47.6 percent of the suburban vote. See Manuscript Election Returns, Sixth Congressional District, 1902, Board of Election Commissioners, Chicago. The *News* and the *Record-Herald* charged that Lorimer had made a bargain with Democratic bosses Sullivan and Hopkins to secure Democratic machine votes, but a check of the ballots revealed that while Lorimer received 1,931 votes on Democratic ballots, Durborow received 2,966 votes on Republican ballots. See *News,* Oct. 24, 28, Nov. 5, 8, 1902, and *Record-Herald,* Oct. 30, Nov. 6, 1902; the cross-voting totals are in an undated note in the Lawson Papers.

[6] *Tribune,* Jan. 27, Feb. 3, 20, 21, 26, 28, Mar. 1–5, 1903; Harrison, *Stormy Years,* 222–223; Ickes, *Autobiography,* 91–99.

[7] *Tribune,* Mar. 28–30, 1903; *News,* Mar. 23–26, 30, 1904; Edwin Burritt Smith, "Street Railway Legislation in Illinois," *Essays and Addresses* (Chicago, 1909), 74–76.

Harrison also maintained that Lorimer controlled Stewart and that if he were elected Lorimer would run the city. Many of the municipal reformers who had backed Harlan for the Republican nomination agreed. They especially feared that a Republican triumph would enable Lorimer to join with Democratic bosses Roger C. Sullivan and John P. Hopkins to elect a bipartisan slate of machine judges. Reformers such as William Kent and Victor Lawson supported Harrison, as did Chicago's two influential independent newspapers, the *Daily News* and the *Record-Herald*.[8]

Lawson and Kent, however, in their attempt to defeat Stewart and block Lorimer, were also engaged in a conspiracy with Allan C. Durborow to deny Lorimer his congressional seat. Durborow, the Democrat whom Lorimer had defeated in the previous congressional election, believed that his loss was due to fraud. He turned to Kent for financial support for a contest. Kent, who envisaged Lorimer's political destruction and Stewart's defeat if Lorimer was unseated, agreed to help him, as did Victor Lawson and wealthy reformer Charles R. Crane.[9] Durborow filed notice of his contest in the Cook County circuit courts, and on February 2 applied to the Board of Election Commissioners for a writ directing the surrender of the congressional election ballots to a notary public for a recount.[10]

When Lorimer was notified of the challenge, he argued to the board that only Congress could order a recount in a congressional election. He also claimed that the ballots would become valueless if surrendered to a notary. However, after hearing Lorimer's points, the board ordered the county clerk to surrender the returns. Lorimer immediately applied to Judge Hanecy for a restraining order until a court of "competent jurisdiction" or the House of Representatives ordered the county clerk to act; Hanecy issued the injunction.[11]

[8] Victor Lawson wrote Judge John Barton Payne, "If Harrison is reelected the proposed bi-partisan judicial scheme will undoubtedly be defeated. If Stewart is elected the danger will undoubtedly be very great that the scheme will be carried out." Lawson to Payne, Apr. 1, 1903, Lawson Papers; William Kent to Editor, *Record-Herald*, Apr. 3, 5, 1903; *News*, Mar. 23, Apr. 2–4, 1903; *Tribune*, Mar. 22, Apr. 5–7, 1903. The *Tribune* supported Stewart.

[9] *Tribune*, Nov. 7, 1902; *News*, Nov. 3, 1902; Victor Lawson to William Kent, June 5, 1903, to Allan C. Durborow, June 25, 1903, to Charles R. Crane, July 4, 1903, Lawson Papers.

[10] *Tribune*, Dec. 21, 1902, Feb. 4, 1903; *Record-Herald*, Dec. 21, 1902, Jan. 15, 1903.

[11] *Tribune*, Feb. 7, 8, 1903; *News*, Feb. 7, 1903.

Hanecy, in granting the injunction, claimed that if the ballots were opened, Illinois law and the intent of the Australian ballot would be violated. But speaking through Judge Orin N. Carter, the election board asserted that if the ballots were not "mutilated or defaced, or their integrity impaired," the board could examine them. In defiance of Hanecy's order, the board set Saturday, March 28, for the recount.[12] On that morning, however, the commissioners heard that deputy sheriffs were assembled to seize the ballots and to arrest the commissioners for violating Hanecy's injunction. Judge Carter declared that "anarchy" prevailed, and called upon Chicago police chief Francis O'Neill for protection. O'Neill dispatched fifty policemen to the city hall, and Carter delayed the recount until over the weekend.[13]

After conferring throughout Sunday, Lorimer and his lawyers decided to ask the election board not to open the returns until the Illinois Supreme Court had ruled upon Hanecy's jurisdiction. On Monday morning the commissioners refused the request. "Right is right," said Judge Carter. "The count will proceed." The board's clerk proceeded to break the seals on one precinct's returns and a notary public counted the ballots. When the notary found no irregularities, the commission announced that it would adjourn until after the city election.[14]

But the affair was not over. Harrison had decided to maximize its benefits. Democratic politicians rumored that Hanecy had issued a writ for the seizure of the ballots by sheriff's deputies. On Monday afternoon, Mayor Harrison ordered 275 more policemen to the city hall. For an hour police patrol wagons raced downtown with their bells clanging to protect the ballots from Lorimer's forces. The attack never came, but the boss was further stigmatized. Speaking for Lorimer, his attorney W. T. Underwood protested that the "attempt to associate the board of election commissioners with Carter Harrison

[12] Lorimer tried to get the federal courts to hear the case but Judge Peter S. Grosscup referred it back to the county. Judge Murray F. Tuley, acting on the appeal of the election board, then found Hanecy's restraining order invalid on the grounds that it was beyond the right of a court of equity to interfere in an election contest, but this was countered by a restraining order by Judge Charles G. Neely, acting on Lorimer's appeal. See *News,* Feb. 9, 10, 18, 26, Mar. 25, 27, 1903; *Tribune,* Feb. 19, 22, 27, 28, Mar. 26–30, 1903.

[13] The board's lawyers tried to secure writs of *habeas corpus* from the clerks of the circuit and superior courts, but found that the clerks, reportedly at Lorimer's instructions, had closed their offices. *Tribune,* Mar. 29, 30, 1903; *News,* Mar. 28, 1903; *Chronicle,* Mar. 30, 1903.

[14] *News* and *Tribune,* Mar. 30, 31, 1903.

and his police force looks like a conspiracy to . . . secure the defeat of Graeme Stewart and the re-election of Harrison for Mayor." [15]

And Harrison did emerge the winner, although whether or not the Lorimer election contest was the decisive element is debatable. The *Record-Herald* and the *Inter-Ocean,* on different sides of the fence politically, believed it an important factor, but the *Tribune* blamed the Democratic victory on independent Republicans who considered Lorimer a "bogey man," and who marked everyone "nominated by a convention in which he controls a delegate . . . for slaughter." [16] The *Tribune* analysis seems most accurate. Harrison's vote was nearly 5 percentage points lower than in 1901, but the Republican vote was down from the 1902 state and congressional elections. Polish, Russian, and Bohemian wards gave Harrison more support than in 1901, while Stewart increased the Republican vote in native-American, Scandinavian, and German wards. Harrison's popularity among ritualistic cultural groups and with independent voters probably contributed more to his victory than did the contested election. [17]

The recount was disposed of after the mayoralty contest. The Supreme Court decided that Hanecy had no jurisdiction in the case since Lorimer's political, not his property or personal, rights were involved. The recount proceeded, an event that the *Daily News* called a "victory for the people." To the surprise of many Chicagoans, however, the irregularities charged by Durborow were not discovered. Lorimer actually gained nine votes. [18] But even though Lorimer retained his congressional seat, his opposition to opening the returns and Stewart's loss further damaged his reputation. Lorimer's candidates had lost four mayoralty elections in a row, and many Republicans increased their determination to depose him. Lawson wrote to Charles R. Crane that he was "well satisfied that the [Lorimer election] investigation has contributed to what now seems to be a reasonably well assured result—the passing of Lorimerism." To his secretary Lawson wrote a "Memorandum" instructing her to enter the expenses

[15] *Tribune,* Mar. 31, 1903; *Record-Herald,* Apr. 1, 1903; Harrison, *Stormy Years,* 223–224. Lorimer later denied that he had contemplated seizing the ballots by force. See *Dillingham Committee Hearings,* VIII, 7538–40.

[16] *Tribune, Record-Herald,* and *Inter-Ocean,* Apr. 8, 1903.

[17] *Daily News Almanac for 1904,* 328–336. Harrison had 146,308 votes (47.3 percent) and Stewart had 138,548 (44.7 percent). The Socialist candidate had 11,124 votes (3.6 percent) and the Independent Labor candidate, 9,947 (3.2 percent).

[18] "The People ex rel. William C. Malley v. Thomas E. Barrett, Sheriff," *Illinois Supreme Court Reports,* CCIII, 99–111; *News,* Apr. 22, 1903; *Tribune,* May 22, 1903.

of the Lorimer-Durborow case in her account book under the heading, "Public Beneficences and Contributions." [19]

The traction question, which had been important in the 1903 mayoralty campaign and which had caused Lorimer difficulties in 1897, now provided a further challenge to his position. The expiration of the general traction ordinances of 1883 in 1903 furnished the Forty-third General Assembly with the knotty problem of traction legislation. While the passage of new ordinances would normally have been controversial, the Chicago electorate further complicated the picture by approving, in 1902, the policy of municipal ownership.[20] The Union Traction Company, which had acquired the Yerkes streetcar lines in 1899, was the principal company involved.

Early in 1903, reportedly acting at the behest of the Union Traction Company in order to block municipal-ownership legislation, Lorimer intervened in the fight over the election of a speaker for the lower house of the General Assembly. Claiming that he was acting in order to insure that the legislature had a "harmonious session" and made a "good record," he put forward as his candidate John H. Miller of McLeansboro to oppose Lawrence Y. Sherman, the speaker from the previous session.[21] Lorimer argued that Sherman's selection would widen the party split, and he and his lieutenants offered key committee assignments and state and federal patronage for Miller votes. The Lorimer forces warned assemblymen that it was "entirely useless for anyone to stand up against their combination of State and Federal patronage." [22] On January 6, 1903, seemingly verifying this claim, the Republican caucus elected Miller speaker by a vote of 49 to 39.[23]

Miller's selection, although a Lorimer victory, contained the seeds

[19] Lawson to Crane, June 25, 1903, to Miss Dewey, "Memorandum," June 24, 1903, Lawson Papers. In late May, at a political rally, Lorimer charged that Lawson was behind Durborow's charges of fraud. "No man can succeed in public life in this city," claimed Lorimer, "unless he bends his knee to Victor Lawson." *Tribune,* May 29, 1903.

[20] *Tribune,* Apr. 2, 1902. The voters approved the referendum by a margin of 5 to 1.

[21] Undated interview wtih Lorimer, Sherman Papers; *Tribune,* Nov. 23, 26, 1902.

[22] Sherman to Shelby M. Cullom, Nov. 26, Dec. 11, 27, 1902, to W. A. Rankin, to John A. Montelius, to W. F. Bundy, all Nov. 17, 1902, to W. M. Owen, Nov. 18, 1902, to Homer Tice, Nov. 21, 1902, J. O. Anderson to Sherman, Jan. 4, 1903, all in Sherman Papers; William Meese to Dawes, Dec. 1, 1902, Wilfred Arnold to Dawes, Dec. 9, 1902, Dawes Papers; *Tribune,* Nov. 23, 1902.

[23] *Tribune,* Jan. 7, 1903; *House Journal, Forty-third General Assembly* (Springfield, 1903), 15–16.

of future trouble. Lorimer's tactics had infuriated Sherman and his thirty-nine followers. Sherman wrote that "the members are getting strung up pretty tight. If there is too much interference by outside influences there is liable to be an explosion among Members . . . [they] resent the ownership of them assumed by men who do not have seats in that body." [24] For many Republicans the question had become "the right of the party to govern itself as against the right of Mr. Lorimer . . . to govern it." [25] The danger for Lorimer was that Sherman's thirty-nine followers would not abide by Republican caucus decisions. The minority would be able to paralyze the party.

In the early spring, after the mayoralty election, traction legislation monopolized the attention of the General Assembly. On April 9, in response to the urging of the Chicago Committee of Fifty on Traction, reformers, and the press, the Illinois Senate approved the Mueller municipal-ownership bill 45 to 0. This unanimity, however, did not represent the true feelings of many senators, who preferred to shift the burden for the bill's defeat to the House. [26]

Lorimer, who had a great deal of influence in the House, relied upon the Committee on Municipal Corporations, controlled by his lieutenants Cicero J. Lindley and Gus Nohe, to block the bill. When a reporter asked Nohe whether there would be traction legislation that session, he answered, "I don't know. I do whatever the old man [Lorimer] tells me to. . . ." [27] In the committee Lindley and Nohe substituted the misnamed Lindley municipal-ownership bill for the Mueller bill. The Lindley bill had poor financing provisions and lacked both a rate clause and provision for city exercise of the right of eminent domain, making municipal ownership practically an impossibility. Those "who are opposed to municipal ownership should vote for the Lindley bill," wrote Charles G. Dawes to Lawrence Y. Sherman, "and those who favor municipal ownership should vote for the Mueller Bill. . . ." [28]

On April 17, a majority of the Committee on Municipal Corpora-

[24] Sherman to Shelby M. Cullom, Nov. 26, 1902, Sherman Papers.
[25] *Dawes Journal*, 334.
[26] Walter L. Fisher to Ida Tarbell, Aug. 25, 1908, Fisher Papers; *Senate Journal, Forty-third General Assembly*, 664; *Tribune*, Apr. 10, 1903.
[27] *Tribune*, Apr. 10, 13, 14, 1903; *News*, Apr. 13, 1903; Smith, *Essays and Addresses*, 77.
[28] *House Journal, Forty-third General Assembly*, 721; *Tribune* and *News*, Apr. 18, 1903; Smith, *Essays and Addresses*, 81; Sherman to Dawes, Apr. 19, 1903, Dawes to Sherman, Apr. 21, 1903, Dawes Papers.

tions reported the Lindley bill to the House. The Committee of Fifty and Mayor Harrison called it unacceptable and demanded the Mueller bill. Lorimer and Colonel E. R. Bliss, spokesman for the Chicago traction companies, offered to confer with the Lindley bill opponents, and on the evening of April 22, groups representing the opposing legislation met in Lorimer's rooms in the Leland Hotel. The city council's transportation committee, its special counsel, Edward Buritt Smith, and members of the Committee of Fifty represented the Mueller bill, while Lorimer, George W. Hinman, editor of the *Inter-Ocean,* and several members of the House organization stood for the Lindley bill.

Lorimer told the Mueller bill proponents that their legislation was "dead and buried" and that only the Lindley measure could pass. He consented, however, to make several amendments, and offered these with the ultimatum, "You must accept the Lindley bill with these amendments, pull down all opposition on the floor of the house and from the Chicago press, and actually support the bill. It is the Lindley bill or nothing." While Stewart and the Republican members of the transportation committee wanted to accept the amended bill, Smith and the others refused. In their eyes passage of the Lindley bill was worse than no legislation at all.[29]

The traction fight now shifted to the House floor. The Mueller bill supporters informed Speaker Miller that they would block all appropriations until the traction question was settled. Several test votes proved their determination; the Democrats had joined with the minority of Republicans led by Lawrence Y. Sherman to frustrate the boss.[30] But Lorimer determined to force the Lindley bill through. On April 23, Miller announced that the Lindley bill had been made special order, and that the amendments agreed upon by Lorimer and the Chicago representatives would be submitted to the House. In spite of protests from the floor demanding a roll call, Miller proceeded to gavel the amendments through on a voice vote. The House erupted in turmoil, and Miller was forced to declare the General Assembly in recess and to retreat in order to escape bodily harm.[31]

But the ninety-six anti-Lindley members, more than a House quorum, refused to leave. They proceeded to elect a speaker *pro tem,*

[29] Smith, *Essays and Addresses,* 79–82; *Tribune,* Apr. 18–21, 1903.
[30] Smith, *Essays and Addresses,* 82–83; *News,* Apr. 22, 1903; *Tribune,* Apr. 23, 1903.
[31] *Tribune,* Apr. 24, 1903; Smith, *Essays and Addresses,* 84–85.

recall the Lindley bill, and table the Lorimer amendments. Section by section they substituted the Mueller bill for the Lindley bill. As their final action, they approved a resolution against Miller:

Whereas: The Speaker of this House has by revolutionary and unconstitutional methods, denied a hearing in this House or a roll call constitutionally demanded upon measures of grave importance, and has attempted by the same methods to force the same beyond the point where they can be amended or calmly considered by this House upon their merits; therefore be it

Resolved: That until the House records shall show a reconsideration of the action of this House on House Bill No. 864 [the Lindley bill] and all amendents thereto and this House shall be assured of the continuous observance . . . of the constitutional right to a roll call on all questions . . . that no further vote can be cast on any pending bill by the members of this House without a permanent reorganization of this House.[32]

That afternoon, the rebels presented the ultimatum to the Speaker.

Miller hurriedly conferred with Lorimer, Hinman, Governor Yates, and Cicero J. Lindley about a course of action, and they suggested that the revolutionary members had been bribed to advance the Mueller bill. Lorimer and Hinman drew up a statement of the bribery charges for Miller to use to justify his refusal to allow a roll call.[33] Miller read the Lorimer-Hinman document to the House, but was greeted by a demand for names. One assemblyman moved that the House consider no legislation until an investigating committee reported on the bribery charges. On the next day, April 24, the committee was appointed and began its hearings.[34]

As its chief witnesses the committee heard Miller, Hinman, Colonel E. R. Bliss, and Cicero J. Lindley. The testimony revealed that the bribery charges were a Lorimer and Hinman fabrication, and that they and the Governor had directed the replacement of the Mueller bill by the Lindley bill. The committee reported the bribery charges "utterly unworthy of notice." [35] On May 1 the House approved the Mueller bill by a vote of 91 to 20, with the Lorimer men voting in the negative. On May 18, ten days after the legislature's close, Yates

[32] *House Journal, Forty-third General Assembly,* 833; *News,* Apr. 23, 1903; *Tribune,* Apr. 24, 1903.

[33] *Tribune,* Apr. 24–26, 28, 1903; *News,* Apr. 24, 25, 1903.

[34] Smith, *Essays and Addresses,* 87; *Tribune,* Apr. 24, 1903.

[35] The first bribery charge had actually been made in the *Inter-Ocean* on Apr. 21, 1903. For the committee testimony see *Tribune,* Apr. 25, 26, 29–30, May 1, 1903; Smith, *Essays and Addresses,* 88–89.

signed the measure, but also affixed a memorandum charging that the Chicago "trust press" had forced the bill's passage "by default in the senate and by riot in the house." He had only withheld his veto, he said, because he was confident that the city council could correct the bill's imperfections.[36]

The Mueller bill episode, combined with Stewart's defeat in the mayoralty election and the fiasco over Lorimer's contested congressional election, brought the boss's prestige to a new low. The decline in his fortunes was reflected in the judicial elections in early June, when the voters rejected his Republican slate and elected Democrats to eleven of the fourteen judgeships being filled.[37] An increasingly large number of politicians believed that "the percentage of republicans who despise Lorimer and Lorimerism is large enough to defeat every ticket he helps nominate." "Strong forces" demanded a reorganization of the party, and many Republicans looked to the gubernatorial candidacy of State's Attorney Charles S. Deneen on a "reform" ticket as the means to accomplish it.[38]

Charles S. Deneen was the son of a college professor and grandson of a Methodist minister. He had grown up in downstate Illinois and attended the Union College of Law in Chicago. Elected to the General Assembly in 1892, he attached himself to Lorimer while developing his own power base in the Scandinavian wards on Chicago's southwest side. Deneen was a wily and careful politician. Charles E. Merriam called "caution" his most characteristic quality.[39] He adhered to Lorimer's leadership in city and county conventions and in return received the support of the organization for Cook County state's attorney in 1896 and 1900. The press and civic organizations praised Deneen as an honest and competent state's attorney, and he combined

[36] Smith, *Essays and Addresses*, 90–91; *Tribune,* May 7, 8, 19, 1903; Lawrence Y. Sherman to Charles G. Dawes, May 3, 1903, Dawes Papers.

[37] Control of the judiciary was especially important to political bosses. Judges appointed masters of chancery, receivers, trustees, and other judicial functionaries. In addition, in Chicago, the county judge regulated election procedures and selected the Board of Election Commissioners. See Edward M. Martin, *The Role of the Bar in Electing the Bench in Chicago* (Chicago, 1936), 264. The *Tribune* opposed Lorimer's slate; Judge Elbridge Hanecy was among those defeated. *Tribune,* Apr. 26, 30, May 25, 1903; *News,* Apr. 25, 27, May 12, 19, 1903. For an evaluation of the judicial candidates by John M. Harlan, Judge Orin N. Carter, Walter L. Fisher, and other anti-Lorimer reformers, see an unsigned and undated document in the May, 1903, letterbook, Lawson Papers.

[38] *Tribune,* June 3, 1903.

[39] Merriam, *Chicago,* 180–181.

loyalty to the organization, which was vital to his political future, with support from groups normally opposed to the machine.

In 1898 strains appeared in the Lorimer-Deneen relationship when Deneen voted with Hertz and Pease for the anti–Allen Law resolutions. Deneen, however, unlike Hertz and Pease, continued to support Lorimer at conventions until 1902, while at the same time reinforcing his own position.[40] By 1903 he and his close friend and adviser Roy O. West were ready to break with Lorimer, and in that year Deneen declared his candidacy for governor. In his campaign he had the support of the anti-Lorimer politicians, of the civic reform groups, and of the independent Republican press.

In later years Lorimer charged that Deneen had sold out to the "trust press," and the accusation had some validity. Deneen consulted with Victor Lawson of the *Daily News,* Frank B. Noyes of the *Record-Herald,* and Robert W. Patterson of the *Tribune,* and he advanced the "good government" measures they favored.[41] But there were also ethnic and religious factors that help explain Deneen's differences with Lorimer. Although Deneen himself was not Swedish (many, however, thought him to be), a majority of the voters in the wards that he controlled were. The pietistic religious orientation of Swedes made them prohibitionists and supporters of reform-oriented government.[42] Lorimer, on the other hand, represented an area inhabited largely by Catholic and Russian Jewish immigrants. These groups regarded government with an occupational and entrepreneurial attitude, and their ritualistic religious orientation caused them to reject an activist reform government. The differences that existed between Lorimer and Deneen stemmed not only from a conflict for power but also from different cultural values in their constituents, a formula that explains many of the political conflicts of the progressive period.[43]

[40] *Tribune,* June 9, 1898, May 13, 14, 1900; Roy O. West to Dawes, Feb. 9, 22, Mar. 4, 1901, Dawes Papers.

[41] *Dillingham Committee Hearings,* VIII, 7433–35. For newspaper influence on Deneen see Victor Lawson to Deneen, May 1, 1905, Apr. 26, 1907, to Roy O. West, June 17, 1905, Aug. 3, 1906, Lawson Papers; Walter L. Fisher to Deneen, May 15, 1905, Fisher Papers.

[42] Reuel Gustav Hemdahl, "The Swedes in Illinois Politics: An Immigrant Group in an American Political Setting" (unpublished Ph.D. dissertation, Northwestern University, 1932), 227, 314, 355, 431, 467; George M. Stephenson, *The Religious Aspects of Swedish Immigration: A Study of Immigrant Churches* (Minneapolis, 1932), 7–10, 19–26.

[43] Hays, "Political Parties and the Community-Society Continuum," 163–164; Hays, "Politics of Reform," 158–161; Miller, "Politics of Municipal Reform in Chicago," 23–43. In "Urban Liberalism and the Age of Reform," *Mississippi Valley*

Lorimer normally would have supported Yates's renomination, but since the Mueller bill revolt he had drawn away from the Governor. Yates's major handicap was his unpopularity in Cook County. William Kent wrote to President Roosevelt and warned that "Yates, if nominated will be overwhelmingly beaten in Cook County by any high minded Democrat. He is the rottenest, puniest spoilsman we have seen in Illinois. . . ." [44] Lorimer and Senator Hopkins conferred with Yates in August, 1903, and tried to persuade him not to seek another term. They argued that Deneen's candidacy threatened to "disrupt the organization" and that only a Chicagoan could preserve it. Yates, however, believed that he was still the choice of the downstate, and insisted on a renomination. [45]

This posed a dilemma for the Blond Boss. If he endorsed Yates he risked defeat in Cook County, but if he shifted to another candidate, the Governor would take away his state patronage. Lorimer decided to accept the patronage loss and break with Yates. As his gubernatorial candidate he supported the handsome Frank O. Lowden, Chicago lawyer and son-in-law of George M. Pullman of sleeping-car fame. Hopefully with Lowden he could defeat both Yates and Deneen and retain party control. [46]

Lowden was a political dilettante. In the 1890's he had dabbled in local reform politics, opposing corruption and advocating civil service. By the turn of the century he had become more ambitious. He drew close to Lorimer, and in 1901 the boss tried to get Yates to support Lowden for Cullom's senatorial seat. [47] But Lowden was not Lorimer's

Historical Review (Sept., 1962), XLIX, 231–241, J. Joseph Huthmacher protests that historians have neglected the role of the urban immigrant masses in progressive reform; John D. Buenker makes the same point in regard to Illinois progressive reform. Both, however, neglect the wider implications of cultural questions. See John D. Buenker, "Urban Immigrant Lawmakers and Progressive Reform in Illinois," in Donald F. Tingley, ed., *Essays in Illinois History in Honor of Glenn Huron Seymour* (Carbondale, 1968), 52–74.

44 Kent to Roosevelt, May 23, 1904, Kent Papers; George C. Rankin to Lawrence Y. Sherman, Dec. 10, 1903, Sherman Papers.

45 *Dillingham Committee Hearings,* I, 324–325 (Yates testifying); Joseph G. Cannon to Richard Yates, Aug. 25, 1903, printed in John H. Krenkel, ed., *Serving the Republic—Richard Yates: An Autobiography* (Danville, 1968), 143–144; *Tribune,* Aug. 11, 25, 31, 1903; J. McCan Davis, *The Breaking of the Deadlock* (Springfield, 1904), 40–47.

46 Although residing in Chicago, Lowden also had support in northern Illinois, where his farm, "Sinnissippi," was located. See Hutchinson, *Lowden,* I, 112–113.

47 Graeme Stewart to Dawes, Jan. 18, 1901, W. S. Louden to Dawes, Apr. 6, 1901, Dawes Papers.

tool; he maintained that if elected he would be his own master. His chief weakness, however, in his critics' eyes, was that his success "would be impossible without carrying with it the success of the Lorimer-Jamieson machine." [48]

Three other candidates, Congressman Vespasian Warner, Attorney General Howland J. Hamlin, and Lawrence Y. Sherman joined Lowden, Deneen, and Yates in the gubernatorial contest. Warner ran at Lorimer's behest to pull votes from the other candidates in central and southern Illinois.[49] Hamlin, however, had a strong following, while Sherman would yield to Deneen to prevent the victory of Lowden, Yates, or Warner. Sherman was the most devoted anti-Lorimerite:

> The Deneen club well laid on is the only weapon that will break that mass of political graft and selfishness known as the 'organization' in Cook. It has made Chicago Democratic and . . . it will do so for the state, if it is not broken up; no amateur milk and water nominee for governor will do it. He must be a big enough man to fill the office and resist the selfish ravenous hordes of vandals who prey on the party and sap its strength among the rank and file. Deneen can stand up. He will be a governor. He will follow the law and let us all live. I can trust him above all men in the field today. While I want to be nominated very much myself, I will be the cheerfulest defeated candidate ever seen in a state convention if I finally have to lose out to him.[50]

Critical in the contest was the attitude of President Roosevelt and the senators and representatives from Illinois. The major gubernatorial contenders declared for the President in his second-term bid, and each insisted that his nomination was essential to a Roosevelt victory in Illinois. Sherman visited the Capital in August of 1903 to convey this message; Fred Busse and Illinois Senator Dan Campbell saw the President for Deneen in December; and Fred Rowe, chairman of the state central committee, spoke to him for Yates in the same month. While each candidate implied that Roosevelt favored him, the President, at least publicly, stayed neutral.[51]

[48] Victor Lawson to H. N. McKinney, June 3, 1904, Lawson Papers.
[49] Lawrence Y. Sherman to Dawes, Dec. 6, 1903, Dawes Papers; *Tribune,* Oct. 1, 1903, Mar. 6, 1904.
[50] Sherman to Dawes, Nov. 10, 1903, Jan. 5, 1904, Dawes Papers.
[51] Dawes to H. L. Stoddard, Dec. 5, 1903, to George B. Cortelyou, June 25, Oct. 27, 1903, to Theodore Roosevelt, July 6, 1903, Dawes Papers; Thomas Worthington to Roosevelt, Feb. 1, 1904, Frank B. Noyes to Roosevelt, Feb. 4, 1904, Roosevelt Papers; *Dawes Journal,* 350; *Tribune,* Dec. 1, 13, 1903.

The senators and representatives were less circumspect about taking sides, even though this meant abandoning old allies. Cullom, who feared Yates as a contender for his senatorial seat, would have been expected to favor Deneen or Sherman, both of whom had supported his re-election in 1901. Cullom, however, backed Lowden as the candidate most likely to win and least likely to oppose his return to Washington. With his own political future involved, Cullom forgot about his opposition to Lorimer. Now "harmony" was the keynote.[52] As for Hopkins, both Lorimer and Yates had helped elect him senator. He now decided, however, that Yates's unpopularity removed him as a serious contender. Hopkins also supported Lorimer's man Lowden, although for the time being he claimed neutrality.[53]

Lowden was also preferred by most of the Illinois Republican representatives and the federal appointees. The favoritism of the "federal machine" for Lowden irritated the other candidates and they complained to the President. Yates, for instance, flooded Roosevelt with letters.[54] These protests caused Roosevelt to issue a public statement denying that he was interfering in the Illinois contest. Roosevelt insisted to Yates that it was an "explicit and authoritative statement," but the President did not limit his Illinois appointees' political actions as he had in the 1902 Dawes-Hopkins senatorial contest.[55] Privately Roosevelt rationalized that in every state "the appointees . . . are in the great majority of cases the allies and friends of the Senators and Congressmen." [56]

The candidates and their supporters suspected that the President favored Lowden. Roosevelt reinforced this impression when, in February, 1904, on the recommendation of Cullom, Hopkins, and Lorimer, he appointed Jamieson as naval officer for the port of Chicago. Reportedly behind the recommendation was the senators' and Lorimer's pledge that the state would be solid for Roosevelt's renomination.[57]

[52] Alonzo K. Vickers to Cullom, Mar. 1, 1904, Cullom Papers; Lawrence Y. Sherman to Dawes, Feb. 9, 1904, Dawes Papers.

[53] Davis, *Deadlock*, 42–43, 150–152.

[54] Yates to Roosevelt, Feb. 21, 27, Mar. 7, 15, 17, 21, 1904, Frank B. Noyes to Roosevelt, May 21, 1904, Roosevelt Papers; Roosevelt to Joseph G. Cannon, May 27, 1904, *Roosevelt Letters*, IV, 805–806.

[55] Roosevelt to Yates, Mar. 17, 1904, *Roosevelt Letters*, IV, 756; John C. Shaffer to William Loeb, Jr. (telegram), Mar. 9, 1904, Roosevelt Papers; *Rockford Star*, Mar. 11, 1904. (Citations to non-Chicago newspapers are from newspaper scrapbooks in the Lowden Papers.)

[56] Roosevelt to Nicholas Murray Butler, May 17, 1904, *Roosevelt Letters*, IV, 799–800.

[57] *Tribune*, Feb. 7, 1904; *Post*, Feb. 8, 1904; *Record-Herald*, Feb. 9, 1904.

The appointment, however, generated a barrage of indignant telegrams and letters to the White House. "Appointment of Jamieson
would be deeply regretted here by very many sincere friends of yours
and of the cause of good government as a recognition of most objectionable political methods and influences," read a telegram from
Walter L. Fisher; another, from Victor Lawson, warned that "the
Lorimer-Jamieson regime in Chicago politics has been repeatedly
condemned by the voters of the party and if not bolstered by the national administration will surely be deposed by the republican voters
of Chicago." Letters and telegrams from William Kent, Frank B.
Noyes of the *Record-Herald,* and Robert W. Patterson of the *Tribune*
repeated these sentiments.[58]

Roosevelt met these protests with a list of Jamieson recommendations which he had solicited from leading Chicago businessmen. To
the question "Are you sufficiently well acquainted with the facts to tell
me that in your judgment Jamieson is an honest man who will do
good service as naval officer?" he received positive replies from
Charles G. Dawes; John C. Black, president of the Continental National Bank; John J. Mitchell, president of the Illinois Trust and
Savings Bank; John C. Shaffer, editor of the Chicago *Evening Post;*
and Federal District Judge Peter S. Grosscup, as well as many
others.[59] Roosevelt also asserted that he had no idea of Jamieson's
factional associations. "Under the circumstances," the President wrote
to William Kent, "I could not do other than appoint him." [60]

The Jamieson appointment was actually more calculated than
Roosevelt admitted. His statement that he was unaware of Jamieson's
factional ties is difficult to comprehend: Jamieson had been Republican national committeeman from Illinois from 1896 to 1900 and
Roosevelt knew of his closeness to Lorimer. More likely Roosevelt
appointed Jamieson to pacify Lorimer, who had been talking about
supporting Senator Mark Hanna for the 1904 presidential nomina-

[58] Fisher to Roosevelt, Feb. 8, 1904, Fisher Papers; Lawson to Roosevelt, Feb. 8,
1904, Lawson Papers. See also William Kent to Roosevelt, Feb. 8, 1904, Kent
Papers; P. Moerdyke to Roosevelt, Mar. 30, 1904, Roosevelt Papers; Roosevelt to
Frank B. Noyes, Feb. 9, 1904, to Robert W. Patterson, Feb. 10, 1904, to Thomas N.
Jamieson, Feb. 13, 1904, *Roosevelt Letters,* IV, 720–723, 728.

[59] Roosevelt to Fisher, to Kent, and to Noyes, all Feb. 9, 1904, to Robert W.
Patterson, Feb. 10, 1904, to Nicholas Murray Butler, May 28, 1904, to Albert J.
Hopkins, Aug. 10, 1904, *Roosevelt Letters,* IV, 718–723, 817–819, 886. For negative
comment on the list of Jamieson backers see Victor Lawson to Roosevelt, Feb. 15,
1904, Lawson Papers, and Kent to Roosevelt, Feb. 11, 1904, Kent Papers.

[60] Roosevelt to Kent, Feb. 9, 1904, Roosevelt Papers.

tion.[61] Furthermore, Roosevelt hesitated to oppose a man recommended by both senators and supported by most Illinois representatives. A telegram from Paul V. Morton of the Santa Fe Railroad, acting as Roosevelt's political emissary, reveals the President's motivation: "Have seen Lorimer & Jamieson," said Morton after Jamieson was informed of his appointment. "There is now no doubt that the Illinois delegation will be for you." [62] In the view of many Illinois Republicans the appointment was a presidential endorsement of the Lowden candidacy.[63]

Probably this is what Roosevelt wanted. After the election he told Lowden that he favored him in the contest. In addition, Roosevelt revealed his disdain for the Deneen backers and preference for party regulars when he wrote Nicholas Murray Butler that "the Chicago machine leaders shine by comparison with the so-called anti-machine people . . . who have done everything they can do to jeopardize even the electoral ticket and gratify their own factional feeling." [64] Although he could not openly endorse Lowden, the Jamieson appointment and Roosevelt's failure to curtail federal officials from working for Lowden indicated his preference.

While the struggle over Jamieson's appointment occupied the front pages, county after county chose convention delegates. To many politicians' surprise, Yates did extremely well in the downstate. Yates's success was partially due to his gubernatorial position. He demanded political work from his appointees and financed his campaign from a "slush fund" assessed from state salaries. He also benefited from downstate resentment of attacks on him by the Chicago press. And he was helped, as Sherman put it, "by the petty jealousies continually exhibited by the other Anti-Yates candidates. . . . Unless the Yates' opposition stops its present course," warned Sherman, "they will renominate him." [65]

Lowden, for a Cook County candidate, did well in the downstate.

[61] Thomas Worthington to Roosevelt, Feb. 1, 1904, Roosevelt Papers; *Roosevelt Letters*, IV, 719n2; *Tribune*, Feb. 7, 1904.

[62] Paul V. Morton to Roosevelt and Thomas Worthington to Roosevelt, Feb. 1, 1904, Roosevelt Papers.

[63] Lawrence Y. Sherman to Dawes, Feb. 9, 1904, Dawes Papers; St. Louis *Republic*, Feb. 22, 1904.

[64] Lowden to Louis A. Coolidge, July 11, 1906, Lowden Papers; Roosevelt to Nicholas Murray Butler, May 17, 1904, *Roosevelt Letters*, IV, 799–800.

[65] Davis, *Deadlock*, 127–128, 138; Alonzo K. Vickers to Shelby M. Cullom, Mar. 1, 1904, Cullom Papers; Sherman to Dawes, Feb. 25, Mar. 6, 19, 1904, Dawes Papers.

He presented himself as a "harmony" candidate and as a man who understood the farmer's problems, since he owned a 600-acre farm in Ogle County. Lowden held several meetings with northern Illinois politicians at "Sinnissippi," as he called his farm, in 1903 and 1904. He also made speeches in 102 counties and had a press bureau distribute publicity to downstate newspapers.[66] Lorimer maintained close contact with his downstate allies like Postmaster Harry B. Ward of Perry County (brother-in-law of Lorimer's secretary) and Frank L. Smith of Livingston County, candidate for lieutenant governor, as well as furnishing transportation to Chicago for downstaters.[67]

Lowden, however, found it difficult to overcome the disadvantage of his Chicago home and his connections with Lorimer and the Pullman Company. Downstate newspapers argued that Lowden's "farm" was really an estate and that Lowden was a plutocrat rather than a farmer. They pictured Lowden as Lorimer's tool and warned their readers that if he were elected Lorimer would dominate Illinois.[68] The results from the downstate areas were: Lowden, 125 delegates, Yates, 505, Hamlin, 120, Sherman, 85, and Warner, 45, with 115 disputed seats. Although Deneen neglected the state outside of Cook County, many of Yates's delegates made him their second choice.[69]

Cook County was decisive for Lowden, Deneen, and Lorimer. Here, because Yates had deprived him of state patronage and thrown many of his adherents out of jobs, Lorimer was in difficulty. Deneen claimed twenty-two of forty-one members of the county central committee, and the organization appeared in danger of disintegrating. During the weeks before the primaries, both Lowden and Deneen spoke throughout the county. They traded charges about which of the two was the real machine politician, with Deneen accusing Lowden of being beholden to Lorimer and to the Pullman Company, and Lowden responding that Deneen had only embraced reform ideas at the bidding of his new master, "the trust press." [70]

[66] Davis, *Deadlock,* 86–97; Hutchinson, *Lowden,* I, 118–122.

[67] Lawrence Y. Sherman to Dawes, Nov. 4, 1903, Dawes Papers.

[68] See, for example, Sterling *Standard,* Feb. 9, 1904, Waukegan *Gazette,* Mar. 19, 1904, Waukegan *Sun,* Mar. 16, 1904, Streator *Monitor,* Feb. 5, 1904.

[69] Davis, *Deadlock,* 87; Hutchinson, *Lowden,* I, 118; Lowden's delegates came from the northwestern Illinois counties.

[70] *Lowden,* I, 116–117; *Tribune,* Jan. 9, Apr. 14, 21, 1904; *Chronicle,* Apr. 12, 15, 19, 1904; Deneen speeches of Apr. 26, 28, 30, 1904, copies in Lowden Papers. It was rumored that Lowden had helped break the Pullman strike of 1894; actually, Lowden had not married into the Pullman family until April, 1896. The Railway Employees' Twentieth Century Club of Illinois, a group that often worked for Lor-

As primary day approached, the Lowden and Deneen camps accelerated their efforts to win votes. The Lorimer organization circulated false ballots marked "Roosevelt and Lowden," and the Lowden newspapers reported that the President favored their candidate. Flyers from the "Business Men's Campaign Committee of Cook County" warned that since Deneen had no downstate delegates, only Lowden could give the city the governorship.[71] The Deneen press, for its part, viewed the contest as a "struggle between two opposing types of party organization, which are so deeply at variance with each other that the outcome is of fundamental importance for good government. . . . Mr. Deneen stands for the organization—which means a strong party. Mr. Lowden stands for the machine—which means fat spoils for its bosses." [72] Cartoon caricatures emphasized the Lorimer-Lowden tie-up. A *Tribune* cartoon, for instance, showed "Bill Sikes" Lorimer saying to "Oliver Twist" Lowden in front of the state capitol building, "You slip in and open the back door for us." [73]

The Deneen forces also challenged Lorimer in his congressional district. Lorimer's opponent was Bernard A. Eckhart, a rich Chicago miller and one of Deneen's financial angels. To discredit Lorimer, the Deneen press recounted his association with Yerkes, his role in the Mueller bill affair, and attacked his record in the Fifty-seventh Congress, where he had voted on only thirteen out of fifty-five roll calls. In addition, they accused Lorimer of profiting from drainage canal contracts to the Lorimer & Gallagher Construction Company. Hopefully these disclosures would discredit both Lorimer and Lowden.[74]

Primary day brought "the most hotly contested primaries ever known in Chicago," as for the first time in eight years Lorimer failed to carry the county. He swept his own West Side areas, the river

---

imer in elections, tried to counter the story that Lowden was anti-labor. See P. E. Conley and N. B. Travis to Dear Sir, May 28, 1904, Lowden Papers; N. B. Travis to Theodore Roosevelt, May 23, 1904, Roosevelt Papers.

71 *Tribune*, Apr. 23, May 4, 1904; *Record-Herald*, Apr. 30, May 4, 1904; *Chronicle*, May 7, 1904; Business Men's Lowden Campaign Committee of Cook County to Dear Sir, May 2, 1904, Lowden Papers.

72 *Record-Herald*, Apr. 27, 1904. See *Record-Herald*, *News*, and *Tribune*, Apr. 27–May 8, 1904, for anti-Lorimer-Lowden material.

73 *Tribune*, May 6, 1904. Nearly every issue of the *Tribune*, the *News*, and the *Record-Herald* from Apr. 27 to May 7, 1904, had an anti-Lorimer cartoon on the front page.

74 Victor Lawson to Bernard A. Eckhart, May 3, 1904, Lawson to Charles M. Faye, "Memorandum," May 4, 1904, Lawson Papers; *Tribune*, Mar. 24–26, 1904; *News*, May 5, 1904.

wards, and several downtown wards for Lowden, but lost in every other part of the city. Jamieson lost not only his home ward on the South Side, but also his seat in the county and state conventions and his place on the state committee. Deneen did best in German, Scandinavian, and native-American areas, while Lowden carried Bohemian, Irish, Russian, and Italian sections. With some exceptions, such as the Polish wards, which John Smulski won for Deneen, Deneen did well in Protestant wards while Lowden did best in Catholic areas, delineating the cultural groups represented in the contest. Lowden secured 187 delegates to the state convention and Deneen approximately 300; most crucial for Lorimer was that Deneen controlled a majority of the delegates to the county convention. Triumphantly, the *Tribune* called the results "a field day for political decency." [75]

The next day at the county convention, Deneen, hoping to gain recruits from the Lorimer men, forced a two-day postponement. On the evening of May 8 the Deneen majority caucused, and for the first time in over a decade the ante-convention caucus of the county majority faction did not include Lorimer, Jamieson, or John M. Smyth. And neither did the slate chosen include any Lorimer men.[76] At the convention on the next day the new leaders of the Cook County party—Deneen, Busse, Pease, and James Reddick of the North Side—put through their slate in forty-one minutes, while Lorimer sat quietly with the Thirty-fourth Ward delegation. "I concede the right of the majority to dictate terms to a defeated minority," he said. "We got nothing, but we are not kicking." [77]

Although Lorimer had lost county control, Lowden was still a strong contender for the nomination. Deneen had a majority of the Cook County delegation, but Lowden had federal faction backing and over a hundred downstate delegates.[78] On May 9 Lowden established headquarters at Springfield's Leland Hotel, the location of most of the other candidates. While the convention proceedings were in the armory, the hotel was the center of political conferences, discussions, and intrigues. Lorimer, who was delayed by Cook County affairs, arrived in Springfield a day later, looking somber in a dark suit and prophetically carrying a large suitcase, as if prepared for a long stay.[79]

[75] *Tribune,* May 7, 1904.
[76] *Tribune* and *Inter-Ocean,* May 9, 1904; *Chronicle,* May 10, 1904.
[77] Chicago *Evening Journal,* May 9, 1904; *Chronicle* and *Tribune,* May 10, 1904.
[78] Walter Reeves to Shelby M. Cullom, Apr. 23, 1904, Cullom Papers.
[79] Davis, *Deadlock,* 162, 167–169. Before the convention Lorimer arranged a meeting of the Illinois congressional delegation which endorsed Senator Charles W.

He did not know it, but this was to be the longest convention in Illinois history.

While delegates boasted that their candidate would win on the first ballot, this was bravado. Of the convention's 1,499 delegates, Lowden, Yates, and Deneen each had approximately 400, while Hamlin, Sherman, and Warner divided up the remainder. A victor would either have to attract other candidates' delegates or make a combination. Which delegation would disintegrate first and what alliances were probable was a constant source of speculation.[80]

The first day of the convention, which opened with packed and noisy galleries, was devoted to speeches and resolutions. On the second day the credentials committee, chaired by Hanecy, announced that the 112 disputed delegates had been split 34 for Lowden and 78 for Yates, a division resulting from a Lorimer-Yates agreement.[81] The first roll call on May 13 was as expected: Yates, 507 votes, Deneen, 368, Lowden, 354, Hamlin, 121, Sherman, 87, and Warner, 45. Unexpected, however, were the slight changes in the subsequent balloting. On the fifteenth and last roll call of the day Yates had 495 votes, Lowden, 405, Deneen, 381, Sherman, 51, Hamlin, 36, and John H. Pierce, president of the Illinois Manufacturers' Association, 21.[82]

It was ten o'clock in the evening when the convention adjourned, but neither Lorimer nor most of the delegates and candidates slept that night. Lowden alone had gained substantially during the day; perhaps other delegates could be persuaded to join him. The support of the "big three," Cullom, Hopkins, and Speaker Joseph G. Cannon, for Lowden, increased his chances. Cullom's lieutenants openly worked for Lowden, while Hopkins and Cannon gave him their tacit backing.[83]

Fairbanks of Indiana for the vice-presidential nomination. Lorimer was concerned with preventing the nomination of Joseph C. Cannon, whom he felt should remain as speaker of the House. Lorimer wrote Senator Cullom, "I am personally of the opinion it would be a great mistake and a great loss to the interests of Illinois, to remove him [Cannon] from the Speaker's chair." See Lorimer to Cullom, May 4, 1904, Cullom Papers; Davis, *Deadlock*, 191–192.

[80] *Inter-Ocean* and *Tribune*, May 9, 1904; Walter Reeves to Cullom, Apr. 23, 1904, Cullom Papers; Davis, *Deadlock*, 175–176.

[81] Davis, *Deadlock*, 182–183; *Tribune* and *Chronicle*, May 11, 1904.

[82] *Chronicle*, May 14, 1904; Davis, *Deadlock*, 224–233.

[83] Davis, *Deadlock*, 186; *Chronicle*, May 7, 1904. Cannon tried to stay impartial in his rulings as chairman. See A. F. Bussard to Cannon, Mar. 14, 1906, Cannon Papers.

Early that morning, Governor Yates met with Hopkins, Lorimer, and Cannon. The details of the meeting are a matter of dispute. Yates claimed that Lorimer and the "big three" offered him the Mexican ambassadorship if he would withdraw in favor of Lowden. Lorimer and Hopkins denied making this proposal; if they did, it was without President Roosevelt's knowledge. While Roosevelt had been asked to appoint Yates to a diplomatic post, Frank B. Noyes, editor of the Chicago *Record-Herald,* made the request in behalf of Deneen.[84] Whatever the truth, the episode strengthened Yates's position, for his supporters now argued that he was so sure of renomination that he could refuse such a tempting offer.

During the entire next week of the convention, the monotonous round of roll calls and conferences, rumors and counter-rumors continued without substantial change in the votes. By the middle of the week, half the delegates had gone home, while the rest, bedraggled and tired, relieved their boredom by horseplay. Permanent chairman "Uncle Joe" Cannon, chewing an ever-present "chew" of tobacco, presided over the uproar with much wit and gavel-banging. It was clear, as Lorimer observed, that "you could not break the deadlock with a Gatling gun." [85]

The problem was the animosity between the three leading candidates. Deneen and Lowden would not combine, for neither Lorimer nor Deneen wanted to see the other receive the power that nomination would bring. On the other hand, the chances of either Deneen or Lowden going to Yates were also slim. Both men had criticized Yates's misgovernment and it would be hard for them to justify giving him the opportunity to serve another term. Yates could win if Hamlin, Warner, and Sherman joined with him, but they would not do this. Rumors circulated that Yates was going to this candidate or that, but they never materialized.[86]

During the first full week of the deadlock, two committees, one representing Lowden and the other Yates, met for discussions. The press reported that at this conference Yates consented to withdraw if Lowden would support his candidacy for senator in 1907 against Senator Cullom. But Lowden would not consider such terms. Cullom

[84] *News* and *Tribune,* May 17, 1904; Davis, *Deadlock,* 257; Frank B. Noyes to Roosevelt, May 21, 1904, Roosevelt to Noyes, May 23, 1904, Roosevelt Papers.

[85] Davis, *Deadlock,* 237, 257, 287–288; *Tribune,* May 15, 1904.

[86] Joseph G. Cannon to William Loeb, Jr., May 24, 1904, Roosevelt Papers; Sherman to Dawes, May 20, 1904, Dawes Papers; Davis, *Deadlock,* 236.

was his ally, and he would not bargain Cullom's Senate seat for his own advancement. The discussion ended without result, and the deadlock continued.[87]

Early on the morning of May 20, Lowden, Yates, and Deneen agreed to adjourn the convention until May 31. The one ballot on this day, the fifty-eighth, showed amazingly little change from the first roll call taken a week earlier.[88] During the ten-day recess, each candidate sought to improve his position. Lowden, after fourteen hours of sleep and a dose of cough medicine, went delegate-hunting in Yates's territory in southern Illinois, while Yates invaded Chicago.[89] The Yates, Deneen, and Sherman forces all tried to get President Roosevelt to intervene for their candidates, or at least to limit the pro-Lowden activities of Hopkins, Cullom, and the federal appointees. "Only one thing remains to make my success overwhelming," wrote Yates in a letter intended for Roosevelt's eyes. "That is to have the President simply say to Cullom and Cannon that I am his friend, as well as they, and that he wants them not to fight me." "I am thoroughly convinced that if Deneen is nominated you need give no further thought to Illinois," wrote Frank B. Noyes to the President. "Can't you find it possible to help us in our fight for better political things in Illinois?" And, wrote Sherman to Dawes, "ask Cortelyou [Republican national treasurer] to suggest my support by Hopkins Cullom and Lorimer as settlement contest. . . ." Even Cannon wrote to Roosevelt warning that Yates's renomination would mean the loss of the state, and asking him to get Deneen and Lowden to agree on a compromise candidate. Roosevelt, however, refused to intercede, and suggested that Cannon take over the role of compromiser.[90]

When the balloting began again on Monday, May 30, the roll calls showed approximately the same totals as those of ten days before. On Wednesday, June 2, however, during the noon recess, Lorimer, Hopkins, Cullom, and other influential Lowden supporters met with

[87] Davis, *Deadlock*, 261–262, 275–280, 299; Chicago *Evening Journal*, May 17, 20, 1904; *Inter-Ocean*, June 9, 1904; Hutchinson, *Lowden*, I, 130.

[88] Davis, *Deadlock*, 303–304.

[89] *Ibid.*, 307–308; Chicago *Evening Journal* and *Tribune*, May 24–25, 1904; Hutchinson, *Lowden*, I, 127.

[90] Yates to Frank S. Witherbee, May 22, 1904, Noyes to Roosevelt, May 21, 1904, Cannon to William Loeb, Jr., May 24, 1904, Roosevelt Papers; Roosevelt to Cannon, May 27, 1904, *Roosevelt Letters*, IV, 805–806; Sherman to Dawes, May 31, 1904, Cortelyou to Dawes, May 19, 1904, Dawes Papers.

several Yates leaders and promised them federal and state positions if they would shift to Lowden. With a Yates victory seemingly impossible, many of the Yates men agreed.[91]

That afternoon the Lowden push began. On the sixty-ninth ballot Lowden jumped from 400 to 573 votes and by the seventy-third he had reached 631, with most of the additional votes coming from the Yates camp. The day's end found Lowden slightly down from his high of 631 votes, but his followers were confident that he would win on the next day. Sherman's pledge to throw his votes to the first candidate who went over 700 aided their optimism.[92]

The prospect of a Lowden victory, which was made particularly distasteful to Yates because of his betrayal by his former allies, forced the Governor to seek out Deneen. Shortly after one A.M. on June 3, Yates warned Deneen that his forces were disintegrating and that unless they acted, Lowden would be nominated. The Governor proposed the same bargain he had suggested to Lowden: he would back Deneen for governor if Deneen would promise Yates support for senator in 1907. Deneen knew that such an arrangement might be distasteful to some of his supporters, but most of them would prefer this to Lorimer's man in the statehouse. Whatever scruples Deneen had on the deal were overcome by his ambition and by the chance to overthrow Lorimer, and he accepted Yates's proposal.[93]

Since Yates's support alone was insufficient to guarantee Deneen's nomination, the two invited the other candidates to participate in the discussions. The new allies forced the convention to adjourn until two P.M. and met in the executive mansion to finalize their plans. After reviewing the situation, they agreed that Deneen was acceptable to them all and especially preferable to Lowden.[94] When the Yates delegates marched back into the convention hall, the Lowden men shouted, "The world hates a quitter," for they knew of their candidate's defeat. Yates announced his withdrawal and asked his friends to

[91] Davis, *Deadlock,* 348–351; *Tribune,* June 2, 3, 1904.

[92] *Tribune,* June 3, 1904; Davis, *Deadlock,* 353–366.

[93] Yates to James E. Babb, June 16, 1904, Yates Papers, Illinois State Historical Library; John C. Shaffer to Albert J. Beveridge, June 4, 1904, Albert J. Beveridge Papers, Library of Congress. Deneen later denied that he promised to support Yates for the senatorship but evidence in the Yates Papers points to a different conclusion. See Yates to Deneen, July 30, 1905, to James E. Babb, Aug. 14, 1906, Lawrence Y. Sherman to Yates, Apr. 24, 1916, Yates Papers.

[94] Davis, *Deadlock,* 372–374; *Tribune,* June 4, 1904.

support the "man who is the choice of a majority of the Republicans of Chicago," Charles S. Deneen.[95] Hamlin, Sherman, and Pierce followed suit, and a roll call confirmed Deneen as the Republican gubernatorial nominee. The next day Yates and Deneen completed the slate by further agreement. The convention nominated Sherman as lieutenant governor and Yates men Len Small and James A. Rose for treasurer and secretary of state.[96]

"It was a fair fight and I am beaten," Lowden said as he moved to make Deneen's nomination unanimous, and Lorimer, although he refused to comment, no doubt agreed.[97] Why Yates was so anxious to beat Lorimer and the other Lowden supporters he later detailed in a letter to his mother:

> The result of the convention is the indirect work of William Lorimer and A. J. Hopkins. They could . . . have supported me. They failed to do so, and forced me to nominate Mr. Deneen, so that after all, in a certain sense, it is their work. They had it in their power to do a noble and honorable thing, and support me, and they failed to do it, and on the contrary made every effort to destroy me, and I had to choose between a man supported by the Chicago newspaper trust on the one hand, and a man who, if nominated, would be the creature of my ungrateful friends and S. M. Cullom and Joe Cannon, on the other; and I made my choice without hesitation.[98]

Lorimer, of course, realized the danger in abandoning Yates for Lowden, but because of the Governor's unpopularity he probably believed he had little choice. What surprised Yates's opponents was his success in winning delegates. Without his ability in this regard, Deneen might never have been nominated.

"What's going to happen to Lorimer?" asked the *Tribune*. The more naive of the reformers answered that he was finished as a political power. "At last the era of primary corruption, assessment of State employees and the prostitution of the State Civil Service is at an end," wrote Dawes in his journal. "The old machine is gone . . . irrevocably both in the county and in the State. They have lost both power and public respect." [99] Other more astute observers, however, recog-

[95] Davis, *Deadlock*, 377–378.
[96] *Ibid.*, 378–390; *Tribune* and *Chronicle*, June 4, 1904.
[97] Davis, *Deadlock*, 382; *Tribune*, June 5, 1904.
[98] Printed in Krenkel, ed., *Richard Yates*, 144–154.
[99] *Tribune*, June 4, 1904; *Dawes Journal*, 372.

nized that a person with Lorimer's political talents could never be discounted. He still held his congressional seat and a base of loyal wards on Chicago's West Side. His power might be circumscribed and his prestige diminished, but he remained a dangerous foe. Whether or not he would be able to return as Cook County boss was a question still to be answered.

★　★　★　★　★　★　★　★　★　★　★

CHAPTER 7

An Urban Politician in the House of Representatives, 1895-1901, 1903-09

Dᴜʀɪɴɢ ᴛʜᴇ ʏᴇᴀʀs from 1895 to 1901, and again from 1903 to 1909, William Lorimer represented a Chicago congressional district in the U.S. House of Representatives. In many ways Lorimer, the local political boss, differed little from the bulk of his Republican colleagues. He generally voted the straight party line on national issues, he seldom spoke, and he represented the needs of his constituents and the industries in his district as he conceived them. The nature of his constituency, however, set him off from his fellows. For Lorimer came from an urban congressional district at a time when rural America elected the great mass of congressmen.[1]

Lorimer's congressional districts, the Second (1895–1901) and the Sixth (1903–09), consisted of several West Side Chicago wards and a number of Cook County towns, the largest of which was Cicero. Both were primarily working-class areas with pockets of middle-class residents toward the outlying sections. A majority of the voters in the two districts were either foreign-born or had foreign-born parents, of mainly German, Irish, English, and Bohemian stock. The Sixth District also contained a large bloc of Russians, the newest arrivals in the area.[2]

[1] The population of the United States in 1890 was 64 percent rural (40,841,000) and 36 percent urban (22,106,000). U.S., Bureau of the Census, *Historical Statistics of the United States* (Washington, 1961), 9.

[2] Although the two districts shared some territory, the Second was much larger than the Sixth. It consisted of the Tenth, Twenty-eighth, Twenty-ninth, and Thirtieth Chicago wards and a number of county towns; the Sixth, formed in 1901 following a Chicago ward reapportionment, consisted of the Thirteenth, Twentieth, and Thirty-fourth wards and several county towns. U.S., *Eleventh Census, 1890,* "Population,"

Many of the residents of the two districts worked in the industries that dotted the eastern sections of the Chicago wards, especially along the drainage canal and the south branch of the Chicago River. Among these industries were the Edward Hines Lumber Company, International Harvester Corporation, the Illinois Steel Company, the W. W. Kimball Company, builder of pianos and organs, and many other manufacturing companies. The vast Union Stock Yards were also located on the West Side and formed part of the Second District.[3]

As an urban congressman, Lorimer, as well as most members of the Chicago delegation, on numerous occasions voted in opposition to their nonurban Illinois colleagues.[4] These were cases in which the metropolis' interests differed from those of the rest of the state. In his study of the Chicago congressional delegation from 1843 to 1925, L. Ethan Ellis notes that Chicago Republicans and Democrats usually voted alike when their city was involved.[5] Lorimer shared this attitude and was well known for his defense of Chicago interests. He obtained federal funds for city projects and introduced legislation to help Chicago businesses or specific groups within the city. "Whenever any bill is introduced affecting any industry in Chicago," Lorimer once commented, "I always make it my business to communicate with the people that may be affected by it." [6]

Since Lorimer's legislative stands were often determined by the

I, 161–181, and *Thirteenth Census, 1910,* "Population," I, 512–514; *Daily News Almanac for 1894,* 313; James A. Rose, comp., *Blue Book of the State of Illinois 1909* (Danville, 1909), 140–141.

[3] The *Inter-Ocean* called the Second District "the largest industrial district in the United States." The Sixth District was more residential. Inter-Ocean, *A History of the City of Chicago* (Chicago, 1901), 477; Pierce, *Chicago,* III, 60–61, 92–93, 140, 156, 163.

[4] When Lorimer took his seat in the Fifty-fourth Congress he was one of a group of seven Chicago congressmen out of an Illinois delegation of twenty-three. Lorimer at thirty-three was the second youngest member of the delegation although the Chicagoans, on the average, were considerably younger than their downstate colleagues. Throughout Lorimer's tenure, there were substantial differences between metropolitan and nonmetropolitan congressmen: 60 percent of the non-Chicagoans were Illinois-born, but only 32 percent of the Chicagoans; 24 percent of the latter were foreign-born but no one in the rest of the delegation; and downstate congressmen were generally better educated than their urban colleagues. U.S., *Biographical Directory of the American Congress 1774–1949* (Washington, 1950).

[5] Lewis Ethan Ellis, "A History of the Chicago Delegation in Congress, 1843–1925," *Transactions of the Illinois State Historical Society for the Year 1930* (Springfield, 1930), 131.

[6] *Ibid.,* 126–128; *CR,* 54th Cong., 1st Sess., XXVIII, 2624–25, XXIX, 14, 2683–85, 56th Cong., 1st Sess., XXX, 56; *Tribune,* Apr. 12, 1896, Feb. 20, Nov. 27, Dec. 7, 1897, Jan. 19, 1899, Mar. 29–30, 1900; *Dillingham Committee Hearings,* VIII, 7781–82.

needs of his district rather than by an adherence to a strict party line, his voting record and the legislation he submitted followed an unusual pattern. In 1897 and in 1909 he supported the high protective tariff, but in 1901 he actively opposed a tariff between Puerto Rico and the United States.[7] The latter stand seemed dictated by political consider- ations and by the wishes of the Chicago meat-packers and sugar- refiners. Although he supposedly was tied to the interests of big busi- ness, in 1896 he introduced legislation that would have prohibited the blacklisting of workers because of strike participation and in 1897 he submitted a bill to establish a postal savings system, a proposal similar to one made by the Populists in their 1892 platform.[8] During the Roosevelt administration, he usually followed his party majority, voting for railroad regulation, for financial reform, and for defense and naval appropriations. He opposed, however, food and drug regulations, and in 1908 and 1909, when many Republicans attacked the President's reform proposals, Lorimer joined them in their op- position.[9]

Although Lorimer occasionally spoke in House debate and several times made set speeches, his most effective congressional work was conducted behind the scenes. He had considerable influence with the two men who held the speaker's chair for most of his congressional

[7] Lewis Ethan Ellis, "A History of the Chicago Delegation in Congress, 1843– 1925" (unpublished Ph.D. dissertation, University of Chicago, 1927), 132, 135–141, 156–157. The dissertation contains a chapter on the tariff not included in the pre- viously cited work by Ellis. Lorimer led a House rebellion against McKinley's pro- posed 15 percent tariff. See Margaret Leech, *In the Days of McKinley* (New York, 1959), 487–503; *Times-Herald,* Feb. 26, 27, Mar. 1, Apr. 4, 6, 12, 1900; William E. Curtis to William McKinley, Feb. 18, 1900, McKinley Papers.

[8] *CR,* 54th Cong., 2nd Sess., XXIX, 35, 55th Cong., 2nd Sess., XXXI, 13, 56th Cong., 1st Sess., XXXIII, 221. Lorimer introduced the postal savings bill at the behest of Victor Lawson. He told Speaker Thomas B. Reed that the legislation "would go a long way toward contradicting the general impression that the Re- publican party had been given over to the corporations." Dennis, *Victor Lawson,* 231–240.

[9] In January, 1906, Lorimer introduced into the House a food and drug bill that forbade interstate commerce in adulterated or misbranded food and drugs, but which allowed the definition of adulteration to be determined by the state of origin. The press attacked the bill as designed to perpetuate existing unsatisfactory conditions. Oscar E. Anderson, Jr., *The Health of a Nation: Harvey W. Wiley and the Fight for Pure Food* (Chicago, 1958), 126–183; *Tribune,* Jan. 26, 31, Feb. 3, 1906; *CR,* 59th Cong., 1st Sess., XL, 1143. For Lorimer's other votes during the Roosevelt administration see *CR,* 58th Cong., 1st Sess., XL, 1142 (Philippine tariff), 58th Cong., 2nd Sess., XXXVIII, 4115, 58th Cong., 3rd Sess., XXXIX, 1136 (army appropriations), 58th Cong., 3rd Sess., XLIX, 2184–85 (Esch-Townshend Act), 59th Cong., 1st Sess., XL, 2207 (Hepburn Act), 60th Cong., 1st Sess., XLII, 6375– 76 (Vreeland bill).

tenure, "Czar" Thomas B. Reed and "Uncle Joe" Cannon, and he used this influence to secure favors for his district. His committee assignments reflected his main areas of legislative concern: agriculture, from where he watched over the concerns of the meat-packing industry; rivers and harbors, which related to his involvement in waterway development; and labor.[10] Working within his committees, in the cloakrooms, and through his friends, Lorimer strove to secure measures helpful to Chicago's interests and to block those that threatened them.

Not all of Lorimer's congressional actions, however, were conducted in private or had only local significance, and there were three main occasions when he involved himself in issues having national importance. In 1898 Lorimer helped lead a House rebellion against President McKinley's Cuban policy; in 1906 Lorimer led the fight against the Beveridge meat-inspection amendment; and from 1905 to 1909 Lorimer fought for federal aid for the construction of a deep waterway from Chicago to the Gulf of Mexico. In the first two instances, American intervention in the Cuban revolution and meat-inspection legislation, Lorimer took positions opposed to those of a President of his own party. In each case, although the issues involved had national ramifications, Lorimer's motivation was related to his district's and city's concerns.

In regard to U.S. intervention in the Cuban revolution, Lorimer made no speech and took no action before March of 1898 that indicated a desire to involve the United States in the conflict between Spain and her rebellious colony. In fact, he disapproved of jingoistic statements by Senator William E. Mason and Governor John R. Tanner of his own state. Lorimer told the Washington correspondent for the Chicago *Record* that a "clique of speculators in Chicago" inspired their actions.[11] In late March, however, at the time of President McKinley's message on the destruction of the battleship *Maine,* Lorimer became a leader among the group of representatives who sought to force McKinley to intervene in Cuba. What sort of factors could have influenced him to become an interventionist activist?

Ernest R. May has suggested that because they lacked any sophis-

10 Lorimer was also appointed a member of the Industrial Commission in 1900.
11 William E. Curtis to Charles H. Dennis, Feb. 19, 1898, Charles H. Dennis Papers, Newberry Library, Chicago; Ernest R. May, *Imperial Democracy: The Emergence of America as a Great Power* (New York, 1961), 138.

ticated method of measuring public opinion, congressmen "may have gauged public views in the unfamiliar area of foreign policy by observing a small cosmopolitan elite." Among the Chicago "foreign policy establishment," May finds merchants such as Marshall Field and Franklin MacVeagh and newspapermen such as Melville E. Stone, formerly Victor Lawson's partner and now general manager of the Associated Press, and Herman H. Kohlsaat. Several lawyers and educators are also in May's list.[12] This "elite" supported McKinley's attempts to resolve the Cuban difficulties without U.S. intervention. It may have restrained Lorimer and the rest of the Chicago congressional delegation from opposing McKinley's policy of restraint for as long as they did, but once the *Maine*'s destruction had aroused public opinion, it lost its influence.

Pro-intervention sentiment had been present in Chicago for some time. A Club Patriotico Cubano, a branch of the Cuban junta, the U.S. representative of the Cuban revolutionary government, encouraged this feeling among labor organizations. The local cigar-makers' union, the municipal Trades Assembly, and the Illinois Federation of Labor all passed pro-Cuban resolves, while the Chicago local of the Typographical Union petitioned the Chicago congressional delegation to oust Spain from Cuba. Some Chicago industrialists such as John W. Gates were "feeling militant," while the Chicago *Tribune* was especially belligerent in its demands. In one editorial appearing after the *Maine*'s destruction the *Tribune* called for "War and Honor, Not Peace and Shame." War, said the *Tribune*, would increase "American patriotism," "eliminate mugwumpery," "wipe out [the] cowardly gamblers of Wall Street," and end the "16 to 1 abomination." [13]

Chicago jingoism reached a new level after the mysterious explosion on the *Maine*. Patriotic outbursts occurred in theaters, and ministers, in their Sunday sermons, demanded intervention in the name of humanity.[14] A significant poll of bankers' opinions appearing in the

---

[12] Ernest R. May, *American Imperialism* (New York, 1968), 75, 225.

[13] Gonzalo de Quesada to Tomas Estrada Palma, Jan. 17, 1899, *Correspondencia Diplomática de la Delegación Cubana en Neuva York durante la Guerra de Independencia de 1895 a 1898*, Vol. V of *Publicaciones del Archivo Nacional de Cuba* (Havana, 1946), 162, hereafter cited as *Cuban Letters; Tribune*, Mar. 28, 1898; May, *Imperial Democracy*, 71; Thomas Beer, *Hanna, Crane, and the Mauve Decade* (New York, 1941), 550; *Tribune*, Feb. 27, 1898; "A War Fever in Chicago," New York *Times*, Feb. 27, 1898.

[14] *Tribune*, Feb. 21, 28, Mar. 14, 1898.

March 24 *Tribune* noted that while the presidents of the Northwest National Bank, the Metropolitan National Bank, and the National Bank of America deprecated war, the influential John J. Mitchell of the Illinois Trust and Savings Bank and E. A. Hamill of the Corn Exchange Bank were for intervention.[15] Victor Lawson's *Daily News* and *Record* pleaded for calm and support for the administration, but admitted "that war fever was rampant in the city." And, as an important indication of the rise of Chicago jingoism, in late March Kohlsaat's *Times-Herald* abandoned its peaceful stand and declared that "intervention in Cuba . . . is immediately inevitable." On April 2 Kohlsaat telegraphed McKinley that "the conservative people here . . . have sustained your policy with vigor but believe the matter should be settled now." [16]

Lorimer and every member of the Chicago congressional delegation save George E. Foss responded to this increase in war spirit by threatening to break with the President's cautious policy. If there was a Chicago "foreign policy establishment," it had lost its influence over the city's congressmen. On March 28, when McKinley delivered a calm message on the destruction of the *Maine* in Havana harbor, Lorimer warned in a newspaper interview that unless the President moved against Spain, Congress would "take action on its own hook." [17] On the next day, he joined with Chicago Representative James R. Mann to organize a meeting of fifty congressmen dissatisfied with the administration's course. Twelve of the fifty were from Illinois and half of these were Chicagoans. In his speech to the group, Lorimer emphasized that "absolute independence" was necessary for Cuba and warned that Republicans should "not allow the

[15] *Ibid.*, Mar. 24, 1898. Julius W. Pratt notes that the "financial interests and their spokesmen" were solidly anti-war up to the beginning of hostilities. This generalization may not be valid for midwestern financial interests. See *Expansionists of 1898* (Quadrangle ed., Chicago, 1964), 235–236.

[16] Robert L. Tree, "Victor Fremont Lawson and His Newspapers, 1890–1900: A Study of the Chicago *Daily News* and the Chicago *Record*" (unpublished Ph.D. dissertation, Northwestern University, 1959), 249–250. Kohlsaat's editorial is quoted in May, *Imperial Democracy*, 146; Kohlsaat to McKinley, Apr. 2, 1898, McKinley Papers. John C. McNulta wrote Charles G. Dawes from Chicago that "The public mind is in a condition without parallel since the surrender of Fort Sumter." Apr. 8, 1898, McKinley Papers.

[17] *Tribune*, Mar. 28, 1898. "The Republicans in Congress feel that if the President will not formulate a policy it must be put forward by the Republican leaders in Senate and House." See William E. Chandler to Paul Dana, Mar. 29, 1898, William E. Chandler Papers, Library of Congress.

party to be awed by so-called business interests into stultifying itself and betraying the wishes of the people of the country." [18]

Lorimer's statement implies that "real" business interests desired intervention while "so-called business interests" opposed it. Some of the latter criticized the large involvement by the Chicago delegation in the dissenting caucus. Thirty-nine Chicago firms, including Marshall Field & Company, John V. Farwell Company, Carson Pirie Scott & Company, Hart, Schaffner & Marx, Phelps, Dodge & Palmer, Armour & Company, the Cudahy Packing Company, and the Chicago Packing and Provision Company, addressed a petition to the Chicago delegation observing that "the patriotic, conservative business elements of our country . . . deprecate war with Spain except as a last resort," and warning that "the views of sensationalists are not cherished by the majority of our thoughtful and conservative citizens. . . ." [19] The *Tribune* observed that most of the signers of the petition were "middlemen," concerned about the injury that war would do to profit.[20]

Lorimer answered the petition. He observed that the only difference between the petitioners and himself was timing. They would temporarily delay action; he would act immediately. The administration had to force Spain to withdraw and recognize Cuban independence because "murder is going on every day by the slow process of starvation on that island." If the administration did not move toward this end, Lorimer would vote for a resolution "on the broad grounds of humanity," recognizing such independence and authorizing armed intervention.[21] The city greeted Lorimer's pronouncement with enthusiasm. "Public sentiment in Chicago and Illinois approves your manly and dignified course," read one telegram printed in the *Tribune;* "Stock jobbers do not represent American sentiment." [22]

By March 31, the ranks of the *Reconcentrados,* as the Republican rebels were now called, had grown to 115. Almost all of the *Reconcentrados* had been in the House only a relatively short time.[23] Their lack of seniority makes their willingness to oppose the administration

---

[18] *Tribune,* Mar. 30, 1898; New York *Times,* Mar. 30, 1898; Arthur Dunn, *From Harrison to Harding: A Personal Narrative, Covering a Third of a Century, 1888–1921* (2 vols., New York, 1922), I, 232.

[19] *Tribune,* Mar. 31, 1898.

[20] *Ibid.,* Apr. 1, 1898.

[21] *Ibid.,* Mar. 31, 1898.

[22] Quoted in *ibid.,* Apr. 1, 1898.

[23] The *Tribune* printed the names of seventy-two members of the group; of this number fifteen were from Illinois, nine from Michigan, eight from Pennsylvania,

all the more striking and suggests that they were responding to strong constituency pressure. The rebel group selected a committee of eleven, including Lorimer, Mann, and Hopkins of Illinois, to meet with the President and secure a clear statement of his policy. Instead, the committee merely returned with a request that Congress postpone action until the President had heard from Madrid concerning his latest armistice proposal.[24]

When several days passed, however, and still McKinley had not acted on Spain's failure to agree to his conditions, the *Reconcentrados* again met to demand action. But while they (with Lorimer prominent) threatened to move independently, they finally agreed to await the President's pronouncement of April 11. On that day McKinley forwarded a message to Congress asking for the authority to use the military to secure peace and a "stable government" in Cuba without recognizing the existing rebel government. He did propose that Congress eventually recognize an independent Cuban regime. According to Walter LaFeber, this message indicated that McKinley "had assumed an inflexible position" and was prepared to accept war.[25]

Congress, however, thought that McKinley was still evading the issue. The Senate received his message with silence and the House greeted it with only slight applause. Lorimer, reflecting the attitude of the House militants, commented that "the President's message is a disappointment. We do not know what kind of government a 'stable government' is, and we propose to find out before we give the President authority to act. . . ."[26] But, as the party whips applied pressure, the House rebels fell into line. When the Committee on Foreign Affairs presented resolutions in conformity with the President's message, the House approved them by a large majority, with Lorimer and most of the *Reconcentrados* rejoining the party fold.[27]

But the Senate proved more recalcitrant. The majority of the Com-

---

seven from New York, six from Iowa, and four from Maryland. Ninety-four percent of the group had been elected since 1892: fifteen in 1892; thirty-three in 1894; and twenty in 1896.

[24] *Tribune* and New York *Times,* Mar. 31, Apr. 1, 1898; Walter LaFeber, *The New Empire: An Interpretation of American Expansion 1860–1898* (Ithaca, 1963), 402.

[25] LaFeber, *The New Empire,* 399–400; *Tribune,* Apr. 2, 7, 8, 11, 12, 1898; New York *Times,* Apr. 4–10, 1898.

[26] William E. Chandler to Paul Dana, Apr. 7, 1898, Chandler Papers; Charles A. Boynton to Benjamin F. Montgomery, Apr. [n.d.], 1898, McKinley Papers; *Tribune* and New York *Times,* Apr. 12, 1898.

[27] New York *Times,* Apr. 13, 1898.

mittee on Foreign Relations reported resolutions tantamount to a declaration of war, while the minority expressly recognized the Cuban Republic. After four days of controversy in the upper house, twenty-four Republicans under the leadership of Senator Joseph B. Foraker of Ohio joined with the Democrats to approve the minority report.[28] The Senate action precipitated a new uprising against the President's policy by the House *Reconcentrados.* Lorimer and other rebels who had reluctantly supported the Foreign Affairs resolutions now threatened to join with the Democrats to force the House to approve the Senate resolutions providing for recognition as well as intervention. They justified their shift by claiming that nonconcurrence with the Senate would further delay intervention. The New York *Times* reported that they were responding to "home sympathy" for the Cubans.[29]

The administration forces worked feverishly to restore discipline. Speaker Thomas B. Reed turned his suite of rooms at the Shoreham Hotel into a headquarters and from there issued warnings that no "loyal" Republican could approve the Senate resolution. He appealed to Lorimer personally to support the administration position, but to no avail. The Blond Boss continued to work with the Illinois delegation to persuade others to join the break.[30] When the House-Senate conference committee arrived at a compromise that accepted the Senate resolution on intervention but eliminated the recognition clause, Lorimer opposed the leadership's position. But few Republicans were willing to continue their rebellion over the question of recognition. On April 18, amidst "unparalleled activity," the House voted 179 to 156 to accept the conference committee's recommendation of intervention without recognition. Only fourteen Republicans, including five Illinois representatives, voted with the Democrats. Lorimer, Mann, Belknap, and White, all from Chicago, were joined by Vespasian Warner to stand fast for recognition of the Cuban Republic.[31]

In *The New Empire,* Walter LaFeber raises a question as to President McKinley's behavior during the Cuban crisis. Why, he asks, was

28 William E. Chandler to Paul Dana, Apr. 13, 1898, Chandler Papers; Everett Walters, *Joseph Benson Foraker: An Uncompromising Republican* (Columbus, 1948), 151.
29 New York *Times,* Apr. 18, 19, 1898.
30 *Ibid.*
31 *Tribune,* Apr. 19, 1898; Paul S. Holbo, "Presidential Leadership in Foreign Affairs: William McKinley and the Turpie-Foraker Amendment, *American Historical Review* (July, 1967), LXXII, 1321–35.

McKinley prepared to accept war in April when he had not been ready in January and February? LaFeber suggests that the reason was the "transformation of the opinion of many spokesmen for the business community who had formerly opposed war." [32] Can the same answer be used to explain Lorimer's emergence as an interventionist leader in mid-March? There is no doubt that Chicago business opinion was becoming more militant but it is debatable that this decisively influenced Lorimer. Steel magnate John W. Gates, who was close to him, had been pro-war for some time, while the meat-packers, to whom Lorimer often looked for guidance, were prominently represented on the businessmen's peace petition of March 31. More plausible is the interpretation that Lorimer and the rest of the Chicago delegation were spurred by political motives in becoming jingoes. [33]

Lorimer and the other Chicago congressmen, all of whom had been elected since 1894, were conscious that Chicago was a Democratic city, and of the need to maintain the GOP gains made in the elections of 1894 and 1896. The administration's hesitant Cuban policy, however, posed difficulties, as the Democrats sought to take advantage of the city's war fever. Whereas the *Times-Herald,* considered an administration spokesman in Chicago, disapproved of Republican Senator Mason's belligerent speeches, the Bryan and Altgeld clubs passed resolutions approving them. During the township and city council campaigns in March, the Democrats used "War with Spain" as their campaign cry. When the Democrats captured the majority of local posts, the *Tribune* editorialized that Republican candidates had suffered "because the Republican national administration has not moved more rapidly in the Cuban question." [34] Concern over the political implications of the administration's indecisiveness rather than any large shift in business opinion drove Lorimer and the Chicago delegation toward militancy.

That Lorimer viewed his militancy as politically important was reflected in his re-election campaign. Lorimer won renomination without opposition; Democrat C. Porter Johnson, a relative unknown, opposed him in the election. Lorimer's campaign theme was the patriotic necessity of a Republican Congress, and he entertained voters at his rallies with patriotic songs and cinematograph pictures of battles. The popular singer Bert Murphy often introduced Lorimer with the

[32] LaFeber, *The New Empire,* 403.
[33] Beer, *Hanna, Crane, and the Mauve Decade,* 550.
[34] *Tribune,* Apr. 1, 4–6, 1898.

spirited refrain, "Who was it fought for Cuba? Who was it cried for vengeance for the murders on the *Maine*? Billy Lorimer, Billy Lorimer," was Murphy's answer. Lorimer's speeches praised the Republican party for freeing Cuba. He also called for the retention of the Philippines and Puerto Rico, the enlargement of the navy, and the building of a Nicaraguan canal. Lorimer's astute mixture of politics and patriotism appealed to the voters and gave him a substantial victory over his Democratic opponent, as he ran well ahead of his party in his district.[35]

In the case of meat-inspection legislation, another issue in which he played a prominent role, Lorimer again opposed a President of his own party. In this instance, however, he acted at the behest of a specific Chicago industrial interest, the meat-packers, and risked public disapproval and censure by his district's voters.

The congresses that met during Theodore Roosevelt's presidency, the Fifty-eighth, Fifty-ninth, and Sixtieth, were characterized by a more active executive direction of affairs than in previous administrations. "Increasingly," Robert H. Wiebe notes, "the important bills . . . were either drafted in an executive department or cleared there before they were introduced." [36] Major innovations rejected by the President seldom survived in Congress. Many of the policies of Roosevelt's administration involved the centralization of decision-making and the scientific solution by experts of social and economic problems. These policies brought the President into conflict with a Congress representative of local interests that resisted these centralizing tendencies and opposed executive interference in legislative affairs.[37]

As a congressman with a strong local orientation, Lorimer voted against legislation that impinged upon the interests of Chicago or city

[35] For accounts of Lorimer's campaign rallies see *Tribune,* June 10, Sept. 13, 15, 20, 22, 23, 27, 1898; *Times-Herald,* Sept. 15, 20, Oct. 5, 8, 1898. Lorimer had 27,151 votes (53.8 percent) and Johnson 23,354 (46.2 percent). See Manuscript Election Returns, Second Congressional District, 1898, Board of Election Commissioners, Chicago. Of the seventy-two *Reconcentrados* in the House, thirteen were defeated in 1898 and thirteen did not run for re-election.

[36] Wiebe, *Search for Order,* 191; John Morton Blum, *The Republican Roosevelt* (Cambridge, 1954), 73–74.

[37] Samuel P. Hays, *Conservation and the Gospel of Efficiency: The Progressive Conservation Movement, 1890–1920* (Cambridge, 1959), 138, 266–271; Jerome M. Clubb, "Congressional Opponents of Reform, 1901–1913" (unpublished Ph.D. dissertation, University of Washington, 1963), 24–39.

industries and for measures that favored them. At other times he usually followed the GOP majority. Rather than insurgency, Lorimer's record was marked by party regularity and nonvoting and nonattendance, as Illinois political concerns kept him from Washington.[38] In 1906, however, issues involving meat inspection drew Lorimer from his customary silence and into the legislative limelight.

In February, 1906, Doubleday, Page & Co. published Upton Sinclair's explosive novel, *The Jungle,* about the life of workers in Chicago's packing town. *The Jungle* had an immediate impact, although not in the manner Sinclair intended. He was concerned with industrial slavery, not the condition of the meat, but public opinion reacted to Sinclair's descriptions of stockyards sanitary conditions. Several journals, such as *Collier's* and *The World's Work,* prepared to publish articles on the question of clean meat and the need for government inspection.[39]

Actually, such inspection already existed. In 1891 Congress had passed legislation requiring ante mortem inspection of all sheep, cattle, and hogs whose meat was intended for export or interstate sale and authorizing post mortem inspection at the discretion of the Secretary of Agriculture. Congress passed further legislation in 1895, and by 1904 the government inspected 84 percent of the beef slaughtered by the Chicago Big Four packers. The packers sponsored this inspection as a means of guaranteeing entrance into European markets.[40]

The Jungle caused the public to question the efficacy of the packer-sponsored meat inspection. Secretary of Agriculture James Wilson, whose Bureau of Animal Industry conducted the inspections, believed that the book contained an "implied criticism" of his department; he

[38] In the Fifty-eighth Congress, Lorimer voted on 25 out of 84 roll calls; in the Fifty-ninth Congress he voted on 47 out of 135. See Victor Lawson to Bernard A. Eckhart, May 3, 1904, and to Charles M. Faye, May 4, 1904, Lawson Papers, for comments on his voting record.

[39] Upton Sinclair, *The Jungle* (New York, 1906); John Braeman, "The Square Deal in Action: A Case Study in the Growth of the 'National Police Power,' " in John Braeman *et al.,* eds., *Change and Continuity in Twentieth-Century America* (Harper Colophon ed., New York, 1966), 44–46; James Harvey Young, *The Toadstool Millionaires: A Social History of Patent Medicines in America before Federal Regulation* (Princeton, 1961), 239. My account follows that in Baerman's excellent study.

[40] Braeman, "The Square Deal in Action," 46; Willard L. Hoing, "James Wilson as Secretary of Agriculture, 1897–1913" (unpublished Ph.D. dissertation, University of Wisconsin, 1964), 193–194; Gabriel Kolko, *The Triumph of Conservatism: A Reinterpretation of American History 1900–1916* (Glencoe, 1963), 99–101.

appointed a committee of departmental experts to investigate the thoroughness of the federal inspection process. President Roosevelt was also aroused by Sinclair's work, and in mid-March, after he received advance proofs of three articles which were critical of government inspection, he decided upon an independent investigation. Upon Secretary Wilson's recommendation, he appointed Commissioner of Labor Charles P. Neill and New York social worker James B. Reynolds as investigators.[41]

By early May, Roosevelt had both the Neill-Reynolds and the Department of Agriculture reports. Each commented upon the lack of cleanliness. The departmental investigators found stacks of brains next to a water closet and men walking over viscera on their way to and from the closet. Some of the abattoirs reminded them, they said, "of the typical country slaughter-house, being indescribably filthy." Neill and Reynolds noted poor ventilation, rotten and blood-soaked tables and meat racks, and a lack of concern for the laborer's health and comfort. The workers themselves showed no concern for the pureness of the meat, walking on it with dirty shoes and spitting and urinating on the floor.[42]

Both reports recommended tighter government inspection, with examination not only at the time of a slaughter but continuously during the packing process. They also suggested that the Secretary of Agriculture be delegated the authority to make rules and regulations for "soundness and fitness" and to forbid the interstate shipment of meats not government approved.[43] Senator Albert J. Beveridge of Indiana introduced a bill embodying these ideas into the Senate, where it was made an amendment to the agricultural appropriations bill on May 25, 1906. Specifically, the Beveridge amendment provided for mandatory post mortem inspection of all meats destined for interstate and foreign commerce, for the dating of canned meat, and for the destruction of products containing harmful substances. It gave the Secretary of Agriculture power to establish sanitary regulations and to provide for inspection. Violations would result in fines of not more than

[41] Braeman, "The Square Deal in Action," 47–49; Hoing, "James Wilson," 194–195.
[42] Both the Neill-Reynolds report and that of the Department of Agriculture are printed in U.S., House of Representatives, *Hearings before the Committee on Agriculture . . . on the so-called "Beveridge Amendment"* (Washington, 1906), 312.
[43] Braeman, "The Square Deal in Action," 32.

$10,000 and/or imprisonment for not more than two years. The Secretary's decision was final in all appeals. The packers themselves would pay the inspection costs through a fee system.[44]

The packers reacted with panic to the Beveridge amendment and to a Roosevelt threat to publish the Neill-Reynolds report unless it passed. Louis Swift of Swift & Company promised that the packers would "guarantee to remedy all the wrongs" if Roosevelt would withhold the report. Mary E. McDowell, director of the University of Chicago settlement, reported to the President that on "every hand [in packing town] there was indication of an almost humorous haste to clean up, repave, and even to plan for future changes." New restrooms, dressing-rooms, and clean uniforms for employees suddenly appeared.[45] Roosevelt commented that this "is good as far as it goes, but it does not go far enough, and it is absolutely necessary that we shall have legislation which will prevent the recurrence of these wrongs." [46] Momentarily stunned, the packers ordered their defenders in the Senate not to impede passage of the amendment.

But it was a strategic withdrawal, not a surrender. The packers planned to weaken the bill in the House Committee on Agriculture through amendments. They had two firm friends on the committee: Chairman James W. Wadsworth, a wealthy New York banker and stock-raiser, and as "Mr. Dooley" characterized him, "Farmer Bill Lorimer [ready] to protect th' cattle inthrests iv th' Gr-reat West. . . ." The stockyards were located in Lorimer's old congressional district, and he acted as the packers' chief House spokesman. Throughout his career he sent them copies of all bills affecting the industry; as the packers' representative on the Committee on Agriculture, he was responsible for increased government appropriations to expand existing inspection. Among his close friends were Edward Tilden of the National Packing Company and Louis Swift of Swift & Company.[47]

On May 26, after the Senate had passed the Beveridge amendment, Roosevelt called a White House conference on the legislation and invited Representatives Lorimer, Cannon, Wadsworth, and Martin B.

[44] *Ibid.*, 52–57; Hoing, "James Wilson," 199–200.

[45] Roosevelt to James W. Wadsworth, May 26, 1906, *Roosevelt Letters*, V, 282–283, 295; *Tribune*, May 26, 1906.

[46] Roosevelt to Wadsworth, May 26, 1906, *Roosevelt Letters*, V, 282–283.

[47] Braeman, "The Square Deal in Action," 61; *Dillingham Committee Hearings,* VIII, 7781–82; *Tribune*, Dec. 21, 1898.

Madden and Senators Beveridge and Cullom. At the conference, Lorimer, reflecting the packer point of view, claimed that expansion of the inspection process would involve large expense for the industry; all meat, intrastate as well as interstate, would have to be inspected since it was impossible to separate the two. He also protested against the "springing" of the measure at the end of a session and as a rider to an appropriations bill. Emphatically Lorimer stated that he would fight the bill, resorting to "every parliamentary dodge to eliminate the senate amendment from the agricultural bill, even if it became necessary to beat the appropriation bill itself." [48]

Lorimer's threats did not bother Roosevelt. At the conference's end he wrote to Wadsworth reaffirming his determination to adhere to the Beveridge amendment and to use the Neill-Reynolds report to compel House action. The situation reported by Neill and Reynolds, he said, was "hideous, and it must be remedied at once." Roosevelt noted that if he released the report, "great damage" would befall the packers and stock-growers; the effect on the export trade in meats "would undoubtedly be well-nigh ruinous." He would therefore hold it, "provided that without making it public I can . . . have the meat inspection amendment that has been put on in the Senate in substance enacted into law." [49]

On May 29, after meeting with Wadsworth, Cannon, and Senator Hopkins, Lorimer announced that the packers would challenge the constitutionality of the Beveridge amendment; by giving inspectors power to close a packinghouse, it violated due process and took private property without just compensation. The packers were not opposed to all legislation: "Have you thought that they [the packers] will benefit enormously from government inspection of all their products?" asked Lorimer. "They will be able to say to foreign markets, 'Every pound of our products has the stamp of approval of the United States.' " But, Lorimer added, while the packers wanted a "rigid" inspection, "they will not permit outsiders to run their business . . . they do not want a law saying unless everything they are doing is approved by an inspector, who may or may not be right, they must close their establishments." [50]

Lorimer's last statement is the key to his and the packers' objections

[48] *Tribune* and *Record-Herald,* May 27, 1906.
[49] Roosevelt to Wadsworth, May 26, 1906, *Roosevelt Letters,* V, 282–283.
[50] *Tribune* and *Record-Herald,* June 1, 1906.

to the Beveridge amendment. Fully cognizant of the value of the government stamp for the meat-export trade, they wanted "nominal" inspection; they did not want interference with their operations by men that were not, in Lorimer's terms, "practical." [51] The battle over the meat-inspection law that followed concerned the question of power: was packer compliance with the law to be voluntary as in the 1891 statute or would the government have the power to shut down the packinghouses in case of violations? The changes Lorimer and Wadsworth made in the Beveridge amendment revealed the packers' preference for a law without teeth.

The Lorimer-Wadsworth version of the Senate amendment restricted inspection to post mortem examination and did not apply to canned meat products; cans did not have to be dated; and the government rather than the packers had to bear the cost of inspection. Most important, the bill provided for court appeals from the decisions of the Secretary of Agriculture and did not provide for mandatory inspection, as did the Beveridge amendment, of meat entering interstate commerce. If the Lorimer and Wadsworth changes were approved by the Congress, "the new law would be no more effective than the old." [52]

Roosevelt reacted with anger when he saw the alterations. He wrote Wadsworth that he thought "that each change is for the worse and that in the aggregate they are ruinous, taking away every particle of good from the suggested Beveridge amendment." He added that since the amendment was so distorted, he did not believe he could reach an understanding with the House committee. Considering this situation, he felt justified in releasing the Neill-Reynolds report to Congress at "an early date." [53]

Faced by the President's rejection of his and Wadsworth's proposals, and by Roosevelt's promise to release the damaging Neill-Reynolds report, Lorimer took a night train back to Chicago for further instructions from the packers. On Monday he returned to Washington with their response. "The Beveridge amendment in its present form is unconstitutional," reiterated Lorimer. "Our amendment provides for

[51] See Lorimer to Governor Yates, Jan. 29, 1902, and Yates to Lorimer, [n.d., 1902], Yates Papers, Illinois State Archives, in which Lorimer warns Yates about violations of the state meat-packing law. The implication was that such violations could bring stricter federal regulation.

[52] *Tribune* and *Record-Herald,* June 1, 1906; Braeman, "The Square Deal in Action," 63.

[53] Roosevelt to Wadsworth, May 31, 1906, *Roosevelt Letters,* V, 291–292; *Tribune,* May 31, 1906.

sanitary regulation and inspection." The Beveridge amendment would drive the small packers out of business since they could not afford to pay the costs of inspection. The Neill-Reynolds report, he said, was a "gross exaggeration of the conditions." The packers would make no concessions.[54]

On the day of Lorimer's return, Roosevelt transmitted the first part of the Neill-Reynolds report to Congress with a message urging adoption of the Beveridge amendment. The second part he held, in case the Committee on Agriculture continued its recalcitrance. In his message he noted that conditions in the Chicago stockyards were "revolting," and demanded "immediate action." [55] Roosevelt's message and the Neill-Reynolds report were hurried to the waiting presses. The public reacted with horror, but the business community with anger. The National Manufacturers' Association and the Chicago Board of Trade sent Roosevelt "violent protests in offensive language," denying the truth of the conditions reported by the President's inspectors. The publisher of the Chicago *Evening Post* wrote Beveridge that Chicago businessmen and bankers were intensely bitter toward the President, and that many had said they "would vote for Bryan in preference to Roosevelt." [56] Fortified by this support, the packers instructed Lorimer to remain firm.

On June 6–8, the House Committee on Agriculture held hearings on the meat-inspection question. Thomas E. Wilson, representative of the Chicago packers, was the first witness. Wilson stated that the packers favored inspection and agreed, except for "minor details," with the Neill-Reynolds recommendations. The "minor details" of disagreement were the requirement for dating cans, the extensive authority given the Secretary of Agriculture to regulate conditions, and packer payment of inspection costs. The significance of Wilson's testimony, aside from his specific objections, lay in his comments on control: "What we are opposed to and what we appeal to you gentlemen for protection against is a bill that will put our business in the hands of theorists, chemists, sociologists, etc., and the management and control taken away from the men who have devoted their lives

[54] *Tribune,* June 5, 1906; *Record-Herald,* July 15, 1906.

[55] *Tribune* and *Record-Herald,* June 5, 1906. Roosevelt's message accompanying the Neill-Reynolds report is printed in *Hearings before the Committee on Agriculture,* 261.

[56] Roosevelt to Lyman Abbott, June 18, 1906, *Roosevelt Letters,* V, 307–308; John C. Shaffer to Albert J. Beveridge, June 12, 1906, Beveridge Papers.

to the upbuilding and perfecting of this great American industry." [57]
In essence, what the packers said, reiterating Lorimer's earlier point,
was that while they wanted government inspection and understood
its value for foreign trade, they wanted to maintain complete control
over their packinghouses.

On June 7 Dr. Charles P. Neill took the stand, and Lorimer and
Wadsworth proceeded to badger him about the charges of unsanitary
conditions in the Neill-Reynolds report. The vigorousness of Lorimer's
attack and the extent to which he put Neill on the defensive is revealed
in the following exchange:

> NEILL: In a word, we saw meat shoveled from filthy wooden floors,
> piled on tables rarely washed, pushed from room to room in rotten
> box carts, and in all of which processes it was in the way of gathering
> dirt, splinters, floor filth, and the expectoration of tuberculous and
> other diseased workers.
>
> WADSWORTH: How do you know it? You write there for the public a
> great word picture and you are involving property rights amounting
> to millions of dollars.
>
> LORIMER: Do you know, as a matter of fact, that the people you refer
> to had tuberculosis?
>
> NEILL: I didn't examine their sputum.
>
> LORIMER: Is it an opinion or a fact?
>
> NEILL: I can only say that I believe, as a matter of fact—
>
> LORIMER: The difference between belief and knowledge is a consider-
> able difference, is it not? . . . You know this report is going to the
> world . . . you know what the effect of it must be to this industry.
> . . . You say, "other diseased workers." This is a report from the
> Federal Government, and it comes to Congress from the President of
> the United States, and if there were other diseased persons in any
> packing houses that you visited the people of the country are entitled
> to the knowledge and to know what sort of diseases they were afflicted
> with.
>
> NEILL: I have made the statement, and I stand on the statement exactly
> as it was written.[58]

At this point Representative Sidney J. Bowie of Alabama objected
to Lorimer's treating Neill "as if he were a culprit or as if he were
being prosecuted." Lorimer responded that he had "not intended to be
discourteous," but that he wanted to discover the basis for the report's

[57] *Hearings before the Committee on Agriculture,* 5.
[58] *Ibid.,* 121–124.

generalizations. When James B. Reynolds took Neill's place on the stand, Lorimer modified his approach. Following Reynolds, a succession of witnesses defended the packers and challenged various provisions of the Beveridge amendment and the hearings ended on this note.[59]

On June 10 Lorimer and Wadsworth held a five-hour conference in the Willard Hotel with Thomas E. Wilson, Louis Swift, and other packers' representatives. They decided that public and political pressure would force them to yield on the Beveridge amendment sections barring interstate shipment of uninspected meats and providing for inspection of canned meats. They would not compromise, however, on the provisions concerning dating the cans, court review, packer payment of fees, nighttime inspection, and immediate civil service for inspectors.[60] On June 13, by a vote of 11 to 7, the committee approved its substitute for the Beveridge amendment. Lorimer commented that the "inspection provided by the substitute is as complete as the human family is capable of making." [61]

The President, however, made public a letter to Wadsworth in which he complained that "the more closely I investigate your proposed substitute the worse I find it. . . ." Roosevelt chiefly objected to the court review provision, which, he said, seemed "deliberately designed to prevent the remedying of the evils complained of. . . ." [62] Here again was the question of control. Congress did not have the power to deprive the packers of their constitutional right of court appeal, but the substitute amendment allowed such broad judicial review that the Secretary of Agriculture was limited to "purely ministerial" functions—the courts would make final decisions on substantive as well as procedural questions. Roosevelt also objected to the other changes in the Beveridge amendment regarding fees, dating, civil service, and nighttime inspection, but he thought the court review provision especially "incompatible with . . . a properly efficient law." [63]

[59] *Ibid.*, 125–128, 150–257. Representative Charles S. Wharton, who had replaced Lorimer as the representative of the stockyards district, objected to the allegations of uncleanliness, and Representative Edgar Crumpacker of Indiana held that Congress could not pass a law that required inspection before the meat became interstate commerce.
[60] Braeman, "The Square Deal in Action," 66–67.
[61] *Tribune* and *Record-Herald*, June 14, 1906.
[62] Roosevelt to Wadsworth, June 14, 1906, Roosevelt Papers.
[63] *Ibid.;* Roosevelt to Wadsworth, June 15, 1906, *Roosevelt Letters*, V, 298–299.

Wadsworth reacted furiously to Roosevelt's letter: "You are wrong, 'very, very wrong,' in your estimate of the Committee's Bill," he wrote. "It is as perfect a piece of legislation, to carry into effect your own views on this question, as was ever prepared by a Committee of Congress." He denied Roosevelt's implication that the committee didn't really want to correct the "evils" in the stockyards and insisted that every member of his committee was "honest and sincere . . . in his desire to secure the passage of a rigid meat-inspection bill." [64] Lorimer called a meeting of the Illinois congressional delegation and defended the committee bill as being fair to both the packers and the public.[65]

Not everyone involved, however, was as obdurate as Lorimer and Wadsworth. "Uncle Joe" Cannon worried about Republican losses in the November elections if the Committee on Agriculture blocked an effective inspection law. Cannon sent Henry C. Adams, a member of the committee who had voted for the substitute, to the White House, where he agreed to accept several changes, including the elimination of the court review provision and the restoration of the dating and civil service sections. Roosevelt agreed that the government would pay the inspection costs, although the Secretary of Agriculture was given the authority to assess fees if Congress made insufficient inspection appropriations. That weekend, while Lorimer and Wadsworth were out of town, Adams and Cannon convinced a majority of the Committee on Agriculture to accept the compromise.[66]

When Lorimer and Wadsworth returned to Washington they breathed defiance, although their weekend trip may have been a face-saving gesture. At a meeting on Monday, June 18, the committee accepted most of the compromises, erasing only the modified fee and dating provisions. It provided a permanent appropriation of $3,000,-000 a year for inspection costs. Roosevelt, rather than "get into an obstinate and wholly pointless fight about utterly trivial matters," agreed to the alterations.[67] On June 19, the House approved the committee's amendments and eventually the Senate accepted the House

[64] Wadsworth to Roosevelt, June 15, 1906, Roosevelt Papers.

[65] *Tribune*, June 15, 1906.

[66] Roosevelt to Wadsworth, June 15, 1906, to Albert J. Beveridge and to Joseph G. Cannon, June 16, 1906, *Roosevelt Letters*, V, 289–298, 300–301; Braeman, "The Square Deal in Action," 70; *Tribune*, June 17, 1906.

[67] *Tribune*, June 18, 19, 1906; Braeman, "The Square Deal in Action," 71–72; Roosevelt to Beveridge, June 16, 1906, *Roosevelt Letters*, V, 300–301; Beveridge to Roosevelt, June 16, 1906, Roosevelt Papers.

version. The President signed the meat-inspection amendment into law on June 30.[68]

Gabriel Kolko has argued in *The Triumph of Conservatism* that because the packers desired government inspection, historians have misinterpreted the fight over the Beveridge amendment and, in fact, "the true nature of progressivism." Kolko maintains that "it is business control over politics . . . rather than political regulation of the economy that is the significant phenomenon of the Progressive Era." [69] The meat-inspection struggle, says Kolko, was not over the principle of regulation but over the questions of who should pay for the inspection and whether or not canned meat should be dated.[70] The statements of Lorimer, the leading congressional defender of the meat industry, and of Thomas E. Wilson, the packers' representative, however, show that the packers themselves considered the main issue to be control over their manufacturing processes and point to the incorrectness of Kolko's interpretation. The packers wanted inspection, but they wanted the inspectors to be their servants, not their regulators. The importance of the new inspection law was not, as Kolko insists, "the size of the appropriation . . . for implementing it," but rather that it provided for the boldest extension of the so-called "national police power" to that time.[71]

Lorimer was forced to defend his stand on the meat-inspection legislation during his 1906 congressional primary. His opponent for the Sixth District Republican nomination was Luther P. Friestedt, a former alderman supported by the Deneen faction. Friedstedt attacked Lorimer as the "legislative agent of special interests" and the enemy of the people. He hammered on Lorimer's opposition to meat inspection as typical of his "baneful influence on nation, state, county, and city. . . ." [72]

Lorimer, realizing the appeal of the meat-inspection issue, met Friedstedt's attack by denying that he and Roosevelt had been in conflict; rather, they had worked "in sympathy" to frame a strong meat-inspection law. The difficulties, said Lorimer, arose from the "absurdities" in the Beveridge amendment. He had brought these to the attention of the President, who had then allowed Lorimer, Can-

---

68 *CR*, 59th Cong., 1st Sess., XL, 8720–29; *Tribune*, June 20, 31, 1906.
69 Kolko, *The Triumph of Conservatism*, 3, 98.
70 *Ibid.*, 106.
71 *Ibid.*, 106–107; Braeman, "The Square Deal in Action," 75–76.
72 *Tribune*, July 1, 15, 17, 19, 1906.

non, and Wadsworth to draft a new measure. They had written a "sensible bill," but Roosevelt had objected to the court review feature. Lorimer insisted on his version and protested that he "would never consent to a bill becoming a law which would place in the hands of the secretary of agriculture the power to close up a great industry without leaving . . . the right to appeal to the courts for protection." As a result, claimed Lorimer, a compromise took final jurisdiction away from the Secretary of Agriculture, and the "Lorimer-Wadsworth-Cannon" meat-inspection bill became law.[73]

Lorimer related his version of the meat-inspection fight night after night in his tent, claiming credit for a measure that provided "rigid inspection." He distributed 45,000 copies of the inspection law with a signed cover letter in which he claimed credit for it. Twenty prominent businessmen in his district issued a circular praising Lorimer's congressional record and saying that his defeat would be a "calamity, because he has labored faithfully and effectively for Chicago." Listed among his accomplishments was the meat-inspection law, called by President Roosevelt "the most rigid and best . . . in the world." [74] Aided by this distortion of the record, on primary day Lorimer overwhelmed Friedstedt by nearly 2,000 votes.[75]

The meat-inspection fight had put Lorimer, although he tried to gloss over the fact, in opposition to President Roosevelt and to a needed reform. In a different sense, the confrontation was between local industries who wanted to maintain control over their property and the centralizing tendencies of an administration attempting to regulate in the public interest. A commitment to local interests, however, did not necessarily involve opposition to the Roosevelt administration or to programs with regional and national implications. In the case of Lorimer's efforts for the Lakes-to-the-Gulf waterway, he was again aligned with local and regional concerns. In this instance, Lorimer stood with the President and his policies; he was to achieve considerable political benefit from his identification with the waterway issue.

Waterway improvements were an important element in the Presi-

---

[73] *Ibid.*, July 18, 1906.
[74] *Ibid.*, July 25, 1906; *Inter-Ocean,* July 21, 1906; *Chronicle,* July 20, 1906; *Post,* Aug. 2, 1906.
[75] *Inter-Ocean,* Aug. 5, 1906.

dent's program to insure planned and scientific use of the nation's resources. In the process of resource development, large corporations often supported the administration's approach and small users opposed it. Urban merchants and manufacturers led the drive for waterway development that began in the late 1890's, prompted by a rise in railroad rates that forced shippers to seek cheaper means of transportation. Local newspapers, chambers of commerce, and civic organizations, who saw low-cost transportation as the means to economic growth, backed them in their endeavors. As Samuel P. Hays notes, "The campaign for waterway improvement . . . took on the character of local patriotism which congressmen were eager to follow by demanding a large share of the federal rivers and harbors appropriation." [76]

The movement for a deep waterway from Chicago to the Gulf by way of the Illinois and Mississippi rivers was a vital part of the program. Such a channel had been suggested before Illinois entered the Union, but the first practical step toward its realization came with the opening of the Chicago Sanitary Canal in 1900. Through the canal, water from Lake Michigan flowed to the Des Plaines River and eventually reached the Mississippi and the Gulf. While the canal's principal purpose was to facilitate the city's sewage problems, many Chicagoans hoped it would also serve as a ship channel, furnishing the first link in a waterway system that would make Chicago queen of the Mississippi Valley. [77]

It was Lorimer who, in his own words, "stopped dreaming and began to work." Lorimer had been interested in waterway matters since his entry into Congress, and during his first terms worked to improve the Chicago River. The Chicago Sanitary Canal flowed through both the Second and the Sixth congressional districts and many Chicago industries were interested in cheap water transportation. Lorimer was much influenced by the ideas of Lyman E. Cooley, the Sanitary District's first chief engineer and an early proponent of the Lakes-to-the-Gulf deep waterway. [78]

[76] Hays, *Conservation*, 92.

[77] Pierce, *Chicago*, III, 312–313; Ellis, "A History of the Chicago Delegation," 116–118; Goodspeed and Healy, *History of Cook County*, II, 96–99.

[78] As early as 1888 Cooley had agitated for a fourteen-foot channel from the Lakes to the Gulf, but the Sanitary Board trustees had rejected his ideas. See Lyman E. Cooley, *The Lakes and Gulf Waterway: A Brief* (Chicago, 1888); speeches by Cooley in Lakes-to-the-Gulf Deep Waterway Association, *Minutes of the Fifth Annual Convention* (St. Louis, 1910), 30–34, 82; Lewis and Smith, *Chicago*, 198.

In 1900 Lorimer secured provision in the rivers and harbors bill for a special board of army engineers to estimate the cost of deepening the Illinois River to fourteen feet and connecting the river with the drainage canal at Lockport. He argued before the House that the waterway would benefit the entire Mississippi Valley by lowering freight rates and attracting industry.[79] While the engineers advised in 1901 that existing lake commerce did not justify the expenditure necessary to create a fourteen-foot channel, in 1902 Congress authorized new surveys for a fourteen-foot depth from Lockport to St. Louis.[80]

For several years politics diverted Lorimer's attention from waterway matters, but in 1905, having become a member of the Committee on Rivers and Harbors, he renewed his campaign. In October he launched a twenty-six-foot gasoline-powered boat named the *Remirol* (Lorimer spelled backwards) on a trip down the proposed waterway route. Two of his sons served as crew, and Illinois Republican Congressmen Martin B. Madden, Joseph Graff, Howard Snapp, and Democrat Henry T. Rainey came as guests. The expedition's purpose was to publicize the project and to establish chapters of a Lakes-to-the-Gulf Deep Waterway Association.[81]

Traveling by day, the boat stopped at the larger towns on the route, where Lorimer made contact with commercial groups and businessmen. With their cooperation, he began forty-three association chapters. At St. Louis, for instance, the powerful Business Men's League backed the project. Manufacturers throughout the valley believed that the waterway, by lowering transportation costs, would open markets to the South and Southwest, and, through the Panama Canal, provide access to the west coast of South America. A number of valley congressmen visited the *Remirol* and pledged to help in the waterway work.[82]

In March, 1906, at a Washington dinner, Lorimer and his asso-

---

[79] *CR*, 56th Cong., 1st Sess., XXXIII, 3008, 4063; U.S., House of Representatives, *House Doc. 263*, 59th Cong., 1st Sess. (Washington, 1905–06); Ellis, "A History of the Chicago Delegation," 118; *Tribune*, Aug. 22, Dec. 12, 1900.

[80] Ellis, "A History of the Chicago Delegation," 118–119.

[81] See Lorimer's speeches to the first and third conventions of the Deep Waterway Association, printed in the minutes of the convention (St. Louis, 1906, 1908).

[82] Deep Waterway Association, *Minutes of the Third Annual Convention* (St. Louis, 1908); Robert A. Waller, "Congressman Henry T. Rainey of Illinois: His Rise to the Speakership, 1903–1934" (unpublished Ph.D. dissertation, University of Illinois, 1963), 40–42; *Tribune*, Dec. 4, 1905.

ciates in the canal venture formally launched the Lakes-to-the-Gulf Deep Waterway Association. The group elected Lorimer chairman of the association and Congressman Henry T. Rainey secretary. The association, announced Lorimer, planned to "organize every commercial city in the country" and to convince the people that river and harbor appropriations were "meritorious and righteous." [83]

The association held its first convention in November in St. Louis under the auspices of the Business Men's League of that city. The convention's main theme was the need for waterways in order to regulate railroad rates. Lorimer told the delegates of his campaign to create interest in the waterway and held that when completed it would so lower transportation costs that the products of the Mississippi Valley would compete in markets throughout the world. To the economic argument Lorimer added the patriotic one that in the event of a war with Great Britain, the waterway would enable the United States to put its navy on the Great Lakes quickly.[84]

Speeches by Deneen, Congressmen Rainey, Champ Clark of Missouri, and Joseph E. Ransdell of Louisiana, president of the National Rivers and Harbors Congress, hammered on the rate regulation theme. The convention passed resolutions urging Congress to provide for a fourteen-foot channel from the drainage canal to the Mississippi and for the dredging of the river from St. Louis south. The delegates elected William K. Kavanaugh of St. Louis as association president and David R. Forgan, Chicago banker, as first vice-president, reflecting the importance of the waterway to these two cities. A majority of the other officials came from states in the lower Mississippi Valley.[85]

At the end of 1905, the army engineers had estimated that the cost of a fourteen-foot waterway covering 327 miles and having nine locks and five dams would be approximately $31,000,000.[86] Lorimer introduced the necessary appropriations bill in the House, and chairman Theodore E. Burton of the Committee on Rivers and Harbors submitted it to the Army Corps of Engineers' Board of Review. Burton had recommended the creation of the Board of Review in 1902 as a means to block unwise proposals; now it advised that the expense of

[83] *Record-Herald,* Mar. 22, May 18, 1906.
[84] Deep Waterway Association, *Minutes of the First Annual Convention* (St. Louis, 1906).
[85] *Ibid.*
[86] *House Doc. 263; Tribune,* Dec. 19, 1905.

a fourteen-foot channel was unjustified by the anticipated traffic and recommended an eight-foot depth.[87] Hoping to bypass the report, Lorimer and his allies pushed for the inclusion of an initial appropriation of $3,000,000 for the fourteen-foot channel in the rivers and harbors bill with future expenditures to $28,000,000.[88] The appropriation, however, met with strong opposition.

Chairman Theodore Burton was the waterway's chief critic. He doubted its economic value and "feared that logrolling would result in congressional approval of unsound projects." Burton held that the Chicago–St. Louis tonnage did not justify extending the drainage canal at federal expense. He also maintained that the water-power revenues produced by the canal would be a "gift" to someone, since they could not be collected by the federal government.[89]

Lorimer challenged Burton's figures and arguments and claimed that the Chicago–St. Louis tonnage was actually fifty million yearly rather than the one million cited by Burton. The water-power question, Lorimer held, was incidental to the project's main purpose, which was to cheapen transportation costs. But Burton's arguments convinced the House of the unsoundness of the project, and it rejected the waterway amendment 145 to 43.[90]

Spokesmen from the Mississippi Valley states indignantly attacked Burton and the Corps of Engineers, accusing them of prejudice against their section and charging that they were being deprived of their fair share of rivers and harbors appropriations.[91] Early in November, 1907, the Deep Waterway Association swung its support behind the idea of a federal waterways commission as the means to bypass congressional opposition. The chief advocate of the commission was W. J. McGee, an influential conservationist and the proponent of multiple-purpose development of rivers that would utilize their hydroelectric and irrigation as well as navigation potential. In March, McGee presented Roosevelt with petitions from the associa-

[87] St. Louis *Globe*, Jan. 4, 1907; Ellis, "A History of the Chicago Delegation," 119; Hays, *Conservation*, 98.

[88] *CR*, 59th Cong., 2nd Sess., XLI, 2376–77, 2383.

[89] Hays, *Conservation*, 93–94; *CR*, 59th Cong., 2nd Sess., XLI, 2408–10; *Inter-Ocean*, Feb. 7, 1907; Burton speech in Deep Waterway Association, *Minutes of the Second Annual Convention* (St. Louis, 1907), 51–52; Forest Crissey, *Theodore E. Burton, American Statesman* (Cleveland, 1956), 180–182.

[90] *CR*, 59th Cong., 2nd Sess., XL, 2410, 2628–31; *Tribune*, Feb. 1, 8, 1907.

[91] Hays, *Conservation*, 98–99.

tion, the St. Louis Business Men's League, and other commercial groups, and two days later the President announced the appointment of the Inland Waterways Commission.[92]

In his letter of appointment Roosevelt espoused the multiple-purpose use of waterways and called for their inclusion "in a comprehensive plan designed for the benefit of the entire country." He specifically referred to the inadequacy of Mississippi Valley rail facilities and the need for "the development of a complementary system of transportation by water." [93] The Deep Waterway Association believed the creation of the Inland Waterways Commission to be a victory for their cause, and on April 4, 1907, the association's Board of Governors passed a resolution formally thanking the President.[94]

Federal action was soon matched by state. In April the Illinois Internal Improvements Commission presented a favorable report on the waterway and Deneen delivered a special message to the General Assembly asking for legislation to implement the report. Illinois Senator Albert C. Clark of Chicago introduced a bill providing for a twenty-foot channel from the end of the drainage canal at Lockport to the Des Plaines River at Joliet.[95] The General Assembly's Joint Waterway Committee held hearings on the bill, and in May Lorimer testified that if Illinois provided for the Lockport-Joliet section, Congress would vote appropriations for the remainder of the waterway. "Nothing," he said, "will give this great work more impetus than a willingness of Chicago to pay for the beginning of it." [96]

Lorimer's and Deneen's cooperation, however, was not enough to pass the waterway measure. Members of the General Assembly were concerned about the disposal of the water power generated on the new section, the same question that had bothered Congressman Bur-

[92] *Ibid.,* 102, 105; Theodore Roosevelt to Theodore E. Burton, Mar. 14, 1907, *Roosevelt Letters,* V, 619–621; Gifford Pinchot, *Breaking New Ground* (New York, 1947), 329. The commission had nine members: Gifford Pinchot of the Forest Service, Frederick H. Newell of the Reclamation Service, Brigadier General Alexander Mackenzie, chief of the Army Corps of Engineers, Herbert Knox Smith, commissioner of corporations, Representative Theodore E. Burton, Representative John H. Bankhead of Alabama, and Senators Francis G. Newlands from Nevada and William Warner from Kansas. W. J. McGee was secretary.

[93] Roosevelt to Burton, Mar. 14, 1907, *Roosevelt Letters,* V, 619–621; Pinchot, *Breaking New Ground,* 328–329.

[94] *Tribune,* Apr. 5, 1907.

[95] Illinois Internal Improvement Commission, *Report* (Springfield, 1907); *Senate Journal, Forty-fifth General Assembly* (Springfield, 1908), 686–689, 830, 1020, 1033, 1067–68; *Tribune,* May 11, 1907.

[96] *Tribune,* May 13, 14, 1907.

ton. Congressman Rainey circulated a letter charging that the bill would give private interests control of the water power and would block the building of a true deep waterway with federal cooperation.[97] Legislators also objected to Deneen's pressure on the issue. Lieutenant Governor Lawrence Y. Sherman wrote that a "great diversity of opinion existed among the down-country members" on the waterway, and that "there was a little feeling against the Governor." "Many thought that his message urging immediate action . . . was too precipitate." The General Assembly adjourned without passing the bill.[98]

In spite of this setback, the waterway campaign continued. Lorimer and other members of the association spoke throughout the Mississippi Valley, and the Inland Waterways Commission explored the waterway route.[99] Most significant was President Roosevelt's formal endorsement of the project. In October he boarded a steamer at Keokuk, Iowa, and in a trip reminiscent of the earlier journey of the *Remirol,* sailed down the Mississippi with the Inland Waterways Commission and a host of waterway boosters including Lorimer. At Memphis, speaking at the second Lakes-to-the-Gulf Deep Waterway Association convention, Roosevelt made a strong plea for the development of the Mississippi River. He commented that "facility of cheap transportation is an essential in our modern civilization," and that waterways could be used to regulate railroad rates.[100] The governors of Illinois, Iowa, Kansas, and Wisconsin, as well as Representative Champ Clark of Missouri and Senator Francis G. Newlands of Nevada, made similar speeches, and the convention passed resolutions calling for the construction of the waterway as a "public necessity, and . . . a national and imperative duty." [101]

Immediately after the convention, Deneen called a special session of the Illinois General Assembly to consider, among other matters, waterway legislation. A bill calling for a constitutional amendment allowing the state to issue $20,000,000 of bonds to develop the Lockport-Utica stretch on the Illinois River embodied his program. The state would retire the bonds from revenues secured from river-

[97] Waller, "Henry T. Rainey," 67–70.

[98] Sherman to Shelby M. Cullom, May 28, 1907, Sherman Papers; *Tribune,* May 16, 17, 1907.

[99] Lorimer speech in Deep Waterway Association, *Minutes of the Third Annual Convention;* Hays, *Conservation,* 106–107.

[100] Deep Waterway Association, *Minutes of the Second Annual Convention,* 36.

[101] *Ibid.,* 51–162; *Tribune,* Oct. 5, 6, 1907.

generated hydroelectric power. The General Assembly approved the bill and scheduled the vote on the amendment for November, 1908.[102]

Lorimer favored the amendment. He spoke for it before the Illinois Senate and set up a statewide organization to develop support. In the fall of 1907 Lorimer opened waterway headquarters at Greenville, Illinois, with Cicero J. Lindley, an influential member of the General Assembly, as manager. During the winter and spring of 1908, Lorimer and Lindley toured the state by auto, forming chapters of the Deep Waterway Association. "We organized every precinct in Illinois outside of the city of Chicago," Lorimer later related. "Whenever a county or a town was made up overwhelmingly of Republicans we installed a Democrat for president of the association; so that every man with whom we talked and worked was impressed with the nonpartisan character of this movement." [103] During his tour, Lorimer gave illustrated lectures with maps and slides and demonstrated how the waterway would bring world trade to Chicago and Illinois.

When the third annual Deep Waterway Association convention met in Chicago in October, the delegates were optimistic about the future of the waterway. The association had grown in size and influence, the Illinois waterway amendment appeared likely to pass, and presidential candidates William Jennings Bryan and William Howard Taft spoke at the convention and endorsed the project. Association president William K. Kavanaugh noted Lorimer's key role in founding the organization and applauded him as "one of the very staunchest and best friends that the movement for water improvement has in this country." In his own address, Lorimer expressed astonishment at the movement's growth, and predicted that Congress would appropriate "as many millions as are required to build the Waterway. . . ." [104]

---

[102] *Senate Journal, Forty-fifth General Assembly,* 1374, 1381; *House Journal, Forty-fifth General Assembly,* 1420, 1423. There was some concern in the state that private power interests would benefit from the waterway. The Economy Power and Light Company planned to construct a dam across the Des Plaines River but the General Assembly blocked the dam by passing resolutions declaring the river navigable. See Deneen's message of Nov. 6, 1907, in *Senate Journal, Forty-fifth General Assembly,* 1443–45, the Senate resolutions in *ibid.,* 1446, 1540–41, and *House Journal, Forty-fifth General Assembly,* 1507–09.

[103] Lorimer speech in *CR,* 61st Cong., 3d Sess., XLVI, 3119; *Tribune,* Oct. 27, 1907, Jan. 16, 19, 1908; Cicero J. Lindley to John G. Oglesby, June 4, 15, 1908, John G. Oglesby Papers, Illinois State Historical Library, Springfield.

[104] Deep Waterway Association, *Minutes of the Third Annual Convention* (St. Louis, 1908).

On election day, November 3, 1908, Illinois voters approved the waterway amendment 692,522 to 107,857, and it appeared that Lorimer's dream was close to reality.[105] But while up to 1908 the waterway issue was free of politics, it lost this immunity after approval of the bond issue. Politicians eagerly competed for control of the $20,000,000 voted for the waterway and for the prestige that would accompany its construction. Lorimer and Deneen offered rival waterway plans that immersed the program in conflict and delayed its beginnings.[106] Further efforts by Lorimer to secure federal action on the project came in 1909, but by this time his House career had ended and his Senate tenure had begun. The challenge to his Senate seat forced Lorimer to neglect the waterway question and at the time of his ouster the necessary legislation had not yet been enacted. It was many years before the project was completed and then in a different form than Lorimer had advocated.[107]

Lorimer's period of service in the House of Representatives was marked by his devotion to the needs of Chicago. His effectiveness in securing benefits for the city caused newspapers that opposed his activities as a local boss to support him for re-election to Congress. An urban congressman with a heterogeneous constituency, he carefully tried to respond to the wants of his district's various interest groups and he astutely utilized his congressional record in his re-election campaigns. In the three cases involving Lorimer's congressional activities examined in this chapter—U.S. intervention in Cuba, meat inspection, and the deep waterway—Lorimer responded to public opinion in the first instance, to the wishes of the packers in the second, and to a combination of the interests of the city's industrial and commercial firms in the third. On those occasions when his response to local pressures caused him to conflict with administration policies and larger national priorities, however, he proved less successful as a congressman than when he acted on purely Chicago matters.

[105] Rose, comp., *Illinois Blue Book 1909*, 392–393.
[106] *News*, Nov. 7, 16, 1908; *Post*, Nov. 7, 1908; *Record-Herald*, Nov. 8, 1908.
[107] A nine-foot barge-navigation channel was completed in 1933. The $20,000,000 bond issue was supplemented by a federal appropriation of $7,500,000 in 1930. See "Lake Michigan–Gulf Water Route Work Begun," *Central Manufacturing District Magazine* (Oct., 1929), XIII, 83; "Completion of Illinois Waterway in 1933 Made Possible Barge Traffic from New Orleans to Port of Chicago," *Blue Book of the State of Illinois 1933–34* (Springfield, 1934), 571–574.

CHAPTER **8**

★ ★ ★ ★ ★ ★ ★ ★ ★ ★ ★

A Boss out of Power, 1904-08

WHAT DOES A BOSS DO when he has lost control of the political structure? What means does he use to regain power? Where does he find allies? These questions faced Lorimer during the years after his defeat in 1904. His prime aim was to restore the strength of his organization, but this would be no easy task. Against him he had Governor Deneen, Roy O. West, chairman of the state central committee, James Reddick, new chairman of the county central committee, and powerful factional chieftains like Fred Busse and James Pease. In addition, a new wave of reformism was sweeping American cities such as Chicago. Progressives pushed measures such as the direct primary, the initiative, referendum, and recall, the short ballot, civil service, charter reform, and legislative reference bureaus both to break the hold of machine politicians over government and to streamline its workings.[1]

Reformers also hoped to change the class and ethnic origins of government officials. Thus, while their rhetoric was often infused with a democratic spirit, the reforms they advocated such as the direct primary were tactical weapons, not ends in themselves. Some progressives, such as Jane Addams and Raymond Robins, believed in democracy, but others, such as Walter L. Fisher and Victor Lawson, were motivated more by a desire for efficient and expert administration than a wish to give power to the people.[2] Overtones of elitism and nativism within the progressive program, as well as the threat

[1] George E. Mowry, *The Era of Theodore Roosevelt, 1900–1912* (New York, 1958), 59–68; Blake McKelvey, *The Urbanization of America 1860–1915* (New Brunswick, 1963), 86–114.
[2] Miller, "Politics of Municipal Reform in Chicago," 38–41; Hays, "The Politics of Reform," 163–164.

172

that some of Deneen's proposals posed to the cultural values of immigrant groups, could erode his strength in Chicago and furnish the
means by which Lorimer could return to power.

Most important in this regard was the parallelism between the
rise of the progressive movement and the renewed interest by American Protestantism in temperance reform. James H. Timberlake has
noted that each time the liquor question became "an object of concern to the public at large" it "coincided with a nation-wide reform
movement." He finds the roots of this coincidence in the "inherently
progressive nature" of evangelical Protestantism and its belief that
the world's corruption could be overcome by law as well as by conversion.[3] Many Protestants believed drinking to be a moral, social,
economic, and political threat to American ideals. Temperance reform and prohibition, with their "elements of moralism, social de-
sirability, meliorism, and scientifically demonstrated need, provided
a perfect vehicle for reform." [4] Law could be used to change the personal habits of Americans and benefit both the nation and the individual.

Some temperance advocates and prohibitionists saw the danger to
American ideals stemming directly from urban areas where saloons,
non-Protestant immigrants, and the laboring classes were concentrated. "In our large cities," observed the Presbyterian Church's Committee on Temperance, "the controlling vote is that of the dangerous
classes, who are readily dominated by the saloon. City government
is 'boss government,' and the boss rules by the grace of the grog
shop." [5] But urban evangelical Protestants were as interested in
temperance reform and prohibition as their rural counterparts. Social
Gospel churches and settlement-house workers often took an anti-
liquor stance, while urban reformers saw the anarchy and disorder
they were opposing as stemming from the imbibing classes.[6]

Because the liquor question was a divisive cultural issue, often
crossing class and party lines, many politicians sought to avoid it.
But avoidance became increasingly difficult in the period after 1904.
During these years the Anti-Saloon League, which had formed an

[3] Timberlake, *Prohibition and the Progressive Movement*, 7, 13.
[4] *Ibid.*, 9–10; John C. Burnham, "New Perspectives on the Prohibition 'Experiment' of the 1920's," *Journal of Social History* (Fall, 1968), II, 53.
[5] Quoted in Timberlake, *Prohibition and the Progressive Movement*, 16.
[6] *Ibid.*, 29–30; Allen F. Davis, *Spearheads for Reform: The Social Settlements
and the Progressive Movement 1890–1914* (New York, 1967), 82–83.

Illinois chapter in 1898, won the adherence of a number of Protestant churches and campaigned for the passage of a local-option law and for the enforcement of the Illinois Sunday closing statute.[7] The movement was strongest among old-stock Americans and centered in rural and suburban areas, although there were also a number of urban adherents. The latter consisted primarily of native-American evangelical Protestants and Swedish Lutherans. While the majority of temperance advocates were Republicans, the Bryan wing of the Democratic party was also dry. The issue thus appealed to ethnic, religious, and cultural rather than political groups.[8]

While Lorimer did not participate directly in the battle over liquor control, the issue colored most Illinois and Chicago political battles after 1906. Lorimer's constituents, as well as a majority of the Chicago population, were mainly Roman Catholic, Jewish, or German Lutheran. Their ritualistic rather than pietistic religious beliefs caused them to oppose attempts to legislate their private morality and to favor personal liberty. As one group of German Lutheran ministers put it, their church could not participate in the temperance movement "because it does not discriminate between secular and ecclesiastical administration, but mixes them together. It is the duty of the secular government to prevent vice with lawful means, but it is the duty of the church to save men by faith in Christ from committing sin. . . . The prohibition movement does not discriminate between proper use and abuse of the gifts of God." [9]

Ritualistic ethnic groups viewed the attack upon their drinking habits as part of a larger attempt by native Americans to strip them of their life-styles. The editor of the *Illinois Staats-Zeitung* complained that the prohibitionists were "continually attempting to prove that as native Americans they are superior to the immigrant." The popular German paper *Die Abendpost* noted that prohibition menaced not only saloon-keepers but also "the activities of all immigrants." And the Bohemian paper *Denni Hlasatel* warned that the "pussyfooting temperance mongers" wanted to "dictate . . . not

[7] J. C. Jackson, "The Work of the Anti-Saloon League," *Annals of the American Academy of Political and Social Science* (1908), XXXII, 485; Timberlake, *Prohibition and the Progressive Movement*, 127–148.

[8] Timberlake suggests that prohibition was a "middle-class" reform but he fails to differentiate between the different religious orientations of immigrant groups. See *ibid.*, 152–153.

[9] *Illinois Staats-Zeitung,* June 21, 1888.

only what to drink but also what to do at all times." [10] Ritualistic ethnic groups joined to fight attempts to regulate their cultural norms and sided politically with whomever sympathized with their goal of personal liberty. To the extent that Deneen became identified with the temperance cause, he was viewed as a threat to ritualistic immigrant cultural norms. The personal-liberty issue eroded the Governor's Chicago support and Lorimer was the beneficiary.

This pattern, however, was not directly apparent. Deneen won the 1904 gubernatorial contest with 59.3 percent of the vote to 27.8 percent for Democrat Lawrence B. Stringer. He secured at least a plurality of the votes in all thirty-five Chicago wards and a majority in twenty-seven. His victory crossed ethnic, religious, and class lines.[11] Although Deneen campaigned mainly on the need to improve state government with emphasis upon primary reform and civil service, he was not associated with cultural issues. In fact, he was not strongly identified as a reformer, since for eight years he had been an important cog in the Lorimer organization. He supported many progressive reforms because of the urging of his press supporters, Victor Lawson, Robert W. Patterson, and Frank B. Noyes.[12]

By the second part of his administration, however, Deneen's reform program, his alliance with the so-called "trust press," and his secretive political methods created enemies. These came from both Chicago and downstate, where there was a strong distrust of programs originating in the metropolis. In areas like Chicago, the liquor issue assumed overriding importance. In 1904, however, the

[10] *Denni Hlasatel,* Feb. 28, 1910, quoting the editor of the *Illinois Staats-Zeitung; Die Abendpost,* Dec. 9, 1907; *Denni Hlasatel,* Dec. 21, 1914; Joseph R. Gusfield, *Symbolic Crusade: Status Politics and the American Temperance Movement* (Urbana, 1963), 6–7.

[11] *Daily News Almanac for 1905,* 354. Deneen's vote correlated at +.659 with percent native American, at +.640 with percent Swedish-Norwegian, and at +.691 with percent English—all high correlations with normally Republican groups. Correlations with normally Democratic ethnic groups, however, were higher (less negative) than usual. Deneen's vote also correlated at +.614 with 1910 school attendance figures. For ethnic groups and figures on illiteracy and school attendance see U.S., *Thirteenth Census, 1910,* "Population," II, 512–514. Roosevelt secured 57.3 percent of the Chicago vote and also did well among ethnic groups that normally voted Democratic on the local level. This illustrated the continued success of the national Republican party in maintaining itself as an integrative mechanism and in shedding its previous image as a party dominated by crusaders with evangelical cultural goals.

[12] Hutchinson, *Lowden,* I, 97, 184, 185; Schmidt, "Chicago *Daily News* and Illinois Politics, 1876–1923."

liquor question was still relatively unimportant, Deneen had state-wide support, and his hold on the Republican party appeared secure.

In contrast to Deneen, Lorimer was relegated to a political base of his West Side wards. Here his organization remained powerful in the immigrant and laboring-class areas. Hopefully these wards would furnish a point from which he could regain power. Lorimer's continued popularity among ritualistic ethnic groups was reflected in his endorsement for Congress by the Chicago *Citizen,* the official paper of the United Irish Societies. The *Citizen,* which supported the Democratic national ticket, noted that Lorimer was "pre-eminently, a man of the people, a self-made man who understands the needs and capabilities of this gigantic metropolis." [13] While Lorimer won re-election, he ran between 10 and 15 percentage points behind Deneen and Roosevelt in his district's Chicago wards and even further behind in the suburbs. These dissident voters were in all likelihood Republicans alienated from Lorimer for cultural as well as political reasons. They cast their votes in protest for the Prohibitionist candidate, who received an astonishing 12 percent of the Chicago vote and 19.5 percent of the suburban vote.[14]

This diminished vote, however, had little impact on Lorimer's strength within his bailiwick. The state senators and assemblymen from the area, all "Lorimer" men, were among the most influential members of the Illinois General Assembly.[15] From positions such as the House Committee on Appropriations, where Lorimerite David Shanahan was chairman, they sniped at and impeded Deneen's legislative program. Lorimer also continued to draw strength from his relations with the "federal machine," composed of Senators Shelby M. Cullom and Albert J. Hopkins, Speaker of the House "Uncle Joe" Cannon, and their federal appointees. These men, who had supported Lowden for governor, opposed the Deneen-Yates entente that

[13] Chicago *Citizen,* Aug. 13, Oct. 15, 22, 29, 1904. The *Citizen* was edited by Long John Finerty, an Irish nationalist and Independent Democrat who served in Congress from 1883 to 1885. In the 1880's he and several other Irish nationalist leaders joined with the Republicans, but by 1900 Finerty again supported the Democratic party. See Thomas N. Brown, *Irish-American Nationalism 1870–1890* (Philadelphia, 1966), 135–143.

[14] Manuscript Election Returns, Sixth Congressional District, 1904, Board of Election Commissioners, Chicago.

[15] Denison Bingham Hull, *The Legislative Life of Morton Denison Hull* (Chicago, 1948), 42–43; Legislative Voters' League of Illinois, *Biennial Report* (Chicago, 1907).

emerged from the convention.[16] For the time being, their alliance was with Lorimer.

Lorimer's activities through 1905 and 1906 involved strengthening his organization and extending his ties with the federal machine. Initially he sought to find jobs for his men, who had been "thrown into the streets" by Yates and Deneen, and his federal machine allies helped him place a number in governmental posts.[17] Lorimer also retained a major voice in senatorial recommendations for federal appointments. In two instances his advice was heeded over that of Deneen's and other Republican congressmen.[18] In the first case, Kenshaw Mountain Landis, a close friend of Lowden's, rather than James Harlan, was picked for a federal district judgeship. James Harlan was the brother of John Maynard Harlan, the 1905 Republican mayoralty candidate. Involved in Harlan's rejection was his brother's refusal to allow any Lorimer men on the 1905 city ticket.[19]

The second case involved a new postmaster for Chicago. The incumbent, Frederick E. Coyne, had supported Deneen in 1904 and continued to work against Lorimer after the election. Lorimer lieutenant Fred M. Blount complained to Senator Cullom that in "regard to Illinois politics, it seems to be the policy of the 'ins' to exterminate the 'outs.' " He referred to Coyne as one who did "politics with an AXE." [20] Deneen, however, wanted Coyne retained, as did several Republican congressmen. But Lorimer demanded his removal and the senators agreed. The problem was finding a replacement.[21]

Former state treasurer and state senator Fred Busse proved suitable. The short, rotund Busse ("Fat Freddie") was not identified with

[16] Hutchinson, *Lowden*, I, 134–139; *Tribune*, Jan. 10, 12, 14, 1906.

[17] William B. Ridgely to Charles G. Dawes, July 7, 1904, Dawes Papers; William Lorimer to Frank O. Lowden, Nov. 24, 1906, Lowden Papers; *Record-Herald*, June 29, July 29, 30, 1906.

[18] The *Tribune* reported that Chicago congressmen were "in revolt" over the senators' policy to consult only Lorimer on patronage appointments. See *Tribune*, Jan. 10, 12, 14, 1906.

[19] Sol H. Bethea wrote Senator Cullom that "the problem was to get the President so that he would be satisfied with Landis, or to get Lorimer so he would be satisfied with James Harlan." Jan. 25, 1905, Cullom Papers; Bethea to Cullom, Feb. 15, 1905, *ibid.*; Victor Lawson to Theodore Roosevelt, Mar. 11, 1905, Lawson Papers; *Tribune*, Jan. 29, Feb. 14, 15, 1905.

[20] Fred M. Blount to Cullom, Dec. 8, 1904, Cullom Papers; *Tribune*, Sept. 17, Nov. 22, 1905.

[21] Sol H. Bethea to Cullom, Dec. 2, 7, 1905, Cullom Papers; *Tribune*, Dec. 11, 1905.

either faction. He had his own organization in Chicago's North Side German area. An astute politician, he reflected the split character of his own near North Side ward. On the east it embraced the luxurious Gold Coast; on the west it was filled with slums, saloons, brothels, and gambling houses. Busse had learned to live with both sections. On the one hand he counted among his close friends the gangster Barney Bertsche, on the other members of the Chicago elite such as Charles G. Dawes and Joseph Medill Patterson and Robert R. McCormick of the *Tribune* family.[22] Busse had supported Deneen in 1904, but Lorimer accepted him because he did not believe the alliance would last. Deneen had the same belief, but he depended upon Busse to help him control the county central committee and could not afford to alienate him.[23]

Busse's appointment as Chicago postmaster had a direct bearing on the struggle for Shelby M. Cullom's senatorial seat.[24] This factional battle was related to the struggle for political power within the party rather than to any cultural or ideological issue. Cullom's challenger was ex-Governor Richard Yates, who supposedly had Deneen's backing. Lorimer entered the contest as chairman of Cullom's Cook County campaign committee and he sought to transform the campaign from one of Cullom versus Yates to one of Cullom *and* Lorimer versus Yates *and* Deneen. He hoped that Yates's unpopularity in Cook County would cut Deneen's strength there.[25]

Deneen perceived the hazards of an all-out campaign for Yates. He could diminish his Cook County strength and further antagonize the federal faction. He also doubted that Yates could defeat Cullom. But Deneen was still saddled with his 1904 pledge to Yates. He decided that the wisest course was public neutrality on the senatorship, even though this meant breaking his commitment. At the same time, he privately tried to establish good relations with Cullom, hoping to restrict Lorimer's influence. In December, 1905, after conferring with state chairman Roy O. West, Sol H. Bethea wrote Cullom that West and Deneen were "quietly doing the best they can to keep

[22] Charles G. Dawes to Lawrence Y. Sherman, Nov. 2, 1903, to George B. Cortelyou, Oct. 27, 1903, Dawes Papers; Ickes, *Autobiography*, 92–93.

[23] Sol H. Bethea to Cullom, Nov. 7, 1905, Cullom Papers.

[24] Albert J. Hopkins to Cullom, Dec. 28, 1905, Cullom Papers; *Tribune*, Dec. 13, 14, 1905.

[25] *Tribune*, Sept. 17, 1905.

him [Yates] out of the fight. . . . They don't want him to come in; they want to be friendly to you. . . ." [26]

Yates was disturbed over Deneen's refusal to take an outright pro-Yates stand. When the *Tribune* reported on July 30 that Deneen would be neutral in the senatorial contest, he wrote an angry letter to the Governor. Yates complained that Deneen was playing " 'foxy' politics." He asked Deneen to end his professed neutrality and let Roy O. West be his campaign chairman. Yates proposed that the campaign be fought on the basis of the "Lorimer Cullom crowd against the Deneen Yates . . . 'organization'—*i.e.* the old (discredited) Chicago machine and the federal oligarchy . . . against the Deneen organization of Chicago decisively put into power by the primaries and the Yates organization of the country decisively upheld by the country primaries." The real issue, Yates held, was: "Shall the federal oligarchy which was beaten at the primaries and convention of 1904 climb back into power by the aid of Lorimer Jamieson Blount Bidwell and Smyth." [27]

While Lorimer wished to use the identical issue, Deneen and Cullom had strong reservations. Deneen insisted upon his neutrality, while Cullom reconsidered his close Lorimer connection. Seeing that Deneen was not hostile, Cullom awakened to "the importance of . . . doing nothing to offend Deneen, the State Administration, or the Chicago organization." [28] When federal appointments were made in the spring of 1906, much to Lorimer's annoyance, Cullom recommended several Deneen men. In addition, Deneen caused Lorimer lieutenant "Billy" Cooke to be rejected as U.S. marshal.[29]

Lorimer could do little. No longer the shaper of political events, he could not punish those who retreated from his alliances. Lorimer continued to emphasize his close Cullom connection, even though Cullom had drawn apart. Yates also preferred the theme of a Cullom-Lorimer alliance, and he barnstormed the state claiming that a vote for Cullom was a vote to return the Blond Boss to power.[30]

[26] Bethea to Cullom, Dec. 2, 7, 1905, Cullom Papers.

[27] Yates to Deneen, July 30, 1905, Richard Yates Papers, Illinois State Historical Library, Springfield.

[28] Sol H. Bethea to Cullom, Dec. 2, 1905, Cullom Papers.

[29] Bethea to Cullom, Dec. 7, 1905, Jan. 6, 1906, Cullom Papers; *Tribune,* Jan. 10, 12, 14, 17, 1906.

[30] *Illinois State Journal,* Jan. 31, 1906, clipping in Yates Papers; Cullom to Charles G. Dawes, Jan. 15, 1906, Dawes Papers.

The county ticket and his congressional seat as well as the senatorial race concerned Lorimer during the spring and summer of 1906. A new primary law, passed by the General Assembly during a special spring session, complicated the situation. Deneen had wanted a direct primary but a combination of the Lorimerites, the federal machine representatives, and some downstate representatives blocked its passage. The resulting law provided for the voter election of delegates but only bound them for one ballot to the candidate receiving a district plurality. The political organizations kept control over the nomination of candidates. The primary vote was merely advisory in regard to the U.S. Senate and the Cook County races.[31] Initially it appeared that Lorimer and Deneen would "harmonize" and avoid a factional fight over the county ticket, but Deneen would not meet Lorimer's demands. Lorimer ran a rival slate in the primary and tied it to the Cullom campaign.[32]

The primaries drew a small proportion of the voters and the rival party organizations largely controlled them. The results clearly indicated a rebound by the Lorimer organization from its 1904 low. Cullom defeated Yates with 60 percent of the Chicago vote, while Lorimer's county candidates ran just behind the Deneen slate.[33] In Lorimer's own congressional race his opponent vigorously challenged him on the basis of his opposition in the House to the Beveridge meat-inspection amendment, but he still swept to a substantial victory— the result of his "highly organized machine that worked methodically and relentlessly in every precinct."[34]

While the *Tribune* claimed that Deneen had won a major victory over Lorimer in the county contests, it also noted that the Deneen leaders were devoting "all their energies . . . to the task of conciliating their late enemies."[35] Lorimer was too powerful to be ignored in the ticket's makeup, and the party caucus gave him a number of county posts on the final slate. At the convention on August 9 the delegates approved the slate after two roll calls, with Deneen receiv-

[31] Carroll Hill Wooddy, "The Direct Primary in Chicago" (unpublished Ph.D. dissertation, University of Chicago, 1926), 22–23; Bogart and Mathews, *The Modern Commonwealth*, 361.

[32] *Tribune* and *Record-Herald*, June 22–27, July 13, 1906; *Inter-Ocean*, June 27, July 5, 10–12, 1906.

[33] Manuscript Election Returns, 1906 Primaries, Municipal Reference Library, Chicago City Hall.

[34] *Record-Herald*, Aug. 5, 1906.

[35] *Tribune*, Aug. 6, 1906.

ing the largest share of offices.[36] The Republicans swept the November elections and secured a majority in the General Assembly for Senator Cullom. Lorimer's men won their county posts with approximately the same percentage of the vote as the other candidates, while his bloc of General Assembly representatives increased. Lorimer also secured 55.4 percent of the vote in his congressional race as compared with 50.8 percent in 1904.[37] He occupied a firm position from which to continue his struggle to return to power.

Lorimer's political activities from 1906–08 centered on blocking Deneen's renomination and impeding the Governor's legislative program. The Deneen agenda included civil service extension, a Chicago city charter, and a direct primary law.[38] Although he tried to stay neutral on the liquor question, the campaign for a local-option law became inextricably associated with Deneen's other proposals. A number of Deneen leaders in the General Assembly, such as Morton D. Hull, Oliver Sollitt, and Walter Clyde Jones, were "drys." In addition, Victor Lawson, Deneen's leading newspaper supporter, was a Sabbatarian. He did not publish a Sunday edition of the *Daily News,* he did not accept liquor advertisements, and he opposed Sunday band concerts.[39] Deneen was saddled with the image of a "reformer" in a cultural as well as a political sense, and this image helped erode his large 1904 majority.

Among ritualistic ethnic groups there was a tendency to equate progressives with prohibitionists. Thus, *Die Abendpost* commented that the "Progressive Republicans . . . are in favor of prohibition almost without exception," while *Denni Hlasatel* warned of "various and sundry 'improvers,' 'correctors,' and 'reformers' " who would take away the liberty of the people.[40] George C. Sikes, a leading member of the Municipal Voters' League, complained of the automatic linking of reform and sumptuary legislation in a 1916 article when he observed that "the trouble now in our large cities is that men who

[36] *Ibid.,* Aug. 6, 8, 9, 1906; *Inter-Ocean,* Aug. 10, 1906.

[37] Lorimer secured 18,163 votes; Democrat Edmund J. Stack, 10,734; Prohibitionist Edward E. Blake, 1,794; and Socialist Walter E. Huggins, 2,082. The Socialist percentage was about the same as in 1904, but the Prohibitionist percentage declined nearly 10 points. See Manuscript Election Returns, Sixth Congressional District, 1906, Board of Election Commissioners, Chicago.

[38] *Tribune,* Aug. 22, 1906.

[39] *Dillingham Committee Hearings,* VII, 7121, 7140, 7141 (Morton D. Hull testifying); Dennis, *Victor Lawson,* 64–70; *Die Abendpost,* Dec. 9, 1907.

[40] *Die Abendpost,* Aug. 26, 1910; *Denni Hlasatel,* Mar. 30, 1915.

are fighting for decency and honest government are suspected of being puritans no matter what they say." [41]

But while some progressives were unfairly identified as coercive cultural reformers, throughout the nation progressivism and temperance, as well as other sumptuary reforms, were often closely linked. This connection is made explicit in studies of prohibition in California, Tennessee, and Washington.[42] Analyses of progressivism in such varied states as Georgia and Indiana note the importance of the anti-liquor crusade in progressive victories. Georgia became the first southern state to adopt statewide prohibition in 1907 during Hoke Smith's regime, while Governor J. Frank Hanly of Indiana was responsible for the passage of legislation controlling the liquor traffic and even the manufacture and sale of cigarettes.[43]

Several elements in the progressive program, in addition to temperance, were susceptible of a cultural interpretation. The direct primary, which was a key part of Governor Deneen's program, was one of these. Lorimer, for instance, observed that the direct primary militated against "representation of the different subdivisions, geographically, or by the different nationalities. . . ." [44] That is, because of the preponderance of Illinois native-American voters, members of minority ethnic groups such as the Bohemians and the Russians would be denied representation on the ticket. The technique of balancing slates in order to attract the votes of multi-groups would be threatened. The civil service system was also viewed as having nativistic or anti-immigrant overtones.[45]

In a different sense, Lorimer and other machine politicians opposed measures such as civil service and the direct primary because

[41] George C. Sikes, "The Liquor Question and Municipal Reform," *National Municipal Review* (July, 1916), V, 417; *Die Abendpost*, Feb. 4, 1911.

[42] Gilman M. Ostrander, *The Prohibition Movement in California, 1848–1933* (Berkeley, 1957), 102, 107–109, 116; Paul E. Isaac, *Prohibition and Politics: Turbulent Decades in Tennessee 1885–1920* (Knoxville, 1965), 139, 151, 264–265; Norman H. Clark, *The Dry Years: Prohibition and Social Change in Washington* (Seattle, 1965), 85, 86, 102, 122–127.

[43] Dewey W. Grantham, Jr., *Hoke Smith and the Politics of the New South* (paperback ed., Baton Rouge, 1967), 162–163, 189–190; Clifton J. Phillips, *Indiana in Transition: The Emergence of an Industrial Commonwealth, 1880–1920* (Indianapolis, 1968), 99–102.

[44] *Dillingham Committee Hearings*, II, 1182.

[45] Handlin, *The Uprooted*, 217–221. Objections to municipal civil service reform are discussed in William Bennett Munro, *The Government of American Cities* (3rd ed., New York, 1920), 280–285.

they threatened to dilute their control over party organization and nominations. "As an organization Republican," said Lorimer, "I believe the direct primary has been a serious obstacle in the way of the Republican organization." [46] In addition, the direct primary threatened the organization hold over nominations for the lower house of the General Assembly. The Illinois cumulative voting system gave the organizations practically monopolistic control. In most cases the majority party in a legislative district received two seats and the minority one. The machines only nominated as many candidates as there were seats and nomination became practically synonymous with election. [47]

The rivalry between the metropolis and downstate formed another basis of opposition to reform, especially when it emanated from Chicago. Downstate politicians wanted to restrict, not extend, Chicago's powers of self-government and they made several attempts during the 1906–08 period to curtail Chicago legislative representation. [48] Downstaters distrusted both the big city's cosmopolitanism and its polyglot population. They believed that the direct primary would give Chicago a disproportionate amount of influence over nominations. As one "Egypt" politician expressed it, the Republicans in his section opposed the direct primary because "they are, by nature, 'short' on all 'reform' measures." [49]

While much of the opposition to Deneen derived from his legislative program, his personality and approach to politics were also complicating factors. Unlike the familiar gregarious professional politician, Deneen was tight-lipped and secretive and often antagonized his associates. One Illinois politician wrote that the Governor was "about as chilly an icicle as has ever been produced in this state . . . he has a winning way of making people hate him." [50] In contrast to Lorimer, Deneen had a reputation for untrustworthiness, as in the 1906 senatorial contest. And politicians also suspected Deneen of duplicity in

[46] *Tribune,* June 17, 1909.

[47] Wooddy, "The Direct Primary in Chicago," 17–18; Blaine F. Moore, *The History of Cumulative Voting and Minority Representation in Illinois, 1870–1919* (Urbana, 1919), 56–57; Charles E. Merriam to James Thomas, Nov. 19, 1907, Charles E. Merriam Papers, Harper Library, University of Chicago.

[48] Philip, "Chicago and the Down State," 50–61; Bogart and Mathews, *The Modern Commonwealth,* 196.

[49] Harry B. Ward to Frank O. Lowden, Apr. 6, 1906, Lowden Papers.

[50] Godfrey G. Leethy to Lawrence Y. Sherman, May 26, 1908, Sherman Papers.

trying to embrace both reform and organization politics simultaneously.[51]

By 1907 the Governor's personality and politics had antagonized many politicians.[52] The local-option bill, an item not in Deneen's legislative program, exacerbated the situation. The Anti-Saloon League, which used the legislation to attack the liquor evil at points of least resistance, applied pressure for local option. The Illinois law provided that the voters of any town, precinct, city, or village could vote their political subdivision dry.[53] The House approved the measure by a vote of 83 to 65 and the Senate by 35 to 6. The Chicago Deneenites supported the bill along with the downstate Republicans, while most Democrats and the Cook County Lorimer Republicans opposed it.[54] Deneen signed the bill into law on May 16 and the Anti-Saloon League immediately began passing petitions to obtain local-option votes at the next election.[55]

The Chicago city charter movement demonstrated the havoc the liquor issue could cause when involved with a reform measure. Chicago reformers organized the charter convention in 1905 to draft a governmental plan suited to the city's modern needs. Deneen supported the reform in his 1905 message to the General Assembly. Early in 1907 framers of the charter submitted it to the General Assembly, where it encountered immediate difficulties. The legislature eliminated several controversial reform provisions such as the direct primary, woman suffrage, and the removal of the party circle from municipal ballots. It retained, however, such items as governmental consolidation and an increase in the city's bonded debt limit, as well as the referendum and the redistricting of the city into fifty wards.[56] But most significant for the future of the charter proposal was saloon regulation. The United Societies for Local Self-Government, an amalgamation of ethnic and cultural groups formed in 1906 to protect personal liberty, petitioned the charter convention and the leg-

[51] *The Outlook* (Aug. 29, 1908), V, 89, 966.

[52] Harry B. Ward to Frank O. Lowden, May 23, 1907, Lowden Papers; Lawrence Y. Sherman to Shelby M. Cullom, May 28, 1907, Sherman Papers.

[53] Bogart and Mathews, *The Modern Commonwealth*, 386.

[54] *House Journal, Forty-fifth General Assembly,* 987; *Senate Journal, Forty-fifth General Assembly,* 719. Elbridge Hanecy was the spokesman for the Brewers' Association against the local-option bill. See *Tribune*, Feb. 21, 1907.

[55] Jackson, "The Work of the Anti-Saloon League," 485.

[56] Milton J. Foreman, "Chicago New Charter Movement—Its Relation to Municipal Ownership," *Annals of the American Academy of Political and Social Science* (May, 1908), XXXI, 639–648. Foreman was chairman of the convention.

William Lorimer, c. 1912.

J. McCan Davis, *The Breaking of the Deadlock* (1904)

Lorimer on his way to the 1904 "deadlocked"
Republican convention in Springfield.

Davis, *Breaking of the Deadlock*

The Leland Hotel in Springfield, center of political activity at convention time.

Davis, *Breaking of the Deadlock*

Republican gubernatorial candidate Frank O. Lowden's headquarters in the Leland Hotel, 1904.

Governor Frank O. Lowden.

Governor Len Small.

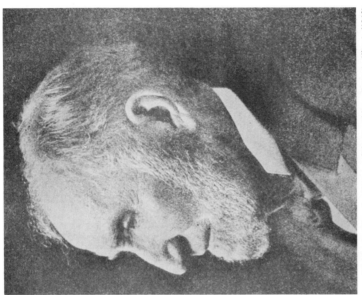

Charles A. Church, *History of the Republican Party in Illinois* (1912)

Joseph G. Cannon, speaker of the U.S. House of Representatives.

Blue Book of the State of Illinois 1909

Edward D. Shurtleff, speaker of the Illinois House of Representatives.

Some of Lorimer's political allies.

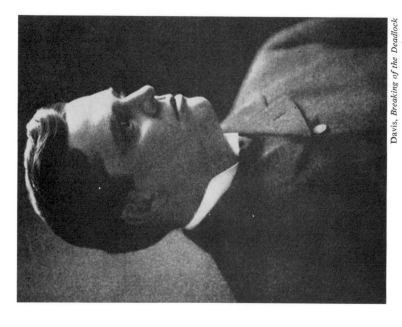

Davis, *Breaking of the Deadlock*

Governor Charles S. Deneen.

Davis, *Breaking of the Deadlock*

Governor Richard Yates.

Church, *Republican Party in Illinois*

U.S. Senator Shelby M. Cullom.

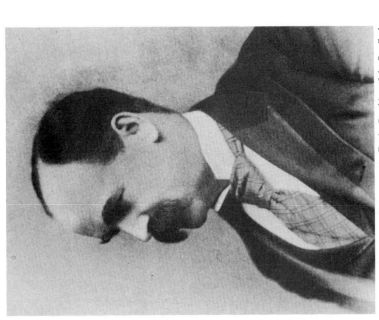

Davis, *Breaking of the Deadlock*

U.S. Senator Albert J. Hopkins.

Some of Lorimer's political friends who became enemies.

Charles G. Dawes, *A Journal of the McKinley Years* (1950)

U.S. Senator Albert J. Beveridge.

Davis, *Breaking of the Deadlock*

Lawrence Y. Sherman, speaker of the Illinois
House of Representatives and U.S. senator.

Charles G. Dawes, U.S. comptroller of the currency.

Among Lorimer's opponents.

U.S. Senator John W. Kern.

The American Magazine, Sept., 1910

Cook County State's Attorney John E. W. Wayman, who led the criminal prosecution of those involved in the Lorimer election case.

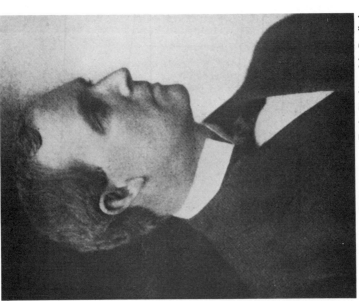

Davis, *Breaking of the Deadlock*

Judge Elbridge Hanecy, Republican candidate for governor in 1900 and mayor of Chicago in 1901, and Lorimer's attorney during the investigations into the charges of corruption in Lorimer's Senate election.

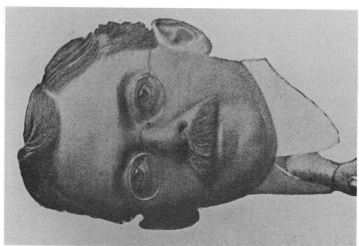

Cosmopolitan Magazine, Oct., 1910

Lumberman Edward Hines, accused of furnishing the money for the Lorimer election "jackpot."

The American Magazine, Sept., 1910

State Representative Charles A. White, who confessed to receiving $1,000 for his Lorimer vote from Lee O'Neil Browne.

The American Magazine, Sept., 1910

State Representative Lee O'Neil Browne, accused by Charles A. White of paying him $1,000 for his Lorimer vote.

The American Magazine, Sept., 1910

Daniel W. Holtslaw.

The American Magazine, Sept., 1910

H. J. C. Beckemeyer.

The American Magazine, Sept., 1910

John Broderick, Illinois senator and saloon-keeper.

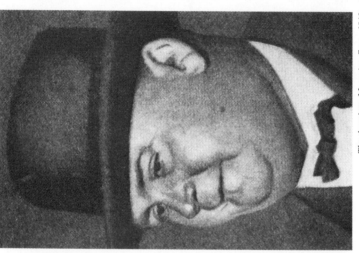

The American Magazine, Sept., 1910

Michael S. Link.

The American Magazine, Sept., 1910

Robert E. ("Bathroom Bob") Wilson.

Members of the Forty-sixth Illinois General Assembly accused of being involved in the Lorimer "jackpot."

Herman H. Kohlsaat, publisher of the Chicago
Times-Herald and *Record-Herald*.

Victor Lawson, publisher of the Chicago *Daily
News*.

Underwood and Underwood

Medill McCormick of the Chicago
Tribune.

Philip Kinsley, *The Chicago Tribune,* III (1946)

Robert W. Patterson of the Chicago
Tribune.

Members of Chicago's "trust press."

Chicago Historical Society

Joseph Medill, publisher of the Chicago
Tribune.

Traction baron Charles Tyson Yerkes.

Banker John R. Walsh.

Two of Lorimer's business allies.

islature for home rule on the issue of Sunday closing. Both the convention and the General Assembly refused the request.[57]

The General Assembly eventually approved the city charter with but one dissenting Cook County Republican vote. Cook County Democrats, however, reflecting the criticism of the charter among many Chicago ethnic groups, were mostly opposed. The Democratic party, the United Societies, and the Federation of Labor joined to fight charter adoption, while the reform press, the Union League Club and the Chicago Club, and most Republicans supported it.[58] The backing of these groups proved insufficient to secure the charter's approval, and in a special election held on September 17, 1907, the voters defeated the charter by a margin of nearly two to one. The charter only won a majority in upper-class and native-American wards, while the newer immigrant wards voted overwhelmingly against it.[59]

While the opposition of small property owners who were apprehensive that the charter would cause a rise in real-estate taxes contributed to its defeat, most critical was the hostility of ritualistic religious and ethnic groups, "who seemed to fear that the adoption of the Charter meant a return to the puritanical Sunday." [60] These groups perceived the charter as a threat to their life-styles and norms rather than as an attempt to secure more governmental efficiency, and they rejected it decisively.[61]

The charter's loss, in spite of Deneen's support, symbolized the growing opposition to his renomination. By the summer of 1907 there were three candidates for the Republican gubernatorial nomination: Judge Willard M. McEwen of Cook County, Edward D. Shurtleff, the speaker of the lower house of the General Assembly, and ex-Governor Richard Yates. McEwen was reputed by the press to be Lorimer's candidate.[62] Shurtleff had been a Deneen supporter, but by 1907 he had become discontented with the Governor's politics and

---

[57] *Ibid.*, 648; *Record-Herald*, May 3, 5, 8, 1907. Foreman called saloon regulation "the most complicated and embarrassing obstacle which the Charter Convention encountered."

[58] *Tribune*, Aug. 11, 1907; *Record-Herald*, May 26, June 5, July 22, Sept. 4, 5, 16, 1907.

[59] *Daily News Almanac for 1908*, 495.

[60] Charles E. Merriam to G. A. Cutherbertson, Nov. 17, 1907, Merriam Papers; *Tribune*, Sept. 18, 1907.

[61] *Die Abendpost*, Sept. 16, 1907, Feb. 25, 1908.

[62] *Tribune*, July 20, 21, 1907; *Post*, Aug. 27, 1907.

policies. He believed Deneen an opportunist—"one of the most notorious humbugs, hypocrites, and four-flushers of the twentieth century"—and was "willing to go to any length to defeat him." [63]
Shurtleff campaigned for the restriction of Chicago's legislative representation, hoping to win in the downstate districts.[64] And the always
dangerous Yates, backed by his "indignant friends," determined to
seek revenge for Deneen's betrayal in 1906.[65]

During the fall of 1907, the fight against Deneen centered on the
passage of a direct primary bill. Deneen believed that without a direct
primary his opponents would block his renomination in the convention.[66] Deneen had fought for primary reform since the beginning of
his term, but neither of the new primary laws passed by the General
Assembly in 1905 and 1906 had actually provided for direct voter
choice. The Illinois Supreme Court found both laws unconstitutional
for technical reasons.[67] In 1907 Deneen and his supporters pushed
the so-called Oglesby primary bill, which provided for direct voter
choice of national convention delegates and for municipal, county,
state, judicial, and congressional nominations by plurality vote.[68]
Shurtleff and the Yates and Lorimer men opposed the bill in the
General Assembly. Old Guard Speaker of the House "Uncle Joe"
Cannon aided them in their fight.

Cannon, who was a candidate for the 1908 Republican presidential nomination, fought the direct primary because he believed it
would destroy party organization and give too much influence to the
large Chicago dailies. These papers opposed his presidential aspirations.[69] Lorimer, Yates, and most downstate politicians, however,
supported Cannon for the nomination, while Deneen stayed on the
fence.[70] Cannon disliked Deneen and believed that he only supported

[63] Shurtleff to John G. Oglesby, Feb. 7, 1908, John G. Oglesby Papers; Harry B.
Ward to Frank O. Lowden, June [n.d.], 1907, Lowden Papers.

[64] Ward to Lowden, Aug. 15, 1907, Lowden Papers; W. T. Norton to Lawrence
Y. Sherman, Sept. 24, 1907, Sherman Papers; *Tribune*, July 28, 1907.

[65] Krenkel, ed., *Richard Yates*, 162; *Tribune*, Dec. 29, 1907.

[66] Charles E. Merriam to Fred Carr, Mar. 26, 1909, Merriam Papers.

[67] Wooddy, "The Direct Primary in Chicago," 15–24; Walter Clyde Jones, "The
Direct Primary in Illinois," *Proceedings of the American Political Science Association* (1910), VII, 138–150.

[68] *House Journal, Forty-fifth General Assembly*, 1415. John G. Oglesby was
chairman of the House Committee on Primary Elections.

[69] Joseph G. Cannon to Captain Henry A. King, Nov. 2, 10, 1907, to Percy C.
Ellis, Nov. 2, 1907, Charles P. Hitch to Cannon, Mar. 11, 1908, Cannon Papers.

[70] Lorimer to William B. McKinley, Mar. 9, 1908, to Joseph G. Cannon, Mar. 9,
1908, Charles P. Hitch to Cannon, Mar. 11, 1908, Cannon Papers.

the direct primary to "make his renomination sure." The Speaker wrote Captain Henry A. King of the St. Louis *Globe-Democrat* that he was "morally certain that he [Deneen] absolutely takes orders from Victor Lawson . . . [who] is not a Republican; does not support Republican tickets, and believes in the disorganization of all parties that he may be a dominating factor." [71]

The General Assembly began struggling with the Oglesby bill in October of 1907. On October 23 the Deneen men in the lower house (the "Band of Hope") joined with the Democrats to pass the measure by the deceptively large vote of 102 to 27.[72] Eighteen of the twenty-seven assemblymen who voted nay on the direct primary had also voted against the local-option bill. The Senate proved more difficult than the House. From headquarters in Springfield's Leland Hotel, Lorimer and Cannon, aided by a number of congressmen, guided the opposition. They were helped by Chicagoans James Pease, Illinois Senator Dan Campbell, and the newly elected Chicago mayor, Fred Busse. Following Lorimer's and Cannon's direction, the Senate enacted amendments that eliminated national elections and convention delegates, as well as party organizational machinery, from the direct primary requirement. The Senate approved the "mangled" Oglesby bill with amendments by a vote of 40 to 8.[73]

The House, however, led by the "Band of Hope," refused to concur in the Senate amendments. The members also rejected a subsequent conference committee report, made by a committee packed with direct primary opponents.[74] It appeared that direct primary legislation was dead for the session. On January 23, however, the Senate passed a measure called the Jones-Oglesby bill, which was the Oglesby direct primary bill minus the provision for national delegates. It was probably the result of a Cannon-Deneen compromise. Senator Hopkins may also have been involved. The bargain was that Deneen accept the elimination of national delegates from the Oglesby bill in exchange for a direct primary for state offices.[75]

It appears that Lorimer was not privy to this deal. Rising from a sickbed, he rushed to the state capitol declaring that he would fight

[71] Cannon to King, Nov. 2, 10, 1907, Cannon Papers.

[72] *House Journal, Forty-fifth General Assembly*, 1483; *Tribune*, Oct. 24, 1907.

[73] Joseph G. Cannon to William Lorimer, Nov. 17, 1907, Cannon Papers; *Senate Journal, Forty-fifth General Assembly*, 1418–23; *Tribune*, Nov. 1, 2, 1907.

[74] *House Journal, Forty-fifth General Assembly*, 1517, 1547–60, 1569–81.

[75] *Ibid.*, 1640–68, 1677, 1680–81; *Senate Journal, Forty-fifth General Assembly*, 1506, 1570; *Tribune*, Jan. 25, 26, 28, 29, 1908.

the Jones-Oglesby bill to "the last ditch." [76] But he could do little with his depleted forces, and on January 29, 1908, the House approved the bill by a vote of 88 to 33. Nineteen Republican assemblymen, including Shurtleff and Lorimerites David Shanahan, Edward J. Smejkal, and Thomas Curran, entered a protest in the *House Journal:* "WE PROTEST, Against the passage of a law that . . . will absolutely destroy this great [Republican] party . . . and in the end, destroy all parties, placing the power of government in the hands of the independent and minority voters. . . . It makes the individual—the personality of some candidate—the party platform, in place of principles. It deprives the citizen of his voice and influence in political affairs." [77] But the protest was an overstatement, as was *Tribune* political columnist Clifford S. Raymond's prediction that the bill would "politically turn Chicago upside down." [78] Walter L. Fisher noted to New York's Mayor Seth Low that "the Illinois law is a very hastily prepared and ill-considered measure, which represents simply the best piece of legislation . . . which could be obtained. . . . [It] is intentionally cumbersome, and carries many provisions to an extreme . . . it was made radical and complicated for the express purpose of discrediting it and of embarrassing Governor Deneen. . . ." [79]

But however cumbersome, the primary law required Lorimer to change his tactics in his fight to deny Deneen renomination. Under the convention system, several candidates opposing Deneen worked to Lorimer's benefit. The direct primary, however, necessitated agreement upon one opponent. On passage of the Jones-Oglesby bill, Lorimer met with Shurtleff, McEwen, and Yates in publisher George W. Hinman's office. Shurtleff and McEwen agreed to withdraw in favor of Yates, and Lorimer to again support the ex-governor.[80] On February 23, 1908, Yates announced his candidacy, and observed that the direct primary provided "an opportunity for the first time in this state, for an effectual and real 'appeal to the people.' " [81] Even Lorimer

---

[76] *Tribune* and *Record-Herald,* Jan. 28, 1908.

[77] *House Journal, Forty-fifth General Assembly,* 1694–95.

[78] *Tribune,* Jan. 30, 1908.

[79] Fisher to Hon. Seth Low, Feb. 24, 1909, Fisher Papers.

[80] *Dillingham Committee Hearings,* I, 254 (Richard Yates testifying); Harry B. Ward to Frank O. Lowden, Jan. 31, 1908, Lowden Papers; *Tribune,* Jan. 30, 31, 1908; *Record-Herald,* Feb. 2, 1908.

[81] *Tribune,* Feb. 24, 1908; Springfield *Register,* Feb. 24, 1908, clipping in Charles S. Deneen Scrapbooks, Illinois State Historical Library, Springfield.

now talked about the need for an "expression from the people." [82] The anti-Deneen forces would try to defeat the Governor with his own weapon.

One uncertain factor was Mayor Busse, who had been nominated and elected in the spring of 1907 with the support, albeit reluctant, of all factions.[83] Busse was German, the first member of that nationality to be nominated by the Republican party. In the election he faced the Irish Catholic reform mayor Edward Dunne, in a contest that pitted members of Chicago's two largest ethnic groups. As a German and a Republican, Busse secured the support of native Americans as well as much of Chicago's large German population. Both men were members of ritualistic ethnic groups, but Dunne had alienated the personal-liberty forces by attempting to enforce the Sunday closing law and by refusing to issue permits for the use of alcoholic beverages at fraternal clubs and festivals. *Die Abendpost* accused Dunne of declaring "war . . . upon the most honorable unions of a social, educational, and benevolent character." [84] The traction issue was also important, with Dunne supporting a municipal-ownership program and Busse promising to make a favorable settlement with the streetcar companies.[85] Busse won the election with 48.6 percent of the vote, an increase of 6.3 percentage points over Harlan's 1905 total. He ran very strongly in the normally Democratic German wards, and became Chicago's first German mayor, the city's first four-year-term executive, and its first Republican mayor in twelve years.[86]

According to the *Inter-Ocean,* Busse's election was "to the advantage of Lorimer." Lorimer had been active in the convention that chose Busse, and a Lorimer man, John R. McCabe, was nominated and elected city clerk. Busse also appointed Lorimer lieutenant Ernest J. Magerstadt as city collector.[87] Several years later, Lorimer claimed that Busse had encouraged him to bring Yates into the

[82] William B. McKinley to Joseph G. Cannon, Feb. 8, 1908, Cannon Papers.

[83] *Tribune,* Feb. 9, 12, 26, Mar. 1, 1907.

[84] *Die Abendpost,* Mar. 10, 16, 19, 26, 1906; "Saloon License Made $1,000 in Chicago," *The Outlook* (Mar. 17, 1906), LXXXII, 587–588.

[85] *Tribune,* Apr. 1, 3, 1907; Ickes, *Autobiography,* 107–109. The Republican press charged that Dunne was controlled by William Randolph Hearst and the Hearst interests.

[86] *Daily News Almanac for 1908,* 316–319. Busse's vote correlated at +.497 with percent German, the highest such correlation for any Republican candidate in the 1901–11 period.

[87] *Inter-Ocean,* Apr. 7, 16, 1907.

gubernatorial race against Deneen. If this was true, and there is little reason to doubt Lorimer, it would suggest that Lorimer and Busse were drawing together and that Lorimer had reason to believe he could defeat Deneen.[88]

The Yates campaign took rapid shape. Len Small of Kankakee, "one of the ablest campaign managers in the state," took charge of the downstate areas, while Lorimerite David Frank was Cook County chairman. Lorimer expected that Yates would score heavily in the immigrant areas of the city because of the support of the Deneenites for local option. Early in the campaign David Frank told Yates that the Brewers' Association would contribute $25,000 to his campaign, but Yates refused the money because he was for local option and hoped to win temperance votes.[89] During the summer, however, both the *Tribune* and the *Record-Herald* reported that Yates had accepted the $25,000 and promised to oppose further local-option legislation.[90] Whether or not Yates had accepted the money is immaterial; what is significant is that the Deneen press saw Yates as the candidate of the liquor interests and the groups that supported personal liberty.[91]

There are indications that Yates implicitly accepted that role. Yates charged that the "newspaper trust" controlled Deneen and that he relied upon the party organization to win him the nomination.[92] In contrast, Yates would go directly to the voters. When taken in conjunction with the refusal of the Chicago reformers in the charter convention and the Deneenites in the General Assembly to permit a Chicago vote on the Sunday closing law, it appeared that Yates, rather than Deneen, trusted the people. In early May the county central committee held a series of pre-primary "conferences" which endorsed Deneen for governor and selected an organization slate. Lorimer refused an invitation to the conferences. He said he wanted nothing to do with "slate making." The *Inter-Ocean* noted that Lorimer's nonattendance implied "that he believes a caucus or conference endorsement a violation of the primary idea."[93] Taking advantage of Deneen's endorsement by a caucus of "bosses," Yates added a

[88] *Dillingham Committee Hearings*, VIII, 7675.
[89] Richard Yates to David Frank, Feb. 18, 1904 [*sic*], printed in Krenkel, ed., *Richard Yates*, 164–165.
[90] *Tribune* and *Record-Herald*, Aug. 5, 1908.
[91] *Record-Herald*, July 31, Aug. 3, 1908; *Tribune*, Aug. 9, 1908.
[92] *Inter-Ocean*, Apr. 9, 19, 1908; *Tribune*, Mar. 21, 29, Apr. 25, 1908.
[93] *Inter-Ocean*, May 5, 1908.

new speech on the "Primary Law Nullifiers" to his repertoire. He pictured the Chicago "bosses" as those who would use their "slate making sledge hammers" to smash the "liberty bell in the direct primary law." The use of the word "liberty" was probably not accidental.[94]

Lorimer also used the personal-liberty theme. On June 21, at a Yates meeting in the Coliseum, he gave an address entitled "Put the False Gods Aside." The "false gods" were the newspaper trust and their kept politicians like Deneen. Lorimer pictured himself as the leader in a move to return the Republican party to a state of original purity: "For ten or twelve years we have been following these false gods in Chicago. . . . We have listened to the campaign of denunciation against all public men *who do not think to suit those who have plied the lash.* This meeting tonight is a protest against that idea, and against such methods." Lorimer and Yates held that they sought to free men from those who would control their thoughts and actions. They would bring the return of "the old Republican party, the party of American progress, the party of the stars and stripes . . . and the best party for the American people." [95]

Speaking in Deneen's home ward on July 29, Lorimer indicted Victor Lawson, the Governor's chief press supporter, as a dictator. He charged that Lawson was "the real head of the ring machine—the man who pulled the wires attached to Deneen. . . . Under their control it has never been possible for any man to get a Republican nomination unless he first crawled up the steps leading to Lawson's office and *accepted the yoke.*" [96] Lorimer again implied that he, unlike Lawson and Deneen, would resist attempts to deprive men of their liberty.

The General Assembly's approval of a committee report on state asylums added to Deneen's difficulties. The report criticized Deneen and charged that "both the spirit and the letter of the [civil service] law . . . have been evaded with the sanction and approval of the executive, who while leading the people of the state to believe that the law is being strictly enforced . . . is evading the law and deceiving the people." [97] Shurtleff and his Republican followers had combined with the Democrats to pass the condemnation. While some

[94] *Ibid.*, May 12, 13, 1908.
[95] *Ibid.*, June 23, 1908 (my italics).
[96] *Ibid.*, July 30, 1908 (my italics).
[97] *Tribune,* May 7, 8, 1908.

of the charges were exaggerated and some untrue, they had enough substance to reflect badly on Deneen. Letters from throughout the state noted that Yates was cutting deeply into the Governor's strength.[98]

Although the main focus was upon the gubernatorial contest, there were also other important offices at stake in the primary. Most crucial for Lorimer were the races for Cook County state's attorney and for U.S. senator.[99] The state's attorney contest pitted the incumbent John J. Healy against challenger John E. W. Wayman. Healy was an especially controversial state's attorney. He tried to enforce the Sunday closing law in Chicago for the first time in over thirty years. The Anti-Saloon League, the WCTU, the Law and Order League, and the Sunday Closing League supported him in his prosecutions.[100] Wayman, on the other hand, took the position that the state's attorney was "powerless" to close the saloons on Sunday. He received the endorsement of the United Societies as well as the German-American Republican Club.[101] While they had no direct ties, Lorimer did what he could to help Wayman.[102]

The state's attorney contest was critical because it reinforced the picture of Deneen as a puritan reformer. Deneen had handpicked Healy as his successor in 1904, and the Governor backed his renomination in 1908. In addition, Deneen's strongest press supporters, the *Tribune,* the *Daily News,* and the *Record-Herald,* backed Healy. Healey would strengthen Deneen among pro-temperance native Americans and Swedes, but further weaken him with Germans, Bohemians, Poles, and Catholic Irishmen, who favored personal liberty.

The primary for U.S. senator, which was advisory rather than binding, presented a different situation. The chief candidates were the incumbent Albert J. Hopkins, Congressman George E. Foss, and ex-Senator William E. Mason. Hopkins, who lacked personal popularity, depended upon his federal appointees and his ties with Busse

[98] Edward D. Shurtleff to John G. Oglesby, Feb. 7, 1908, Oglesby Papers; Frank C. Bruner to Frank O. Lowden, Mar. [n.d.], 1908, Ralph E. Bradford to Lowden, Apr. 10, 1908, Lowden Papers; Seth F. Crews to Lawrence Y. Sherman, May 14, 1908, Sherman Papers.

[99] Lorimer was opposed in his own congressional primary by Deneenite Dr. Carl L. Barnes. Barnes charged that Lorimer was an "alien." *Tribune,* May 31, Aug. 8, 1908.

[100] *Record-Herald,* Jan. 7, 30, Feb. 6, Mar. 17, Apr. 7, 1908; "Chicago's Sunday Closing Fight," *The Outlook* (Mar. 7, 1908), LXXXVIII, 524.

[101] *Die Abendpost,* May 24, 1909; *Record-Herald,* Aug. 1, Oct. 10, 1908.

[102] *Dillingham Committee Hearings,* VIII, 7839.

and Lorimer for victory. Against him he had the three leading Chicago reform newspapers, the *Tribune,* the *Record-Herald,* and the *Daily News,* as well as an influential group of Chicago progressives. Most of the latter supported Foss, who was associated with the Union League Club and other elite Chicago organizations. Although newspaper pundits predicted a Hopkins victory, the situation was uncertain.[103]

The senatorial contest intermeshed with the gubernatorial. Hopkins was under pressure to make a choice between Deneen and Yates, however reluctant he was to do so. Under the rules of politics, Hopkins was obligated to Lorimer and to Yates, who had made possible his election in 1903. But Hopkins had decided that self-interest dictated that he help Deneen. As early as June, 1907, Lawrence Y. Sherman wrote Cullom that "Hopkins' friends, to my certain knowledge are making efforts to join with Deneen and pull down the fight all along the line. Hopkins, of course, to be Senator and Deneen Governor under this arrangement." [104] Hopkins and Deneen, as the primary approached, drew closer in their cautious embrace, although many of the more progressive Deneen backers would not swallow the red-headed Senator at any price. They intended to work for Foss.[105]

Although Lorimer became aware of Hopkins' desertion, he gave no outward sign and his slate's sample ballots appeared with a cross next to Hopkins' name. Several years later, Lorimer claimed that Hopkins as well as Busse had urged him to enter Yates against Deneen in the primary.[106] He related that he was astonished when he discovered evidence of Hopkins' flirtation with Deneen, since he and Yates had made Hopkins senator. "I would not believe Senator Hopkins would turn on friends such as we had been to him . . . in a struggle that would decide which crowd would go down forever," said Lorimer. Lorimer decided to "use all the influence" he had to win Hopkins the nomination and call for a reckoning after the pri-

---

[103] William E. Mason to Lawrence Y. Sherman, Feb. 3, 1908, Sherman Papers; Ira C. Copley to Mrs. Copley, Aug. 3, 1908, Ira C. Copley Papers, used through the permission of Mr. James Copley, San Diego; *Tribune,* June 21, July 12, Aug. 3, 7, 1908. The leaders of the Chicago reform group tried unsuccessfully to get William Kent to run against Hopkins in the primary. See William C. Boyden to Kent, Mar. 21, 1908, Ira C. Copley to Kent, Apr. 1, 1908, Kent Papers.

[104] Sherman to Cullom, June 5, 1907, Sherman Papers.

[105] *Dillingham Committee Hearings,* VII, 7126 (Morton D. Hull testifying), VIII, 7686, 7689.

[106] *Ibid.,* VIII, 7675-77.

mary. Then the course that Hopkins followed would be clear.[107]

On primary day the political organizations in the normally Democratic areas pulled out a heavy vote, while in the large Republican wards the tally was light, reflecting the Governor's unpopularity. In the three wards in Lorimer's congressional district, the Thirteenth, Twentieth, and Thirty-fourth, Yates had an average percentage of 66.4; in the Ninth, Tenth, and Eleventh wards, all river wards and Lorimer territory, Yates secured an astonishing 85.9 percent. High correlations between the Yates vote and the Democratic votes in 1904, 1905, and 1907 showed Yates's large appeal in Democratic areas, as well as the work of the Lorimer organization. The initial Yates returns were so favorable that the late evening edition of the *Inter-Ocean* proclaimed a Yates majority of from 15,000 to 20,000. By the next day, however, the final totals showed that Deneen had won a narrow victory, with 51.75 percent of the Chicago vote and 51.4 percent of the state vote.[108]

Deneen was helped in Chicago by politicians such as John Smulski in the Sixteenth Ward and Fred Busse in the Twenty-third, who swung their wards for him in spite of their ethnic composition. The Sixteenth Ward had more Poles than any other in the city and there Deneen secured his largest percentage of the vote. The Twenty-third, the first German ward, also went to Deneen by a slight margin.[109] This suggests that Deneen might not have been as tarred with the anti–personal-liberty brush as Lorimer had hoped. The vote for state's attorney reinforces this conclusion. Wayman won this race over Healy and Edward R. Litzinger with 47.4 percent of the vote. Although the Deneen vote correlated with the Healy vote at +.760, Healy lost the Sixteenth and Twenty-third wards.[110] Generally where Yates did well, so did Wayman, and their vote had a high correlation. Thus in contests involving a clear question of personal liberty, ritualistic cultural groups rallied to defend their norms and life-styles.

In the senatorial contest, Hopkins emerged the victor with 43.3 percent of the statewide vote. Foss followed him with 30.6 percent and

---

[107] *Ibid.*, 7676.

[108] *Inter-Ocean*, Aug. 9, 1908; Manuscript Election Returns, 1908 Republican Gubernatorial Primary, Municipal Reference Library, Chicago City Hall.

[109] Deneen had 73 percent of the vote in the Sixteenth Ward and 51.6 percent in the Twenty-third Ward.

[110] In the Sixteenth Ward Healy had 43.7 percent of the vote and in the Twenty-third, 34.5 percent.

Mason with 22.3 percent. But these totals do not reflect the large amount of anti-Hopkins feeling in the state. Hopkins lost his own city and county as well as Chicago and Cook County to Foss. He did well in the wards where Yates and Wayman were strong (and also Lorimer) and poorly in the Deneen-Healy areas. Hopkins' strength was largely in Democratic areas and his vote, like Yates's, correlated highly with the 1904, 1905, and 1907 Democratic votes. Foss, on the other hand, did well in the normally Republican areas. His vote correlated significantly with the 1907 Republican mayoralty vote and with the Deneen and Healy primary votes.[111]

Because of Hopkins' poor showing, Foss claimed that the primary vote was a repudiation of the Senator and that the General Assembly should not be bound. Before the primary Hopkins had refused to pledge himself to abide by its results; now he demanded that his victory be honored. A *Tribune* poll of assemblymen revealed that twenty-four considered the primary binding, but this was far less than was needed to elect.[112] Colonel Ira C. Copley of Aurora, one of Hopkins' bitterest foes, wrote his mother that "the fight we have put up against Mr. Hopkins will defeat him, even though he . . . [did] get more votes at the Primary than any other candidate." [113]

Even more significant were Lorimer's feelings. He was certain that "Hopkins had turned against his friends," and that Deneen would have lost the primary if it had not been for Hopkins' betrayal. Lorimer decided that "there was no obligation running from me to Mr. Hopkins." "I withdrew my support," said Lorimer, "and I was glad at any time or at any place to aid in electing any other Republican United States Senator from the State of Illinois." [114]

Lorimer also blamed Busse for Yates's loss and pointed to Deneen's majorities in the Busse wards. Lorimer's removal from the county executive committee in mid-August reinforced his bitterness against Busse, Hopkins, and Deneen.[115] Lorimer's course after this is in dispute. Rumor had it that he supported the Democratic candidate for governor, former Vice-President Adlai Stevenson. Illinois Assem-

---

[111] Foss had 36.3 percent of the Chicago Republican primary vote, Hopkins, 30.9 percent, and Mason, 29.1 percent. Manuscript Election Returns, 1908 Republican Senatorial Primary, Municipal Reference Library, Chicago City Hall.

[112] *Tribune,* Aug. 11, 25, 1908.

[113] Ira C. Copley to Mrs. Copley, Aug. 17, 1908, Copley Papers.

[114] *Dillingham Committee Hearings,* VIII, 7676–77.

[115] *Inter-Ocean,* Aug. 20, 1908.

blyman Thomas G. Tippit, an important Democratic factional leader, later related that Lorimer had made an agreement with the Democratic state central committee to help Stevenson. Lorimer, however, denied it.[116] But regardless of what he did, many of Lorimer's friends made no secret of their intention to try to defeat Deneen. Gus Nohe, for instance, boasted that he and his friends had organized a "band of hope . . . for the sole and express purpose of retiring Governor Charles S. Deneen to private life." Elbridge Hanecy, who attacked Deneen as the "destroyer of real Republicanism," organized a Taft-Stevenson club. And on October 30, on its front page, the *Inter-Ocean* printed a sample ballot which included instructions on "How to Vote AGAINST DENEEN And Yet Vote The REPUBLICAN TICKET." [117]

On election day, while it predicted a "smashing victory for Governor Deneen," the *Record-Herald* still noted "a swishing sound, as of the sharpening of knives," arising from the Lorimer wards.[118] And the cutting occurred, as Deneen lost the city of Chicago to Stevenson, running over 9 percentage points behind Republican presidential nominee William Howard Taft. Deneen finally won the election by his downstate majorities, but his total was 83,953 votes less than his 1904 vote.[119] "The fight on the Governor here [Chicago] was the most distinct lineup we have ever seen," wrote William C. Boyden to William Kent. "The trade of Bryan for Stevenson was the most open ever known. In the Lorimer wards, in the forenoon of election-day, there were open offers of two Taft votes for one Stevenson vote." [120]

But there was more than factional politics involved in the willingness of some Republicans to vote for Stevenson. Cultural conflict was also a factor. Deneen was touched with the image of the coercive reformer, while Stevenson ran on a personal-liberty platform. The Deneen forces were conscious of this element. Roy O. West, Deneen's campaign manager, observed that the Governor's "chief obstacle in

116 *Dillingham Committee Hearings*, V, 4264–65, 4279 (Thomas Tippit testifying), VIII, 7864–65.

117 *Inter-Ocean*, Oct. 27, 30, 1908; Chicago *Examiner*, Oct. 30, 1908.

118 *Record-Herald*, Nov. 3, 1908; *Tribune*, Oct. 25, 27, 29, 30, Nov. 1, 1908.

119 Deneen had 45.3 percent of the Chicago vote to 54.5 percent for Taft. Stevenson had 47.2 percent of the Chicago vote and Bryan 38 percent. *Daily News Almanac for 1909*, 382.

120 William C. Boyden to William Kent, Nov. 7, 1908, Kent Papers; Louis F. Post to William Jennings Bryan, Nov. 12, 1908, Louis F. Post Papers, Library of Congress.

this campaign is likely to be the demon rum." [121] Stevenson also appealed to those Democrats who objected to Democratic presidential candidate William Jennings Bryan because of his evangelical Protestant tendencies, and he ran 9 percentage points ahead of Bryan in Chicago.[122] A large source of Stevenson's Chicago strength was those voters who had backed Yates in the Republican primary. The Democratic candidate's vote correlated at +.550 with the Yates primary vote, while Deneen's vote correlated with the Yates primary vote at —.661.

In the state's attorney race, both the Democratic candidate, Jacob J. Kern, and the Republican Wayman were "wets," and large numbers of pietistic Republicans voted for the Prohibitionist, who secured 11.2 percent of the county vote. The Prohibitionist vote correlated at +.676 with the Deneen vote, showing the cultural roots of his support, and at +.681 with the Healy primary vote. Wayman, who emerged the victor, drew his support from a different base than he had in the primary. His vote in the general election correlated negatively with his vote in the primary, but positively with the Healy primary vote. A number of Republicans overcame their aversion to Wayman's opposition to Sunday closing to vote a straight party ticket.[123]

The events of the 1904–08 period revealed Lorimer's considerable strength, in spite of the fact that he was no longer boss. Notwithstanding the many predictions of his demise made after Deneen's victory in 1904, Lorimer had revived by carefully building upon his base of West Side wards and utilizing his ties with the federal machine to restore his organization. Lorimer also benefited from the controversial nature of Deneen's reform program, as the Governor's proposals created bitter political enemies. Possibly even more important in eroding Deneen's strength was the intrusion of cultural issues such as prohibition into Illinois politics, and Lorimer astutely capitalized upon such questions in the Republican primary. Yates's near victory in the 1908 Republican primary testified to the diligence of Lorimer's rebuilding effort.

[121] *Tribune,* Oct. 17, 1908.

[122] Macrae and Neldrum, "Critical Elections in Illinois," 679; Paolo E. Coletta, *William Jennings Byran I,* 433–435.

[123] Wayman had 48.6 percent of the Cook County vote and 46.9 percent of the Chicago vote; Kern had 35.9 percent of the Cook County vote and 36.2 percent of the Chicago vote; the Prohibitionist had 11.2 percent in Cook County and 10.3 percent in Chicago.

But, because he had come so close to defeating Deneen and yet failed, Lorimer was left in a bitter and dangerous mood. He believed that he had been deprived of victory by the treason of Hopkins and Busse. That he won his own congressional contest by his largest margin offered slight comfort. Lorimer now determined to prevent Hopkins' re-election as senator and to harass Deneen during his second term.

★ ★ ★ ★ ★ ★ ★ ★ ★ ★ ★

CHAPTER 9

William Lorimer: U.S. Senator from Illinois

THROUGHOUT THE NATION during the winter and spring of 1908–09, struggles between opposing political factions upset the normal patterns of two-party politics.[1] Historians have generally interpreted these conflicts in ideological terms as pitting progressives against conservatives, but this narrow framework overlooks important cultural and sectional divisions. While issues such as the direct primary, civil service, women's rights, and business regulation split political groups, questions such as local option and prohibition, rural-urban tension, and the cultural overtones of many progressive reforms intensified the competition. Bitter personal rivalries, devoid of ideological or cultural content, also played an important role.

Both political parties in the Forty-sixth Illinois General Assembly split over regional and cultural as well as political questions. The divisions were most marked in the Assembly or lower house. The Republican delegation divided into three factions which, for the sake of convenience, will be called the Deneen, the Lorimer, and the Hopkins factions. There were about fifty Deneenites, about thirty Lorimerites, and approximately twenty-five men tied to Hopkins, although lines were not always rigid between the three groups. For, as Democratic boss Roger C. Sullivan commented, "Well, sometimes they are enemies and sometimes they are friends . . . the checkerboard is moving all the time . . . and the men who are strong enemies to-day may be friendly six months from now." [2]

---

[1] Mowry, *The Era of Theodore Roosevelt,* 72–82; Russel B. Nye, *Midwestern Progressive Politics: A Historical Study of Its Origins and Development 1870–1958* (Harper Torchbook ed., New York, 1965), 212–214.
[2] *Dillingham Committee Hearings,* V, 4403; *Tribune,* Nov. 6, 13, 1908; Hutchinson, *Lowden,* I, 179.

The "Band of Hope," as the Governor's followers were known, composed the "progressive" group in the Assembly. Many of the Deneenites were first- or second-term members, some without previous political experience. Twelve of the fifty were from Cook County and half of them represented upper-class or wealthy suburban areas. The "Band of Hope" supported Deneen's legislative program and reforms such as the direct primary and civil service extension. Most of the members of the Deneen faction who had been in the Forty-fifth General Assembly voted for the local-option bill.[3]

The group of assemblymen obligated to Hopkins included the followers of Mayor Fred Busse and Postmaster Dan Campbell of Chicago. Observers assumed that the Deneenites and the Hopkins faction would cooperate out of necessity but there was considerable friction between the two. Many of the "Hopers" disliked Hopkins' conservative Senate record and his political methods in the state, while Busse and Campbell distrusted Deneen. In addition, Busse hesitated about alienating any powerful group in the legislature and sparking a retaliatory investigation into his vulnerable Chicago administration.[4]

The Lorimer faction included those assemblymen personally loyal to the Congressman, the followers of Edward D. Shurtleff, speaker in the previous session, and the friends of Richard Yates. Approximately half the group came from Cook County and it included several eastern European Jews and a Bohemian. All of the Lorimerites who had been in the Forty-fifth General Assembly voted against the direct primary and over half of them voted against local option. Their stands on the so-called progressive legislative measures caused the reform press to label them as "reactionaries." [5]

While issues such as the direct primary, statewide civil service, and local-option legislation continued to divide the three factions in the Forty-sixth General Assembly, new questions had also arisen. The Deneen and the Lorimer factions, for instance, disagreed about how to spend the $20,000,000 waterway bond money and each submitted rival plans to the General Assembly. In addition, the Lorimerites

---

[3] There are biographies of the members of the General Assembly in James A. Rose, comp., *Illinois Blue Book 1909*, 196–247; *House Journal, Forty-fifth General Assembly*, 987, 1484.

[4] *Tribune*, Dec. 6, 17, 20, 1908; Hutchinson, *Lowden*, I, 179.

[5] Rose, comp., *Illinois Blue Book 1909*, 196–247; *House Journal, Forty-fifth General Assembly*, 987, 1484; *Record-Herald*, Jan. 7, 1909.

supported a Democratic challenge to the validity of the 1908 gubernatorial returns. And, on the senatorial question, the Lorimer
followers opposed Hopkins' return, while the Deneen faction split,
with many members favoring Foss. On most of these questions aside
from the Senate election, the Hopkins group moved in the direction
that best suited its interests.

The Democrats in the Assembly also suffered from disunity. There
were three Democratic factions: the Browne, the Tippit, and the Sullivan. Of the approximately thirty members of the Browne faction,
about one third came from Cook County; the eight Sullivan men were
Chicagoans; and most of the twenty-six members of the Tippit faction
were from downstate.

The major issue between the Browne and the Tippit groups was
the liquor question. Lee O'Neil Browne was an attorney for the
Liquor Dealers' Protective Association of Illinois and supposedly the
choice of the brewing interests for Democratic minority leader.[6] Assemblyman Anton J. Cermak, secretary of the powerful United Societies for Local Self-Government, supported Browne for this position.
Thomas G. Tippit, on the other hand, represented those downstate
Democrats "who did not believe in being dictated to or turning over
the democratic organization of Illinois to . . . [the brewing] interests." [7]

The Sullivan Democrats, however, complicated this neat dichot-
omy. They were beholden to boss Roger C. Sullivan, Illinois Democratic national committeeman, who opposed the selection of Browne
as minority leader. The friction between Browne and Sullivan, however, was personal and political and had nothing to do with issues.
For although they allied with the Tippit faction on some questions,
the Sullivanites opposed any liquor legislation.[8]

Uniting the three Democratic factions was a hatred of Hopkins and
a desire to unseat Deneen and make Stevenson governor. Hopkins'
record of vilification of the Democratic party made him the state's
most unpopular Republican among the Democrats. George W. Alschuler, for instance, Democratic assemblyman from Hopkins' home

[6] *Dillingham Committee Hearings*, V, 4254, 4261 (Thomas Tippit testifying),
4939 (Lee O'Neil Browne testifying).

[7] *Ibid.*, 4254 (Thomas Tippit testifying).

[8] *Ibid.*, 4260 (Thomas Tippit testifying), 4879, 4881 (Lee O'Neil Browne testifying).

town of Aurora, ran for the General Assembly solely to organize opposition to Hopkins' re-election.[9] The Democrats also hoped to unite with the anti-Deneen Republicans to unseat the Governor and put Stevenson in his place.

The Forty-sixth Illinois General Assembly therefore presented a shifting factional mosaic. The most critical questions involved the seating of Deneen, the election of a U.S. senator, and Deneen's legislative program; they were complicated matters that promised no easy solutions. The actions of men and of factions were unpredictable and would be swayed by many influences, including personal and cultural as well as political and ideological factors.

Deneen's precarious position caused him and his lieutenants to make unusual efforts to capture the organization of both houses of the General Assembly. In the Senate, where the Lorimerites were weak, the so-called "yearling insurrection" secured the important committees and pledged a liberal rules revision.[10] In the House, Deneen intervened directly to prevent Shurtleff's re-election as speaker. The Governor and his lieutenants used personal pressure and patronage to force House members to pledge to abide by the Republican caucus choice of a speaker. On December 1, 1908, the Deneenites announced that forty-eight Republicans, more than a caucus majority, had signed.[11]

But while Deneen had his majority, his methods created much animosity. Senator Cullom wrote Federal Judge J. Otis Humphrey that there was "considerable feeling against him [Deneen] in the legislature, almost to the extent of swearing vengeance against him. I doubt a little whether Deneen's action in trying to control the legislature by whatever means he can will result in any good to the party. He ought to have some regard for the constitution and the rights of the legislative department . . . and not stoop to the lowest kind of politics to control it." [12] Shurtleff angrily told a caucus of his supporters that "the unfair, un-American, and un-Republican method

---

[9] *Ibid.*, 4276 (Thomas Tippit testifying), VI, 6077, 6079, 6083 (George Alschuler testifying).

[10] *Tribune*, Nov. 15, 19, 1908.

[11] *Ibid.*, Nov. 15, 19, Dec. 2, 1908; *Inter-Ocean*, Dec. 3, 1908; *Dillingham Committee Hearings*, II, 1088 (Deneen testifying), V, 4558 (Shurtleff testifying), VII, 7132–58 (Morton D. Hull testifying), VII, 7162–65 (John Wilkes Ford, Jr., testifying), VIII, 7200 (John L. Flannigen testifying).

[12] Cullom to Humphrey, Nov. 11, 1908, Henry Emrich to Cullom, Nov. 2, 1908, Cullom Papers.

that has been resorted to to defeat me for speaker . . . will in the end defeat itself," and rumors circulated in Springfield that he would appeal to the Democrats for votes.[13]

On January 4, the fifty-five Deneen assemblymen chose Edward J. King of Galesburg, Deneen's personal choice, as their candidate for speaker. King offered Shurtleff a share of committee chairmanships and patronage if he would withdraw his candidacy, but Shurtleff refused. Shurtleff, who found King personally as well as politically objectionable, had conferred with Lorimer and they had decided to try for election with Democratic votes. The next afternoon, thirty-two Republicans, supposedly at Lorimer's instructions, bolted the caucus.[14]

That evening, January 5, the Democrats met to choose a minority leader and candidate for speaker. The competition was between Thomas Tippit and Lee O'Neil Browne, but Tippit upset the caucus by presenting a resolution calling for Shurtleff's election as speaker. Browne vehemently protested and, at the request of Charles Boeschenstein, chairman of the Democratic state central committee, Tippit withdrew his motion. The caucus then elected Browne minority leader.[15]

Browne's objections to Tippit's motion, however, did not signify opposition to Shurtleff. Browne had already promised Shurtleff his support for the speakership, and he and Tippit now joined to ask the Democrats to support the Republican.[16] There was little dissent; most Democrats thought well of Shurtleff and also saw his election as a means to disrupt the Republican party. In addition, Shurtleff promised the Democrats patronage and choice committee assignments in return for their backing.[17]

On January 6, after standing for Browne for two ballots, fifty-nine

[13] *Inter-Ocean*, Dec. 3, 5, 1908; *Tribune*, Dec. 3, 18, 21, 1908, Jan. 1, 1909. Thirty-two Republican assemblymen also announced that they would vote with the Democrats in demanding a recount of the gubernatorial ballots.

[14] *Post*, Jan. 5–6, 1909; *Record-Herald*, Jan. 6, 1909; *Tribune*, Jan. 5–6, 1909; *Dillingham Committee Hearings*, II, 1086, 1208–09 (Deneen testifying), V, 4559, 4563 (Shurtleff testifying), VII, 7203 (John L. Flannigen testifying). Lorimer denied that he was involved in planning the bolt. See *ibid.*, VIII, 7395–96. Shurtleff held a conference with Busse in Chicago in December and at that time Busse promised to keep his men out of the caucus. *Ibid.*, V, 4557–58 (Shurtleff testifying).

[15] *Ibid.*, V, 4243–46 (Thomas Tippit testifying); *Record-Herald* and *Tribune*, Jan. 6, 1909.

[16] *Dillingham Committee Hearings*, V, 4867 (Lee O'Neil Browne testifying).

[17] For Shurtleff's popularity with the Democrats see *ibid.*, IV, 3302 (Daniel D. Donahue testifying), IV, 3871 (Robert E. Wilson testifying), VI, 5422, 5432–33

Democrats threw their votes to Shurtleff, and the "Band of Hope" became the "Band of Lost Hope." In addition to the fifty-nine Democrats, twenty-five Republicans voted for Shurtleff, and for the first time in Illinois history the House was organized on bipartisan lines.[18]

Shurtleff's bipartisan election greatly complicated the senatorial picture. If Democrats joined with Republicans to elect a speaker, might not they also do so to elect a senator? "Shurtleff has just been elected Speaker of the House," wrote Judge K. M. Landis to Lowden. "As I understand it this means that 'hell has broke loose.' I do not see how it is possible the Senatorship has failed to become involved in the fuss . . . everybody seems to regard Hopkins' re-election as seriously jeopardized."[19] But before the senatorial balloting began, Deneen had to be declared governor, and even this was uncertain.

Deneen thought Shurtleff's election the prelude to an attempt to oust him as governor. He and his lieutenants suspected that the Republican-Democratic coalition planned to seize control of the joint session of the General Assembly that would canvass the returns, recognize Adlai Stevenson's contest petition, and make him governor. In order to block such a move, the Senate, which Deneen controlled, refused to attend the joint session until Shurtleff promised fair play. Deneen would agree to a recount of the vote, but only after he was declared elected.[20]

On January 13, Lorimer, Roger C. Sullivan, and House Democratic and Republican leaders met and agreed to Deneen's condition. The joint session canvassed the returns, declared Deneen elected, and temporarily filed Stevenson's contest petition.[21] Deneen, however, still

---

(John Griffin testifying), VI, 6113, 6116–17 (George Alschuler testifying). For the agreement on patronage and committee assignments see *ibid.*, V, 4248–50 (Thomas Tippit testifying), V, 4867, 4874–75 (Lee O'Neil Browne testfying).

[18] *House Journal, Forty-sixth General Assembly* (Springfield, 1909), 6–13; *Tribune*, Jan. 7, 1909.

[19] K. M. Landis to Lowden, Wednesday [Jan. 6, 1909], W. D. Mack to James R. Cowley, Jan. 4, 1909, Lowden Papers. Lowden had a representative in Springfield, John A. Corwin, during the course of the senatorial election. His letters, and also those of James R. Cowley, furnish an almost daily, and sometimes hourly, record of the early months of the contest. Many of the letters are dated with only the day of the week, but in most cases their contents give a clue to the correct date. See Hutchinson, *Lowden*, I, 180.

[20] *House Journal, Forty-sixth General Assembly*, 15, 17, 22; *Post*, Jan. 7, 1909; *Inter-Ocean* and *Tribune*, Jan. 8, 1909

[21] *Senate Journal, Forty-sixth General Assembly*, 46–47; *Post*, Jan. 11–12, 1909; *Tribune*, Jan. 13, 1909.

faced ouster at any time by the bipartisan coalition; Lorimer and Shurtleff undoubtedly intended to use the threat to wring concessions from the Governor.

Deneen's position was further threatened when, on January 12 in the Republican state central committee meeting, the Hopkins faction refused to support the Governor's request for a caucus agreement on legislation and committee appointments. Hopkins, believing he could count on Deneen's support for the senatorship, did not want to antagonize Shurtleff.[22] Unexpectedly confronted by the erosion of his forces and badly in need of allies, Deneen decided to make overtures to Lorimer. The two had been close political friends for years; perhaps they could restore the alliance.

At five o'clock on the evening of January 13, for the first time in five years, Lorimer and Deneen met for a private conference; it was the beginning of a series of meetings that continued until May. As the two rivals, one the leader of the state's progressive forces, the other the state's most noted machine politician, talked, they moved warily from reminiscences into the discussion of issues such as the waterway, the primary law, and Hopkins' and Busse's negative attitude toward the Governor. If the two can be believed, neither mentioned the gubernatorial contest or the Senate election, although these were important topics in later conversations.[23] The meeting ended without any definite plans, but Lorimer and Deneen had established the basis for future communications.

In the meantime, the senatorial balloting approached; Hopkins was a shaky favorite, and Deneen, Shurtleff, and Congressmen George E. Foss, Frank O. Lowden, and William B. McKinley were mentioned as possible alternatives. Both the *Tribune* and the *Record-Herald* suggested that Lorimer might be elected, but he denied that he wanted the post.[24] Two theories of the primary law complicated the election: that legislators should vote for Hopkins because he had won a statewide primary majority, and that they should vote according to their district majorities. Before the primary Hopkins had re-

[22] *Dillingham Committee Hearings,* II, 1089–90, 1106–09, 1225–27 (Deneen testifying), VIII, 7400; *Record-Herald* and *Tribune,* Jan. 3, 1909.

[23] Deneen said it was Roy O. West who first suggested the meetings. See *Dillingham Committee Hearings,* II, 1099–1110, 1193–94 (Deneen testifying), VIII, 7399–7401. Lorimer said that much of the first conversation was concerned with ways and means to block Busse's increasing Chicago power

[24] *Record-Herald* and *Tribune,* Jan. 15, 1909.

fused to bind himself to its results, but he now insisted that it made his election mandatory. Few members agreed; they would vote as they saw fit. Hopkins' attempt to force a senatorial caucus failed, and his prospects grew more uncertain.[25]

Lorimer directed the anti-Hopkins campaign. "I was opposed to Mr. Hopkins from the time I found out how he had acted in the Yates campaign," Lorimer later related, "and I was willing to cooperate with anybody to defeat Mr. Hopkins at any time." [26] There were no other roots to Lorimer's opposition; he admitted that he and Hopkins agreed on the "essentials of government." In combating Hopkins, Lorimer added to his own forces some members of the "Band of Hope" who found Hopkins unpalatable. These legislators represented districts that Foss won in the primary, and they claimed they were abiding by their primary instructions in voting for him.[27]

Lorimer had thus developed a force that could possibly deadlock the senatorial contest. The test of his group's cohesiveness came on January 19, when the two houses of the General Assembly balloted separately on the senatorship. Lorimer's bloc held firm: Hopkins received a majority in the Senate, but fell sixteen short in the House.[28] That night only 75 of the 126 Republican members attended a senatorial caucus, and Lorimer appeared close to vindication.[29]

The Assembly vote was unusual in that seventeen of the legislators who had supported Shurtleff for speaker voted for Hopkins and fifteen members of the "Band of Hope" supported candidates other than Hopkins. Eleven "Hopers" voted for Foss and claimed they were obeying their primary instructions, but the vote also suggested Deneen's lack of enthusiasm for the Senator. Lorimer later claimed that the Governor could have elected Hopkins on the first ballot, and this was possibly so.[30] Until the disposal of the gubernatorial contest, however, Deneen and his followers would attempt to forestall Hopkins' election. Deneen claimed that his lieutenants feared that Hopkins' men might join with the Lorimerites and the Democrats to

[25] *Dillingham Committee Hearings*, V, 4517–18 (Ira C. Copley testifying), VIII, 7696; *Tribune*, Jan. 15–16, 1909.

[26] *Dillingham Committee Hearings*, VIII, 7447, 7685–87, 7713.

[27] *Tribune*, Jan. 21, 1909.

[28] *House Journal, Forty-sixth General Assembly*, 68–69; *Senate Journal, Forty-sixth General Assembly*, 96–97.

[29] *Post*, Jan. 19, 1909; *Tribune*, Jan. 20, 1909.

[30] *Dillingham Committee Hearings*, VIII, 7711.

Chicago *Tribune*, Jan. 19, 1909

install Stevenson as governor; until Hopkins pledged to support Deneen, the Governor would play coy.[31]

While Deneen helped block Hopkins' re-election, Lorimer and others began a movement to make the Governor senator. Lorimer suggested this to Deneen at one of their conferences and promised his support. With Deneen senator, Lieutenant Governor John G. Oglesby, a member of the Lorimer faction, would become the chief executive and Lorimer would regain statewide influence.[32] Lorimer would also get his waterway scheme through the legislature without fear of a veto. As things stood, however, the waterway was stalemated, with the Deneen-sponsored Schmitt bill in the Senate and a Lorimer-sponsored measure in the Assembly. The Schmitt bill provided for a state-built fourteen-foot waterway aimed toward the production of water power, while Lorimer's measure forbade the expenditure of state money without federal cooperation.[33]

Deneen rejected the idea of his becoming senator as "imbecilic, idiotic, and insane." With Oglesby governor, Lorimer would again dominate the state Republican party and, through the waterway, have access to ample patronage and lucrative contracts.[34] The newspaper publishers and editors who supported Deneen, especially Victor Lawson of the *Daily News* and Frank B. Noyes of the *Record-Herald,* were adamant against Deneen accepting. "Lawson will never permit Deneen to be Senator & turn [the] state over to Lorimer and John Oglesby," wrote one knowledgeable Springfield political observer to Frank O. Lowden. "The newspaper bosses in Chicago are standing that off." [35]

On January 20, the House and Senate met in joint session and took

[31] *Ibid.,* II, 1141–42 (Deneen testifying), VIII, 7400–7401, 7411. Douglas Southerland, the Springfield reporter for the *Evening Post,* told the author on Feb. 21, 1961, that Deneen had never really been for Hopkins.

[32] *Dillingham Committee Hearings,* VIII, 7414.

[33] Deneen's plan had been drawn up by Isham Randolph, chief engineer of the Chicago Sanitary District. Lorimer's plan was the work of Lyman E. Cooley. For the plans in the General Assembly see *House Journal, Forty-sixth General Assembly,* 303; *Senate Journal, Forty-sixth General Assembly,* 165; *Dillingham Committee Hearings,* II, 1214–20 (Deneen testifying), VIII, 7442–43; *Tribune,* Jan. 29, Mar. 19, 1909.

[34] *Dillingham Committee Hearings,* II, 1221–23 (Deneen testifying); *Record-Herald,* Jan. 7, 1909; *Tribune,* Jan. 21, Feb. 28, 1909; "The Revolt of the Illinois Legislature," *The World Today* (Feb., 1909), XVI, 130–132. Lorimer supposedly told Deneen that he could appoint the state waterway commission if the Governor would approve Lorimer's waterway plan.

[35] John A. Corwin to Lowden, Jan. 29, 30, 1909, Andrew J. Lester to Lowden, Jan. 29, 1909, Lowden Papers.

five senatorial ballots; Hopkins' total fell from eighty-nine on the first to eighty-five on the last. Several other Republicans also received votes, including Shurtleff, Mason, and Congressmen Foss, Lowden, and W. B. McKinley.[36] The press mentioned Congressman Rodenberg and W. J. Calhoun as likely dark-horse candidates. Concerned over his vote loss, Hopkins frantically attempted to get legislators to pledge to deadlock the General Assembly until he was elected; Busse and Campbell descended on Springfield to help, but to little avail. Seven ballots on January 21 resulted in no important change in the totals, and the General Assembly adjourned until the 26th.[37]

On Friday, January 21, satisfied with the situation, Lorimer left for Washington, accompanied by rumors that he was going to contact Lowden or some other possible candidate. Hopkins telegraphed Lowden that Lorimer was on his way "to get you or some other Congressman to enter the field against me," but warned that "Busse, Campbell and Deneen have United to Elect me I have the votes and shall win. . . ."[38] Lorimer, however, when questioned, insisted that waterway matters brought him to Washington. The deadlock, he said, was "an enigma which I am not able to solve at present, nor is anybody else whom I have seen able to do so. It is simply impossible to tell what is going to happen."[39]

Lorimer's statement was no doubt straightforward, but obviously he would attempt to shape the situation. By Sunday he was back in Springfield, conferring with Shurtleff, Browne, and other members of the legislature. Lorimer shared Shurtleff's suite of rooms at the St. Nicholas Hotel and he met with the Speaker and with Browne at least once every day that he was in Springfield. On Tuesday night Lorimer spoke with Deneen, as did Hopkins, Busse, and Foss, but the conferences changed nothing. The deadlock continued throughout the week and Hopkins reached a low of seventy-two votes on Thursday. Clifford S. Raymond, writing in the *Tribune*, compared Lorimer

[36] *House Journal, Forty-sixth General Assembly*, 74–82.

[37] *Ibid.*, 84–97; *Post, Record-Herald*, and *Tribune*, Jan. 21–23, 1909.

[38] Hopkins to Lowden, Jan. 23, 1909, John A. Corwin to Lowden, Jan. 24, 1909, Lowden Papers; *Record-Herald*, Jan. 24, 1909. Lowden was probably the most prominent of the dark-horse candidates. He took the position, however, that he would not try for the senatorship until Hopkins was out of the race. "If it shall finally appear that Hopkins cannot be elected," wrote Lowden, "there may be an opportunity; if so we ought to seize it." See Lowden to K. M. Landis, Feb. 6, 1909, to J. L. Pickering, Mar. 2, 1909, Lowden Papers.

[39] *Tribune*, Jan. 25, 1909.

to a "great human magnet [who] drew the Hopkins vote away by threes and fours. . . ." [40] John A. Corwin, Lowden's political observer in Springfield, wrote him that Hopkins was "dead" and that Lorimer had the *only deliverable strength.*" [41]

The chief talk of the following week concerned Hopkins' possible election by Democratic votes. A group of Democrats formed the "Fourteen Club" (Hopkins needed approximately fourteen votes to win) and supposedly offered their votes for sale. Colonel Ira C. Copley, one of Hopkins' bitterest foes, heard of the movement and told Shurtleff and Deneen. He also telephoned Roger C. Sullivan to come to Springfield and prevent the defection. Sullivan, Shurtleff, and Deneen halted the plan and the "Fourteen Club" dissolved.[42]

The weekend of February 6–7 found Hopkins and Lorimer in Washington, Lorimer because of waterway affairs, Hopkins to seek the aid of the outgoing President and whoever else would help. They returned to Springfield on Monday preceded by stories that the February 10 vote would be crucial. Several factors indicated this. On February 9 Theodore Roosevelt declared for Hopkins' re-election because of his primary victory and because he had been a "constant and loyal" supporter of Roosevelt's policies.[43] On the same day, a *Tribune* editorial called for Hopkins' re-election for the identical reasons. Lorimer confirmed the importance of the vote on the 10th, and predicted Hopkins' defeat if he did not win on that day.[44]

Preparations were again made to halt Hopkins. The *Record-Herald,* probably at Deneen's instigation, editorialized that Hopkins

[40] *Ibid.,* Jan. 28, 1909.

[41] John A. Corwin to Lowden, Friday [Jan. 29, 1909], Lowden Papers; *Tribune,* Jan. 28, 29, 1909; *House Journal, Forty-sixth General Assembly,* 127.

[42] John A. Corwin to James R. Cowley, Feb. 6, 1909, Corwin to Lowden, Feb. 15, 1909, Lowden Papers; *Dillingham Committee Hearings,* II, 1920–22 (James Keeley testifying), III, 2276–78 (Lawrence B. Stringer testifying), V, 4373 (Roger C. Sullivan testifying), V, 4523–26 (Ira C. Copley testifying), V, 4570 (Shurtleff testifying), VII, 6831 (Homer E. Shaw testifying). Hopkins denied he tried to secure Democratic votes. See *ibid.,* I, 316, 318–320.

[43] *Post,* Feb. 5, 1909; *Inter-Ocean* and *News,* Feb. 8, 1909; *Tribune,* Feb. 9, 1909; J. R. C. [James R. Cowley], "Memo for Mr. Lowden," [n.d.], John A. Corwin to Cowley, Feb. 9, 1909, Lowden Papers; Theodore Roosevelt to Cornelius J. Ton, Feb. 15, 1909, *Roosevelt Letters,* VI, 1521; A. C. Bartlett to Albert J. Beveridge, Feb. 27, 1909, Beveridge Papers. The Beveridge Papers contain a number of letters on the senatorial deadlock from A. C. Bartlett, a Chicago businessman, and John C. Shaffer, publisher of the *Evening Post,* to Beveridge. Both Bartlett and Shaffer were mentioned as possible candidates to break the deadlock.

[44] *Tribune,* Feb. 8, 1909; see also Ira C. Copley to Mrs. Copley, Feb. 8, 1909, Copley Papers.

was not the party choice; Roy O. West, Republican state central committee chairman, went to California to escape Hopkins' ire; and Browne warned the Democrats to stay in their own camp. The February 10 vote produced no substantial change; on the next day Hopkins received only fifty-six votes on the thirty-first joint ballot, his lowest total yet.[45] That evening, for the first time, Lorimer announced he believed Hopkins "undoubtedly beaten." He told his lieutenant Harry B. Ward that there would be no election until after the presidential inauguration in March, and that he had no candidate. Knowledgeable Springfield political observers agreed with this diagnosis, as did Washington opinion.[46]

As the senatorial contest moved from ballot to ballot with little substantial change, other matters involved the General Assembly. Shurtleff and Lieutenant Governor Oglesby appointed a joint contest committee which commenced hearings on February 18. Assemblymen friendly to Deneen were a majority on the committee, indicating that Lorimer and Shurtleff had decided to remove the threat of ouster.[47] A joint waterway committee also began hearings, and on February 17 heard Lorimer testify on the need for federal-state waterway cooperation. In Washington the House Committee on Rivers and Harbors reported a bill containing several Lorimer provisions to advance the waterway project.[48]

On February 25, the Illinois Senate agreed not to conduct any business until March 10. Since Hopkins' term expired on March 4, he would become an "ex"-senator. Conferences held in Springfield, Chicago, and Washington during the interim failed to solve the deadlock. Lorimer, Hopkins, and Copley each spent hours speaking to Deneen. Hopkins tried to enlist President Taft's aid but the new executive refused to intervene. "Taft is for Hopkins," lamely announced the Senator's supporters, "and is his personal friend. . . . Senator Hopkins does not ask President Taft to meddle in the Illinois

[45] John A. Corwin to James R. Cowley, Feb. 9 (one letter, one telegram), Feb. 10, 1909, Lowden Papers; *Dillingham Committee Hearings*, VIII, 7423; *House Journal, Forty-sixth General Assembly*, 168–170, 176–177.

[46] John A. Corwin to James R. Cowley, Feb. 11, 1909, Lowden Papers; Albert J. Beveridge to A. C. Bartlett, Feb. 11, 1909, Beveridge Papers; *Tribune*, Feb. 12, 1909.

[47] *House Journal, Forty-sixth General Assembly*, 163–165, 173–174; *Senate Journal, Forty-sixth General Assembly*, 259–260; *Dillingham Committee Hearings*, II, 1251–59 (Deneen testifying); *Post*, Feb. 10, 1909; *News*, Feb. 11, 1909; *Record-Herald*, Feb. 14, 1909.

[48] *Tribune*, Feb. 18, 20, 1909.

contest, but is satisfied to have his moral support." [49] Moral support, however, was insufficient, and when the balloting resumed on March 10 the deadlock still held.

During the weeks of March 15 and 22, an attempt to elect Deneen as senator nearly broke the impasse. On March 18, a joint session of the General Assembly adopted the majority report of the Stevenson contest committee, which found insufficient grounds for a recount. Deneen's title was secure.[50] That evening, Deneen, Roy O. West, and Lorimer met, and, according to Lorimer, Deneen agreed to accept the senatorship. By March 23 Lorimer and West had lined up 160 votes, more than enough to elect. Late that night, however, West told Lorimer that Deneen's election was off. Lorimer hurried over to the executive mansion, where Deneen reported that his Chicago newspaper "friends" were unwilling to give control of the state government to Lorimer and Oglesby. Deneen would remain governor.[51]

With Deneen's withdrawal, Lorimer suggested other names to the Governor. Over a period of three weeks during April while the deadlock continued, they discussed Shurtleff, Chicago businessman A. C. Bartlett, W. J. Calhoun, and Congressmen Boutell, Lowden, McKinley, and Rodenberg. Lorimer preferred Shurtleff, but Deneen balked; his feud with the Speaker could not be compromised. Deneen also objected to most of the other men either because they were unknown or too close to Lorimer or Busse, while Lorimer refused to consider Calhoun.[52] According to Lorimer, the Governor urged him to become a candidate; he felt they had worked together in the past and could in the future. But Lorimer demurred—he had seniority and influence in the House of Representatives and he wanted to complete the waterway; this meant more to him, he said, than being senator.[53]

The inability of Lorimer and Deneen to agree upon a candidate

49 *Ibid.*, Feb. 26, Mar. 3, 8, 9, 1909; *Inter-Ocean*, Feb. 27, 1909; *Record-Herald*, Mar. 6, 1909; *House Journal, Forty-sixth General Assembly*, 267–268.

50 *House Journal, Forty-sixth General Assembly*, 307–311, 316–317.

51 Charles H. May to Lowden, Mar. 18, 1909, W. Schwartze to James R. Cowley, Mar. 24, 1909, Lowden Papers; *Dillingham Committee Hearings*, VIII, 7416–21; *Inter-Ocean, Record-Herald*, and *Tribune*, Mar. 24, 1909.

52 A. C. Bartlett to Albert J. Beveridge, Feb. 15, Apr. 12, 1909, Beveridge Papers; *Dillingham Committee Hearings*, VII, 7425–29. Calhoun's name was suggested to Lorimer by William G. Beale, a Chicago *Tribune* trustee.

53 *Dillingham Committee Hearings*, II, 1124, 1134, 1311 (Deneen testifying), VII, 7424; *Post*, Mar. 27, 1909. Deneen denied that he had encouraged Lorimer to seek the senatorship.

appeared to preclude the deadlock's settlement that session. Unless the two joined forces, or unless the Democrats voted for a Republican, Hopkins could prevent a choice. And neither Lorimer nor Deneen would support a candidate that would increase the strength of the other.[54] In the meantime, the General Assembly was stalemated.

The deadlock's continuation concerned Washington as well as Illinois. Senator Cullom complained that "we ought to elect some first-class man, whoever he may be, and send him down here for work. There is plenty for him to do. Matters are held up awaiting the result of the contest." [55] Illinois business interests were bothered because the state was not fully represented in the crucial congressional tariff debate. The House passed the Payne bill, which accomplished "substantial reductions" in rates, in early April, while Senator Nelson Aldrich introduced his tariff bill into the Senate on April 12. The Aldrich measure contained several hundred upward revisions over the Payne bill, causing a heated Senate struggle between low-tariff Republican insurgents and the regular organization.[56] Hopkins, a strong protectionist with close steel connections, would undoubtedly have supported Aldrich, but most senators acknowledged the impossibility of Hopkins' re-election. With every tariff vote crucial, the Old Guard leadership hoped to find a suitable replacement.

Lorimer understood the importance of the tariff fight and the need for a second Illinois senator in Washington. A protectionist, he had opposed cutting tariff rates in the House and voted for higher duties on goods such as lumber and hides.[57] In the beginning of April, Lorimer's friend, Edward Hines, president of the National Lumber Manufacturers' Association and Washington lobbyist for a high lumber rate, told Lorimer that Senators Nelson Aldrich and Bosie Penrose wanted his help in electing a conservative Illinois Republican. Hines also said that Aldrich told him that the President wanted a senator chosen as quickly as possible. Lorimer and Hines discussed several candidates who were protectionists and Lorimer suggested them to Deneen, but the Governor was unenthusiastic. In further conversa-

---

[54] Frederick H. Smith to Lowden, Apr. 13, 24, 1909, William Meese to Lowden, Apr. 24, 1909, Lowden Papers; A. C. Bartlett to Albert J. Beveridge, Apr. 26, 1909, Beveridge Papers; interview with Douglas Southerland, Feb. 21, 1961, Chicago.

[55] Cullom to Lawrence Y. Sherman, Feb. 24, 1909, Sherman Papers; *Tribune*, Feb. 23, 1909. Hopkins had also requested a halt on post office appointments until the deadlock ended.

[56] Mowry, *The Era of Theodore Roosevelt*, 242–245.

[57] *CR*, 61st Cong., 1st Sess., XLIV, 1299, 1301.

tions, Hines asked Lorimer if he would consider the position, but Lorimer declined; the waterway was too important.[58]

In late April, however, Lorimer reconsidered his decision. The deadlock seemed to preclude victory by any of the announced candidates; Illinois would be without a second senator until the fall legislative session and the Old Guard could be deprived of a crucial vote. Lorimer sympathized with the Senate establishment and was attracted by the prestige and power of the upper house; he could also continue his waterway work in the Senate. As he assessed his chances, he grew cautiously optimistic. Along with the votes of his own faction, he might gain the backing of some of the "Hopers." And, most crucial, his popularity among the Democrats would draw strong support from that quarter.[59]

In the beginning of May, Lorimer began to talk of his candidacy. Around May 10 he met with his leading supporters to count votes and to plan strategy. Shortly after, he secured the critical support of Lee O'Neil Browne by promising that, if elected, he would not aid Browne's Democratic factional rival, Roger C. Sullivan.[60] During the following week, Lorimer and his followers used every art of persuasion and political cajolery to secure votes; all his past favors and friendships now paid off. Lorimer was his own most effective worker; he carefully compiled a card file of legislators and how they could be influenced. "I think I myself knew," said Lorimer, "about the time that I became a candidate, more about the situation and what each man would probably do than almost any man in Springfield." He spoke with nearly every member of the General Assembly: "I will say that I had conference with maybe a dozen men some days and maybe 50 men other days. I had more or less conference all the time. . . . I talked a good deal with members of the legislature during the session—every day, sometimes two or three times." [61] As the days passed, Lorimer accumulated votes, although he would not let his name be voted upon until sure of victory.

On the evening of May 13, Lorimer spoke to Deneen about his

[58] *Dillingham Committee Hearings*, I, 812–817, 821 (Edward Hines testifying), II, 1648–50 (Senator Nelson Aldrich testifying), II, 1791–93 (Senator Bosie Penrose testifying).

[59] *Ibid.*, V, 4577–79 (Shurtleff testifying); *Tribune*, May 10, 1909.

[60] *Dillingham Committee Hearings*, V, 4886–90 (Lee O'Neil Browne testifying), VIII, 7585, 7788.

[61] *Ibid.*, VIII, 7587, 7594. See *ibid.*, 7584–51, for Lorimer's analysis of why men voted for him.

candidacy. According to Lorimer, Deneen promised support and encouraged him to see his followers; if they were hesitant to back Lorimer, said the Governor, he would speak to them. This account, however, seems spurious, and Deneen denied that he had made such a promise. But, regardless of Deneen's attitude, Lorimer discussed his Senate bid with most of the Governor's followers. He believed he could secure some of their votes.[62]

Deneen, faced by Lorimer's election, finally decided that he preferred Hopkins as senator. He knew that Lorimer was a more astute politician than Hopkins and constituted a stronger threat to his state control. On May 25, Hopkins, with the Governor's support, made a last try. He secured eighty-eight votes, but fell fourteen votes short of election. Lorimer concluded that Deneen "could not control the situation" and he could be elected.[63]

A new source of influence aided Lorimer. On May 23, 25, and 26, Lorimer received telegrams from Edward Hines stating that President Taft and Senators Aldrich and Penrose wanted him to become a candidate. "Highest authorities want you elected before legislature adjourns," read the May 25 telegram. "Important Republican Party Illinois politics have strong, experienced man, friendly to powers here, elected immediately; needed here now." [64] Lorimer showed the telegrams to many legislators as evidence of his administration support.[65] Hines called Deneen and told him of Washington's interest in Lorimer, but, according to Lorimer, this information did not change the Governor's attitude.[66]

Whether or not the telegrams swayed many votes is problematical. Lorimer did not believe so: ". . . it was not necessary for me to show them to anybody . . . to get the support of the men that voted for me. They were for me whether Senator Aldrich or Senator Penrose or the President were for me or not." [67] Most likely he was correct. Men supported him because of a multitude of considerations: friendship, promises of patronage, the waterway campaign, and sheer weariness. The last was a critical factor, for the senatorial voting had

[62] *Ibid.*, II, 1135–37 (Deneen testifying), VIII, 7433, 7436–38.
[63] *Ibid.*, VIII, 7438; *House Journal, Forty-sixth General Assembly,* 1023.
[64] Edward Hines to William Lorimer, May 23, 25, 26, 1909, printed in *Dillingham Committee Hearings,* I, 827, 833.
[65] *Ibid.*, VIII, 7461, 7467.
[66] *Ibid.*, I, 833–834 (Hines testifying), II, 1147–50 (Deneen testifying), VIII, 7463–66.
[67] *Ibid.*, VIII, 7468.

degenerated into a farce, as legislators voted for newspaper reporters, clerks, and absent members. Richard Yates, who was in Springfield working for Lorimer's election, related:

> I think they [the legislators] were absolutely tired out. It had gotten to be an absolute joke. Everybody voted for everybody. I think there were 150 of us that got about one vote apiece at a time. It got to the point where the papers had cartoons representing senators as saying: *I vote for that bald-headed man up in the gallery. I vote for that messenger boy coming down the hall,* and so on. It was a well known fact that the legislature was thoroughly tired out, and wanted to settle the matter.[68]

The news that Lorimer expected to secure sixty Democratic votes caused consternation among Democratic party leaders, or at least they made it appear that way. Roger C. Sullivan, Democratic state chairman Charles Boeschenstein, and John McGillen, secretary of the Democratic Cook County committee, instructed the Democrats not to vote for Lorimer. McGillen warned that "ignominious oblivion awaits an act of perfidy on the part of any Democratic legislator in this matter," and sent telegrams asking the Democrats to stick by Democratic senatorial candidate Lawrence B. Stringer.[69] But although Sullivan and the Democratic leaders took a public stand against Lorimer's election, members of the Sullivan, Browne, and Tippit factions prepared to vote for him. Lorimer's willingness to do favors for men regardless of party and his reputation for fairness made him the most popular Republican among Democrats in the state. Lee O'Neil Browne related that "Senator Lorimer was thought very kindly of by the Democrats . . . he was regarded through his bailiwick . . . as almost as much a Democrat as he was a Republican. . . . And he stood very high throughout the State, by his reputation, his life, and his acts politically. He had the reputation—that very few, if any, political leaders in the State of Illinois then had or now have—that he always kept his word." [70] His "indefatigable efforts" for the waterway also convinced many that he had the welfare of the state at heart.[71]

[68] *Ibid.,* I, 262.

[69] *Ibid.,* III, 2322–23 (Lawrence B. Stringer testifying), V, 4377 (Roger C. Sullivan testifying); *Record-Herald,* May 16, 1909; *Tribune,* May 16, 20, 1909.

[70] For Lorimer's popularity with the Democrats see *Dillingham Committee Hearings,* IV, 3201–02 (Thomas Campbell testifying), IV, 3308–09 (Daniel D. Donahue testifying), V, 4401 (Roger C. Sullivan testifying), VI, 5527, 5543 (Albert E. Isley testifying), V, 4923 (Browne testifying).

[71] *Ibid.,* V, 4540 (Ira C. Copley testifying), V, 4922–23 (Browne testifying).

Hopkins' failure to win on the ninety-fourth ballot convinced Lorimer that it was time for him to make his bid. All during the night of May 25, politicians descended on Springfield for the Lorimer push. All of Lorimer's influential friends worked for him, as well as Cook County Deneenites Chauncey Dewey and John R. Thompson, both of whom believed that Lorimer "was the strongest man and could be elected, and nobody else could be. . . ." [72] Many Democrats also labored for Lorimer, such as Thomas Tippit, who argued that it was "good politics" to do so, and Louis Stevenson, son of Adlai Stevenson, who was repaying Lorimer's support for his father in 1908.[73] Throughout the evening of May 25 and on the morning of the 26th, Lorimer conferred with Democratic and Republican legislators in the Speaker's room in the capitol building. As the joint session approached, Lorimer committed himself to try for the toga on the ninety-fifth ballot.[74]

At twelve o'clock "The Honorable the Senate" filed into the House chamber. Politicians of note, as well as the elite of Springfield, who had come as if to a "gala society event," packed the galleries. Lorimer remained in the Speaker's room, but his aides stood ready to supply minute-by-minute reports. On the platform behind Speaker Shurtleff sat ex-Governor Yates, looking forward to Hopkins' downfall.[75]

The Senate began the roll call. Members who had previously voted for Hopkins or Foss now changed their votes to Lorimer, as did Democrats who had voted for a variety of candidates. Some legislators were angry over the shifts, and Democratic Senator Albert E. Isley of Jasper County warned Jeremiah-like that a "crisis" faced his party: "I would rather see my right arm paralyzed than to vote in absolute opposition and antagonism to the party to which I belong for a candidate who will not represent the Democratic party." Deneenite Senator Walter Clyde Jones of Cook County also thundered of the dangers of a "bipartisan conspiracy or plot" which would "destroy the integrity of the Republican party," and some paid him heed: the Senate roll call ended with Hopkins, 31, Lorimer, 12, and Stringer, 7.[76]

[72] *Ibid.*, II, 1276–77 (Deneen testifying); *Post*, May 25, 1909; *Tribune*, May 26, 1909; Hutchinson, *Lowden*, I, 186.
[73] *Dillingham Committee Hearings*, V, 4264–65, 4270 (Thomas Tippit testifying).
[74] *Ibid.*, IV, 3230, 3234 (John M. Peffers testifying), IV, 3250–51 (Henry Terrill testifying), IV, 3319–20 (Henry A. Shephard testifying), VI, 5772–73 (George B. Welborn testifying), VIII, 7241–42 (John A. Logan testifying).
[75] *Tribune*, May 27, 1909.
[76] *Ibid.; House Journal, Forty-sixth General Assembly*, 1058.

Before the crucial House roll call, Lee O'Neil Browne addressed the joint assembly. He reviewed the five "long, weary months" of balloting, and held that a "call of duty" from the people now demanded the election of a senator: "The people of the State want results. *You can not cash theories. You can not cash dreams.* You wake up and you haven't got them. What the people want is results. . . ." And Lorimer could secure them: "His word is as good as a gold bond. You can cash it any place—among his enemies or among his friends. . . . He loves his friends, and he puts in his life demonstrating it." Browne also noted that Lorimer was a "model man in his home, in his daily life, with his associates, and in business," and the "father and mother" of the waterway. Because of the "duty" he owed his state, Browne would vote for Lorimer.[77]

"Manny" Abrahams of Chicago, later identified as the Democratic "bellwether," started the Lorimer trend among the assemblymen.[78] Democrat after Democrat voted for Lorimer, as did a number of Hopkins men. However, Democratic Assemblyman George W. English, from Egypt, refused to join his colleagues, and scathingly attacked Browne and the other turncoat Democrats. Did they intend, he asked, "to tell the whole reason" for their Lorimer votes? "You can say that . . . principles can not be cashed and that dreams can not be cashed," said English. "What, then, can be 'cashed' on the floor of this assembly? Nothing but votes, I take it." [79] Other Republicans and Democrats also defended or attacked the Lorimer votes, but the words made little difference, as the shift continued, with Shurtleff casting the 101st vote for Lorimer, one short of the necessary majority. The Lorimer forces wanted a majority of Republicans in the Lorimer total, and, amid confusion, a number of legislators changed. When the Lorimer vote reached 108, Shurtleff banged his gavel down: Lorimer had been elected U.S. senator.[80]

[77] *Tribune*, May 27, 1909 (my italics).

[78] *Dillingham Committee Hearings*, III, 2921 (H. J. C. Beckemeyer testifying).

[79] In the *Dillingham Committee Hearings* English testified that he made his comments about "cash" because "I felt at the time that the probabilities were that the remark that he [Browne] had made, 'You can not cash dreams here,' was of a double meaning. . . . My inference was that perhaps if there was anything of a corrupt nature as an influence to secure votes for Senator Lorimer in speaking of cash it might be interpreted as a real cash deal; to those that were not it was simply to be a metaphor." VI, 5256.

[80] *House Journal, Forty-sixth General Assembly*, 1058–59. In the *Dillingham Committee Hearings* Lorimer commented that "if the speaker had not dropped the gavel when I got 108 votes, I probably would have gotten 150 votes." VIII, 7429.

Chicago *Tribune*, May 27, 1909

An analysis of the senatorial vote reveals the complexity of the election and of the shifts that occurred during the four months of the deadlock. In the final totals, Lorimer received 108 votes (55 Republican and 53 Democratic), Hopkins 70, and Stringer 23. The Hopkins vote was quite complicated. On the last ballot, he received the support of twenty-four senators and forty-five assemblymen. Only thirty-five legislators who voted for Hopkins on the first ballot also voted for him on the last. Thirty-eight assemblymen who backed Edward J. King for speaker in January (the "Band of Hope") voted for Hopkins on the last ballot, as did four assemblymen who voted for Shurtleff for speaker. Five legislators who supported Foss on the first tally were for Hopkins on the last.

Lorimer received the vote of eighty-nine assemblymen and nineteen senators. Sixty-four assemblymen who voted for Shurtleff for speaker supported Lorimer, as did sixteen assemblymen who had backed Deneenite Edward J. King for the post. From the Republicans, there were twenty-five legislators who were for Hopkins on the first ballot but for Lorimer on the last; ten Foss supporters eventually voted for Lorimer. From the Democrats, Lorimer received the votes of forty-five assemblymen who voted for Browne for speaker and forty-six legislators who backed Stringer on the first ballot.[81]

This dissection of the vote reveals that the Hopkins men were more willing to go to Lorimer than the Deneenites, although Deneen could not hold all his forces. Factional lines were fluid and no absolute correlations existed between the Speaker's fight or positions on legislation and the Senate election. Legislators made their decisions on cultural and sectional as well as personal and political grounds. Lorimer, the representative of Chicago's West Side, secured the votes of fifty-three of the seventy-six Cook County General Assembly representatives, making it clear how important his Chicago origins were.[82]

With Lorimer's election, excited friends rushed into the Speaker's room to tell him of his victory and to bring him before the General Assembly. With a red rose in his lapel, and looking "benign, innocent, grateful, [and] wishing good to all men," Lorimer addressed the body. He commented that although his bipartisan election was a "new precedent," it was unimportant since "the parties have been growing

---

[81] *House Journal, Forty-sixth General Assembly,* 6–13, 68–69, 1058–59; *Senate Journal, Forty-sixth General Assembly,* 96–97.
[82] *House Journal, Forty-sixth General Assembly,* 1058–59.

in their great principles closer and closer together every day until now we are separated by just a few great principles." One of these, he said, was the tariff, but since the Republican party had declared for a lower tariff he would abandon his protectionism and strive for a Senate measure similar to the Payne bill just passed by the House. He also promised to work to complete the waterway, a matter important to both Democrats and Republicans. In closing, he invited both those who had voted for him and those who had not to call on him for "any service" he could render.[83]

Shortly after his speech, Lorimer called on the Governor. He was still interested, said the new Senator, in "harmonizing the party" and in working with Deneen. He wished to "wipe the slate," to forget past differences, and "to start a new book." He would, he said, speak to his friends and "see if the fight that had been going on for so long in Illinois could not be stopped." Deneen replied that he thought he and Lorimer could cooperate—that "there was need of it in Illinois." [84]

And thus it seemed that one of the most disruptive events in Illinois political history would lead to a new era of peace and harmony. As for Lorimer, through a lifetime of making political friends and building his influence, he had reached the pinnacle of his political career.

Enthusiasm marked the statewide reaction to Lorimer's election. Lorimer received hundreds of congratulatory letters and telegrams from businessmen, politicians, clergymen, and judges. Some were from past political enemies, such as Charles G. Dawes and John Maynard Harlan, as well as friends. Father Francis C. Kelley, president of the Catholic Church Extension Society, and Samuel R. Rabinoff, president of the Jewish Political League of Chicago, sent letters that reflected Lorimer's strength among Chicago ethnic groups. Rabinoff commented that "no people in the State of Illinois have as much reason to rejoice at your success as the Jews," while Kelley said he joined his many Catholic friends who admired Lorimer in applauding his election. Other letters praised Lorimer's "practical good sense," his "ability, eminent public service, and integrity," and predicted "an exceedingly able and efficient administration of the duties of the office by you." [85]

[83] *Ibid.*, 1060–62.

[84] *Dillingham Committee Hearings,* II, 1143–44 (Deneen testifying), VIII, 7441–42.

[85] The congratulatory letters are printed in *Dillingham Committee Hearings,* VIII,

But there were some dissenters. The *Tribune,* the *News,* and the *Record-Herald* expressed mild unhappiness over Lorimer's election, while William Randolph Hearst's Chicago *Examiner* thundered "Lorimerism Degrades the State." Reformer William C. Boyden wrote to William Kent that "the worst has happened. . . . Lorimer was elected Senator. . . . It is a permanent set-back. The cheap and nasty elements of the community are overjoyed." Kent agreed that "the very worst had come . . . the state . . . is everlastingly disgraced. . . ." [86] A bitter Albert J. Hopkins wrote to President Taft about Lorimer's bipartisan election and warned that Lorimer would be disloyal to Taft's administration and would attempt to depose all of Hopkins' federal appointees. Taft responded soothingly that Hopkins' "suspicion with respect to his [Lorimer's] attitude may not be well founded," and that he would "consult both Senators" in regard to appointments. [87]

The first year of Lorimer's brief and tumultuous Senate career witnessed his accumulation of political power in Illinois and his adherence to the Senate establishment in Washington. Lorimer took his seat at a time of heated political emotions, as progressives strove with the Old Guard for party control; he immediately took his stand with the stalwarts. As he later remarked, conservative leader Nelson Aldrich was his "bellwether":

> We have our bellwether here [the Senate]; we have the Democratic bellwether; we have the "insurgent" bellwether, and we have the "stalwart" bellwether. When I happen to be absent from this Chamber and the bell rings announcing the roll call, if I chance to step in the door in time to hear the name of Senator ALDRICH called, he is my bellwether. I know where my vote belongs, and I vote as he votes. If he happens to be absent, I listen to the roll call until the clerk comes to the name of my distinguished colleague, the Senator from Illinois, and . . . Senator CULLOM becomes my bellwether. . . . Then we go along a little

7554–61. In addition to those already mentioned, there are also letters from Judges Adams A. Goodrich, Theodore Brentano, John Gibbons, Richard S. Tuthill, W. N. Gemmill, and Jesse A. Baldwin, all dated May 27, 1909, as well as Solicitor General Lloyd W. Bowers, June 4, 1909, and ex-Governor Joseph W. Fifer, May 30, 1909.

86 All newspaper comments are May 28, 1909; William C. Boyden to William Kent, May 27, 1909, Kent to Boyden, June 7, 1909, Kent Papers.

87 William Howard Taft to Albert J. Hopkins, June 4, 1909, William Howard Taft Papers, Library of Congress.

further, and if I happen to come in after he has answered the roll call, I wait until Senator LODGE has voted. Then, if I find that he and Senator LA FOLLETTE have voted the same way, I wait for somebody else to vote, and then somebody else becomes my bellwether.[88]

On the spectrum of progressive legislation presented during the Sixty-first Congress, ranging from child labor and railroad regulation to political, tax, and tariff reform, Lorimer followed Aldrich's lead. In so doing, he voted with a majority of his party—the so-called "opponents" of reform—who came from states largely located east of the Mississippi River and were devoted to industry rather than agriculture in their economic life.[89]

Lorimer demonstrated his allegiance to the Senate establishment on the issue of tariff revision. The Payne bill, passed by the House with Lorimer's support, represented a substantial downward revision from the rates of the 1897 Dingley tariff.[90] But under Aldrich's direction, the Senate Committee on Finance revised hundreds of rates upward. The insurgents, led by midwesterners Albert J. Beveridge, Albert B. Cummins, Jonathan P. Dolliver, and Robert M. La Follette, who were from largely agricultural states, attacked these revisions on the Senate floor. They accused Aldrich of a betrayal of the Republican campaign promise of a revision.[91]

Lorimer, no insurgent he, noted that he was "satisfied that Mr. Aldrich and the finance committee are revising the schedules downward wherever they can and doing the best possible for the country where it is manifestly impossible to cut them." [92] Representing an in-

---

[88] CR, 61st Cong., 3rd Sess., XLVI, 3122. Lorimer had intended to remain in the House until the tariff was disposed of, but was called to the Senate because his vote was needed by the Old Guard on the tariff and the income tax. See News, June 18, 1909; Tribune, June 9–10, 16, 1909. He was assigned to the committees on manufacturing, private land claims, Pacific islands and Puerto Rico, and made chairman of the Committee on Naval Expenditures. His seat was in the "Cherokee strip." See CR, 61st Cong., 1st Sess., XLIV, 3437, 3486.

[89] Clubb, "Congressional Opponents of Reform, 1901–1913." Clubb lists Lorimer among his "opponents of reform" in the Sixty-first Congress, using as a basis his vote on the tariff, tax, and political reform, and railroad regulation (Mann-Elkins Act). See 107–108, 144, 153, 183, 245, 282.

[90] CR, 61st Cong., 1st Sess., XLIV, 1118–19; Mowry, The Era of Theodore Roosevelt, 243.

[91] Mowry, The Era of Theodore Roosevelt, 243–248; Stanley D. Solvick, "William Howard Taft and the Payne-Aldrich Tariff," Mississippi Valley Historical Review (Dec., 1963), L, 430.

[92] Tribune, June 9, 10, 18, 1909.

dustrial state and standing close to Chicago business, Lorimer was a firm protectionist. Of his thirty-two votes on the tariff schedules, thirty-one were identical with Aldrich's.[93]

Throughout the tariff debate, Lorimer kept in touch with the Chicago lumbering and meat-packing industries. Lorimer often conferred with Edward Hines, president of the National Lumber Manufacturers' Association, who was in Washington lobbying for a $1.50 rate on lumber, while he communicated with the packers by telegram.[94] Although President Taft wanted hides and lumber on the free list, Lorimer, protecting the interests of these Chicago businesses, supported the high finance committee rates. He also voted for a substantial tariff on wood pulp, a move which worsened his already bad press relations.[95] Although he voted for the final Payne-Aldrich tariff, Lorimer expressed dissatisfaction with it. "Downward revision," he claimed, had been "a foolish cry for the Republican party to have construed and heeded." [96] Lorimer had repudiated his pledge to work for a lower tariff made upon his Senate election.

Lorimer's Senate record had implications for Illinois politics. Initially upon Lorimer's election most newspapers predicted that a Lorimer-Deneen combine would rule the state, disposing of federal officials such as Dan Campbell and Henry L. Hertz and supporting a mayoralty candidate against Busse, but this alliance did not occur.[97] Deneen's newspaper supporters as well as important members of his faction were committed to the progressive program and would not tolerate an agreement that might benefit Lorimer.[98] In addition, Lorimer assured a clash with Deneen by planning to restore his organization and extend his statewide influence. "The contest between Lori-

---

[93] There is a record of all Senate yea-nay votes on the tariff in *CR,* 61st Cong., 1st Sess., XLIV, 4792–4818.

[94] Charles E. Ward [Lorimer's secretary] to Edward Hines, July 5, 1909, printed in *Dillingham Committee Hearings,* I, 896; Lorimer to Edward Tilden [president, National Packing Company], July 22, 1909, printed in *ibid.,* VIII, 7781; Charles E. Ward to Shelby M. Cullom, July 26, 1909, printed in *ibid.,* 7783.

[95] For Lorimer's tariff votes see *CR,* 61st Cong., 1st Sess., XLIV, 4792–4818. Lorimer offered one amendment to the tariff bill providing for duties on photographic films. He presented it at the request of his political ally Ernest J. Magerstadt, who was in the movie business. See *ibid.,* 4181; *Tribune,* June 25, July 8, 1909.

[96] *Tribune,* July 24, 31, 1909.

[97] Chicago *American,* Chicago *Examiner, Inter-Ocean,* and *Tribune,* all May 27, 28, 1909.

[98] "In my conference with the Governor yesterday he assured me most emphatically that there was nothing in the report concerning the combination between the Governor, Shurtleff and Lorimer." John E. Wall to Lawrence Y. Sherman, July 10, 1909, Sherman Papers.

mer and Deneen, for state control, is now on," wrote Lorimer lieutenant Harry B. Ward to Frank O. Lowden, "and the former is sure
to win. . . . Lorimer is steadily growing stronger with the people." [99] But more important for Lorimer than "the people" were the
politicians, and almost immediately upon taking office he began a
campaign of "molelike work" undermining Deneen.

First he rewarded his supporters in the Senate election and pun-
ished his enemies. Although he stated that he did not believe "in
driving men from the political map because they do not agree with
me," his actions proved otherwise. To those who had voted for him
he gave jobs and patronage; those who had opposed him he ousted
from positions.[100] Lorimer also pressured federal office-holders,
especially postmasters, to aid him politically; he replaced those who
refused. The vision that some politicians had of Lorimer, "striding"
across the state "like a Cyclops, with broad-ax, scimitar, bludgeon
and gibbet, thundering 'Fee, fi, fum . . .' and crushing the helpless
populace under his ponderous feet," seemed justified. Lorimer had
put Deneen on the defensive.[101]

Lorimer's political prestige was markedly increased when, on July
31, Frank O. Lowden, Illinois Republican national committeeman,
designated him his proxy on the national committee. Lowden gave ill
health as his reason to President Taft, but he also sympathized more
with Lorimer's politics than Deneen's. To the press he pontificated
that his move would bring peace between the party factions. "It is
time that all the elements of the Republican party of Illinois get together and work together. I think there is no one better fitted for the
post of leader . . . than is Senator Lorimer." [102] Lorimer promised

[99] Ward to Lowden, Sept. 6, 1909, Lowden Papers.

[100] The Lorimer statement is in *Post*, May 31, 1909. For Lorimer's use of the
patronage see Homer Tice to Lawrence Y. Sherman, July 11, 1909, Sherman Papers;
William P. Welker to Albert J. Beveridge, Jan. 16, 1911, Beveridge Papers; George
B. Welborn to Lorimer, July 3, 9, 1909, printed in *Dillingham Committee Hearings*,
VI, 5773–74; Lee O'Neil Browne to Charles A. White, Oct. 24, 1909, printed in
ibid., III, 2537.

[101] Lawrence Y. Sherman to Shelby M. Cullom, Aug. 9, 1909, Sherman Papers;
Inter-Ocean, Aug. 3, 1909; *Tribune*, Aug. 24, 1909.

[102] Lowden to Taft, July 30, 1909, to Chairman and Members, Republican National Committee, July 31, 1909, Lowden Papers; *Tribune* and *Inter-Ocean*, Aug. 1,
1909; Hutchinson, *Lowden*, I, 188–189. Lowden wrote Colonel Charles Bent on
Aug. 16, 1909 (copy in Lowden Papers), "When I see you I shall be glad to tell
you fully all of my reasons for making Senator Lorimer my proxy. Of course my
health was partly responsible, but there were other reasons as well." While Lowden
added that he wanted a "re-united party in Illinois," he may have regarded Deneen's

to do his best to advance "harmony," and the pro-Lorimer *Inter-Ocean* predicted a new era of party peace. The reform press questioned Lorimer's interpretation of harmony, but agreed that "the move admittedly puts Senator Lorimer at the head of the Republican party in Illinois." [103]

Not all Republicans, however, would accept Lorimer's leadership. Busse, for one, fought Lorimer's Chicago organization. The Senator retaliated by attacking Busse's allies in federal posts and by fielding prospective mayoralty candidates.[104] If Lorimer gained control of city hall, his power in the state would be practically unlimited. Taking its lead from Lorimer, the *Inter-Ocean* began a series of exposés of fraud in the Busse administration.[105]

The chief response to Lorimer's attacks on Busse came in the *Tribune*. Here the ailing Robert W. Patterson had been replaced as editor-in-chief by the imperious Medill McCormick. McCormick, like his grandfather Joseph Medill, aspired to control the Illinois Republican party. With Busse as mayor, McCormick had influence; with Lorimer in power in the city he would have none. A reformer as well as an elitist, McCormick represented that brand of progressive that wanted to impose his life-style and direction on others.[106] Under his orders, the *Tribune* printed a steady barrage of articles critical of

espousal of progressive measures such as the direct primary as the chief divisive factor. See, for instance, Lowden to Lorimer, Aug. 25, 1911, Lowden Papers.

[103] Chicago *Examiner, Inter-Ocean, Record-Herald,* and *Tribune,* all Aug. 1, 1909; *News,* Aug. 2, 3, 1909.

[104] *News,* Aug. 2, 1909; *Post,* Aug. 20, 1909; *Tribune,* Sept. 19, 1909. The candidacy of Frederick ("Poor Fred") Lundin was boosted in the Swedish-language press. See *Svenska Amerikanaren,* July 15, 1909; *Svenska Tribunen-Nyheter,* Aug. 10, 1909.

[105] In the beginning of November, 1909, the *Inter-Ocean* exposed fraud in the granting of the city shale contracts. These exposés led to investigation of city expenditures by the Merriam Commission of the city council. The commission discovered extensive fraud in city contracts and purchases, and evasion of civil service. Eventually a number of Busse's officials resigned. See *Inter-Ocean,* Nov. 1, 2, 1909; William C. Boyden to William Kent, Nov. 20, 1909, Feb. 5, 1910, Raymond Robins to Kent, Mar. 22, 1909, Kent Papers; Charles E. Merriam, "Investigations as a Means of Securing Administrative Efficiency," *Annals of the American Academy of Political and Social Science* (May, 1912), XLI, 281–303. For the political motivation of the *Inter-Ocean* exposé see Martin J. Hutcheons [editor, Chicago *Daily Journal*] to Senator Thomas H. Carter, July 26, 1910, Thomas H. Carter Papers, Library of Congress; "Chicago's Graft Inquiry," *The Outlook* (Mar. 5, 1910), XCIV, 509–511.

[106] For portraits of Medill McCormick see Ralph A. Stone, "Two Illinois Senators among the Irreconcilables," *Mississippi Valley Historical Review* (Dec., 1963), L, 445; Frank C. Waldrop, *McCormick of Chicago: An Unconventional Portrait of a Controversial Figure* (Englewood Cliffs, 1966), 67–68.

Lorimer and charging him with wanting to restore the "old bipartisan, politico-business organization" that had formerly ruled the city.[107]

McCormick's anti-Lorimer drive focused upon the campaign to choose Lorimer's successor in the Sixth Congressional District. Lorimer's candidate was oleomargaine manufacturer William J. Moxley. Speaking at the nominating convention, Lorimer put the election in the context of the insurgent–Old Guard struggle: Speaker of the House Cannon needed Moxley in Congress to help him against the insurgent attack. Reflecting the party split, Independent Republican Carl L. Barnes ran on a platform opposing "Lorimerism" and "Cannonism." The Democratic candidate, personally selected by boss Roger C. Sullivan, was city paymaster Frank S. Ryan.[108]

The English-language reform press endorsed Barnes and charged that bosses Lorimer and Sullivan, "Tweedledum and Tweedledee," had made a bargain to elect Moxley. The newspapers attacked Moxley ("Whispering William—Muscle Orator") as the symbol of "Lorimerism" and "Cannonism." [109] The Bohemian press, however, representing the largest ethnic group in the district, backed Moxley. *Denni Hlasatel,* for instance, noted that Moxley was Lorimer's choice and therefore, from the perspective of the Czechs, "most agreeable." [110] Lorimer's business allies also supported Moxley. Lumberman Edward Hines obtained signatures from forty district corporations for a Moxley petition. In a telegram requesting an endorsement from International Harvester, Hines noted, "Very strong interests in town back of this." [111]

On election day the Chicago wards of the Sixth District gave Mox-

---

[107] *Tribune,* Aug. 24, 25, Sept. 12, 14, 19–21, 1909; James Weber Linn, *James Keeley: Newspaperman* (New York, 1937), 139–140; *Dillingham Committee Hearings,* II, 1947–48 (James Keeley testifying). William C. Boyden wrote William Kent that "since Medill McCormick returned to town, he has been playing with the Mayor, and I suppose this [anti-Lorimer] editorial is in the nature of a warning to the blond boss. It is fairly certain that the feud between Lorimer and Busse at the present time is quite real. I have never believed it would last. It has always seemed to me that those two would get together." Aug. 24, 1909, Kent Papers.

[108] *Tribune,* Oct. 23, Nov. 4, 1909. Because the Illinois Supreme Court had declared the Oglesby primary law unconstitutional, there were no formal parties in the election. The Republican and Democratic machines, however, controlled their respective "nonpartisan" conventions.

[109] *Ibid.,* Oct. 23, 28, 30, Nov. 4, 9, 10, 17–20, 1909.

[110] *Denni Hlasatal,* Nov. 14, 24, 1909.

[111] Edward Hines to C. S. Funk [general manager, International Harvester Corporation], Nov. 16, 1909, printed in *Dillingham Committee Hearings,* VIII, 7360.

ley a large majority, while Barnes, who finished second, did best in the native-American suburbs. Exulting, Cannon hailed Moxley's victory as a blow to insurgency. The election also damaged Medill Mc-Cormick's campaign to stop Lorimer, and clearly illustrated that in Chicago's ritualistic immigrant wards, Lorimer's personal popularity and organization outweighed the call for reform.[112]

While Lorimer's growing strength upset the progressives, it also bothered orthodox Republicans such as Senator Shelby M. Cullom, who resented Lorimer's bipartisan election. When Lowden gave Lorimer his national committee proxy, Cullom wrote Lawrence Y. Sherman and commented ironically "that Frank Lowden has taken it upon himself to designate a leader for the republican party in Illinois who will make great changes . . . in the interest of republicanism, notwithstanding the leader designated secured his position by the aid of the democrats." "What," inquired Cullom, "do the friends out there think and say about this?" [113]

Sherman responded pessimistically about the Republican party's predicament, and forecast a possible Democratic sweep in the next election. "A union of non-caucus Republicans with machine Democrats does not mis-lead the Republican voter," he said. "Any harmony that produces good results must come from those in the first instance who abide by the settled rules of party procedure." Bitterly Sherman commented that it was from the disloyal Republicans "that most of the specious talk for 'harmony' comes." But "it is they who make discord. Having done so, harmony is proffered at the price of forgiving them offense and leaving them in possession of the party assets taken from loyal Republicans by joining with Democrats to do so. General amnesty to bolters and a surrender to them of all the fruits of party organization and control is a summary of the offer." [114] Cullom answered in the same tone. "It seems to me," he said, that "our party is in bad shape when it has got to be harmonized by such fellows as the speaker of the Illinois legislature and my colleague . . . the party should rise up and express the feeling . . . that Republicans should run the party." [115]

During the following weeks, Cullom wrote a number of letters to

112 *Tribune,* Nov. 24, 1909.
113 Cullom to Sherman, Aug. 2, 1909, Sherman Papers.
114 Sherman to Cullom, Aug. 9, 1909, Sherman Papers.
115 Cullom to Sherman, Aug. 12, 1909, Sherman Papers.

his Illinois lieutenants asking their opinion of the political situation. Their responses were mixed. As one writer said, "I found everybody pretty much at sea as to what the future situation was going to be." [116] Several letters blamed Deneen's appointment policy for the party distress, while others mentioned the heated Yates campaigns.[117] Many, however, held Lorimer responsible for the party's difficulties. "The coalition between Shurtleff, Lorimer and the democrats to over-ride the Republican majority in our legislature," wrote one Stark County correspondent, "has caused intense bitter feeling. Many of our people look upon these two men as false to our party. . . ." [118] Another wrote from the same county that "the idea of electing a man like Lorimer as a yoke-fellow with a man like yourself has disgusted thousands of Republicans. There is disgust, discontent and discord all along the line." [119]

The responses disturbed Cullom. "I have felt very uneasy about the situation," he wrote to Sherman. "The party seems to be split up and in danger of remaining so." [120] Cullom believed Lorimer the main cause of party dissension, and decided to circumscribe his power by bypassing him on federal appointments. In the fall he made a number of patronage recommendations to President Taft without consulting Lorimer.[121]

Lorimer complained to Taft that Cullom was violating senatorial courtesy. Taft investigated, and then wrote a letter of apology to Lorimer:

> The Attorney General [Wickersham] . . . told me of the mistake which was made with reference to the Illinois appointments, which was quite annoying, for I only sent in those appointments which as I supposed had been concurred in by both Senators. . . . I hope you will find it pos-

116 Robert M. Farthing [Jefferson County] to Cullom, Nov. 3, 1909, Cullom Papers.

117 George T. Turner [Vandalia] to Cullom, Nov. 5, 1909, S. S. Tanner [Cass, Menard, and Tazewell counties] to Cullom, Nov. 6, 1909, E. V. Reed [Livingston County] to Cullom, Nov. 6, 1909, Cullom Papers.

118 A. G. Hammon to Cullom, Nov. 8, 1909, Cullom Papers.

119 B. F. Thompson to Cullom, Nov. 6, 1909, Cullom Papers. See also W. R. Hunter [Kankakee County] to Cullom, Nov. 1, 1909, Cullom Papers. Hunter wrote that "real Republicans have no use for Shurtleff, Lorimer, Yates, Small, Cannon and others of that ilk who have stood with the party solely for self advancement."

120 Cullom to Sherman, Oct. 3, 1909, Sherman Papers; *Tribune*, Sept. 20, 21, 1909.

121 William Howard Taft to William Lorimer, Dec. 21, 1909, Taft Papers; *Tribune*, Dec. 21, 1909.

sible to come to Washington before the session opens in order that I may have a full opportunity for conversation with you. I am very anxious to work in co-operation with both the Senators from your State and not to do anything which is not the result of full and free consultation with both.[122]

During the first months of 1910, however, to Taft's irritation, the Lorimer-Cullom patronage dispute continued. Taft's sympathies were with Lorimer. He told Postmaster General Frank H. Hitchcock to help Lorimer "as far as it is possible," and he complained to Secretary of the Treasury Franklin MacVeagh that Cullom had "no business to ask our action without consulting Lorimer, because it always creates a row." [123]

By late April, presidential pressure forced Cullom to compromise with Lorimer over the patronage. Taft appointed Lorimer men to federal positions, some of whom Lorimer recommended as a reward for voting for him for the Senate.[124] Lorimer, by triumphing over Cullom and with the aid of Taft, was closer to full control of the Illinois Republican party.

Lorimer matched his political triumphs with success in blocking Deneen's waterway plans and advancing his own. The Forty-sixth General Assembly had ended with the Lorimer and Deneen proposals stalemated between the Senate and the Assembly.[125] In Congress,

---

[122] Taft to Lorimer, Dec. 21, 1909, Taft Papers.

[123] Taft to Frank H. Hitchcock, Mar. 2, 1910, to Franklin MacVeagh, Apr. 14, 1910, to Lorimer, Mar. 4, Apr. 16, 1910, Taft Papers.

[124] In Chicago Taft removed Hertz as collector of internal revenue and appointed Samuel M. Fitch in his place; he appointed Len Small subtreasurer, and John C. Ames collector of customs. See Taft to Lorimer, Feb. 19, Apr. 26, June 6, 21, 1910, Cullom to Taft, Dec. 1, 1910, Taft Papers. Lorimer agreed to Fitch's appointment at Taft's request. See Taft to Lorimer, Feb. 9, June 9, 1910, Taft to Franklin MacVeagh, June 17, 1910, *ibid.* Edgar Bancroft, president of the Illinois State Bar Association, wrote Attorney General George Wickersham that Small's appointment would "be a scandal." See Wickersham to Charles D. Norton, July 5, 1910, Charles S. Deneen to Norton, Sept. 29, 1910, as well as other comments on the appointment in the "Len Small" file, *ibid.* Lorimer recommended William H. Behrens as U.S. marshal for the Illinois Southern District as a reward for his Lorimer vote in the Forty-sixth General Assembly. See Charles DeWoody to S. W. Finch [chief, Bureau of Investigation], Nov. 14, 1910, Finch to the Attorney General [Wickersham], Nov. 18, 1910, Wickersham to Charles D. Norton, Nov. 25, 1910, *ibid.* Wickersham noted, "I am . . . satisfied that his [Behrans'] endorsement by Senator Lorimer for the office of United States Marshal was compensation for Behrens' vote for Mr. Lorimer as Senator."

[125] *House Journal, Forty-sixth General Assembly,* 1328, 1335, 1385–86; *Dillingham Committee Hearings,* VIII, 7442–43, 7451; *Tribune,* June 12, 25, 1909; *Post,* July 12, 1909.

however, Lorimer and Cannon packed the House Committee on Rivers and Harbors with men who favored an immediate Lakes-to-the-Gulf appropriation.[126] During the fall of 1909 Lorimer toured European waterways as a member of the National Waterways Commission, returning to participate in the fourth annual convention of the Lakes-to-the-Gulf Deep Waterway Association at New Orleans.[127]

A grand cruise down the Mississippi preceded the convention. President Taft, 29 governors, 34 senators, and 278 congressmen participated, testifying to the popularity of the waterway idea. The convention, however, was not harmonious. Lorimer made his usual enthusiastic waterway speech, but Taft dampened the delegates' spirits by warning of pork-barrel appropriations. The convention ended on a sour note, as Congressman Henry T. Rainey sought unsuccessfully to secure a resolution expressing the "bitter disappointment and sorrow" of the Deep Waterway Association with the President's stand.[128]

But Lorimer was not dissuaded. In February, with the help of Edward Hines, he persuaded the Senate Committee on Commerce to make a waterways appropriation.[129] The resulting rivers and harbors bill contained $1,000,000 for a special Army Corps of Engineers commission to survey the project. Although Lorimer and Senator Theodore E. Burton clashed on the Senate floor over the wisdom of the grant, Lorimer prevailed.[130] He appeared to be on his way toward achieving another of his goals, the construction of the waterway.

In the same months that Lorimer solidified his political power and pushed the waterway appropriation through the Senate, he also embarked upon a new business venture. In late 1909 and early 1910, Lorimer joined with downstate banker and grain merchant Charles B. Munday to plan a chain of statewide banks. The center of the chain was a Chicago trust company and a national bank which would clear for Munday's downstate institutions. Lorimer would be presi-

[126] *Tribune,* Aug. 6, 1909; *News,* Aug. 7, 1909; Hays, *Conservation,* 212.

[127] *Tribune,* Sept. 19, Oct. 11, 20, 1909; Crissey, *Burton,* 183–189. Burton was chairman of the commission. Lyman E. Cooley accompanied Lorimer on the trip.

[128] Deep Waterway Association, *Minutes of the Fourth Annual Convention* (St. Louis, 1910); *Tribune,* Oct. 27, 30, Nov. 2, 1909; Waller, "Henry T. Rainey," 117; Henry F. Pringle, *The Life and Times of William Howard Taft* (2 vols., New York, 1939), I, 466–467.

[129] Lorimer to Hines, Feb. 22, 1910 (two telegrams), Feb. 23, 1910, printed in *Dillingham Committee Hearings,* I, 897; *Tribune,* Feb. 28, 1910.

[130] *CR,* 61st Cong., 2nd Sess., XLV, 4801–18; Crissey, *Burton,* 191; Hays, *Conservation,* 221.

dent of the Chicago banks, with his main function to draw political deposits.[131]

Attracted by the idea of increasing his already considerable fortune and also furnishing his sons with a business career, Lorimer approached his more eminent friends and asked them to consider bank directorships. The resulting list was impressive and included William C. Browne, president of the New York Central Railroad, John M. Roach, president of the Chicago Railways Corporation, Frank J. Baker, vice-president of the North Shore Electric Company, as well as other leading bankers and businessmen. Elbridge Hanecy and William J. Moxley were also directors.[132] Munday sent letters to hundreds of Lorimer's political friends and acquaintances, offering them stock in the new banks. "I have been instructed by Senator Lorimer," wrote Munday, "to inform you that in organizing the La Salle Street National Bank and the La Salle Street Trust Company, he is desirous of giving his personal friends the first opportunity of becoming stockholders in the new banks." Many politicians responded, including some who had voted for Lorimer as senator. They understood the potential profits in political banking.[133]

Thus, by the spring of 1910, Lorimer had achieved the pinnacle of his power and influence. He was a member in good standing of the U.S. Senate; he had put his political opponents, especially Deneen and Cullom, on the defensive; he had obtained a large federal deep waterway appropriation; and his new banks promised to multiply his wealth. Good fortune, indeed, seemed to shine upon the Blond Boss.

[131] *Tribune,* Apr. 14, 1916.

[132] *Ibid.,* Feb. 6, Apr. 13, 1910.

[133] Munday's letter is printed in *ibid.,* May 11, 1910. A list of politicians who were stockholders is in *ibid.,* June 13, 1914.

CHAPTER **10**

★ ★ ★ ★ ★ ★ ★ ★ ★ ★ ★

From Exposé to Senate Vindication

"DEMOCRATIC LEGISLATOR CONFESSES HE WAS BRIBED TO VOTE FOR LORIMER FOR UNITED STATES SENATOR," read the April 30, 1910, *Tribune* headline. "Charles A. White, Member of Illinois Assembly, Tells How Support Was Bought. Gives $1,000 As Price." The signed White story, written in his own words and illustrated with pictures of the bribers and the bribed, filled the first two pages of the paper. The *Tribune* published other parts of his story on the next two days.[1]

Who was Charles A. White, and what was the background to his confession? White was a slight, rather handsome fellow with grandiose ideas. Born in Knoxville, Tennessee, in 1881, he attended public school there and the Knoxville Business College, although not lingering long enough at either school to obtain a diploma. After drifting through several jobs with Knoxville and St. Louis mercantile firms, in 1903 he became a conductor on the East St. Louis & Suburban Railway Company. Like Lorimer when he worked on the streetcars, White was active in the local union; in 1907 he was chosen as its Springfield legislative representative. Most of White's ideas and attitudes stemmed from his labor experience, and he generally confined his reading to labor papers such as the *American Federationist,* the *Industrial Workers of the World,* and the *Western Federationist.* He favored, he said, "a great deal of the Socialist idea." [2]

In 1908 White was elected as a Democrat to the Illinois General Assembly from the Forty-ninth District. He became a member of

---

[1] *Tribune,* Apr. 30, May 1, 2, 1910.
[2] The best source for White's life and for the background to the bribery story is his testimony in the *Dillingham Committee Hearings,* III, 2404–2826.

DEMOCRATIC LEGISLATOR CONFESSES HE WAS BRIBED TO VOTE FOR LORIMER FOR UNITED STATES SENATOR.

Charles A. White, Member of Illinois Assembly, Tells How Support Was Bought.

GIVES $1,000 AS PRICE

Writes Details of His Experience, Alleging Lee O'Neil Browne Participated in the Deal.

SAYS HE GOT $900 IN 'POT'

The *Chicago Tribune* has in its possession and will submit to the proper authorities—Governor Deneen, Attorney General Stead, or State's Attorney Wayman—a sworn statement made by Charles A. White, a member of the lower house of the Illinois legislature from the Forty-ninth district, charging that William Lorimer was elected to the United States senate last summer by bribery and corruption; that a large number of the members of the last legislature received money for their votes on various bills; that he, White (a Democrat), received $1,000 for voting for Lorimer and that he also received $900 as his share of the "jackpot," a term applied to the general corruption fund distributed at the close of each session.

White admits his criminality—says he accepted the money so that he might expose the corruption and rascality of the legislature. He knows he will be charged with attempted blackmail by Senator Lorimer and Lee O'Neil Browne, Democratic leader of the last legislature, because he wrote certain letters to these persons. White denies the blackmail theory, and alleges that the letters were written in furtherance of his plan of exposure.

THE TRIBUNE is thoroughly conversant with this and other features of the case.

White's manuscript has been in the possession of THE TRIBUNE for a month. A most thorough and searching investigation has been made, the results of which will be given by THE TRIBUNE to its readers day by day.

Minute Account of Reputed Dealings in St. Nicholas Hotel and Briggs House.

BRINGS OTHERS' NAMES

Pen Picture of Excitement in Joint Session Last Year When "Blonde" Leader Won Victory.

SAYS HIS PURPOSE WAS GOOD

Author of the Statement; a Colleague: and a Telegram.

Telegram summoning White to St. Louis

CHARLES A. WHITE

ROBERT E. WILSON

Chicago Tribune, Apr. 30, 1910

the Browne faction and supported him for minority leader, although he did not vote for Shurtleff for speaker. During the course of the senatorial deadlock, White consistently backed Democratic candidate Lawrence B. Stringer. On May 26, however, for the first time that session, White voted for a Republican, William Lorimer.[3]

In his confession White claimed that Lee O'Neil Browne gave him $1,000 for his Lorimer vote. He related that Browne first asked him if he could support Lorimer on the evening of May 24; while Browne mentioned nothing about a specific sum of money he did say " 'it wouldn't be any chicken feed.' " The next day after the inconclusive ninety-fourth ballot Browne promised him $1,000 for his Lorimer vote and "almost a thousand more . . . from the jackpot." On May 26, after Browne reminded him that this "comes off on the first ballot," White voted for Lorimer. He received $100 from Browne in Springfield shortly after the legislature adjourned and $900 in Chicago in June.[4] The "jackpot" share, consisting of contributions paid by corporations for legislation, came in July.

On July 15, 1909, White's confession continued, he met Democratic legislators Robert E. Wilson of Chicago, Joseph S. Clark, Michael S. Link, Charles S. Luke, and Henry A. Shephard at the Southern Hotel in St. Louis, and also encountered H. J. C. Beckemeyer on a street near the hotel. All had voted for Lorimer. In the bathroom of his hotel room, Wilson, acting for Browne, gave White $900 as his "jackpot" share. White implied in his story that Wilson also paid the other legislators. White explained that he accepted the Lorimer and the "jackpot" money to expose the corrupt plot: "The actual act of taking the money was dishonorable; it was dishonest; but the ultimate end was to result in good. That is the way I had it figured out." [5]

White began preparing his tale of corruption in the late summer of 1909. While writing he stayed in communication with Browne; he borrowed small sums of money from him, and even persuaded Browne to intercede with Lorimer to get him a political job.[6] In January, White finished his story. Entitled "The Jackpot," it in-

[3] *Ibid.*, 2496 (White testifying); *House Journal, Forty-sixth General Assembly*, 1058–59.

[4] *Dillingham Committee Hearings*, III, 2469–73, 2480–86; *Tribune*, Apr. 30, 1910.

[5] *Dillingham Committee Hearings*, III, 2594; *Tribune*, Apr. 30, 1910.

[6] Lorimer got White a position in the office of deputy county comptroller James L. Monaghan, but White refused it. See White to Lorimer, Oct. 19, 1909, in which White suggests that he would like a job in the "Secret Service," Browne to White,

cluded not only the bribery narrative, but also pages of moralistic philosophizing and poetry. After several publishers declined the manuscript, White turned to the *Tribune*.[7]

At the *Tribune,* White saw the editor-in-chief, James Keeley, an Englishman of little education but an expert journalist. Keeley "was a great driver of men, imperious . . . in disposition and . . . jealous of recognition." [8] Keeley wanted to wrest control of the paper from the McCormicks and the Pattersons and he possibly saw the Lorimer bribery story as a means to increase his prestige. He told White he would buy the manuscript if it could be verified. *Tribune* reporters, private detectives, and *Tribune* counsel Alfred S. Austrian interrogated a number of the legislators mentioned in the manuscript. The information they unearthed convinced Keeley of the story's truth, and he purchased it from White for $3,250, a much smaller sum than White had anticipated. After eliminating most of White's philosophy and poetry, the *Tribune* published the "essential features" of the manuscript.[9]

Accompanying the White story was a statement that the *Tribune* would submit the bribery evidence to the "proper authorities": Governor Deneen, Attorney General William H. Stead, and State's Attorney John E. W. Wayman. Actually, both Deneen and Wayman had known about the manuscript for over a month. Deneen acknowledged to the press that it was a "startling story," and recommended that a "searching investigation should be made. . . ." At the end of the White narrative, at the bottom of the second page, was a notice that Lorimer would be president of the La Salle Street National Bank and the La Salle Street Trust and Savings Company.[10]

Oct. 24, 1909, Nov. 2, 1909, White to Browne, Nov. 5, 1909, James L. Monaghan to Browne, Nov. 1, 1909, all printed in *Dillingham Committee Hearings,* III, 2533–41; *Tribune,* May 2, 1910.

[7] The manuscript was declined by Doubleday, Page & Co., *Everybody's Magazine,* and the Kerr Publishing Co. of Chicago. See the correspondence printed in *Dillingham Committee Hearings,* III, 2567–78.

[8] Waldrop, *McCormick of Chicago,* 95. See also Linn, *James Keeley.*

[9] Linn, *James Keeley,* 143–149; *Dillingham Committee Hearings,* II, 1889–96 (Keeley testifying). In *An American Dynasty,* 87, John Tebbel notes, "It was Lorimer's bad luck to run afoul of Keeley, whom he had never antagonized, at a time when the *Tribune's* editor needed him for his own career." The only part of the White manuscript that the author has been able to locate is the last page, which is in the James Keeley Papers, Chicago Historical Society. It contains the poem "A Curse on the Traitor" by Thomas More.

[10] *Tribune,* Apr. 30, 1910; *Dillingham Committee Hearings,* II, 1884–91 (Keeley testifying).

Denials of the story's validity came immediately. Lorimer maintained that it was "absolutely false from start to finish," and charged a *Tribune* plot to "wreck the financial institutions which I am . . . starting," and to destroy him politically. "The *Tribune*'s animus and purpose," noted Lorimer, "should be plain to anybody who noticed that White's pack of lies was printed right next to the announcement that I was to be president of the two banks that I am organizing." White's tale was "so impossible that its falsehood is apparent at a glance." "Anybody who was in Springfield during the senatorial contest . . . would know in a minute that it could not be true. Such fantastic things don't happen."

Lorimer told how in the winter of 1910 he received a mysterious letter from White telling of his intention to "write a story of his life in the legislature." White said he had written 50,000 words and had an offer of $2.50 a word. "As this would mean $75,000 [*sic*]," said Lorimer, "I concluded that the man was crazy." Ignoring a statement by his secretary that it was a "blackmail letter," Lorimer blandly responded that he "was glad [White] was doing so well." [11]

All the other politicians mentioned in White's narrative—Browne, Beckemeyer, Clark, Link, Shephard, and Wilson—also rebutted White's charges. Browne accused White of "blackmail" and said he was the kind of man "who wants to live high without working." The real but innocent target of White's story, said Browne, was Lorimer. [12]

In spite of protestations of innocence, legal action quickly followed publication of White's manuscript. State's Attorney Wayman subpoenaed White and the other assemblymen mentioned in the confession to appear before a special Cook County grand jury; in Springfield, Sangamon County State's Attorney Edmund Burke also issued subpoenas for White. [13] On May 2, White appeared before the Cook County grand jury. He was nervous and distraught and added nothing to his published story of bribery. Beckemeyer, Link, Clark, and Shephard, who followed him, denied any complicity. On May 6, however, after his initial denial, Assemblyman Beckemeyer admitted

[11] *Inter-Ocean*, May 3, 1910. See White to Lorimer, Dec. 4, 1909, Lorimer to White, Dec. 13, 1909, printed in *Dillingham Committee Hearings*, III, 2556–57.

[12] *Tribune*, May 1, 1910.

[13] *Ibid*. Wayman and Burke clashed over the questions of jurisdiction and the subpoena of witnesses. Waymen would not let White answer a Sangamon County subpoena. See *Inter-Ocean*, May 6–13, 1910; *Dillingham Committee Hearings*, V, 4673–83 (Burke testifying), VI, 5752–57, 5799–5804 (Wayman testifying).

that Browne gave him $1,000 with the comment, "Here is the Lorimer money." Beckemeyer also said he received $900 from Wilson in the now-famous Southern Hotel bathroom.[14] The grand jury subsequently brought indictments against Browne, Link, and Wilson for bribery and for falsely testifying about the "jackpot." Faced by perjury charges, and guaranteed immunity by Wayman if he changed his testimony, Link confessed that he had received money from Browne and Wilson, although he did not tie it to his Lorimer vote.[15] After hearing from several other assemblymen, none of whom had anything startling to reveal, the grand jury concluded its investigation.

The White, Beckemeyer, and Link confessions proved costly to Lorimer. On May 8, when his new bank opened, deposits were far less than expected, and so many pledged bank subscriptions were withdrawn that Lorimer had to cancel his plans for a state trust company.[16] And how would the bribery story affect Lorimer's political fortunes? As the days passed without a Lorimer statement, rumors circulated in the Senate cloakroom about the implication of his silence.[17]

Raymond Robins, a radical social worker, tried to supply an answer as to how Lorimer could counter the *Tribune*'s charges. A romantic adventurer, Robins had worked as a coal-miner, attended law school, and made a fortune in the Alaskan gold fields before joining Graham R. Taylor in his settlement house, Chicago Commons. In 1905 Mayor Edward Dunne had appointed Robins, Jane Addams, Louis Post, and other Chicago reformers to the city school board. The board had attacked the school land leases held by several firms, including the Chicago *Tribune* Corporation. The *Tribune* responded by calling Robins and his board colleagues "freaks, cranks, mono-

---

[14] *Tribune*, May 6, 7, 1910. Beckemeyer confessed after Wayman granted him immunity from prosecution. The *Inter-Ocean* claimed that Wayman was pursuing the bribery case with great zeal because Levy Mayer, a *Tribune* attorney, was the power behind Wayman. The bribery case was also a convenient cover, claimed the *Inter-Ocean*, for the fraud being exposed in the Busse administration. See *Inter-Ocean*, Apr. 28–30, May 2–4, 1910.

[15] The Link testimony is printed in *Dillingham Committee Hearings*, VI, 6142–57. The *Tribune* reported that Link said he had been paid for his Lorimer vote. This is a distortion of the testimony. See *Tribune*, May 8, 1910.

[16] *Tribune*, May 9, 1910, Mar. 21, 1916; *Inter-Ocean*, May 9, 10, 1910.

[17] C. P. Barnes to Ira C. Copley, May 3, 1910, Copley Papers; Senator La Follette speaking in *CR*, 62nd Cong., 1st Sess., XLVII, 1435.

maniacs, and boodlers." In 1907, when Fred Busse was elected mayor with *Tribune* support, he ousted Robins, along with twelve others, from the board.[18] These incidents caused Robins to question the *Tribune*'s role as a moral leader in the Lorimer fight. He viewed the bribery charges as part of a political power struggle between the *Tribune* and Busse, and Lorimer and the *Inter-Ocean*, and he was glad to strike a blow through Lorimer at the *Tribune*.[19]

On the morning of May 14, Robins visited the Blond Boss and suggested that the *Tribune* school-lease "steal" story be used to discredit the paper. Lorimer listened carefully. "He seemed to be impressed with my suggestions," Robins wrote his wife. "If the Tribune Lease Steal were ventilated from the floor of the U.S. Senate and the speech franked all over Illinois . . . I would be willing to rest . . . with the feeling that principal and a good interest had been paid on the old Tribune score." [20]

After several days during which the progressive press demanded his resignation and cries rose for a Senate investigation, Lorimer decided to use Robins' material. He saw Robins on the evening of May 20 and told him to prepare the speech. Robins, working "overtime on the dope," finished late the next afternoon, just before Lorimer left for Washington. The whole affair, as described by Robins to his wife, had a melodramatic tone.

Dearest, Blessed Margaret:

It is so dark that I have the gas lit and it is only five o'clock. Rain has been falling in torrents and it is cold. I have just finished the mss of the vindication speech of the Senator in the most difficult moment of his career. An inner circle politician sat here in our little flat while his big automobile waited across the street for thirty minutes while I finished copying the "dope". . . . The whole situation has been remarkable from start to finish. I have worked under great pressure and feel limp. Of course we cannot know that he will have the courage in the last

---

[18] For the school board fight see Margaret D. Robins to Lincoln Steffens, Nov. 6, 1906, to Mary Dreier, [n.d.], 1907, printed in Mary E. Dreier, *Margaret Dreier Robins: Her Life, Letters, and Work* (New York, 1950), 29–31, 35–37; Allen F. Davis, "Raymond Robins: The Settlement Worker as Municipal Reformer," *Social Service Review* (June, 1959), XXXIII, 139–140.

[19] For Robins' views on the Lorimer exposé see Robins to Margaret D. Robins, May 12, 22, 24, 1910, Raymond Robins Papers, State Historical Society of Wisconsin, Madison.

[20] Robins to Margaret D. Robins, May 14, 1909 (two letters), Robins Papers.

hour. He seems willing to go the limit. . . . Come what may I have done my best to help pay a big debt to the Chicago Daily Tribune.[21]

On May 28 in Washington, looking "ministerial" in a double-breasted gray suit and white evening tie, Lorimer rose on a point of personal privilege to give his maiden Senate address—his "vindication speech."[22] Among the spectators in the crowded gallery were his wife and children, who listened intently throughout the several hours and thousands of words of Lorimer's defense.

Lorimer maintained that the White story was part of a *Tribune* conspiracy to drive him from public life and to ruin him financially because he would not place himself "under the absolute control and dictatorship of the *Tribune*." Involved in the plot were Governor Deneen and Medill McCormick, *Tribune* publisher.[23] White was McCormick's "depraved tool." Deneen was in the conspiracy because Lorimer had blocked his waterway plans and prevented the "squandering of $20,000,000 of the people's money. . . ." Browne, one of the plot's victims, was actually a "strong, high-minded, God-fearing, honorable man . . . [who] believed the Bible from cover to cover."

The root of the struggle, said Lorimer, was the attempt of the newspapers to "break up party organization and destroy party fealty" so they could control politics. Lorimer recounted his major political battles from 1886 to 1910, and in every case he saw the *Tribune* opposing the Republican "organization" and resorting to "lies and slander" to create the impression that the organization was devoted to plunder. Lorimer described the 1909 General Assembly session as "a last stand against the *Tribune* newspaper combination" by true Republicans. His own election was a symbol of rebellion against the newspaper dictatorship.

The *Tribune*'s true motivation, held Lorimer, was "revenue," not principle: "It acknowledges no party, proclaims no principles, and

---

[21] Robins to Margaret D. Robins, May 24, 1909, Robins Papers. See also letters of May 21, 22 (two letters), 23, 1910, *ibid.*

[22] *Tribune,* May 29, 1910. The Lorimer speech is in *CR,* 61st Cong., 2nd Sess., XLV, 7019–21, 7064–70.

[23] Actually, Medill McCormick had left the *Tribune* just before the White story broke. Robert R. McCormick was treasurer of the *Tribune* company. In his memoirs he claimed that "the responsibility for the Lorimer fight was mine, but the executive work was done by James Keeley. . . ." *Tribune,* July 11, 1954. Keeley's biographer notes, however, that McCormick relied completely on Keeley in the Lorimer case. See Linn, *James Keeley,* 155.

sails the political sea a pirate craft with the black flag nailed to the mast. Its only purpose is to gather money for its owners. . . ." It even preyed upon Chicago's schoolchildren, and here followed Robins' story of how the *Tribune* stole $100,000 each year from the public treasury. Other men had been lashed "into subjection" by the "pirate craft," or bought off, but not Lorimer. He would not surrender his "manhood" or "accept dictation." So the *Tribune* continued to oppose him: ". . . they fear I may aid in reviving the spirit of manhood in the Republican party, through which men of courage and honesty will be placed in public office and put a stop to their nefarious plundering of public office and the public treasury. . . ." [24] Here lay their motivation in publishing the White confession.

At the conclusion of his speech, Lorimer offered a resolution asking the Committee on Privileges and Elections to investigate the *Tribune* bribery charges and report back to the Senate.[25] On June 18, in response to Lorimer's resolution as well as a petition from the Illinois Legislative Voters' League, the Committee on Privileges and Elections designated a subcommittee to make the inquiry. The subcommittee consisted of Republicans Julius C. Burrows of Michigan, chairman, William P. Dillingham of Vermont, Robert J. Gamble of South Dakota, Weldon B. Heyburn of Idaho, and Democrats James B. Frazier of Tennessee, Thomas H. Paynter of Kentucky, and Joseph F. Johnston of Alabama. Their task was broader than that suggested by the Lorimer resolution: they were to investigate the whole question of whether "corrupt methods or practices" had been used in Lorimer's election rather than confining themselves to the *Tribune* charges.[26]

Meanwhile, in Chicago, the *Tribune* had responded to Lorimer's accusations with a blanket denial: White had written every word of his story, no politicians were involved with its publication, and the school board lease was legally obtained. In the same issue where it printed the full text of Lorimer's speech, it also published Democratic state senator Daniel W. Holstlaw's confession that Democratic state

---

[24] *CR*, 61st Cong., 2nd Sess., XLV, 7070.

[25] Senate Res. 247, *ibid.*

[26] The Voters' League resolution was written by James Keeley of the *Tribune*. See *Dillingham Committee Hearings*, II, 1903 (Keeley testifying); *CR*, 61st Cong., 2nd Sess., XLV, 7528. An amendment by Senator Borah adding the word "immediate" to the Senate resolution was defeated. See *ibid.*, 8452, 8501; New York *Times*, June 8, 19, 1910.

senator John Broderick of Chicago had paid him $2,500 for his Lorimer vote.[27] The *Tribune* now offered a $5,000 reward for "legal proof of the identity of all the members of the 'syndicate' which put up the money for Lorimer's election to the United States Senate." In view of the Holstlaw confession, Lorimer's long-winded effort at vindication seemed wasted.[28]

Simultaneously with the new revelations, Browne's attorneys unsuccessfully tried to have his bribery indictment quashed, claiming a lack of state jurisdiction. The lawyers chose a jury from a list of over a hundred veniremen, with a "small army of detectives" watching to prevent tampering. The trial began on June 14 with White as the first witness. There were no surprises in his testimony, and he did not make a strong impression. Especially damaging to him was the introduction of his two letters to Lorimer, which made White seem a blackmailer. The Chicago *Evening Post* commented editorially that White was "the most despicable character that has come to the notice of the people of Illinois in this whole bribery affair. He is an ingrate. He is a confessed bribe taker and is telling the truth now, if he is . . . because he is getting paid for it. . . ." [29]

Other members of the General Assembly followed White and repeated their stories essentially as given to the grand jury. Beckemeyer and Link still insisted that while they had received money from Browne, they had voted for Lorimer for nonmonetary reasons. Link, who weighed 300 pounds and agitatedly waved a fan as he testified in the hot courtroom, tearfully explained that he had only confessed to the grand jury after Wayman showed him a picture of his wife and of the penitentiary, and told him to make a choice. Link did not find it a difficult decision. A new witness, Assemblyman George W. Myers, testified that Browne had solicited his vote with the comment that there were "lots of state jobs to be had and also plenty of ready necessaries." [30]

Neither Browne nor Lorimer took the stand. Charles E. Erbstein, a brilliant young criminal lawyer, and P. M. O'Donnell made the

[27] Holstlaw also confessed to receiving $700 from the "jackpot" and $1,500 for his vote on a furniture contract for the General Assembly. Holstlaw's statement is printed in *Dillingham Committee Hearings*, III, 3045–46. He resigned from the General Assembly after his confession.

[28] *Tribune*, May 29, 30, 1910.

[29] *Post*, June 16, 1910; *Tribune*, May 25, 27, June 7, 8, 1910.

[30] *Tribune* and *Post*, June 17, 18, 1910.

defense summation before a packed courtroom with Erbstein reading from the New Testament about Christ's betrayal by Judas. Lorimer, rather than Browne, said the flamboyant defense attorney, had been chosen for the sacrifice, and the jury had to prevent another crucifixion.[31]

On June 29, after 115 hours of deliberation, the jury announced that it was divided eight to four and could not reach a decision. Four jurors preferred not to be classed with the Romans. The long period of decision was marked by discovery of an "observation plant" from which defense detectives watched the jury room and by a Wayman charge of jury-bribing. Judge William H. McSurely rebuked Wayman for his comments, but the District Attorney began preparations for another trial.[32]

The second trial ran into immediate difficulties. Judge George Kersten, who had taken McSurely's place, disclosed that nearly every prospective juror had been approached by detectives, supposedly employed by Browne's attorneys. Kersten discharged several panels before the jury was completed. Again White, Link, and Beckemeyer related their bribery stories. A Detective Keeley, from Wayman's staff, appeared as a defense witness and testified that an assistant district attorney had instructed him to treat Beckemeyer "right." To him this had meant taking Beckemeyer to a brothel and getting him drunk. Another defense witness, George Gloss, testified that White told him that he had not received the "big job" he expected for his Lorimer vote and was therefore "going to get even." The "jackpot" story was the result. Wayman and the defense attorneys clashed a number of times, and the judge fined two of the latter, Charles E. Erbstein and W. S. Forrest, for contempt of court. After a defense summation marked by "Lincolnesque panegyrics" of Lorimer, the case went to the jury for a second time.[33]

While the jury deliberated, other explosions were forthcoming, caused by ex-President Theodore Roosevelt. Roosevelt was concluding a western tour, and would cap a Chicago visit with a dinner at

[31] *Tribune*, June 21, 22, 1910.

[32] *Ibid.*, June 26–Aug. 1, 1910; New York *Times*, June 30, 1910; Ira. C. Copley to Frank E. Armstrong, June 25, 1910, Copley Papers.

[33] *Tribune*, Aug. 17–20, 27, Sept. 1, 2, 7, 8, 1910; New York *Times*, Aug. 17, 27, Sept. 1, 2, 7, 8, 1910. Wayman petitioned for and obtained a special grand jury to investigate perjury and jury-fixing. One witness, George Gloss, was indicted but never tried. See *Tribune*, Aug. 27, 31, Sept. 3, 1910.

the Hamilton Club. While ostensibly he intended the trip to heal the conservative-progressive split in the Republican party, it had the opposite effect. Roosevelt's speeches demanded advanced socioeconomic legislation. In Denver he struck at the Supreme Court as a block to social justice, and in Osawatomie, Kansas, he delivered his famous "New Nationalism" speech, calling for elevation of public welfare over private interests.[34] The press speculated whether he would use his Hamilton Club dinner speech to make new radical proposals.

Lorimer was scheduled to be seated at the Hamilton Club speaker's table. Roosevelt knew of the charges against Lorimer through the newspaper accounts and through privileged information he had received from Herman H. Kohlsaat. In the middle of August, in Chicago, Kohlsaat had told Roosevelt that Edward Hines had asked C. S. Funk, the general manager of International Harvester, to contribute $10,000 to a $100,000 Lorimer election fund.[35] Funk told the story to Kohlsaat in confidence because he did not want to involve his company in the bribery case. Kohlsaat, however, had broken the confidence and repeated Funk's story not only to Roosevelt, but also to Victor Lawson of the *Daily News* and James Keeley of the *Tribune,* and both had used it obliquely in their editorials on the Lorimer case.[36]

Roosevelt was informed of Lorimer's presence at the Hamilton Club head table by a John McCutcheon cartoon in the September 8 *Tribune.* The front-page cartoon showed the speaker's table and the faces of Lorimer, Roosevelt, and the chief of police. The caption said, "The Hamilton Club is giving a banquet tonight. Among those at the speakers' table will be the Chief of Police." Roosevelt claimed that Lorimer's presence insulted him, and demanded that club president

[34] George E. Mowry, *Theodore Roosevelt and the Progressive Movement* (New York, 1946), 141–144.

[35] *Dillingham Committee Hearings,* I, 440–442 (Kohlsaat testifying); Kohlsaat to Elihu Root, Jan. 17, 1911, printed in *ibid.,* VIII, 7333. See also J. A. Stewart to Roosevelt, Aug. 15, 1910, Roosevelt Papers; Roosevelt to Henry Cabot Lodge, Aug. 17, 1910, *Roosevelt Letters,* VII, 114–117.

[36] *Dillingham Committee Hearings,* I, 440–444 (Kohlsaat testifying); *CR,* 62nd Cong., 2nd Sess., XLVIII, 8771 (speech of Senator Dillingham). The *Tribune* headline on May 10, 1910, read, "Was It Sawdust? Who Furnished the Dust . . . to Bribe the Legislators to Elect William Lorimer to the United States Senate?" and also, "What Lumber Company Built Lorimer's Senate Chair?" See *Tribune,* May 10, 11, 29, 31, June 1–6, 1910.

THE HAMILTON CLUB IS GIVING A BANQUET TONIGHT. AMONG THOSE AT THE SPEAKERS' TABLE WILL BE THE CHIEF OF POLICE.

Chicago *Tribune*, Sept. 8, 1910

John H. Batten either withdraw Lorimer's invitation or he would not attend.[37] Batten thereupon telegraphed Lorimer: "Colonel Roosevelt positively declines to sit at the same table with you. Our invitation to you for this evening is hereby withdrawn." Lorimer had no comment, but two days later he resigned from the Hamilton Club.[38]

That night at the club dinner Roosevelt delivered a scathing attack on corruption in Illinois. He had read, he said, the reports of the various investigations and of the indictments and confessions: "Read that, and I defy an honest man . . . not to come to the conclusion that the legislature whose doings have been exposed was guilty of the foulest and basest corruption, and therefore of the most infamous treason to American institutions." He asked the "men of Illinois" to "purify" their politics. The implication was plain: get rid of Lorimer.[39]

Roosevelt's action received a mixed response throughout the nation. The *Tribune* editorial said it was "A Needed Precedent," the Springfield *Republican* called Lorimer "the best snubbed man in America today," and the Baltimore *Sun* credited Roosevelt with giving the country "an excellent lesson in sound morals." Ex-Senator Albert J. Hopkins wrote the former president that his sons "never tire of talking of the rebuke you gave to my successor." [40]

Others, however, criticized Roosevelt's snub, particularly because after leaving Chicago Roosevelt dined with Cincinnati's Boss Cox. The New York *Times,* as well as other papers, commented adversely on Roosevelt's lack of "consistency in morals," while the *Inter-Ocean* charged that Roosevelt was still angry over Lorimer's role in the meat-inspection fight; he had played a "dirty trick and was not ashamed." [41] One politician wrote Lorimerite Len Small that "it was the meanest & dirtiest little trick I ever known [sic] a big man to do. . . . After

[37] *Tribune*, Sept. 8, 1910.

[38] *Ibid.*, and New York *Times*, Sept. 9, 10, 1910. During the same month Hines was also snubbed because of his involvement in the Lorimer election. At the National Conservation Congress in St. Paul, Minnesota, the Illinois delegation voted 28 to 5 to remove Hines from the convention credentials committee. Hines charged that behind this action were Walter L. Fisher, Alfred E. Baker, and Isham Randolph, all of whom were "radically Pinchot-Roosevelt men." See Hines to Charles D. Norton, Nov. 1, 1910, and attached resolutions, Taft Papers.

[39] *Tribune* and New York *Times*, Sept. 9, 1910.

[40] There is a survey of press comment on the Hamilton Club episode in the New York *Times*, Sept. 12, 1910. See also Albert J. Hopkins to Roosevelt, Sept. 29, 1910, Harry Bird to Roosevelt, Sept. 12, 1910, Roosevelt Papers.

[41] See New York *Times*, Sept. 12, 1910, for press comment; *Inter-Ocean*, Sept. 9, 1910.

Teddy refusing to sit with Senator Lorimer & wined and dined with Boss Cox that is twice over as vicious & foul as Lorimer ever was." [42] Roosevelt himself explained that he had acted because of Lorimer's corrupt election, not because he was a boss: ". . . it became in my judgment a duty for someone to take the lead in showing that the people of his own party unqualifiedly condemned what he had done." [43]

But while observers may have expected Roosevelt's action to affect the Browne jury's deliberations, Browne was acquitted in his second trial. The jury, said the foreman, doubted White's and Beckemeyer's testimony.[44] Lorimer now commented that "Col. Roosevelt spoke for one man—Col. Roosevelt. Twelve good and true men have spoken for me." It was an expensive vindication; Lorimer had contributed $10,000 to pay Browne's defense costs. But it was necessary. Lorimer was "convinced that the whole machinery of the State's Attorney's office was used at the behest of Mr. Austrian . . . and the Chicago *Tribune* to destroy me and not to put Lee O'Neil Browne in the penitentiary." [45]

Browne's acquittal came at an opportune time, the opening of the primary campaign for county, assembly, and congressional nominations. Lorimer and the "jackpot" were the major issues in both Republican and Democratic primaries. Deneen made a statewide campaign asking for the retirement of the assemblymen who had voted for Lorimer for senator. "The issue," said the Governor, "is to rid the state of the members of the general assembly who represent the interests concealed behind the jackpot." On primary day the *Tribune* reminded voters to "remember the bathroom in St. Louis," and to

[42] Joe King to Len Small, Sept. 13, 1910, Small to King, Sept. 29, 1910, Lennington Small Papers, Illinois State Historical Library, Springfield.

[43] Theodore Roosevelt to Alfred Borden, Nov. 2, 1910, *Roosevelt Letters*, VII, 153.

[44] The jury did not hear of Rooosevelt's action before coming to its decision. See *Tribune*, Sept. 10, 11, 1910. On Oct. 30, 1910, one of the Browne jurors, Grant McCutchen, confessed to the Cook County grand jury that he had been promised a county job and paid $125 by Erbstein in return for a vote for acquittal. Erbstein was later indicted for bribery but never tried. See *Tribune*, Oct. 28–31, Nov. 1–6, 1910.

[45] Lorimer's comment on the Browne decision is in *Tribune*, Sept. 10, 11, 1910. His statement about the reasons for his $10,000 contribution to the Browne defense is in *Dillingham Committee Hearings*, VIII, 7576–78. See also William C. Boyden to William Kent, June 13, 1910, Kent Papers. Boyden wrote, "I have little confidence in Wayman, but Levy Mayer is the attorney of the Tribune, and he is supposed to control Wayman, and the Tribune will . . . move heaven and earth to put Lorimer out of business. Furthermore, it is fortunate that Wayman is most ambitious politically."

ask themselves if they were "in favor of making a bathroom the legislative chamber of the state of Illinois?" But the voters seemed to have a plumber's mentality; most of the Lorimer-Shurtleff-Browne group were renominated.[46]

The same pattern repeated itself on election day in November. Forty-one of the fifty Lorimer supporters up for re-election were victorious. Browne, Broderick, Chiperfield, Shanahan, Shurtleff, and "Bathroom Bob" Wilson returned to the General Assembly. Throughout the state, as in the nation, Democrats won, and the Deneenites fared no better than the Lorimerites among the Republicans. If the Lorimer affair had redounded to anybody's benefit, it seemed to be that of the Democratic party.[47]

But the Senate and its investigating committee, not the voters, controlled Lorimer's future, and while the politicians were preparing for the election, the Burrows Committee had begun its deliberations. Perhaps Lorimer's future was not as secure as the Browne acquittal and the elections might have indicated.

The Burrows Committee first met on September 22, 1910, in the Chicago Federal Building. Judge Hanecy appeared for Lorimer and Alfred S. Austrian represented the *Tribune*. Since the committee had no attorney, Austrian assumed the role of prosecutor, and the committee only called witnesses offered by him.[48] Acrimonious and heated clashes between the two counsels, especially over the admissibility of evidence, marked the three weeks of the Chicago hearings. Frazier was the committee's sharpest questioner, while Paynter, Gamble, and Johnston seldom spoke.

Three crucial points developed at the beginning of the hearings: Austrian admitted that he would not directly connect Lorimer with the payment of money; the committee decided not to inquire into the "jackpot" aside from Lorimer's election; and the committee ruled that hearsay evidence was unacceptable. Austrian said he would attempt to show that Lorimer's election was corrupt, but he would not inquire into the corruption's source or the extent of malfeasance in the Gen-

---

[46] *Tribune*, Sept. 15, 17, 18, 1910. Seventy assemblymen who had voted for Lorimer ran for renomination; fifty were successful.

[47] *Tribune*, Nov. 9, 1910; Mowry, *Theodore Roosevelt and the Progressive Movement*, 155–156. The Democrats swept the Cook County ticket and gained five Illinois congressional seats. Only in western states where the progressives were in control of the party did the Republicans do well.

[48] *CR*, 62nd Cong., 2nd Sess., XLVIII, 8772 (speech of Senator Dillingham).

eral Assembly.[49] These three decisions, as well as the committee's self-imposed restriction to Austrian's witness list, severely limited the scope of the investigation.

The hearings generally went badly for the anti-Lorimer forces. Hanecy claimed that the *Tribune* was engaged in a conspiracy against Lorimer, and the admission by the first witness, president Clifford W. Barnes of the Legislative Voters' League, that editor James Keeley had prepared his petition calling for a Senate investigation supported the charge.[50] The identity or testimony of the other witnesses created no surprises. Almost all were Illinois legislators mentioned in the White manuscript. White, who spoke so softly that Burrows had constantly to ask him to speak louder, made a poor impression. He put one more name on the bribery list, that of Democratic Assemblyman Joseph S. Clark of Vandalia, but aside from this added nothing to his published confession.[51]

Daniel W. Holstlaw, who followed White, now maintained that while he received $2,500 for his Lorimer vote, he would have voted for Lorimer whether paid or not.[52] Beckemeyer and Link, each of whom had received $1,000 from Browne, took the identical position. They voted for Lorimer because he was the best Republican before the General Assembly.[53] Assemblyman Henry A. Shephard admitted that he had voted for Lorimer in return for the right to name his home-town postmaster but denied any knowledge of money payment. And while Henry Terrill, Republican state senator, testified that Chicago Democrat John Griffin told him he could get $1,000 for a Lorimer vote, Griffin denied it.[54]

On October 6, Broderick and Browne, both of whom were under indictment for bribery in Springfield, testified. Broderick denied paying Holstlaw $2,500 for his Lorimer vote, but refused, on the advice of counsel, to answer any other questions. Browne also rebuked the bribery charges. He said he supported Lorimer for patronage and to disrupt the Republican party. He insisted that men "would have voted

---

[49] See the discussion and committee rulings in U.S., Senate, *Senate Report 942*, Pt. 2, 61st Cong., 3rd Sess. (Washington, 1911), 41–105, hereafter cited as *Burrows Committee Hearings*.

[50] *Ibid.*, 19–32; *Tribune*, Sept. 23, 1910.

[51] The White testimony is in *Burrows Committee Hearings*, 82–195.

[52] Holstlaw's testimony is in *ibid.*, 195–224.

[53] See *ibid.*, 218–219, 224–261, for Beckemeyer's testimony, and 281, 295–296, for Link's.

[54] See *ibid.*, 318, 322, for Shephard's testimony, and 498, 680–681, for Terrill's.

for him [Lorimer] as soon as his name was mentioned . . . independent of party, party leaders, or anybody else." Shurtleff, who followed Browne, agreed that Lorimer's personal popularity, not money or patronage, caused his election.[55]

No important witnesses followed Shurtleff ("Bathroom Bob" Wilson was missing from Chicago), and on October 9 the Burrows Committee ended its Chicago hearings. Early in December, however, in Washington, "Bathroom Bob" appeared before the committee. He said he had been in a Michigan rest home and did not know that a subpoena had been issued for him. Wilson testified that he was in St. Louis on July 15, 1909, the date when he supposedly distributed the "jackpot," to arrange a banquet in honor of Lee O'Neil Browne, and that he knew nothing of Lorimer money. As for his own Lorimer vote, he was responding to a sickbed plea by Democratic sheriff Tom E. Barrett that he help Lorimer.[56]

Wilson's testimony marked the formal end of the Burrows Committee hearings. The committee spent the next ten days considering the evidence preparatory to making a final report. The investigation had produced no new information. Surprising, however, was the committee's failure to call as witnesses Lorimer, Governor Deneen, Edward Hines, reputed to have financed Lorimer's election, and Herman H. Kohlsaat, who instigated the rumor that Hines had done so.[57] The responsibility for the restriction of the witness list belonged to *Tribune* attorney Alfred S. Austrian, since the committee only called witnesses suggested by him. Chicago lawyer Otto Gresham charged that Austrian deliberately neglected to call Hines; he wrote President Taft that the "firm of lawyers he [James Keeley of the *Tribune*] employed to present his case to the Committee on Privileges and Elections . . . had business connections that would not desire a verification of the rumors as to whence some of the money came." [58] The supposed conspiracy to oust Lorimer from the Senate was matched by a counter-conspiracy to keep the investigation from affecting

---

[55] See *ibid.*, 548, 551–557, for Broderick's testimony, and 662, 696, for Browne's.
[56] *Ibid.*, 727, 740–744. The request was supposedly made in 1904.
[57] Hines wrote presidential secretary Charles D. Norton that "the Chicago Tribune or the Prosecution did not call me, although prior to that, in their paper, I was pictured most strongly as the one alleged to have furnished the money for the Senator's election. Had I been called, under oath, I would have felt justified in making perfectly plain my exact connection with his election." See Hines to Norton, Nov. 1, 1910, Taft Papers.
[58] Gresham to Taft, Mar. 13, 29, 1911, Taft Papers.

certain vested interests. The case against Lorimer could only involve the bought and not the buyers.[59]

The Burrows Committee completed its consideration of the testimony on December 17, 1910. It reported to the Committee on Privileges and Elections that it found no evidence that Lorimer had engaged in bribery or that his election was corrupt. The report maintained that even if the White, Beckemeyer, Link, and Holstlaw confessions were true, Lorimer had the necessary majority of uncorrupted votes to validate his right to his Senate seat.[60]

Four days later, over Senator Beveridge's protest, the Committee on Privileges and Elections, by a vote of 10 to 2, accepted the Burrows Committee report. Republicans Bulkeley, Burrows, Depew, Dillingham, Gamble, and Heyburn, and Democrats Bailey, Fletcher, Johnston, and Paynter composed the majority. Beveridge, a Republican, and Frazier, a Democrat, reserved the right to submit minority reports.[61] Beveridge maintained that he needed more time to study the voluminous testimony and briefs and that he would delay a final decision until after the Christmas holidays.[62]

The majority agreed with the Burrows Committee that Lorimer had not engaged in bribery and that there were insufficient corrupt votes to change the election results. They challenged the veracity of White's story, commented upon his "corrupt character," and cast doubts upon the trustworthiness of the Beckemeyer, Holstlaw, and Link confessions. Most controversial, however, was their insistence that corrupt votes had to be subtracted from the quorum majority as well as the Lorimer total. Thus, even if seven votes were tainted, Lorimer had enough for election.[63]

The Lorimer case monopolized the attention of the Capital in the period before Beveridge completed his deliberations. The case intruded into a Senate torn by intra-party strife. The Republican split between insurgents and regulars, reflected in the Payne-Aldrich tariff debate, was exacerbated by the Ballinger-Pinchot conservation con-

[59] See the remarks by Senator Dillingham in *CR*, 62nd Cong., 2nd Sess., XLVIII, 8772–73.

[60] New York *Times* and *Tribune*, Dec. 18, 1910.

[61] See *Senate Report 942*, Pt. I, for the report of the majority.

[62] *CR*, 61st Cong., 3rd Sess., XLVI, 552–554.

[63] Senator Heyburn presented a concurring opinion in which he noted that the state was responsible for the actions of its own officers, and that since the courts had found no one guilty of wrongdoing in the Lorimer election, the Senate had no basis for action. The Heyburn opinion is included with the majority report.

troversy and the unsuccessful attempt of Taft and the Old Guard to purge the insurgents in the 1910 congressional elections. The struggle between insurgents and Old Guard had reached a peak, and progressives such as Beveridge and La Follette sought issues to use against their foes.[64]

The Lorimer case was a natural for the Senate insurgents. Their hero, Theodore Roosevelt, had sparked the anti-Lorimer cause by refusing to sit with him at the Hamilton Club banquet. They could use the charges of legislative corruption in Lorimer's election as evidence of the need for the direct election of senators. Lorimer was not only a "boss," a figure odious to the progressive mind, he was also a firm ally of the Senate establishment. Conservatives Aldrich, Penrose, and Murray Crane of Massachusetts defended Lorimer's right to his seat. They accepted Lorimer as a "regular," who had to be protected from the progressives. The Republican majority of the Committee on Privileges and Elections, aside from Beveridge, also reflected establishment opinion, further proving to the insurgents that the Senate was an Old Guard "club" which protected its own.

And yet the Lorimer case did not precisely reflect the insurgent–Old Guard split. The Burrows Committee testimony convinced President Taft that Lorimer's election was corrupt. However, Taft had not always taken this position. He had been irritated by the "decided hit" Roosevelt made when he refused to sit with Lorimer at the Hamilton Club, and told his aide Archie Butt that he "felt it very cruel to have judged Lorrimer [*sic*] in advance . . . that every man was entitled to his day in court, and it was not giving the Senator a square deal." [65] During the Burrows Committee hearings, however, Taft disassociated himself from Lorimer. When Otto Gresham asked Taft if it was true, as rumor had it, that in 1909 he had favored Lorimer's election, Taft denied it. "It is possible that I may have expressed my anxiety that the matter should come to an end, but as I did not know Senator Lorimer and did know Senator Hopkins . . . there was no special reason why I should favor Senator Lorimer. I should have preferred to have had Governor Deneen to any of them." In his own hand Taft added, "My recollection now is that I was asked by

64 Mowry, *Theodore Roosevelt and the Progressive Movement*, 36–156.
65 Archie Butt to Dear Clara [Mrs. Lewis F. Butt], Sept. 11, 1910, in Archie Butt, *Taft and Roosevelt: The Intimate Letters of Archie Butt* (2 vols., Garden City, 1930), II, 509.

telegram to express an opinion in favor of Lorimer and declined to take any part." [66]

Undoubtedly Taft, the legalistic conservative, was shocked by the revelations of corruption in the Illinois General Assembly, but he was also anxious to prove that the progressives had no monopoly on political virtue. At Christmas he wrote his brother Horace that he was "perfectly disgusted with the committee report on the Lorimer case."

> There is, in my judgment, ample evidence to require the vacation of his seat, but he commands the support of the Packers of Chicago, of the Lumbering industry of the whole country, the oleomargarine people and the Brewing interest. So Bailey and all the Democrats except one on the committee have rallied to his support. When I think of their position in regard to Lorimer, and contrast it in respect to Ballinger, the more I think of dogs. Of course this is a Senate question and I have to be careful not to be public in my efforts, but I am doing everything I can to force some regulars to the attack. It is neither right nor politic that the insurgents should be left alone to uphold the cause of decency in this case.[67]

To prevent the progressives from capturing the credit in the Lorimer case, Taft encouraged regulars Theodore E. Burton, Knute Nelson, and Elihu Root and progressives William E. Borah and Coe Crawford to join the anti-Lorimer fight. Burton and Root agreed to make Senate speeches. Taft wrote Roosevelt of his efforts but warned him to be cautious in his own actions lest "outside interference" push the Democrats to Lorimer. Roosevelt responded that he would act with caution.[68]

---

[66] Taft to Otto Gresham, Sept. 8, Oct. 11, 1910, Taft Papers; W. Werner to Victor Lawson, Sept. 16, 1910, Lawson Papers. Judges Peter S. Grosscup and K. M. Landis both told Gresham that Taft had approved of Lorimer's election.

[67] Taft to Horace Taft, Christmas, 1910, F. A. Delano to Charles D. Norton, Jan. 3, 1911, Taft Papers. Delano wrote, "Just as a suggestion for the New Year don't let insurgents get all the credit for opposing Lorimer." Written across the bottom of the letter was the note, "The President has seen."

[68] Taft to Roosevelt, Jan. 6, 1911, Taft Papers; Roosevelt to Taft, Jan. 7, 1911, *Roosevelt Letters*, VII, 203–204. Taft, hearing that Roosevelt was about to write a "strong article on the Lorimer case and publish it in *The Outlook*," warned him not to. Roosevelt responded that he had "not the slightest intention of writing any such article." Taft wrote to John C. Shaffer, publisher of the Chicago *Evening Post*, "We are doing what we can to purge the Senate and Illinois. Of course, I can not take an open part in the matter, because I do not want to give the friends of Lorimer an opportunity to change the issue from one of corruption to

Roosevelt was already at work behind the scenes, partially as a result of his own interest and partially as a result of the urging of John Callon O'Laughlin, the *Tribune* Washington correspondent. O'Laughin, who had been Roosevelt's Assistant Secretary of State, believed that the Lorimer case represented "one of the last battle-grounds of privilege." O'Laughlin asked Roosevelt to speak to Senator Henry Cabot Lodge about Lorimer.[69]

Lodge, who usually stood with the Old Guard, was convinced by his Massachusetts colleague Murray Crane that Lorimer was the victim of newspaper persecution. Neither Lodge nor Crane liked the insurgents and they viewed the attack on Lorimer as part of the fight against the Senate establishment. Lodge maintained that since Lorimer was not connected with the bribery and since he had a majority of uncorrupted votes, he should not be ousted. Without this rule, he wrote Roosevelt, "innocent men" would be put "at the mercy of blackmailers and unscrupulous political enemies. . . ."[70]

Roosevelt disagreed. In his opinion the evidence showed "that there was universal corruption." He maintained that when "overnight a Republican who the day before had received one vote suddenly received fifty-five Republican and fifty-three Democratic votes, it is simply out of the question to treat the man as honest."[71] At Roosevelt's urging, Root spoke to Lodge and assured him that Lorimer "must have known of all that was going on and that . . . it was bribery that determined the election. . . ." Lodge responded that if this could be shown, "the case becomes pretty clear." The "good name of the Senate" was at stake.[72]

Beveridge prepared to defend his chamber's "good name" by care-

_____

one of invading the prerogative of the Senate by the Executive. . . ." See Taft to Shaffer, Jan. 7, 1911, to John V. Farwell, Jan. 7, 1911, Taft Papers.

[69] O'Laughlin also asked Roosevelt to influence Beveridge. He noted that "Lorimer represents better than anyone else the alliance of Big Business and Politics. The Lumber Trust, the Steel Trust, the Railroads, the Beef Trust, and allied interests, have exerted their influence." See O'Laughlin to Roosevelt, Dec. 15, 22, 31, 1910, Roosevelt Papers.

[70] Lodge to Roosevelt, Dec. 31, 1910, Jan. 7, 1911, Roosevelt Papers.

[71] Roosevelt to Lodge, Jan. 3, 1911, *Roosevelt Letters*, VII, 200. Roosevelt later wrote Lodge: "The Lorimer case is just as clear as the case against Tweed. It will stand as one of the test cases in our history. It is not in the least a difficult case to understand. It needs no special study of the testimony. The incontrovertible facts show at a glance what was done." Roosevelt to Lodge, Jan. 27, 1911, Roosevelt Papers.

[72] Lodge to Roosevelt, Jan. 7, 1911, Roosevelt Papers; Roosevelt to Lodge, Jan. 12, 1911, *Roosevelt Letters*, VII, 204–205.

fully studying, during the recess, the "evidence of the law." [73] Important friends, such as financier George W. Perkins and newspaper publisher Frank Munsey, encouraged him, while President Samuel A. Harper and Professor A. C. McLaughlin of the University of Chicago wrote in "appreciation of your attitude . . . [in] the Lorimer investigation." [74] On January 9, when the Senate resumed its session, Beveridge was ready.

Lorimer began discussion of the case by reiterating his innocence; he announced he would remain in the chamber during the debate. After a race with Senator Owen as to who would be first to present the anti-Lorimer resolution, Beveridge offered his minority report produced by a "careful and judicial" reading of the evidence.[75] Beveridge maintained that "far more than enough bribery was practiced in this election to invalidate the same. . . ." He believed that seven votes were "tainted": those of the bribed, Beckemeyer, Holstlaw, Link, and White, and those of the bribers, Browne, Broderick, and Wilson. According to "the law," said Beveridge, taking issue with the Committee on Privileges and Elections, the corrupted votes should be subtracted from Lorimer's total but not from the quorum majority. This gave Lorimer one less than a majority. Realizing that he was on weak ground, Beveridge suggested the establishment of a new Senate precedent: "If only one case of bribery be clearly established in the election of a Senator, [the] entire election was invalid." Beveridge resolved that Lorimer's election be declared void.[76]

The arguments and rationale of the majority and minority reports set the tone and issues of the Senate debate that stretched over the next month and a half. Lorimer was present most of the time. The principal questions argued by the Senate concerned the number of bribed votes and the reliability of the bribery testimony; the formula to be used in determining whether or not Lorimer had a majority of noncorrupted votes; the connection of the "jackpot" to

[73] Beveridge to Albert Shaw, Dec. 24, 1910, to A. C. Bartlett, Dec. 26, 1910, Beveridge Papers.

[74] See the following letters to Beveridge, all in Beveridge Papers: A. C. McLaughlin, Dec. 22, 1910, Albert Shaw, Dec. 23, 1910, Samuel A. Harper, Dec. 30, 1910, David H. Jackson, Dec. 22, 1910, Norman G. Flagg, Dec. 26, 1910, Richard Lloyd Jones, Dec. 30, 1910, and Harry McGartney, Jan. 3, 1911.

[75] See Albert Shaw to Beveridge, Dec. 23, 1910, Beveridge Papers. Beveridge to Shaw, Dec. 24, 1910, Beveridge Papers.

[76] *CR*, 61st Cong., 3rd Sess., XLVI, 657. The Beveridge minority report is printed as *Senate Report 942*, Pt. 3, the Frazier report as Pt. 4. Frazier maintained that there were seven tainted votes, giving Lorimer less than a majority.

the Lorimer election; and whether Lorimer knew of the bribery. Subsidiary issues were the wisdom of allowing the *Tribune* to present the case to the subcommittee, and the bearing of the case upon the honor of the Senate and the direct election of U.S. senators. Intermingled and involved with the discussion was legislation concerning tariff reciprocity, a tariff commission, and the direct election of senators.

In the debate the Republican insurgents and progressive Democrats opposed Lorimer, as did Republican regulars Burton and Root, whom Taft and Roosevelt had influenced. The Republican Old Guard, led by members of the Committee on Privileges and Elections and by Murray Crane, and a number of southern Democrats, led by Joseph Bailey of Texas, supported Lorimer. Some of the Old Guard defended Lorimer because they considered the case an unjustified insurgent attack on the Senate establishment. Others, strongly influenced by Senate tradition, believed that Senate precedent did not justify unseating Lorimer.[77] The pro-Lorimer southern Democrats worried that the Senate might upset precedents opposed to federal interference in local elections. They also reflected that sentiment which makes the southern senator "pre-eminently *the* 'Senate man,' " preoccupied with an "almost mystical meaning" of Senate precedent and tradition.[78]

Each side in the case made a number of set speeches. Eight senators, five Democrats and three Republicans, all of whom save one were members of the Committee on Privileges and Elections, made pro-Lorimer speeches. There were eleven anti-Lorimer speeches, seven by Republican insurgents, two by Republican regulars, and two by Democrats.[79] Lorimer spoke near the debate's end and attempted to answer the charges made in the previous addresses.

Both before and during the debate, powerful outside forces worked

---

[77] See William Dana Orcutt, *Burrows of Michigan and the Republican Party* (2 vols., New York, 1917), II, 292–293.

[78] William S. White, *Citadel: The Story of the U.S. Senate* (New York, 1956), 67–79; Claude E. Barfield, Jr., "The Democratic Party in Congress, 1909–1913" (unpublished Ph.D. dissertation, Northwestern University, 1965), 244.

[79] Senators Bailey, Burrows, Robert J. Gamble, Duncan U. Fletcher, Weldon B. Heyburn, Joseph F. Johnston, Thomas H. Paynter, and F. M. Simmons made pro-Lorimer speeches. All but Burrows, Gamble, and Heyburn were Democrats and all but Simmons were members of the Committee on Privileges and Elections. Beveridge, William E. Borah, Joseph L. Bristow, Norris Browne, Theodore E. Burton, Coe Crawford, Albert B. Cummins, Robert M. La Follette, Robert L. Owen, William A. Smith, and William J. Stone spoke against Lorimer. All but Owen and Stone were Republicans.

to shape its outcome. The nation's media, for example, were generally convinced of Lorimer's guilt. They condemned the report of the Committee on Privileges and Elections and applauded Beveridge for his minority stand. The press concluded that the Burrows Committee investigation revealed corruption in Lorimer's election. According to the Springfield *Republican,* the case "should add new strength to the movement for popular election of Senators." *The Outlook,* voicing the opinions of Theodore Roosevelt, denied that the Senate was "bound by the technical procedure of the criminal courts. . . . " It should act "to purge the august body . . . of the contamination that would come from their admission to membership of any man whom they are morally certain is guilty of corrupt election practices." [80] Placed on each senator's desk during the debate was a small booklet entitled "Comment on the Lorimer Case," containing 123 newspaper editorials demanding Lorimer's expulsion. *Tribune* correspondent "Cal" O'Laughlin, who supplied a number of senators with anti-Lorimer material, was probably responsible.[81]

Letters attacking Lorimer's election and demanding his ouster deluged senators and the President.[82] When Cyrus H. McCormick of International Harvester heard that the Secretary of the Navy intended to appeal to the President for Lorimer, he wrote Taft's secretary warning that he would "greatly regret to have him do anything on that side of the case . . . our Company does not stand for, nor have any sympathy with that kind of politics." [83] Walter L. Fisher sent one extremely important letter to Senator La Follette, while Herman H. Kohlsaat sent another to Root at Fisher's request. Both

[80] "Lorimer's Suspended Vindication," *The Literary Digest* (Jan. 7, 1911), XLII, 2–3; New York *Times,* Jan. 12, 1911; *The Outlook* (Dec. 31, 1910), XCVI, 987 (Jan. 7, 1911), XCVII, 13–14 (Jan. 21, 1911), XCVII, 88–89.

[81] Roosevelt to Lodge, Jan. 12, 1911, *Roosevelt Letters,* VII, 204–205. There is a copy of the booklet in the Elihu Root Papers, Library of Congress. James Keeley of the *Tribune* came to Washington and spoke to a number of senators. See *Dillingham Committee Hearings,* II, 1905, 2079 (Keeley testifying).

[82] See the following letters to Beveridge, all in Beveridge Papers: Norman G. Flagg, Dec. 26, 1910, William P. Welker, Jan. 16, 1911, J. A. Eichler, Feb. 13, 1911. Also Albert T. Capps to Elihu Root, Jan. 4, 1911, Root Papers; A. N. Williams to Senator Thomas H. Carter, Dec. 24, 1910, Carter Papers. When James Keeley heard that several Illinois congressmen were soliciting pro-Lorimer letters to be sent to Senator Cullom, he had his friends send anti-Lorimer letters. See *Dillingham Committee Hearings,* II, 1923 (Keeley testifying).

[83] McCormick to Charles D. Norton, Jan. 20, 1911, Taft Papers. Attached to the letter was the following note: "The President said Secretary Norton could handle this himself. Show to Mr. Meyer when he calls—*OK.*"

letters told of Hines's $100,000 Lorimer election fund. Fisher wrote: "The story is that shortly before Mr. Lorimer's election, $100,000 was raised and expended through Mr. Hines in the interest of Mr. Lorimer, and that after Lorimer was elected . . . Hines went to the representatives of large interests in Chicago and stated to them that the money raised by him and others had been in the nature of an underwriting, because it had been necessary to raise it very quickly. . . ." Fisher added that Hines's activities in Springfield and Washington corroborated the story. Although both Fisher and Kohlsaat declined to reveal their source, their letters strengthened the determination of Root and La Follette in the case.[84]

The Lorimer forces, however, were not without resources. As *The Outlook* noted, "powerful special interests are exerting their influence in behalf of Senator Lorimer." Hines, who admitted speaking and writing to senators, was most active. According to Senator La Follette, he "waylaid Senators at every turn . . . [and] was brazen and impudent in his work."[85] W. C. Brown, president of the New York Central Railroad and a director of Lorimer's La Salle Street bank, wrote Root that he had known Lorimer "intimately for twenty-five years," and that he was "one of the cleanest men in every respect that I have ever known."[86] A former House member, J. Adam Bede, warned Taft that Lorimer's friends controlled Illinois and might vote against him in 1912 if the Senate's "cleanest member" was ousted.[87]

Especially significant because of what it implied about the cultural overtones of the Lorimer fight was the threat by Father Francis C. Kelley, president of the Catholic Church Extension Society, to deprive Taft of the Catholic vote if the Senate unseated Lorimer. Kelley

[84] Kohlsaat to Root, Jan. 17, 1911, Root Papers; Fisher to La Follette, Jan. 17, 1911, Fisher Papers. See also Kohlsaat to Shelby M. Cullom, Feb. 10, 1911, printed in *Dillingham Committee Hearings*, VIII, 7334. On Feb. 15, 1911, the *Record-Herald* carried an editorial which asked, "Do we know all that we might about the Illinois jack pot? Do we know all there is to be known concerning the $100,000 fund that was raised to pay for Lorimer's votes?"

[85] *The Outlook* (Jan. 21, 1911), XCVII, 88–89; New York *Times*, Jan. 10, 1911; *Tribune*, Jan. 12, 13, 14, 17, 1911. The La Follette comment is in *CR*, 62nd Cong., 1st Sess., XLVII, 1549. Hine's is in *Dillingham Committee Hearings*, II, 1840–42, 1873–75. He specifically named Senators Borah, Cullom, Jones, and Piles.

[86] W. C. Brown to Root, Jan. 20, 1911, Root Papers. Brown wrote at Hines's request. See *Dillingham Committee Hearings*, II, 1838 (Hines testifying).

[87] J. Adam Bede to Taft, Jan. 15, 1911, Taft Papers. See also F. F. Hanley to Taft, Jan. 26, 1911, *ibid.*

was a close friend of Hines, who was a prominent Catholic layman. Taft angrily replied to Kelley that "if the entire Catholic Church stood before me I should not be moved in my attitude towards Lorimer [*sic*]." The President complained to Archie Butt that "the beef packers . . . the Catholic interests and all the lumber interests," as well as Vice-President James Sherman, were for Lorimer.[88]

The speeches in the Senate debate ranged in interpretation and emotion. Burton and Owen, for instance, supported Beveridge's opinion that a single bribed vote invalidated an election.[89] Five senators maintained that seven corrupt votes deprived Lorimer of his majority, and one, Senator Cummins, called the ruling that the tainted votes had to be subtracted from the quorum total "the most alarming and dangerous proposition ever made in the Senate. . . ."[90] Five senators also insisted that Lorimer knew of the bribery, and all the anti-Lorimerites believed the "jackpot" and the Lorimer fund connected.[91] Some used the case as justification for the direct election of senators, and all insisted that Senate honor required Lorimer's ouster.[92]

Burrows gave the first speech defending his committee's report. He praised Lorimer for seeking the investigation: "Crime does not seek exposure and publicity; criminals do not invite judgment and disgrace." The only applicable question, Burrows maintained, was whether there were enough tainted votes to destroy Lorimer's majority, since precedent supported the committee's ruling that the mere presence of corrupt votes did not invalidate an election.[93] A number of senators from the pro-Lorimer group discussed the same point in detail. All were disgusted by White, a "low and vile" creature who followed a "sinuous, slimy course." In contrast, Senator Paynter found Browne "a man of great intellect . . . of marvelous intellect." While several of the pro-Lorimer speakers admitted there was

---

88 Taft to Father Francis C. Kelley, Jan. 30, 1911, attached to Victor Lawson to Herman H. Kohlsaat, Aug. 23, 1911, Lawson Papers; Archie Butt to Dear Clara [Mrs. Lewis F. Butt], Jan. 28, 1911, in Butt, *Taft and Roosevelt*, II, 584–585; Max Pam to Taft, Feb. 2, 1911, Taft to Pam, Feb. 3, 1911, Taft Papers. Pam, who served as Taft's liaison with various Chicago ethnic groups, was also friendly with Kelley. He wrote Taft not to worry about the Catholic vote since Kelley "*is not indispensable to my influence in 'that' quarter of my control of 'that situation.'*"
89 *CR*, 61st Cong., 3rd Sess., XLVI, 665, 1980.
90 *Ibid.*, 1531.
91 *Ibid.*, 717, 728.
92 *Ibid.*, 665 (Owen), 1106 (Borah), 1635–36 (Davis), 3525 (Crawford).
93 *Ibid.*, 1042–49.

corruption in the General Assembly, they denied that it was connected with Lorimer's election.[94]

Root's powerful speech on February 5 bolstered the anti-Lorimer cause. Although he opposed many progressive reforms, Root believed self-policing necessary if the Senate was to forestall criticism and changes such as the direct election of senators. Speaking before crowded galleries, he attacked the members of the Burrows Committee for their narrow "view of the scope and nature of their duties" and for abdicating to the *Tribune* the "guardianship of our honor and the preservation of the integrity of our Government." Root held that Browne was Lorimer's agent and that the Senate should reject all thirty of his faction's votes. Unless the Senate unseated Lorimer, warned Root, the people would lose faith in representative government: ". . . it rests with the Senate . . . to do its duty now, and . . . purge itself of this foul conspiracy against the integrity and purity of our government." [95]

Taft wrote Root after his speech that it "was great, one of the greatest things you have done," and reported that Senator Lee S. Overman had told him "that when you finished, it seemed to him that Lorimer couldn't have a vote except the committee and that they would be glad to get out of it." O'Laughlin, writing to Roosevelt in thanks for influencing Root's speech, calculated that the vote would be 51 to 39 against Lorimer.[96]

These optimistic predictions were premature. The "Lorimer lobby" continued hard at work. According to the New York *Times* it included Hines, representatives of the Chicago, Milwaukee & St. Paul Railroad, Standard Oil, the Illinois Central Railroad, the packers, the president of the Kimball Piano Company, "Uncle Joe" Cannon, and most of the Illinois congressional delegation. In the Senate, Bailey and Crane labored in Lorimer's behalf, while letters from Lorimer supporters bombarded Senator Cullom.[97]

[94] *Ibid.*, 1280, 1416, 1420, 1894, 2060.

[95] *Ibid.*, 1886–93.

[96] Taft to Root, Feb. 4, 1911, Taft Papers; J. C. O'Laughlin to Roosevelt, Feb. 4, 1911, Roosevelt Papers; O'Laughlin to Root, Feb. 3, 1911, Root Papers. See also J. H. Wilson to Root, Feb. 6, 1911, J. H. Blount to Taft, Feb. 3, 1911, Root Papers; William B. Ridgely to J. Otis Humphrey, Feb. 3, 1911, J. Otis Humphrey Papers, Illinois State Historical Library, Springfield.

[97] New York *Times* and *Tribune*, Feb. 13, 1911; J. C. O'Laughlin to Roosevelt, Feb. 6, 1911, Roosevelt Papers; Kohlsaat to Cullom, Feb. 15, 1911, Lorimer to David Shanahan, Jan. 18, 1911, printed in *Dillingham Committee Hearings*, VIII, 7334–35, 7840.

Barely a week after his supposedly definitive speech, Root wrote to Kohlsaat seeking more information about the bribery fund and asking if his "friend" upon "whom Mr. Hines called" could testify. Kohlsaat responded that his "friend's testimony would greatly help . . . but it would absolutely ruin him to take the stand. He was approached as an officer of the company [International Harvester] . . . and could not come out in the open without the consent of the directors, some of whom are friendly to Lorimer. . . . The weakness of the anti-Lorimerites," added Kohlsaat, "is that the Chicago Tribune is back of the fight to unseat Lorimer." [98]

On February 13 and 14, Bailey's eloquent and forceful speech further damaged the anti-Lorimer cause. The eccentric Bailey, a combination of populist and conservative, wore his usual costume of string tie and sparrow-tail suit. He attacked the "errors" and "misstatements of fact" in the anti-Lorimer speeches. Bailey contended that Lorimer's election was valid even with eleven tainted votes, since the corrupt votes had to be deducted from the quorum total as well as Lorimer's. The "courage" rather than the "integrity" of the Senate was on trial, concluded Bailey; "this Republic is menaced more by cowardice than by corruption." He challenged his colleagues "to be brave enough . . . [to] dare to do what we believe is right and leave the consequences to God and to our countrymen." [99]

Bailey's speech changed at least one vote, that of Benjamin R. Tillman, and probably that of several other Democrats. Once Lorimer's expulsion seemed guaranteed; now it appeared doubtful. On February 17 Crane wrote Nelson Aldrich: "There will be a safe vote against declaring Lorimer's seat in the Senate vacant. The insurgents are all opposed to him, also Root, Burton, and Lodge. Nearly all the others will vote for him and enough Democrats to make his position safe. This, however, is contrary to the general expectation but is my private opinion." [100]

Before the vote, however, Lorimer and Beveridge delivered their speeches. Beveridge began on February 21 and finished on February

[98] Root to Kohlsaat, Feb. 11, 1911, Kohlsaat to Root, Feb. 15, 1911, Root Papers; Kohlsaat to La Follette, Feb. 21, 22, 1911, to Senator Murray Crane, Feb. 20, 22, 1911, printed in *Dillingham Committee Hearings*, VIII, 7332–33.

[99] *CR*, 61st Cong., 3rd Sess., XLVI, 2474–75, 2483–88.

[100] Crane to Aldrich, Feb. 17, 1911, Nelson Aldrich Papers, Library of Congress; Lodge to Roosevelt, Feb. 21, 1911, Roosevelt Papers; *Tribune*, Feb. 17, 1911; Sam Hanna Acheson, *Joe Bailey, the Last Democrat* (New York, 1932), 291.

23–24. Lorimer spoke on the 22nd, and delivered his defense in "a deliberate, dignified manner," with an "air of sincerity." His friends packed the galleries.

In a "clear, strong voice," Lorimer told of his election. He denied that he had organized or could have organized the General Assembly to choose a U.S. senator, and insisted that Deneen, not he, had blocked Hopkins. He had been selected by the General Assembly because it could not elect anyone else. Fifty-three Democrats had voted for him not because of bribery but because of personal friendship, his waterway efforts, and anti-Hopkins feeling.[101] Pulling on a rich store of boyhood and adult recollections, he detailed the factors that had caused many Democrats to support him. They were his friends, said Lorimer, not Browne's hirelings, and would have acted the same regardless of Browne's inclinations. Lorimer denied that he had ever used money to effect an election "or for any corrupt purpose." "On my word as a man and on my word as a Senator," he concluded, "I am not guilty. . . ."[102]

The galleries vigorously applauded Lorimer's moving appeal and it left Senator Tillman in tears, but it did not affect the vigor with which Beveridge, making his last major Senate speech, spoke. Proclaiming that *"American institutions . . . the character of the American people is on trial,"* Beveridge derided Lorimer's defense. "It was a novel and an undoubtedly truthful account of peculiar popular strength; but *it did not touch the issue we are to determine here."* ("The flowers that bloom in the spring, tra la, have nothing to do with the case.") He attacked the "weird rulings" of the subcommittee on evidence and insisted that White's story was *"corroborated at every material point."* In addition, the committee erred in holding that Lorimer had a legal majority in spite of the corrupt votes. Quoting from scripture and warning that the Republic was in danger, he concluded with the prophecy that "the congregation of hypocrites is desolate and fire has consumed the tabernacles of bribery."[103]

---

[101] Lorimer listed twenty-three Democrats who had voted for him out of personal friendship, eight because of the waterway, and two because of anti-Hopkins feelings. See *CR,* 61st Cong., 3rd Sess., XLVI, 3118–23.

[102] *Ibid.,* 3124.

[103] *Ibid.,* 3279–3306. See also Roosevelt to Beveridge, Feb. 24, 1911, Beveridge to Roosevelt, Mar. 3, 1911, to William A. Ketcham, Feb. 27, 1911, Beveridge Papers. The Beveridge Papers contain a file of letters congratulating Beveridge for his stand on the Lorimer case.

As the debate on the Lorimer case ended, the anti-Lorimer forces shifted their tactic from rushing a vote to delaying one, thereupon revealing the uncertainty of their position. They believed that their chances of ousting Lorimer would improve in the new session with the lame-duck Lorimer supporters gone.[104] But their wishes in this regard became intertwined with their desire for Canadian reciprocity and tariff commission legislation, both of which followed the Lorimer case in the regular order. The Senate establishment could threaten to block them until the Lorimer vote.[105]

During the last two weeks of February, for instance, the reciprocity advocates and the pro-Lorimer forces sought an agreement. Lumberman Edward Hines, spokesman for the National Lumber Manufacturers' Association, was one of the chief anti-reciprocity lobbyists, and according to the New York *Times,* he agreed to reduce his opposition in return for Lorimer support. *Tribune* editor Keeley met presidential secretary Norton on the Washington train and told him that Lorimer would "keep his seat because of trading of votes against reciprocity." [106]

More obvious was Bailey's delay of a vote on the tariff commission to block a threatened filibuster on the Lorimer case. Taft and the insurgents favored the commission as a scientific method of setting tariff rates, while the Democrats, who viewed the commission as a Republican subterfuge to bypass tariff revision, and the Old Guard, who saw it as an attack upon protectionism, opposed it.[107] On February 25, and again on February 27 during a late-night session, when insurgents Bristow and Crawford commenced delaying tactics, Bailey announced he would insist upon the regular order if they continued.[108] This would have prevented a vote on the tariff commission

---

[104] See *CR,* 61st Cong., 3rd Sess., XLVI, 776, 1216–17, 1636, 2489–90, 3309; New York *Times,* Feb. 24, 26, 27, 1911.

[105] Crane to Aldrich, Feb. 17, 1911, Aldrich Papers; L. Ethan Ellis, *Reciprocity 1911* (New Haven, 1939), 103.

[106] New York *Times,* Feb. 19, 1911; *Tribune,* Feb. 1, 1911; Charles D. Norton to Taft, Feb. 22, 1911, Taft Papers; Ellis, *Reciprocity,* 103. Supporting reciprocity were the nation's newspaper publishers, Taft, the Democrats, Roosevelt and Beveridge, and Crane, Penrose, Reed Smoot, and George Wetmore of the Old Guard. Opposing it were the lumber interests and insurgents Borah, Cummins, and La Follette, as well as a number of regular Republicans. See Ellis, *Reciprocity,* 88, 95; Pringle, *Taft,* II, 594.

[107] Pringle, *Taft,* 599–600; Barfield, "Democratic Party in Congress," 244.

[108] *CR,* 61st Cong., 3rd Sess., XLVI, 3406, 3580, 3584, 3586–88; New York *Times,* Feb. 27, 1911; *Tribune,* Feb. 28, 1911.

that session. Bristow angrily wrote William Allen White: "The machine crowd in the Senate . . . will sacrifice anything to seat Lorimer. They have given, by assistance of Bailey and others on the Democratic side, the Lorimer case right of way over the pension bill and the tariff commission . . . seemingly preferring to take the chance of a defeat or failure to act upon any important legislative measure, rather than take chances of failing to seat Lorimer during this session." [109]

With Bailey and the pro-Lorimer forces in command, the insurgents decided to allow the Lorimer vote in return for the tariff commission legislation. On February 28, the Senate agreed to consider the tariff commission before the session ended and scheduled the vote on the Lorimer case for the next day, March 1. Significantly, on the 28th, by a vote of 54 to 33, the Senate defeated the joint resolution providing for the direct election of senators. Lorimer voted nay on the proposed amendment.[110]

On March 1, meeting before packed galleries, the Senate voted 46 to 40 to retain Lorimer in his seat. Thirty-six Republicans and ten Democrats voted for him; twenty-two Republicans and eighteen Democrats against. All the insurgents opposed him, along with regulars Root, Lodge, and Burton. The pro-Lorimer position of the ten lame-duck Republican senators proved decisive. Most Republicans who voted for Lorimer were also anti-reform on economic, social, and political questions. They came predominantly from more urban and industrial states than Lorimer's opponents, and were older, of more limited formal education, and of longer Senate tenure. These differences, however, did not apply to the Democrats.[111]

Senator Cullom supported his colleague although, according to Taft, he would have voted differently if the trend had been against Lorimer. Cullom explained that he had done what he thought was his "duty in the premises, and with as clear a conscience as I ever did anything

[109] Joseph L. Bristow to William Allen White, Feb. 27, 1911, White Papers.

[110] CR, 61st Cong., 3rd Sess., XLVI, 3639, 3669.

[111] Ibid., 3760; New York Times and Tribune, Mar. 2, 1911. Based upon the classification of "supporters" and "opponents" of reform used by Jerome M. Clubb, "Congressional Opponents of Reform," 183–186, nineteen Republican "opponents" of reform voted to retain Lorimer and six to eject. From the Democrats, four "supporters" of reform voted to retain Lorimer, fifteen Democrats classified as "most favorable" to reform voted to eject, five "most favorable" voted to retain, and two did not vote. See also Howard W. Allen, "Geography and Politics: Voting on Reform Issues in the United States Senate, 1911–1916," *Journal of Southern History* (May, 1961), XXVII, 216–228.

in my life." Lorimer, convinced that Senator Bailey had saved his seat, telegraphed the Texan that he had kept him "from a fate worse than death." [112]

Why was Lorimer retained in spite of the opposition of Taft, Roosevelt, Root, Lodge, all the insurgents, and most of the nation's press? The bitter division within the Republican party between the progressives and the Old Guard, the concern of Republican and Democratic traditionalists for Senate precedent, and the personal influence of Bailey were all important factors. The Old Guard saw the Lorimer case as a further insurgent onslaught upon the Senate establishment; its members believed the case a test of their ability to maintain control. Senators such as Burrows and Heyburn thought Lorimer unconnected with the bribery and they stood by Senate precedent in insisting that unless a direct tie could be shown, Lorimer should not be ousted. And, in an age rife with press attacks upon Senate ethics and charges of corruption, many senators were bothered by the *Tribune*'s zeal in the case.[113]

Most press comment scathingly criticized the Senate's action. The *Tribune* warned that while "the interests" had "won a glorious victory," it would be "the costliest in the history of government by big business in this country." The Springfield *Republican* noted that "not for many years, has the Senate done anything more displeasing to the moral sense of the American people," while the New York *Globe* said that "the whole body is besmirched and bemired." Many newspapers insisted that Lorimer was guilty regardless of his Senate exoneration.[114]

Those papers that defended the decision, such as the New York *Sun* and the *Inter-Ocean,* maintained that "justice has been done— literal, abstract, exact justice." [115] But, while this was the Old Guard voice speaking, others, besides the conservatives, believed the judg-

[112] J. Otis Humphrey to Taft, Feb. 19, 1911, Taft to Humphrey, Feb. 21, 1911, Taft Papers; Cullom to Kohlsaat, Mar. 11, 1911, Herman H. Kohlsaat Papers, Illinois State Historical Library, Springfield; Lorimer to Bailey, Mar. 5, 1911, quoted in Acheson, *Joe Bailey,* 292.

[113] Orcutt, *Burrows,* II, 292–293; *CR,* 61st Cong., 3rd Sess., XLVI, 1042–43, 1286–87, 1896. For concern over the role of the *Tribune* in the case see Lodge to Roosevelt, Jan. 28, 1911, Roosevelt Papers; Otto Gresham to Taft, Mar. 13, 1911, Taft Papers; Kohlsaat to Root, Feb. 15, 1911, Root Papers.

[114] There is a survey of press opinion in *Tribune,* Mar. 5, 1911; "Lorimer Plucked from the Burning," *The Literary Digest* (Mar. 11, 1911), XLII, 443–445.

[115] "Lorimer Plucked from the Burning," 445; *Inter-Ocean,* Mar. 2, 1911.

ment fair. Otto Gresham noted to President Taft that while he believed "Lorimer's seat was purchased," that alone "is not evidence."

> The weakness in the case against Mr. Lorimer was the failure to make some showing as to where Lee O'Neil Brown [*sic*] received the money which Charles White says Brown gave to him and the other Members of the Legislature. . . . Aside from the importance of corroborating White on this part of his confession from a legal standpoint, it became vitally important to do so after it developed that under the contract between White and the Tribune, White had received money from the Tribune and was to receive more.

"The logic" of the situation, continued Gresham, was to "refer the case back to the Committee on Privileges and Elections, with . . . instructions to . . . make an investigation on their own responsibility, and also to get the evidence that was manifestly in existence and would supply the missing link." The handling and outcome of the case showed the error in having a newspaper as "Prosecuting Attorney." [116]

Meanwhile, in Chicago, the Lorimerites rejoiced. On March 5, when Lorimer returned from Washington, a parade of exuberant followers escorted him from the train station to his home. The imposing figure of parade marshal William ("Big Bill") Thompson led over two hundred automobiles, three brass bands, and thousands of people through the city streets. At Lorimer's home Hines and Hanecy told of the "Band of Hope" that had labored for Lorimer in Washington, and Father Michael Bonfield greeted the Senator as "one honored by all citizens regardless of creed or nationality." [117]

Father Bonfield's comment suggests that many Chicago immigrant groups, especially Roman Catholics, considered the attack on Lorimer an attack upon them by puritan progressive reformers. They, like Father Francis C. Kelley, had sprung to his defense. A number of Protestant ministers, on the other hand, prominently condemned the Lorimer vindication. In Rockford a group of ministers approved a resolution criticizing the Senate decision, as did the Aurora Federation of Men's Church Clubs. Rockford churches tolled their bells forty-six times, once for each pro-Lorimer vote. The Congregationalist ministers of Boston demanded an explanation from Senator Mur-

---

[116] Gresham to Taft, Mar. 13, 29, 1911, Taft Papers.
[117] *Tribune*, Mar. 5–6, 1911.

ray Crane for his stand, while Philadelphia ministers denounced the pro-Lorimer vote of Senator Boise Penrose. Many Chicago ministers condemned the Senate in their Sunday sermons.[118]

During the Senate debate, several senators referred to this cultural conflict, although it was not prominent in the discussion. Both Senators Coe Crawford and Robert L. Owen pointedly referred to John Broderick and "Manny" Abrahams as "saloonkeepers from Chicago," and as typical of the "evil and sinister forces" that ruled American cities. Crawford commented that Governor Deneen was more trustworthy than Lorimer because he was a "Methodist minister's son," conveniently overlooking the fact that Lorimer was the son of a Presbyterian minister. And Senator Root mentioned "Manny" Abrahams so prominently in his speech that Lorimer charged him with trying to "create prejudice." [119]

In his comments to his Chicago admirers, however, Lorimer concentrated on the "trust press." "There is a 'trust' among newspaper men all over the land," he said: "Senators were threatened with annihilation if they voted for me. . . . Never have I known such a combination determined on the destruction of one man. Never have I been able to understand how, in the face of such a tremendous combination, it has been possible for one man to escape absolute destruction." But Lorimer survived, and because of the "disposition to live up to the everlasting truth," he would now "go forward from this day with more courage than ever before." [120]

There remained, however, one obstacle to complete celebration. On the day after Lorimer's vindication, the Helm Committee of the Illinois Senate, in response to Senate Resolution No. 17, began its hearings on "acts of bribery and official misconduct" in the Forty-sixth General Assembly.[121] Lorimer's ordeal was still incomplete.

[118] *Ibid.*, Mar. 5–14, 1911.

[119] *CR*, 61st Cong., 3rd Sess., XLVI, 717, 721, 1288, 3122, 3523–25, 3755.

[120] *Tribune*, Mar. 5–6, 1911. "Yes, right has again prevailed," wrote Lorimerite Len Small, "and our friends throughout the State have reason for rejoicing." See Small to Alexander McLean, Mar. 4, 1911, Small Papers.

[121] *Senate Journal, Forty-seventh General Assembly* (Springfield, 1911), 5, 127–129, 138; *Tribune*, Jan. 5, Mar. 3, 1911.

CHAPTER **11**

The Lorimer Case Reopened

THE DENEEN-CONTROLLED STATE SENATE formed the Helm Committee on January 17, 1911, to investigate "alleged acts of bribery and official misconduct" by members of the General Assembly. Its creation reflected the widespread feeling of dissatisfaction with the Burrows Committee and its failure to trace the source of the "jackpot." [1] The committee consisted of Republicans Douglas W. Helm, chairman, John C. McKenzie, Logan Hay, and Samuel Ettelson, and Democrat Frank W. Burton. John J. Healy, former Cook County state's attorney, a man whom Lorimer called one of his most "violent and bitter enemies," was counsel. The Lorimerites, again in control of the General Assembly, tried to block the investigation, but to no avail.[2] The Deneenites and the progressives were determined to gain a maximum of political mileage from the case.

Throughout the state the Lorimer case caused a growth of progressive sentiment. In June, 1910, for instance, in reaction to the White confession, a "People's Conference" of leading progressives met in Peoria and demanded the enactment of the initiative, referendum, and recall, corrupt practices legislation, and statewide civil

[1] *Senate Journal, Forty-seventh General Assembly,* 5, 127–129, 138. The Helm Committee proceedings and final report are printed as U.S., Senate, *Election of William Lorimer. . . . A Copy of the Report . . . ,* Senate Doc. 45, 62nd Cong., 1st Sess. (Washington, 1911), hereafter cited as *Helm Committee Hearings.* The typed transcript is in the Illinois State Archives, Springfield.

[2] *House Journal, Forty-seventh General Assembly,* 107; Ralph A. Straetz, "The Progressive Movement in Illinois, 1910–1916" (unpublished Ph.D. dissertation, University of Illinois, 1951), 69–71; *Tribune,* Mar. 4, 1911. In the lower house of the General Assembly, Browne, Shanahan, Shurtleff, and Smejkal, among others, were allowed to select their seats "as a mark of esteem and recognition of their long service as members of the House of Representatives. . . ." See *House Journal, Forty-seventh General Assembly,* 107.

service. George E. Cole called it an "Illinois rebellion."[3] Now Lorimer's vindication caused a further reaction, as "mass meetings" throughout Illinois condemned the decision.[4]

Lorimer's enemies expected the Helm Committee to provide a number of revelations regarding corruption in the Senator's election. They especially anticipated explosive testimony from Edward Hines, the committee's first witness. Hines, however, with the sharp-tongued Elbridge Hanecy as his attorney, provided a different kind of revelation than expected. He insisted that he had intervened in the Illinois contest as the agent of President Taft and Senators Aldrich and Penrose. They all had been anxious to have a protectionist senator from Illinois for the tariff debate.[5]

In Washington, Taft read Hines's testimony with consternation. Anxious to refute Hines's allegation that he wanted Lorimer to become a candidate, he dictated a "memorandum" detailing his relation to the election. Taft related that during the tariff fight "several Senators" ("I have forgotten who they were") asked him to "express an opinion in favor of the election of Lorimer," but that he had refused to do so. He only desired two Republican senators from Illinois. Taft refuted the validity of Hines's charge and released to the press a letter he had written in 1910 in which he denied any involvement in Lorimer's election.[6]

On March 29, Herman H. Kohlsaat appeared before the Helm Committee. The committee had subpoenaed him because of his *Record-Herald* editorial of February 15, 1911, which had asked, "Do we know all that there is to be known concerning the $100,000 fund that was raised to pay for Lorimer votes?" Kohlsaat testified that a "close friend" informed him of "the raising of $100,000 to bring about the election of Mr. Lorimer," but he would not supply his friend's name; he could not "violate that confidence." Frustrated by the publisher's stand, the committee ruled that unless he supplied his informant's name within a week, it would hold him in contempt.[7]

---

[3] Louis Post to William Allen White, Mar. 17, 1911, White Papers; *Tribune*, June 28, 29, 1910; Straetz, "Progressive Movement in Illinois," 35–38.

[4] *Tribune*, Mar. 13, 1911.

[5] *Helm Committee Hearings*, 25–35.

[6] "Memorandum by the President," Mar. 29, 1911, Taft to Gresham, Oct. 11, 1910, Mar. 31, 1911, Taft Papers. See also New York *Times* and *Tribune*, Mar. 30, 1911.

[7] *Helm Committee Hearings*, 56–62. The *Record-Herald* editorial of Feb. 15, 1911, is printed in *Dillingham Committee Hearings*, I, 522. See also *Record-Herald*

Hearing of Kohlsaat's predicament, Funk decided to testify voluntarily. On April 8 he appeared before the Helm Committee and told its members that Hines had tried to solicit $10,000 from him for a $100,000 Lorimer election fund. "Well, we put Lorimer over down at Springfield," Hines supposedly said, "but it cost us about a $100,000 to do it. . . ." Hines wanted $10,000 from Funk because "you people [International Harvester] are just as much interested as any of us in having the right kind of a man at Washington." Funk was to pay the money to Edward Tilden, president of the National Packing Company and a close friend of Lorimer.[8]

In response to Funk's charges, Hines publicly denied that he ever "put up or asked for a dollar for any fund to be used for the election of Mr. Lorimer to the United States Senate." [9] In Washington, however, in response to Funk's testimony, La Follette introduced a Senate resolution naming a special committee to investigate whether "corrupt methods and practices" were used in the Lorimer election.[10] "It looks as though," wrote William Kent, "Brother Lorimer would get his," and while some papers felt that La Follette's resolution was not "judicious or fair," most agreed that the case should be reopened.[11]

Meanwhile, back in Springfield, evidence injurious to Hines and to Lorimer accumulated. Several lumbermen testified that both Hines and his brother-in-law C. H. Wiehe, secretary of the Edward Hines Lumber Company, had boasted of aiding Lorimer's election. One of those so testifying was Wirt H. Cook, a partner with Hines, William

---

editorial of Jan. 20, 1911, which asks, "Who got the $100,000 Lorimer election money?" printed in *ibid.*, VIII, 7776–77.

[8] Kohlsaat to Senator Helm, printed in *Helm Committee Hearings*, 65–67, and Funk's testimony, 67–74. Funk also said that after the publication of the *Record-Herald* editorial of Feb. 15, 1911, Hines visited him at his office and tried to refresh "his recollection" of their previous meeting. Hines denied that he had mentioned any money and said that he had merely discussed the general situation in Springfield.

[9] *Tribune,* Apr. 6, 1911.

[10] *CR,* 62nd Cong., 1st Sess., XLVII, 101. La Follette's resolution named five freshman senators, John D. Works, Charles E. Townsend, George P. McLean, John W. Kern, and Atlee Pomerene to make the investigation. During the previous session La Follette had prepared a resolution asking that the case be stayed until further information was secured on the $100,000 election fund. He had not presented it because he could not persuade Kohlsaat to testify about the fund. See La Follette's comments in *ibid.*, 1665; Kohlsaat to La Follette, Feb. 21, 22, 1911, printed in *Dillingham Committee Hearings,* VIII, 7332.

[11] Kent to Stanley Washburn, Apr. 10, 1911, Kent Papers; New York *Times* and *Tribune,* Apr. 8, 1911; "Lorimer Case Open Again," *The Literary Digest* (Apr. 22, 1911), XLII, 769–770.

O'Brien, and the Weyerhaeuser interests in the Virginia & Rainy Lake Lumber Company.[12] Cook related that Hines had told him that he had spoken with Senator Aldrich about Lorimer's election and that it was "all fixed"; Hines would "furnish all the money . . . required."[13] Wiehe, however, who followed Cook, denied the truth of the charges about Hines and himself. Angrily he waved a pistol when a photographer tried to take his picture. While Wiehe acknowledged that Hines believed himself responsible for Lorimer's election, it was through his influence, not his money.[14]

While the public tried to absorb this testimony, the Illinois Senate, by a vote of 40 to 7, found Edward Tilden, whom Funk had identified as the collector of the Lorimer fund, in contempt because of his refusal to produce his books for the Helm Committee.[15] On April 28 Tilden was arrested but freed on a writ of *habeas corpus* by "Lorimer" Judge Adelor J. Petit. During the next few days counsel for Tilden and for the Helm Committee argued before Judge Petit over the committee's subpoena powers. On May 6 Petit issued a decision upholding the writ on the grounds that the committee's actions were unconstitutional: the Senate could investigate its own members but not individuals unconnected with the legislature. Such investigation was the province of the judicial branch.[16]

Petit's decision meant that witnesses called by the Helm Committee could disregard its subpoenas with impunity. A Chicago *Evening Post* editorial reflected the outrage of the anti-Lorimerites: "It was a gross impropriety for Judge Petit to consent to take the Tilden case in the first place, in the light of his well-known personal and political re-

[12] *Helm Committee Hearings*, 149–153; Cook to F. C. Weyerhaeuser, Feb. 7, 1911, printed in *Dillingham Committee Hearings*, I, 636–637. According to Weyerhaeuser, Hines and Cook had argued, and Hines carried a gun because he feared violence from Cook. See Ralph W. Hidy, Frank Ernest Hill, and Allan Nevins, *Timber and Men: The Weyerhaeuser Story* (New York, 1963), 196. In contrast to this, however, there is also evidence that Hines was a short-tempered and vindictive man. On Oct. 29, 1963, Mr. Richard G. Brennan, former secretary to Alfred E. McCordic, who was Cook's lawyer, wrote the author that after McCordic had testified in the Dillingham Committee hearings, Hines hired detectives to follow him and seek out evidence to "disgrace or ruin Mr. McCordic if possible."

[13] *Helm Committee Hearings*, 142–146.

[14] *Ibid.*, 175–186; *Tribune*, Apr. 26, 1911.

[15] *Senate Journal, Forty-seventh General Assembly*, 982–990, 1026–29. George M. Benedict, cashier of the Drovers Deposit National Bank, and William C. Cummings, president, were also held in contempt. Lieutenant Governor John G. Oglesby, president of the Senate, refused to accept responsibility for the arrests.

[16] Petit's decision is reprinted in *ibid.*, 1225–38; *Tribune*, Apr. 29, May 1–4, 1911.

lationships. . . . But his decision is not only bad taste; it is indefensible law, an abuse of the judicial position too flagrant to be allowed to pass." [17] The Illinois Senate passed a resolution critical of Petit's decision, but the Judge had effectively nullified the Helm Committee investigation.[18] The committee decided to end its hearings and compile a final summation.

The committee report, approved by all members, concluded that "the election of William Lorimer would not have occurred had it not been for bribery and corruption." It accepted as fact the Funk-Hines conversation involving the $100,000 fund, noted the refusal of Tilden to produce his books, and criticized Judge Petit's ruling. On May 18, by a vote of 39 to 10, the Illinois Senate approved the report and asked the U.S. Senate to investigate Lorimer's election further.[19]

The Senate insurgents, with their ranks strengthened by the 1910 elections, grasped the Helm Committee revelations as a means to reopen the Lorimer case. On May 22 Robert M. La Follette began an exhaustive four-day review of the Lorimer case and of the Helm Committee's evidence.[20] La Follette pleaded for the appointment of a special committee (an "unprejudiced jury") to make a new investigation. He noted that of the fifteen members of the Committee on Privileges and Elections, nine had voted for Lorimer. La Follette's resolution, which he had introduced on April 6, named five freshman senators as the investigating body.[21]

La Follette's action precipitated a spate of other resolutions and speeches on the question of who should conduct the new Lorimer inquiry, although no senator questioned its necessity. Democratic minority leader Thomas S. Martin's resolution was the principal one opposing La Follette's. Martin, who had voted against Lorimer, resolved that Privileges and Elections conduct the investigation and inquire into the "jackpot." [22]

---

[17] *Post,* May 8, 1911.

[18] *Senate Journal, Forty-seventh General Assembly,* 1288, 1367; *Tribune,* May 10, 1911.

[19] *Senate Journal, Forty-seventh General Assembly,* 1431. The Helm Committee report is in *ibid.,* 1380–88; *Tribune,* May 19, 1911.

[20] La Follette had conferred with Illinois progressives Charles E. Merriam, Charles R. Crane, and Walter Rogers between the sessions. Belle Case and Fola La Follette, *Robert M. La Follette* (2 vols., New York, 1953), I, 326.

[21] *CR,* 62nd Cong., 1st Sess., XLVII, 1600–1610, 1628–46, 1654–82, 1732–34.

[22] *Ibid.,* 1482.

Martin was trying to compromise between the Democratic Old Guard, consisting of members such as Bailey and Tillman, who had supported Lorimer, and Democratic "insurgents" such as Luke Lea, Robert L. Owen, and Atlee Pomerene, who favored the La Follette suggestion. On May 22 the Democratic caucus approved the Martin resolution with the understanding, arrived at with the Republican leadership, that the investigation would be conducted by a subcommittee of Privileges and Elections consisting of five original members and three freshmen. Four of the original would be Lorimer supporters and the fifth an anti-Lorimerite. The three new senators would come from each party's progressive wing. Although the Republican insurgents and several Democrats opposed the compromise, on June 1 the Senate approved it 48 to 20.[23]

One week later, the Senate accepted a committee consisting of Republicans William P. Dillingham of Vermont, chairman, Wesley L. Jones of Washington, William S. Kenyon of Iowa, and Robert J. Gamble of South Dakota, and Democrats John W. Kern of Indiana, Duncan U. Fletcher of Florida, Luke Lea of Tennessee, and Joseph F. Johnston of Alabama. Dillingham, Johnston, Fletcher, and Gamble had voted to retain Lorimer in his seat, Jones had voted against, and Kern, Lea, and Kenyon were freshman members. The resolution instructed the committee to inquire into the "jackpot" and its relation to the Lorimer election.[24]

Lorimer, whom the press had criticized for not appearing before the Burrows Committee, telegraphed Dillingham that he had previously not testified because "nothing was charged against me personally." Now, however, he would appear in order to "refute any charges that may be made or any suspicions that any one may have as to the validity of my election." [25] Still upholding the system that had produced his election, on June 12 Lorimer voted against the Borah resolution for the direct election of U.S. senators.[26] But the Senate approved the reform, indicating its changed composition since the preceding session. It was not a good omen for Lorimer.

---

[23] See Martin's comments in *ibid.,* 1676–77—the vote on the compromise is 1682; New York *Times,* May 26, 1911; *Tribune,* May 28, 30, June 2, 1911; Barfield, "Democratic Party in Congress," 246. During the debate Senator Jeff Davis commented that Lorimer was "either the biggest ass that ever disgraced the Senate or the biggest knave that ever disgraced the Senate."

[24] *CR,* 62nd Cong., 1st Sess., XLVII, 1732–34.

[25] Lorimer to Dillingham, June 3, 1911, quoted in *Tribune,* June 4, 1911.

[26] *CR,* 62nd Cong., 1st Sess., XLVII, 1924.

The so-called Dillingham Committee began its hearings on June 20, 1911, and completed them on February 9, 1912. It met from June 20 to August 9 in Washington; from October 10 to November 22 in Chicago; and from December 5 to February 9 again in Washington. The committee heard 186 witnesses, ranging from Senators Aldrich and Penrose to the cigar clerk at the Chicago Union League Club. Most witnesses discussed one of three topics: the "jackpot," conditions in the Forty-sixth General Assembly, or the validity of Funk's charges against Hines. Some also testified about a *Tribune–* International Harvester conspiracy against Lorimer. The published record of the hearings consisted of nearly 9,000 pages and filled eight large volumes.

In contrast to the Burrows Committee, the Senate provided counsel for its investigating body. Appearing for the Dillingham Committee were former Cook County state's attorney John J. Healy, who had served the Helm Committee in a similar capacity, and John H. Marble, chairman of the Board of Review of the Interstate Commerce Commission. Judge Hanecy again directed Lorimer's defense, while W. J. Hynes represented Edward Hines. The attorneys wrangled considerably less than in the Burrows hearings. The committee, discarding the rule of the previous investigation, agreed to accept "hearsay" evidence.[27] Kern and Kenyon were the most active questioners.

Except for a few weeks in Chicago, the hearings took place in a small room, which was often filled with the press and congressional aides, on the ground floor of the Senate office building. The audience was usually loyal to Lorimer and it applauded when Hanecy scored. Lorimer, who attended all the committee sessions, sat in the front row looking, according to the *Tribune,* "bland and humble, the picture of innocent martyrdom." Hines and Hanecy sat next to him.[28]

On Saturday, June 24, after the appearance of several pro- and anti-Lorimer witnesses, the ubiquitous Kohlsaat took the stand. He told the committee of his lifelong opposition to "Lorimerism," which he defined as "the affiliation, cooperation, and cohesion of Democrats and Republicans for party pelf and for private pelf." He related how Funk had told him of the Lorimer election fund, and of his pledge not to release it. He did admit, however, that he *had* told Victor

---

[27] *Dillingham Committee Hearings,* I, 3–5; *Tribune,* June 10, 13–16, 19, 1911.
[28] See the description of the hearing room and of Lorimer in Claude G. Bowers, *The Life of John Worth Kern* (Indianapolis, 1918), 229–231.

Lawson of the *Daily News* and that it affected that paper's editorial policy, and that he *had* told Theodore Roosevelt and that it was responsible for Roosevelt's refusal to sit with Lorimer at the Hamilton Club. Kohlsaat also admitted writing to Senators Root, Crane, and Cullom of the corruption fund.[29] While some observers approved of Kohlsaat's "public-spirited" busybodyism, others found him more akin to an "assassin of character." [30]

Funk appeared before the committee on the following Monday. His testimony was unchanged since the Helm Committee hearings; he insisted that Hines had solicited $10,000 from him for a $100,000 Lorimer election fund. Funk characterized Hines as a "man quite inclined to boast of his achievements, quite disposed to be familiar on short acquaintance, and quite anxious to have people think he was a large factor in large matters." [31] Funk's description helped explain Hines's supposed willingness to boast of electing Lorimer. But while some witnesses testified that Hines had talked of using money in the Lorimer election, others denied that he had done so.

The testimony of the two principals supposedly connected with the Lorimer fund, Edward Tilden of the National Packing Company and Edward Hines, reflected the committee's problem in obtaining uncontradicted evidence. Tilden, for instance, denied any knowledge of such a fund. He explained that he had refused to let the Helm Committee see his books because they were his "personal private affairs." He added, to the amazement of some committee members, that he entered all his transactions on loose sheets of paper, even though he often made investments of $100,000 or more.[32]

Hines followed Tilden on the stand, and while he again admitted his interest in the Illinois senatorial contest, he still denied that he had used money to influence it. He reiterated that President Taft and

---

[29] *Dillingham Committee Hearings,* I, 433–437, 439–440.

[30] See the comments by Senator Duncan U. Fletcher in *CR,* 62nd Cong., 2nd Sess., XLVIII, 8689.

[31] *Dillingham Committee Hearings,* II, 549, 607–609, 615–619. Funk said that since his testimony in the Helm Committee inquiry he had been followed by private detectives. On October 14, 1911, a John Hennings brought suit against Funk in the Cook County circuit court charging alienation of his wife's affections. Mrs. Hennings later confessed to the grand jury that she had been paid $100 by a lawyer, Daniel Donahoe, to bring the suit. See *Tribune,* Oct. 15–17, 1911, June 26, 29, 1912; Charles Collins, "The Funk Case—a Plot That Failed," *ibid.,* May 2, 1954.

[32] *Dillingham Committee Hearings,* I, 773–786. See the comments by Kern and Gamble, I, 777–778.

Senators Aldrich and Penrose, who needed protectionist votes for "certain schedules" in the tariff bill, inspired his intervention. With Aldrich's authorization, claimed Hines, he telegraphed Lorimer of the administration's interest in him; he sent the telegram from the office of George Reynolds, president of the Continental Commercial Bank.[33] Most startling was Hines's rebuttal of Funk's story. He maintained that Funk had asked him to contribute to Lorimer's election, not the reverse. Since he knew, said Hines, that Funk and the McCormicks of International Harvester were Lorimer's enemies, he suspected Funk of currying favor with the new Senator.[34]

In his testimony Hines minimized his political role and tried to picture himself as merely a messenger boy for Aldrich. There is much evidence, however, that he regarded himself, as Senator Reed put it, as "a sort of guardian . . . for the United States . . . as a man whose guiding hand and whose genius control in the Senate . . . and in the House of Representatives." [35] In March, 1911, for instance, in a circular letter to the members of the National Lumber Manufacturers' Association, Hines boasted that reciprocity had failed "chiefly because of our efforts." In June, 1910, he wrote Senator Aldrich that the "lumber interests" of Washington and Oregon would "dictate" the selection of new senators in those states. He suggested to Aldrich the "importance" of assisting him "in trying to frame a course that will bring about results satisfactory to our mutual interest." Some of Hines's talk was undoubtedly idle boasting—even Wiehe admitted his brother-in-law talked too much—but clearly Hines consistently attempted to affect legislation and elections.[36]

Hines's reavowal of Taft's role in Lorimer's election irritated the President. "They are at present charging me with being responsible for Lorimer's election," wrote Taft to brother Horace. "I can stand

[33] *Ibid.,* I, 813–817, 823–824, 833–835, 837.

[34] *Ibid.,* I, 842, 847–849.

[35] See *CR,* 62nd Cong., 2nd Sess., XLVIII, 8889.

[36] The letter on reciprocity was cited by Senator Reed in *ibid.,* 8889; Hines to Aldrich, Sept. 13, 1910, copy of letter furnished to the author through the courtesy of Professor Jerome Sternstein, Columbia University. Wiehe's comment is in *Dillingham Committee Hearings,* II, 1769. Wirt H. Cook charged that Hines was also involved in the primary election of Senator Isaac Stephenson of Wisconsin. Robert J. Shields, employed by Wiehe to secure witnesses for the Lorimer investigation, worked for Hines in the Stephenson primary. See *ibid.,* IV, 3805–13 (Shields testifying); U.S., Senate, *Election of Isaac Stephenson . . . , Senate Doc. 312,* 62nd Cong., 2nd Sess. (2 vols., Washington, 1912), II, 1391 (Shields testifying), 1567, 1571, 1575 (Hines testifying); *Tribune,* Oct. 18–20, 1911.

a good many things, but this really rather passes the limit." [37] Before Hines testified to the Dillingham Committee, Taft told Senator Kenyon of his relationship to Hines and the Lorimer election:

> I never had any conversation with Mr. Hines on the question of Lorimer or the Senatorship in Illinois. Several senators spoke to me—among others, Senator Aldrich—with reference to the necessity of securing a Republican in the vacancy that the deadlock in Illinois made, and to all of them I expressed the hope that the deadlock might be ended and that a Republican might be sent. I said that I had no choice in the matter except that I preferred Governor Deneen if Mr. Hopkins was not to be elected. . . .
>
> Mr. Aldrich came to me and wanted to know whether I would object to Mr. Lorimer for Senator, and I said that I was not making any selection of Senators and that any Republican would suit me. . . .
>
> I had a conversation with Senator Aldrich after Mr. Hines made the statement before the [Helm] committee . . . in which Senator Aldrich did not hesitate to say to me that Hines had lied on the subject of the number of interviews he had with him (Aldrich) on the subject. He said it was perfectly evident that Hines was attempting to exaggerate at the other end the interest which he (Aldrich) and the administration had in Lorimer's election, and that Hines came to him to urge upon him the importance of Lorimer's election and inquired whether it would be agreeable to the Administration, and all that he did was to come to see me, when I told him that I would be satisfied with any Republican and would not object to Lorimer. . . . My recollection was that I had some . . . request that I send a telegram urging the election of somebody—it may have been Lorimer—and that I declined to act. . . .[38]

After Hines's appearance before the Dillingham Committee, Taft angrily wrote Kenyon that Hines was "guilty of the most wilful perjury" in seeking "to give the impression that I was in favor of Lorimer and urged against his will that he become a candidate. . . ." Taft asked Kenyon to show Dillingham his letter and volunteered to appear before the committee in executive session. He also released to the press the "memorandum" about his relationship to the Lorimer election prepared after Hines's Helm Committee testimony. Hence-

[37] Taft to Horace Taft, June 30, 1911, Taft Papers.

[38] Taft to Kenyon, June 27, 1911, Taft Papers. Taft altered this statement on his relationship to the Lorimer election from the "memorandum" of Mar. 29, 1911. In the "memorandum" Taft held that he had forgotten the names of the senators who came to him about the Illinois senatorship.

forth, Taft remained in communication with Kenyon, helping him frame questions that would clarify his relationship to the controversial election.[39]

On July 13, after a twelve-day recess, the Dillingham Committee resumed its Washington hearings. Lorimer was again present, looking, according to Senator Cullom, "perfectly quiet and cool and apparently confident. . . ." [40] Deneen, the first witness, added nothing new to the record. He admitted that Lorimer had tried to persuade him to take the senatorship, but he claimed that this was only because the liquor industry, the electrical utilities, the Illinois Central Railroad, and "a gas company" wanted him out of the state. These were the interests, suggested Deneen, along with the packers, the Pullman Company, and the grain elevator companies, who supplied the legislative "jackpot." Deneen maintained that he had supported Hopkins throughout the deadlock and opposed Lorimer, but he knew nothing about the use of money in the election.[41]

During the week of July 17, a variety of witnesses, many in the lumber business, gave conflicting and confusing testimony about the Funk and Hines meetings and about Hines's and Wiehe's supposed boasts about electing Lorimer.[42] They were followed on the stand by banker George Reynolds and Senator Nelson Aldrich. Reynolds looked smug and collected as befitted one of the nation's most influential financiers. He testified that Hines claimed that Senators Aldrich and Penrose asked him to tell Deneen that they and the President wanted Lorimer elected, and that Hines believed himself "very influential" in Lorimer's victory.[43] After his testimony, the

---

[39] Taft to Kenyon, June 30, July 11, 21, 1911, Kenyon to Taft, July 20, 1911, Taft Papers; *Tribune,* July 1, 1911.

[40] Cullom to William B. Ridgely, July 23, 1911, Cullom Papers. During the recess Lorimer voted against Canadian reciprocity. See *CR,* 62nd Cong., 2nd Sess., XLVII, 3175.

[41] *Dillingham Committee Hearings,* II, 1089–92, 1113–23, 1134.

[42] For testimony that Hines *had* boasted of electing Lorimer see *ibid.,* II, 1335 (William M. Burgess testifying), 1386–90 (Herman H. Hettler testifying), 1412 (Donald M. Frame testifying). For testimony that Hines *had not* boasted of electing Lorimer or requested a contribution from Funk for the Lorimer election fund see *ibid.,* II, 1382 (Henry Turrish testifying), 1449–55 (Isaac Baker testifying), 1490, 1518 (Charles McGowan testifying), 1523–24 (Bolling A. Johnson testifying), 1553, 1583 (John B. Price testifying), 1606–07 (Samuel J. Cusson testifying), 1630, 1643 (C. H. Wiehe testifying).

[43] *Ibid.,* II, 1590–93. Reynolds also testified that several months before the White confession, Medill McCormick told him that $128,000 had gone "from Washington to Springfield" to elect Lorimer.

banker wrote Taft and apologized for using his name. He commented that "it is infamous that either your name or mine should have been mentioned by anyone in the matter and the only reason was because of the *unwarranted action of fool friends*." [44] Reynolds clearly referred to Hines in this statement.

Aldrich's testimony reinforced Reynolds' estimate of Hines as a "fool friend." Aldrich maintained that while he had spoken with Hines regarding the Illinois senatorial contest, he had not urged or said that Taft had urged Lorimer's election; he had told Hines that he and the President wanted "some Republican" and that Lorimer was not "objectionable." Aldrich also insisted that Lorimer's tariff views were "immaterial" to him and that he took "no special interest" in "senatorial elections in various States." [45]

The latter statement was remarkably disingenuous. In March, 1910, Aldrich, Taft, and other Old Guard leaders had agreed to raise a fund to elect conservative congressmen and senators. Aldrich was responsible for corporate aid.[46] Telegrams (some in code) in the papers of George W. Perkins, a partner in J. P. Morgan & Company, suggest that Aldrich contacted Morgan and that he agreed to contribute. But the Lorimer exposé on April 30, 1910, upset the Aldrich-Morgan arrangement. On May 12, 1910, George W. Perkins cabled the following to Henry P. Davison, also a Morgan partner: "Developments in Illinois senate matter continue. Looks as though Senator elected year ago would be forced to resign. Have seen Funk who says looks as though there would be still further developments involving Standard Oil Co. He says no one representing his concern [International Harvester] has ever suggested they would help in any such way as your friend [Hines?] mentioned to you and that under no circumstances will they do anything." Perkins urgently advised that the "matter [be] dropped entirely and at once. . . ." [47]

[44] Reynolds to Taft, July 20, 1911 (my italics), Taft to Reynolds, July 21, 1911, Taft Papers.

[45] *Dillingham Committee Hearings*, II, 1648–53, 1659, 1661, 1666, 1670; Taft to Aldrich and to Kenyon, July 21, 1911, Taft Papers. Taft thanked Aldrich for "the very clear statement you made before the Committee."

[46] Archie Butt to Dear Clara [Mrs. Lewis F. Butt], Mar. 7, 1910, in Butt, *Taft and Roosevelt*, I, 299–300; Mowry, *Theodore Roosevelt and the Progressive Movement*, 99.

[47] These telegrams were brought to the attention of the author by Professor John Braeman of the University of Nebraska. The code is translated on the telegrams themselves. See Perkins to Davison, May 12, 1910, Davison to Perkins, May 13, 1910, George W. Perkins Papers, Columbia University Library, New York. On

J. P. Morgan, Jr., when told of the situation, agreed with Perkins. He cabled Davison that he "strongly" felt "the extreme inadvisability getting ourselves mixed up in matter." [48] Morgan, Sr., saw the necessity of withdrawal. He cabled his son to "communicate" to Aldrich:

> H. P. D. [Henry P. Davison] has laid before me situation in regard to matter discussed with you. In view of disturbed condition and increased political agitation which have engendered personal bitterness both parties . . . I am convinced after personal consideration that it is most unwise and unsafe, and may prove prejudicial to the very interests we want to protect, to adopt plans which we considered when situation was not so acute. In view of all this my personal judgment is that nothing should be done either by individuals or by corporations. I had understood that any commitment made by me had been cared for.[49]

A Morgan partner, probably Perkins, wrote that J. P. Morgan's decision brought the "greatest possible relief and gratification." [50]

These telegrams from the Perkins Papers reveal a direct tie between corporations and the senatorial election of 1910. Possibly the same connections existed in 1909 when Aldrich and the Old Guard were involved in the tariff fight. It is difficult to accept Aldrich's assertion that Lorimer's tariff views were "immaterial" to him. However, while the evidence points to Aldrich's interest in Lorimer and the Illinois senatorial contest, it also shows that Hines was more than Aldrich's agent. The lumberman, no novice at election manipulation, had the same interest as the Senator in electing Lorimer, in fact, even more, since Lorimer was his friend. As for Taft, Hines probably exaggerated his involvement in order to secure support for Lorimer in the General Assembly.[51]

May 13 Perkins cabled Davison that the "Illinois matter I referred to has important bearing on Wisconsin situation." The reference to Wisconsin seems to apply to the disputed election of Senator Isaac Stephenson. See Perkins to Davison, May 13, 1910, *ibid.*

[48] "Chargeless" [J. P. Morgan, Jr.] to Davison, May 13, 1910, Perkins Papers.

[49] Cable from J. P. M. to J. P. M., Jr., May 14, 1910, "Centipedal" [H. P. Davison] to "Cheliform" [Perkins?], [n.d. but probably May 14, 1910], Perkins Papers.

[50] Cable, [no names, n.d.], Perkins Papers.

[51] Hines still insisted that Taft had said he would "aid in the election of Senator Lorimer. . . ." He maintained that Congressman Henry S. Boutell had told him this, but Boutell denied it. See *Dillingham Committee Hearings,* II, 1845–47; *Tribune,* July 26, 1911. Hines was subsequently expelled from the Union League Club because of his supposed involvement in the Lorimer "jackpot." See *ibid.,* Jan. 4, Feb. 24, 1912; pamphlet *Edward Hines to the Union League Club* (n.p., n.d.).

During the last week of July and the beginning of August, the Dillingham Committee heard *Tribune* editor James Keeley and confessed bribe-takers White, Beckemeyer, and Holstlaw. Their lengthy testimony added little to the known facts. White appeared more self-possessed than in the Burrows hearings. He spoke audibly and held his own in exchanges with Hanecy, who attempted to discredit White's moral character. White admitted that he had lied to Browne and Lorimer, but justified the lies as intended to expose corruption: "A man's personal sins do not affect a community or nation . . . a man that will sell his vote . . . [helps] enslave the people of a nation. . . ." White undoubtedly enjoyed the spotlight. Beckemeyer and Holstlaw were less comfortable, but Hanecy did not succeed in breaking down their stories.[52]

The testimony of the admitted bribe-takers ended the Dillingham hearing's first phase, with the question of the corruptness or honesty of Lorimer's election still confused. The committee took a two-month recess and reconvened in Chicago on October 10. In Chicago, the committee examined thirty-seven witnesses including a number of assemblymen and Cook County politicians such as Fred M. Blount and John E. W. Wayman. But the Chicago testimony was as inconclusive as that in Washington. The vagueness and memory lapses of many of the witnesses suggested a desire to conceal rather than to enlighten.

Cyril R. Jandus, for example, a Democratic assemblyman from Chicago's West Side, told of keeping $5,300 in a little "tin box" in his office vault, but was unable to account for the money's origins. W. C. Blair, Democrat from Mount Vernon, admitted having a roll of $100 bills at a ball game, but could not remember how many, even though it was unusual for him to have bills of that size. Blair was intoxicated when he appeared before the committee and had to be excused. Fred Sterling, editor of the Rockford *Register-Gazette,* recalled that Democrat James H. Corcoran told him that men were getting $2,500 for Lorimer votes, but Corcoran could not remember it. Ira C. Copley, Edward D. Shurtleff, Roger C. Sullivan, Thomas G. Tippit, and Lee O'Neil Browne, while supplying election back-

<hr/>

[52] *Dillingham Committee Hearings,* II, 1879–81, 1898–1900, III, 2051–53, 2067–70 (James Keeley testifying), 2611, 2619–20, 2669–71, 2685–87 (Charles A. White testifying), 2838–3013 (H. J. C. Beckemeyer testifying), 3018–19, 3109–14, 3116 (Daniel W. Holstlaw testifying).

ground, denied knowledge of corruption. And the last Chicago witness, State's Attorney Wayman, surprised the audience by claiming that he was friendly toward Lorimer and had hoped that his "investigation would disclose the falsity of White's story." He was only following his "plain duty as State's Attorney of Cook County." [53]

After recessing its Chicago hearings, the committee reconvened in Washington on December 5. The stream of contradictory witnesses resumed, and nothing of substance was added to the record. Observers looked forward with expectation to Lorimer's testimony after the Christmas holidays, believing that he would be the last, and perhaps most sensational, witness.

Lorimer took the stand looking bland and self-confident. He spoke in a quiet, well-modulated voice; there was "nothing theatrical" in his manner and he did not attempt "to appeal to sympathy or partisanship. . . ." [54] Lorimer began his testimony under Hanecy's guidance and denied that he had paid or authorized anyone to pay "any money or other thing of value for any vote," or that he knew of any attempt to purchase votes. [55] He adhered to this position for his six days on the witness stand. Most of his testimony concerned conditions in the Forty-sixth General Assembly and the reasons for his election. Lorimer also discussed his early life, his entrance into politics, and his political career; his frank testimony provided a penetrating insight into the activities and mind of a political boss.

Lorimer said he determined to defeat Hopkins because of his failure to keep "the faith" in the 1908 election. Deneen still could have elected Hopkins on the first ballot, insisted Lorimer, but he preferred to preserve the deadlock. [56] Lorimer discounted Hines's role in his election. In fact, said Lorimer in an insightful slip, "I never had any opinion that he [Hines] was the right man to select for a political mission of any sort." [57] As for the Washington authorities, Lorimer maintained it was "common knowledge" in Springfield that Taft,

[53] *Ibid.*, IV, 3455–72, 3510–11 (Blair testifying), 4000–4008 (Jandus testifying), V, 4918, 4931, 4981–82, 4973–74 (Browne testifying), VI, 5441–49 (Sterling testifying), 5454 (Corcoran testifying), 5763–67, 5792–93, 5803, 5914 (Wayman testifying).

[54] *Tribune,* Jan. 10, 1912.

[55] *Dillingham Committee Hearings,* VIII, 7391.

[56] *Ibid.*, 7405–07, 7711.

[57] *Ibid.*, 7460.

Aldrich, and Penrose wanted him elected. This information, however, was not a crucial factor.

His election by fifty-five Republicans and fifty-three Democrats, said Lorimer, resulted from political friendships and political favors, and he demonstrated his grasp of Illinois politics by explaining the motivation behind each of the 108 votes. His explanations ranged from declarations that men were Republicans and would vote for any Republican who could win to extended discussions of boyhood friendships. As for the Democrats, Lorimer said he had always obtained Democratic votes. And, he added, "the ward workers of the political parties, both Democratic and Republicans . . . are very, very friendly to me. . . . In every campaign some of the ward workers in the Democratic Party were for me." [58]

Lorimer's discussion of how he had won votes from Hopkins in spite of his primary victory disturbed Senator Kern. A Bryan progressive who had been vice-presidential candidate on the 1908 Democratic ticket, Kern had replaced Beveridge as senator from Indiana in 1911 and seemed determined to match Beveridge's role in the Lorimer case. Kern questioned Lorimer about the relationship between the voters and their representatives:

> SENATOR KERN: Were the voters of the district for you or for Senator Hopkins?
> SENATOR LORIMER: It would be egotistical on my part . . . to say that the people of their districts were for me in preference to Senator Hopkins. I never consulted them about it. . . .
> SENATOR KERN: The voters were the ones to whom they [the legislators] were under obligations for support?
> SENATOR LORIMER: Oh, yes. *That is the way men talk who reach the clouds, you know, when they are making that kind of a speech: That the voters are the men that they are responsible to. Of course they are. But voters are human beings.*
> SENATOR KERN: If they [the voters] have not independendent judgments and are not to be considered in a free government on the question of influencing their representatives, they do not count very much in the game.
> SENATOR LORIMER: That may be the way it strikes you, Senator, but my friends have a great deal of influence with me, and men that help

[58] *Ibid.*, 7638–39.

me in the world have a great deal of influence with me, and they can very frequently get me to do things that if I were just left to myself I would not do. . . . I do not think I am owned body and soul by the men that influence me just because I sometimes do things that, if I were left to myself, I would not do. . . . I am just a human being.[59]

In this exchange lay the essence of the distinction between the political boss's conception of politics and that of the progressives. Progressives often spoke of politics and government in an idealistic and moralistic sense. They believed that political machines and bosses were evil and a distortion of the democratic process, and that they responded to the wishes of corrupt interests rather than those of the disinterested citizen. The political boss, on the other hand, saw politics as devoid of idealism. Men were influenced by concrete factors; voters were "human beings," not abstractions.[60]

Lorimer concluded his testimony on January 30, 1912, having supplied information regarding his career and his political motives, and Illinois political conditions. Those committee members who were predisposed toward believing Lorimer innocent probably found that his testimony reinforced their convictions; those who wanted to believe him guilty also had their opinions reinforced. The unexpected events of the last few days of the hearings had a similar contradictory effect.

On January 31, 1912, and for several days after, detective William J. Burns, his operative Arthur C. Bailey, and stenographer James E. Sheridan told of investigating the validity of Charles McGowan's testimony. McGowan was the young Canadian who supposedly heard Wiehe boast of paying $10,000 toward a Lorimer election fund. In July, 1911, however, before the Dillingham Committee, McGowan denied hearing such a conversation. Suspicious of perjury, and urged on by Keeley, the committee counsel hired Burns to inquire into McGowan's story.[61]

Burns's operatives Bailey and Sheridan testified that McGowan had admitted to them that he had lied about Wiehe's boast. McGowan wrote Bailey that "I made them [Hines and Wiehe] come across . . .

---

[59] *Ibid.*, 7632 (my italics); Bowers, *Kern,* 157–187.

[60] See Hofstadter, *Age of Reform,* 213–225, 254–269.

[61] *Dillingham Committee Hearings,* II, 1490, VIII, 7917–18. The committee had discharged Burns after several months of inconclusive investigation, but Keeley retained him to continue his inquiry.

and I had a hell of a time getting it, too, had to threaten him [Wiehe] with all kinds of exposure." [62] Sheridan had secretly taken notes of a McGowan conversation over a "dictagraph," and from them he read a McGowan statement that he had received $1,500 for his perjured testimony.[63] The committee's official stenographer charged, however, that the dictagraph notes were "an absolute fake." The committee tested Sheridan's ability to record over the dictagraph but the test proved inconclusive, and its members were left to reach their own conclusions about the truth or falsity of McGowan's testimony.[64]

Aside from further denials by McGowan, Hines, and Wiehe about their involvement in bribery, the stenographic test marked the end of the Dillingham Committee hearings. At the last public meeting, Hanecy announced that he would enter a plea of *res adjudicata,* since the Lorimer election had already been investigated, discussed in the Senate, and the charges "not sustained." He maintained that the Dillingham Committee had not discovered enough new evidence to overturn this conclusion.[65] The committee took his plea under advisement. It would be several months before it finished considering the voluminous testimony and deciding if Hanecy's plea was justified.

In the months between the end of the Dillingham hearings and the beginning of the Senate debate on his case, Lorimer ran a slate in the Illinois political primaries. It was an inopportune time. The White confession and the revelations of the Dillingham hearings linked him in the public eye with corruption, and many politicians attempted to disassociate themselves from the Lorimer taint.[66]

By 1911 three factions within the Illinois Republican party opposed Lorimer: the Deneenites, who controlled the state administration; the "regular" organization composed of Cullom's and Hopkins' federal appointees and the Busse-Campbell Cook County group; and the progressives, led by Charles E. Merriam, Raymond Robins, and

---

[62] *Ibid.,* VIII, 7974, McGowan to Bailey, Nov. 19, 1911, printed in *ibid.*
[63] *Ibid.,* 8228–30.
[64] *Ibid.,* 8236, 8240–41, 8276, 8279, 8283 (Milton W. Blumenberg testifying). The transcripts of the tests are printed in *ibid.,* 8561–63. The majority of the Dillingham Committee noted in their report that the test was "disastrous" for Sheridan.
[65] *Ibid.,* 8583. Hines appeared as the committee's last witness to deny that he had tried to bribe a telegraph operator to let him see a telegram sent by Detective Bailey. See *ibid.,* 8510, 8556–71.
[66] Len Small to W. Harvey Duff, Nov. 7, 1911, Small Papers.

Illinois Senator Walter Clyde Jones, and financed by Charles R. Crane and Julius Rosenwald.[67]

Besides their anti-Lorimer stand, the three factions had little in common. Merriam, for instance, lost the 1911 mayoralty election to Carter H. Harrison in a campaign in which the regulars gave him only nominal support and the Busse-Campbell faction opposed him.[68] In addition, by the summer of 1911, the Merriam progressives were disillusioned with their former ally, Deneen. They formed their own statewide organization, the Illinois Progressive Republican League, and pressed for statewide civil service, the initiative, referendum, corrupt practices legislation, and a presidential primary.[69] On the national level, the Merriam faction affiliated with La Follette and supported the Senator's presidential ambitions.[70]

The regulars disliked both Deneen and Merriam. They fought Lorimer, but their opposition was based on expediency rather than aversion to his politics. The regular organization, of necessity, allied with the Taft administration and benefited from the President's refusal to accept Lorimer's recommendations for Illinois federal posts. Lorimer opponents such as Postmaster Dan Campbell continued to hold their positions, imposing a further check on Lorimer's power.[71]

Lorimer was cognizant of the disintegration of his support and the need to buttress his organization. Perhaps the split between the Deneenites, the progressives, and the regulars would allow his faction to gain control of the Republican nominations. In the summer of 1911, while the Dillingham hearings were in recess, Lorimer and thirty of his followers formed the Lincoln Protective League, renamed by the press the "Lorimer-Lincoln League." Important in the league were William ("Big Bill") Thompson, ex-congressman Fred-

[67] "Memorandum," Charles D. Hilles to William Howard Taft, May 28, 1911, Charles D. Hilles Papers, Yale University Library, New Haven; Straetz, "Progressive Movement in Illinois," 70–107.

[68] Straetz, "Progressive Movement in Illinois," 86; Ickes, *Autobiography*, 136–137; Harrison, *Stormy Years*, 282–284, 293–294. According to Harrison, Lorimer offered to back him if he promised to name James McAndrews commissioner of public works. Lorimer later said of the campaign that he felt that "Mr. Merriam did not want me to speak for him." See *Dillingham Committee Hearings*, VIII, 7659.

[69] E. B. Fletcher to Merriam, July 1, 1911, Merriam Papers; Raymond Robins to Charles S. Deneen, Sept. 3, 1912, Robins Papers.

[70] La Follette to Charles R. Crane, Jan. 2, 1911, Charles R. Crane Papers, Institute of Current World Affairs, New York; "Memorandum," Hilles to Taft, May 28, 1911, Hilles Papers; Straetz, "Progressive Movement in Illinois," 67.

[71] Taft to Charles P. Taft, May 1, 1911, Frank H. Hitchcock to Charles D. Hilles, Dec. 7, 8, 1911, Hilles to Taft, Dec. 16, 1911, Taft Papers.

erick ("Poor Fred") Lundin, and long-time Lorimer stalwarts Joe Bidwell, "Billy" Cooke, William J. Moxley, and Judge Petit. The influential Negro minister Archibald J. Carey, who opposed the direct primary as detrimental to the interests of his race, was also an original league member.[72]

The Lincoln League was markedly anti-progressive; its platform stated that it believed "in perpetuating the doctrine of Abraham Lincoln" and safeguarding "American constitutional rights" through the advocacy of "responsible representative government." The league opposed the initiative, referendum, and recall, and charged that the direct primary, "the dream of weaklings," would "lead to racial and religious alignments in our politics." [73]

Lorimer needed a gubernatorial candidate to head the league's slate in the 1912 primaries. He first called on his old friend Frank O. Lowden to lead the fight to prevent the substitution of "a pure democracy for the representative government created by the Fathers," but Lowden was too recently recovered from illness to risk the campaign.[74] In the fall of 1911, Lorimer selected U.S. Subtreasurer Len Small as the Lincoln League candidate. Small, who detested Deneen, was powerful in his home county of Kankakee. He had been a follower of Richard Yates and became state treasurer in 1904 as part of the Yates-Deneen convention bargain. An expert political organizer, he helped Lorimer manage Yates's 1908 campaign for the gubernatorial nomination.[75]

Lorimer and Small organized the Lincoln League throughout the

---

[72] *Tribune*, July 11, 12, 28, Aug. 2, 3, 16, 17, 1911; Lloyd Wendt and Herman Kogan, *Big Bill of Chicago* (Indianapolis, 1953), 75. Lundin was in charge of the Lincoln League in Cook County. See Small to S. H. Bransky, Mar. 2, 1912, Small Papers. Carey and Lorimer became close political friends. On July 15, 1916, the Negro newspaper the Chicago *Defender* wrote, "It can truthfully be said that the Race has seldom had a more loyal and consistent friend, in season and out of season, than William J. Lorimer. . . ." See Joseph A. Logsdon, "The Rev. Archibald J. Carey and the Negro in Chicago Politics" (unpublished M.A. thesis, University of Chicago, 1961), 43–46. The Rev. N. J. McCracken wrote Taft, "I make no hesitancy in saying that no man in public life in this State is closer to the hearts of the colored people of Illinois than Senator William Lorimer." See McCracken to Taft, June 26, 1911, Taft Papers.

[73] The platform of the league is printed upon its stationery, many pieces of which are in the Small Papers; *Tribune*, July 19, 1912.

[74] Lorimer to Lowden, Aug. 6, 1911, Lowden to Lorimer, Aug. 25, 1911, Lowden Papers; Hutchinson, *Lowden*, I, 243–244.

[75] Cal M. Freezer to S. B. Roach, Sept. 14, 1911, Small Papers; "Memorandum," Hilles to Taft, May 28, 1911, Hilles Papers; Wooddy, *Case of Frank L. Smith*, 156–158.

state, paying the costs out of their own pockets. The league's purpose involved defending Lorimer as well as promoting Small, and copies of Lorimer's and Bailey's Senate speeches were mailed to the voters along with subscriptions to the *Inter-Ocean*.[76] Lorimer and Small spoke all over Illinois, with Lorimer the main attraction. He warned his listeners against "the Socialistic doctrines of . . . 'progressive Republicanism' which has [*sic*] come sweeping in upon us from out of the west . . . [bringing] anarchy and chaos." He demanded the elimination of Deneen, the end of "trust press" control of politics, and "more representative government and . . . less hypocrisy."[77]

The widespread anti-Lorimer feeling handicapped Small. "There seems to be an impression existing to the effect that Mr. Small is backed by Lorimer," wrote one politician. Unless "that idea can be knocked out, I should say it would be much better for Mr. Small's interest that he do not declare himself a candidate . . . the sentiment against Billy Lorimer . . . is simply gigantic. . . ."[78] Lorimer and Small hoped that by meeting voters personally they could counter this spirit and convince the people that Lorimer was persecuted because he stood for the things that were "right."[79]

The Republican presidential rivalries complicated the Illinois picture. Cullom, the federal appointees, and the Cook County organization backed Taft. Most Illinois progressives supported La Follette, and the Senator's managers considered Illinois in their column.[80] Deneen characteristically equivocated, taking no stand. In January, 1912, Roosevelt boosters such as Frank Knox, and James Keeley and J. C. O'Laughlin of the *Tribune,* formed a Roosevelt National Com-

[76] See Small to Harry B. Ward, Jan. 15, 1912, to E. M. Gullick, Apr. 1, 1912, Small Papers. As of Apr. 3, 1912, Lorimer had contributed $10,000 to the Lincoln League treasury, Small $5,000, and Thompson $1,000. See "Treasurer, Lincoln-Protective League" to Lincoln Protective League of Illinois, Apr. 3, 1912, *ibid.*

[77] Small to J. V. Stevenson, Oct. 20, 1911, to John W. Lewis, Feb. 17, 1912, Small Papers; *Tribune,* Aug. 21, 25, Sept. 2, 6, 8, 16, 23, 1911. Lorimer wrote one potential supporter, "The election of Hon. Len Small, the Kankakee farmer and banker, as Governor means the substitution of a business administration for the ruinous and spendthrift policy of the present Governor." See Lorimer to James M. Lawrence, Mar. 25, 1912, Small Papers.

[78] R. C. Wallis to C. R. Miller, Nov. 6, 1911, Allen Walker to Luther Bratton, Oct. 26, 1911, Small Papers.

[79] Small to W. Harvey Duff, Nov. 7, 1911, to John W. Lewis, Feb. 17, 1912, Small Papers.

[80] Max Pam to William J. Calhoun, May 6, 1911, Taft Papers; Lewis H. Miner to Taft, May 11, 1911, George S. Wood to Charles D. Hilles, Nov. 2, 1911, Hilles Papers.

mittee with Chicago headquarters. Early in February, when La Follette suffered a nervous breakdown, a number of his supporters flocked to the Roosevelt standard.[81] The primary in Illinois, as well as in the rest of the nation, became a Taft-Roosevelt contest.

Who would Lorimer support? Both the President and the ex-President had sought his ouster from the Senate. His first inclination was to remain aloof. Congressman William B. McKinley of Illinois, Taft's campaign manager, told presidential secretary Charles D. Hilles that Lorimer was a puzzle and could not "be judged by any known standards." [82] Ultimately Lorimer endorsed Taft, because, he explained, the President believed, as he did, in "constitutional and representative government." [83]

On February 10, the Lincoln League announced its slate of Taft for president, Cullom for senator, and Small for governor, as well as a complete roster of Cook County candidates. Lorimer proclaimed that the league had been formed "to perpetuate the ringing of freedom from the mountain sides," and to block "socialistic fallacies like the initiative, referendum, and recall. . . . Today is our Gettysburg, and April 9 [primary day] will see the surrender of the enemies of our nation. Our battle is to rehabilitate the Republican party and snatch it from the men who sold it to the trust press. . . . On April 9 yon flag, with its stars and stripes, will be as spotless as it was in the hands of the silent soldier who held it in his hands at Appomattox." [84]

The bitter primary campaign, with five candidates, Deneen, Small, John E. W. Wayman, progressive state senator Walter Clyde Jones, and perennial Richard Yates, revolved about the Lorimer issue. Small defended and the others attacked, accusing Small and each other of being corrupted with "Lorimerism." [85] All except Small paid lip service to the doctrines of progressivism. He and Lorimer toured the state appealing to voters who rejected progressive doctrines. Most important were conservative downstate farmers who disliked progressivism as a big-city product, and Chicago ritualistic immigrant groups who believed that progressivism's Anglo-Saxon "reform" emphasis threatened their cultural norms and life-styles. Bohemian, German,

[81] O'Laughlin to Roosevelt, Jan. 8, 1912, Roosevelt Papers; Mowry, *Theodore Roosevelt and the Progressive Movement*, 205–208.

[82] "Memorandum," Hilles to Taft, May 28, 1911, Hilles Papers; Max Pam to William J. Calhoun, May 6, 1911, Taft Papers.

[83] *CR*, 62nd Cong., 2nd Sess., XLVIII, 8899.

[84] *Tribune*, Feb. 11, 13, 1912.

[85] *Ibid.*, Feb. 26, Mar. 1, 14, 21, 31, 1912.

and Polish newspapers, for instance, often equated progressivism with prohibitionism and nativism. They viewed the progressives as "narrow-minded enemies of immigrants," "hypocritical reformers," and "Pharisees." [86]

Lorimer and Small confronted more than state rivals in the campaign. Late in March, after the General Assembly approved a presidential primary, Theodore Roosevelt toured Illinois and stimulated anti-Lorimer and anti–Lincoln League feeling. He linked Taft with Lorimer, charging that the Lincoln League controlled the Taft campaign.[87] Taft protested in his letters that he was being "misrepresented," and that "Lorimer's people" were supporting him not "because they love me . . . [but] because they hate Roosevelt more. . . ." [88]

While Lorimer and Small seemed confident of victory, on primary day Deneen secured nearly twice Small's vote total. Wayman and Yates trailed behind, and Jones, the progressive candidate, finished last. Small only won four Chicago wards—the Fourth, Tenth, Eleventh, and Twentieth—all machine wards with a large Catholic and Jewish immigrant population.[89] In the presidential primary, Roosevelt also doubled Taft's total, with La Follette third. Senator Cullom, trying for a sixth Senate term, but suffering from his vote to retain Lorimer, lost to Lawrence Y. Sherman. And, for the first time in his political career, Lorimer was defeated for the county central committee.[90]

Roosevelt's and Deneen's victories in Illinois and the defeat of Taft, Cullom, and Small warned many politicians that "Lorimerism" was a difficult burden for any candidate. "There is only one conclusion to come to in this State Primary," wrote a supporter to Lawrence Y. Sherman, "and that is, that the people are sore at Lorimer and Lorimerism." [91] Taft attributed his defeat to "Roosevelt's ability to

---

[86] Small to P. F. Brown, Mar. 25, 1912, Small Papers; Henry May, *The End of American Innocence: A Study of the First Years of Our Own Time 1912–1917* (New York, 1959), 121–132; *The Western Catholic,* Mar. 22, 1912; *Die Abendpost,* Aug. 26, 1910, Nov. 11, 1910, Feb. 4, 1911; *Denni Hlasatel,* Oct. 21, 1912, Mar. 30, 1915; *Dziennik Zwiazkowy Zgoda,* Mar. 17, 1910.

[87] New York *Times,* Apr. 7, 19, 1911; *Tribune,* Mar. 28, Apr. 7, 9, 1911.

[88] Taft to Kohlsaat, Apr. 1, 1912, Taft Papers.

[89] For Lorimer's and Small's expectations of victory see Lorimer to Judge Solon Philbrick, Apr. 4, 1912, Small to R. H. Mann, Apr. 4, 7, 1912, to W. S. Meyer, Apr. 8, 1912, to Charles Davis, Apr. 8, 1912, Small Papers. The 1912 primary returns are in the Chicago Municipal Reference Library, Chicago City Hall.

[90] *Tribune,* Apr. 10, 11, 1912.

[91] Emery Andrews to Sherman, Apr. 11, 1912, Sherman Papers.

turn the anti-Lorimer sentiment against me," while Roosevelt claimed a "victory for clean and straight governmental methods and . . . a stinging rebuke to the alliance between crooked business and crooked politics. . . ." [92] Lorimer, however, held that Illinois voted against Taft because of his espousal of Canadian reciprocity and free trade. "Lorimerism" was a matter of principle that would hurt no man. [93]

The lesson of the Illinois primary strongly impressed Roosevelt, and he linked Taft's name with Lorimer's in other state primary campaigns. "The bosses," said Roosevelt repeatedly, were for Taft: "A vote for Mr. Taft is a vote for the bosses; it is a vote for Lorimer, Penrose, for Guggenheim, for Gallinger, and for all the rest of them. . . ." [94] Taft, angered by the accusation, released correspondence that showed he had worked against Lorimer in the first Senate case. But he made little impression and Roosevelt retorted that Taft had acted "so feebly that Mr. Lorimer, as is shown by his actions, regarded Mr. Taft as his friend." [95]

Roosevelt's charge that Taft was allied with Lorimer and other bosses contributed to his image of Taft the reactionary and undoubtedly helped him win victories in those states with presidential primaries. Believing he was the people's choice, Roosevelt bolted the Republican party when denied the nomination and formed the Progressive party. [96] By this time, however, the Lorimer case was up for decision.

The Helm Committee and the Dillingham Committee hearings had the effect, as the 1912 primaries suggested, of convincing large numbers of voters that Lorimer had bought his way into the Senate. Some

[92] Taft to Howard C. Hollister, Apr. 11, 1912, to J. C. Hemphill, Apr. 12, 1912, Taft Papers; Roosevelt to Medill McCormick, Apr. 10, 1912, *Roosevelt Letters*, VII, 533–534. For press comment see "Meaning of the Illinois Primary," *The Literary Digest* (Apr. 20, 1912), XLIV, 792–795.

[93] *CR*, 62nd Cong., 2nd Sess., XLVIII, 8899. The only two Taft delegates from Illinois came from Lorimer's congressional district.

[94] New York *Times*, Apr. 11, 23, 24, 1912; *Tribune*, Apr. 28, May 11, 1912; "President Taft's Denunciation of Mr. Roosevelt," *The Literary Digest* (May 4, 1912), XLIV, 922–923. Taft wrote his brother: "It is only when they support me that bosses are wicked. Considering the use which Roosevelt made of bosses in the past one would think the hypocrisy of such attacks would be seen, but not in the case of a popular idol." Taft to Horace Taft, Apr. 14, 1912, Taft Papers.

[95] Roosevelt to Augustus P. Gardner, Apr. 18, 1912, to Henry Cabot Lodge, Apr. 24, 1912, *Roosevelt Letters*, VII, 534–536; Taft to Horace Taft, Apr. 14, 1912, to Kohlsaat, Apr. 16, 1912, Taft Papers; New York *Times* and *Tribune*, Apr. 24, 1912.

[96] Mowry, *Theodore Roosevelt and the Progressive Movement*, 229–255.

felt that the existence of corruption in the Forty-sixth Illinois General Assembly, even though not directly connected with Lorimer, was enough to justify his ouster. The belief was widespread that the Senate had erred in retaining him in his seat in 1911. Whether or not enough senators agreed with this judgment to reverse the earlier action was yet to be seen.

CHAPTER **12**

Senate Expulsion

THE PRELIMINARIES to the Lorimer Senate debate began before the end of the 1912 primary campaign. On March 18 Judge Hanecy filed a 114-page brief with the Dillingham Committee in which the doctrine of *res adjudicata* was central: the Senate should dismiss the case against Lorimer because of the lack of new evidence. Hanecy maintained that the confessions of White, Beckemeyer, Link, and Holstlaw were inadmissible because the men were perjurers, that Funk's story was mythical, and that there was no proof of a corruption fund. Senators should ignore the "public prejudice" generated by the press, he said, and remember the injustice of the decisions of Pontius Pilate and the judges of Joan of Arc.[1]

Ten days after Hanecy filed his brief, the Dillingham Committee, in a long and heated session, voted 5 to 3 that the new evidence did not justify reversing the Senate's former action. Dillingham, Gamble, Fletcher, Johnston, and Jones composed the majority and Kenyon, Kern, and Lea were the minority. By the same vote, the committee also held that there was no proof of a Lorimer election "jackpot" or of Hines's involvement in a corrupt election plan.[2]

In its lengthy report, submitted to the Senate on May 20, the majority restated the doctrine of *res adjudicata* and repudiated the Funk story as lacking "conclusiveness." The report attacked White as a

[1] *Tribune*, Mar. 2, 19, 20, 1912.
[2] The proceedings of the committee were secret. The report of the minority, however, contains an account of the committee's discussions. The minority report is U.S. Senate, *Senate Doc. 769*, Pt. 2, 62nd Cong., 2nd Sess. (Washington, 1912), and is printed in U.S., Senate, *Compilation of Senate Election Cases from 1798 to 1913*, *Senate Doc. 1036*, 62nd Cong., 3rd Sess. (Washington, 1913), 1098–1113; *Tribune*, Mar. 29, 1912; Bowers, *Kern*, 239–241.

dissipated blackmailer, and dismissed the Beckemeyer, Holstlaw, and Link confessions as unrelated to their Lorimer votes. The Lorimer election, concluded the majority opinion, logically evolved from Illinois political conditions.[3]

During the weeks after the committee vote, the minority also prepared its report. Kern's ideas shaped the argument. "Morally positive" of Lorimer's guilt before the Dillingham hearings, the testimony reinforced Kern's convictions. He, Kenyon, and Lea (Kern called them "my boys") worked night after night to produce their short but hard-hitting dissent from the majority opinion.[4]

The essence of the minority position was that fifteen men were bribed to vote for Lorimer. While the minority admitted that Lorimer himself did none of the bribing, they held him as guilty as the fifteen. The report found Hines "an accessory to the corruption that resulted in the election of William Lorimer to the Senate." On the day that the majority and the minority submitted their reports to the Senate, Lea resolved that the "corrupt methods and practices" employed in the Lorimer election made it "invalid." [5]

The 5-to-3 committee decision in March had precipitated a nationwide uproar. The press almost unanimously treated it as "a second coat of whitewash" and vehemently criticized Senator Jones, who had shifted his vote since 1911.[6] Roosevelt charged that the reactionaries of both parties produced the decision, while Taft blamed the "tactics of the *Tribune* [which] awakened opposition and an unnecessary sympathy with Lorimer." [7] When the majority and minority gave their reports to the Senate, much of the press demanded that Lorimer resign or be ousted. A Senate poll showed a likely majority against Lorimer, and on May 24 in Chicago, Vice-President Sherman

[3] The majority report is *Senate Doc. 769*, Pt. 1, and is also printed in *Senate Election Cases*, 1031–97

[4] Bowers, *Kern*, 231–244.

[5] See the report of the minority, *Senate Election Cases*, 1098–1113; New York *Times* and *Tribune*, May 21, 1912; Bowers, *Kern*, 231–244.

[6] Kohlsaat wrote Taft: "Our people are thoroughly wrought up over the 5 to 3 Lorimer Committee decision—the things they are saying of Senator Jones would not add to that gentleman's happiness if he could hear them." See Kohlsaat to Taft, Apr. 10, 1912, Taft Papers. There were rumors in Chicago that federal patronage swayed Senator Jones from an anti- to a pro-Lorimer position. Taft denied it. See Kohlsaat to Charles D. Hilles, Mar. 30, 1912, Taft to Kohlsaat, Apr. 1, 1912, *ibid.*

[7] Taft to Kohlsaat, Apr. 1, 1912, Taft Papers. There is a survey of newspaper opinion in *Tribune*, Mar. 31, 1912. See also "Another Lorimer Vindication," *The Literary Digest* (June 1, 1912), LXIV, 1147–48.

asked Lorimer to step down to spare senators the embarrassment of voting. Lorimer refused; he expected vindication.[8]

On June 4 Senator Kern began Senate discussion of the case. Lorimer sat listening carefully; he was flushed and still not recovered from a severe attack of the grippe.[9] Irritated by Kern's remarks, several times he interrupted with questions. But the small, intense-looking Kern, with a long hatchet-like face and eyes set closely together, could not be dissuaded from his relentless speech. Over a period of four days he hammered at Lorimer and the circumstances behind his election. Kern theorized that in April and May of 1909, the "great interests" of the country decided that they needed Lorimer's vote in the Senate. Hines was their representative, and he had bought the votes of the Democrats who supported Lorimer.

Kern did not believe that Lorimer, with "his good heart, his humane impulses, [and] his domestic happiness," was an evil man. Rather, the difficulty stemmed from the "corrupt field" of Chicago politics which had thrown Lorimer into contact with "notorious characters" such as "Hinky Dink" Kenna, John Broderick, Cyril Jandus, and "Manny" Abrahams. For Kern, these city machine politicians were atypical of the mass of Americans. "O Mr. President, it would have been better if this kindly man [Lorimer] had been born and reared elsewhere. It would have been better had he been brought up on the prairie, in the forest, or amongst the mountains, that he might have been closer to nature, that he might have known more of the people of this land . . . and that he might have profited thereby." [10] Given contact with the "real" people of the nation, said Kern, Lorimer would not have developed the contempt for "popular government" he expressed in the Dillingham hearings. The fault, concluded Kern, lay not in the man but in "the system of which William Lorimer is a part, *the system* which undertakes by corrupt methods to thwart the popular will." That system had to "receive condemnation at the hands of the American Senate." [11]

At the end of Kern's speech, the Senate delayed further consideration of the case until July 6, and in the intervening weeks the Re-

[8] *Tribune*, May 25, 28, June 1, 3, 4, 1912. There is a survey of anti-Lorimer press opinion in *ibid.*, May 30, 1912. See also Taft to Helen H. Taft, July 13, 1912, Taft Papers.

[9] See S. R. Slaymaker to Senator Shelby M. Cullom, May 16, 1912, Lorimer to Cullom, May 19, 1912, printed in *CR*, 62nd Cong., 2nd Sess., XLVIII, 6969.

[10] *Ibid.*, 7848.

[11] See *ibid.*, 7700–7704, 7781–84.

publicans and the Democrats held their conventions.[12] The Senate resumed the Lorimer debate after the conventions. Because Washington was in one of its proverbial summer hot spells, the gallery spectators often outnumbered the senators on the floor. Very possibly many senators had already decided their votes.

Senator Dillingham spoke first after the recess and gave the major defense of the committee's pro-Lorimer decision. The conservative Vermonter, deeply concerned with Senate precedent, spoke from July 6 to 9. His remarks echoed the committee report. Illinois political conditions rather than corruption explained Lorimer's election. He attacked Funk's tale as particularly insidious because it was circulated without a legal test and had incited Roosevelt against Lorimer. The Hamilton Club dinner incident, held Dillingham, more than any other factor, generated anti-Lorimer public opinion. The evidence, however, proved Lorimer's innocence. Because he stood for what was "right and true and just," and because he would not be swayed by lies and public opinion, Dillingham supported Lorimer's title to his seat.[13]

Other pro-Lorimer senators made much the same points. Porter J. McCumber, Old Guard Republican from North Dakota who followed Dillingham, questioned the prerogative of the Senate "to try and retry again and again the right of a Senator to a seat. . . ." Lorimer's prosecution was a "political murder," he said, "initiated by the greatest blackmailer and criminal yet unhung" and pursued with a "spirit of malice unequaled in American journalism."[14] Two southern senators, Duncan U. Fletcher of Florida and Joseph S. Johnston of Alabama, maintained that the "vital facts" of Lorimer's life militated against his stooping "to the vulgar, disreputable business of purchasing votes. . . ." Fletcher attacked Kohlsaat as an "assassin of character . . . with the disposition of the snob," and observed that Roosevelt "could enjoy a luncheon with Booker Washington . . . but could not afford to dine in the same room with Mr. Lorimer. . . ." "Justice" demanded Lorimer's retention.[15]

[12] For the Republican convention split and the formation of the Progressive party see Mowry, *Theodore Roosevelt and the Progressive Movement*, 237–273. For the Democratic convention see Arthur S. Link, *Woodrow Wilson and the Progressive Era* (New York, 1954), 12–13.

[13] *CR*, 62nd Cong., 2nd Sess., XLVIII, 8871–73.

[14] *Ibid.*, 8672, 8677.

[15] *Ibid.*, 8813 (Johnston), 8689–92 (Fletcher).

Especially significant were the remarks of "turncoat" Senator Jones. Whereas in the first case Jones had thought Lorimer's election the result of a general corruption fund, now he believed it the product of conditions in the General Assembly.[16] The new testimony before the Dillingham Committee, he held, changed his opinion. Jones had actually doubted his original position soon after the Dillingham hearings commenced. On August 11, 1911, he wrote a friend that the Lorimer case "may be decided upon the preconceived notion and ideas of Members of the Senate. There are no indications yet that there will be secured any more damaging testimony against Lorimer than was secured before . . . the country, however, seems to have its mind pretty well made up in regard to the matter *regardless of the real facts of the case,* and this will probably influence a good many votes in the Senate." [17] Jones now maintained that the "jackpot" had no relation to the Lorimer election. One should not overturn, he said, the character of a man like Lorimer ("honest, true, and courageous in politics") with the testimony of a scoundrel like White. He concluded that "a spirit of intolerance abroad in the land" had denied Lorimer a "square deal." [18]

At the conclusion of Jones's speech, the Senate had been in session for seven hours and the floor was nearly empty. The situation was identical when debate renewed on the next day. The weather continued hot and humid and senators sought relief from the stifling Senate chamber. Lorimer, however, stayed in his seat, determined to hear every word spoken on his case.

After another southern Democrat, Thornton of Louisiana, spoke in Lorimer's defense, two freshman Democrats, Lea of Tennessee and Reed of Missouri, appeared in succession for Lorimer's ouster. Lea's position was significant because he had been elected by a coalition of thirty-four Democrats and thirty-two Republicans. He was known as "Young Thunderbolt" because of "his pugnacity in battling for whatever he considered right," but his later career involved less commendable activities.[19] Lea insisted that only two questions should

[16] See *CR,* 61st Cong., 3rd Sess., XLVI, 2051–52.

[17] Jones to A. G. Foster, Aug. 11, 1911, quoted in William Stuart Forth, "Wesley L. Jones: A Political Biography" (2 vols., unpublished Ph.D. dissertation, University of Washington, 1962), I, 182 (my italics).

[18] *CR,* 62nd Cong., 2nd Sess., XLVIII, 8818–24, 8848.

[19] Bowers, *Kern,* 211. Lea was an important figure in the campaign to secure Woodrow Wilson the Democratic presidential nomination in 1912. See Arthur S. Link, *Wilson: Road to the White House* (Princeton, 1947), 440, 445. During the

be considered: did the doctrine of *res adjudicata* apply and did corruption occur in the Lorimer election? On the first Lea held that since the Senate was a continuing body, *res adjudicata,* a technical plea, did not apply. As for corruption, the testimony conclusively showed the existence of a bribery fund to elect Lorimer, and the seven admitted corrupt votes gave Lorimer less than a legal majority. The Senate, Lea held, must establish "no unsound precedent." [20]

After Reed had made the last speech against him, Lorimer entered the center aisle of the Senate chamber. He wore a blue suit with an American flag in his buttonhole, a white tie, and tan shoes. Only half the Senate membership was present, but House members filled the empty seats. Lorimer's wife and children, as well as many of his friends, sat in the crowded galleries. Lorimer began in a tremulous voice, but rapidly grew more eloquent. His defense was remarkable, not only for its arguments and its passion, but also for its abuse of President Taft, ex-President Roosevelt, and many of his Senate colleagues. Speaking for fourteen hours over a period of three days, Lorimer made a remarkable attempt to reverse a conclusion already held foregone.[21]

Lorimer began his speech by attacking the McCormicks of the *Tribune,* Herman H. Kohlsaat, and Victor Lawson—the proprietors of the "trust press" who were organized in a "plunderbund" to steal from Chicago taxpayers and schoolchildren by cheating on taxes. He again described how the *Tribune* paid low rent on school land, and also accused Lawson of being a "hypocrite and a thief" who dodged full taxes on his paper and his home. "Long, long ago could I have been the white-haired boy," said Lorimer, "if I had climbed the steps of the offices of the Newspaper Trust editors and bent my knee at their bidding, became their subservient tool, and helped them plunder the public treasury in the State of Illinois." [22] But because he would

---

1920's he was involved in several corrupt deals with the Tennessee state administration; in 1931 a federal court in Asheville, North Carolina, sentenced Luke Lea to serve from six to ten years in the penitentiary for conspiracy to violate the national banking laws. See William D. Miller, *Boss Crump of Memphis* (Baton Rouge, 1964), 149–151, 162.

[20] *CR,* 62nd Cong., 2nd Sess., XLVIII, 8885–88.

[21] For descriptions of the Senate chamber and Lorimer's speech see New York *Times* and *Tribune,* July 12, 1912; Bowers, *Kern,* 249–251; H. Beaumont Williams, ed., *A Many-Colored Toga: The Diary of Henry Fountain Ashurst* (Tucson, 1962), 18.

[22] *CR,* 62nd Cong., 2nd Sess., XLVIII, 8893–97.

THE SENATOR SEEMS TO BE OVERLOOKING THE CHIEF CONSPIRATOR.

[Copyright: 1912: By John T. McCutcheon.]

Chicago *Tribune*, July 13, 1912

not concede, the trust press had joined in a conspiracy with Deneen and Wayman, its compliant and corrupt tools, to drive him from politics. Beware, Lorimer warned his colleagues, for "the guillotine" was waiting for them too if they refused to "bend . . . [their] knees to the trust press of this country." [23]

Lorimer spent a good deal of time pointing out errors and distortions in other Senate speeches. He concentrated his attack on Senator Kern, whom he claimed had "slimed and smeared this record all over with suspicion" and never sought the truth. He challenged Kern to point to "any wrongdoing, either in private, in commercial, in financial, or in political life" during his career; if Kern could do this, he said, he would resign and spare the Senate the embarrassment of voting on his case. Kern did not accept the challenge. [24]

Some of Lorimer's most scathing remarks were made about Taft and Roosevelt. Both, he said, had interfered unfairly in his case. On the second day of his speech, July 12, Lorimer quoted a statement Taft had made about his case in a letter to Roosevelt. "I want to win, so do you," Taft had exclaimed. "Win what?" Lorimer asked. "Win a contest? What sort of a contest? In the open? . . . Was the sword and shield handed to me, and was I then notified to defend myself, that a battle was on? O, no; there was no opportunity, no knowledge of what was coming, they were going to win, win, win." "How?" asked Lorimer. By striking him from behind like a "thief in the dark," giving him no chance to defend himself. Taft, Roosevelt, and William Jennings Bryan, charged Lorimer, had joined with the trust press "in the conspiracy to misstate the facts . . . to poison the mind of the citizenship of this Union in order that one man might be destroyed. . . ." [25]

What were the facts? asked Lorimer. Browne never paid one dollar for Lorimer. Funk ("his tongue seemed to be hung in the middle, and it ran at both ends at the same time") and White were liars. He had been elected, held Lorimer, not because of bribery but because he knew "the people." Almost every Democrat who voted for him was his "warm, close, personal friend." He did not have to resort to "corruption to secure the support of the friends of his boyhood, his

[23] *Ibid.*, 8897.
[24] *Ibid.*, 8943–46.
[25] *Ibid.*, 8936.

playmates, his playfellows, those whom he has helped, and those with whom he has worked." [26]

If the Senate did choose to eject him, said Lorimer, on the last day of his speech, he would excuse his colleagues. The perjury purchased by the *Tribune* had made it impossible for them to make a correct judgment. If he were ousted, he would return home where his family would supply his "own reward." "They will not feel that they are disgraced with me if I am turned from this Chamber. It will draw them closer about me; they will love me all the more; they will form a hollow square around me and defend me against the world." [27]

Lorimer knew that "no man cast a corrupt vote" for him. Knowing that, he would not resign. He would not be "a coward." "If I go from this body," he concluded, "it will be because more Senators vote in favor of that resolution than against it. My exit will not be from fear. . . . It will be because of the crime of the Senate of these United States." "I am ready," said Lorimer. And, amidst the sound of sobs from the gallery and the floor, by a vote of 55 to 28, the Senate ousted Lorimer from his seat.[28]

Did Lorimer deserve to be ejected from the Senate? asked many who were moved by his speech. "I've no doubt it's just, but I can't help feeling sorry for the man," was a common remark. Congressman Ira C. Copley, who played a prominent role in the election deadlock, wrote to several friends that Lorimer had "made a wonderful speech. . . . That speech alone ought to have saved his seat in the Senate, providing what he said was true." "Evidently," added Copley, "two-thirds of the Senators didn't agree with him." [29] Senator Henry F. Ashurst, freshman from Arizona who voted against Lorimer, wrote in his diary that Lorimer spoke "bravely"; six months later he added the comment that the Lorimer case was an example of how "civic virtue demands a victim, seizes one, crushes and ruins him, and civic virtue then falls asleep." [30] Senator Cullom, whose career was so intertwined with Lorimer's, reversed his earlier position and voted against his colleague. He explained that "the evidence was very strong . . . that his election was the result of fraud by many mem-

[26] *Ibid.*, 8944, 8984.
[27] *Ibid.*
[28] *Ibid.*, 8985–87.
[29] Copley to Edward Cortlett and to Fred Bennett, July 13, 1912, Copley Paper•
[30] Williams, ed., *Diary of Henry Fountain Ashurst*, 18, 22.

The Chicago Sunday Tribune.

THE WORLDS GREATEST NEWSPAPER

| VOLUME LXXI.—NO.28. | JULY 14, 1912. | ★ PRICE FIVE CENTS. |

WIDOW READS 1,500 MARRIAGE OFFERS BUT NONE WINS HER

Mrs. Brown, Who Asked New York and Boston Mayors to Find a Husband, Gives Up.

MAKES LETTERS PUBLIC

Says "Corned" Westerner May Be Better for Matrimony than Easterner.

SHE TELLS OF UNIQUE EXPERIENCE

Mrs. Clara Lee Brown, yesterday told a Tribune reporter she has decided that after all with her starry again just yet. She is the wealthy Kansas City widow who wrote the mayors of Boston and New York asking them to help her find a husband. She wanted a wan, also said, with a good income and had settled all necessary and on the road, she enjoyed the uplifting and cultivating influences of the office east.

Mrs. Brown's confession was in many ways arrived at late yesterday after she had finished the perusal of some 1,500 love letters that had come to her at the Congress hotel from all parts of the country as the result of the publication of her appeals to the mayors.

LORIMER OUSTED FROM SENATE; VOTE 55 TO 28

BRIBE CHARGES HELD PROVED

Long Fight to Save Honor of Upper House Ends in Victory.

BITTER IN FINAL PLEA

Illinoisan Accuses All Against Him of Having 'Plotted' His Ruin.

DRAMATIC SCENE AT CLOSE

BY JOHN CALLAN O'LAUGHLIN.
Washington, D. C., July 13.—[Special.]—
The great fight for civic decency and against corruption which has centered for more than twenty-six months upon William Lorimer and Lorimerism has triumphed.

By the crushing vote of 55 to 28—with eight other senators paired and two not voting—Lorimer was ousted from the senate chamber on the ground that he never had a legal right to occupy a seat therein.

Thus has ended successfully a long drawn out struggle begun and carried on by The Tribune to cleanse the United States senate of the exit of Lorimerism.

It was a struggle, as Senator Root said, for the preservation of the American government as handed down by the fathers, for a body which would insist upon the retention on one of its members of a man elected by corruption and bribery, as Lorimer was, could not hope to stand.

It was a struggle in which became enlisted all the men and all the forces in this American republic toting their country's welfare at heart, and opposed to them were the predatory interests, laboring to retain their grip upon the upper branch of congress in order that they might continue to profit at the expense of the people.

Final Vote in the Senate.

AGAINST LORIMER: 55.

REPUBLICANS

Wm. E. Borah ....Idaho	Asle J. Gronna..North Dakota
Jonathan Bourne Jr...Oregon	W. S. Kenyon ....Iowa
Frank O. Briggs..New Jersey	R. M. La Follette...Wisconsin
Joseph L. Bristow....Kansas	Henry Cabot Lodge....Mass.
Norris Brown ......Nebraska	Knute Nelson ......Minnesota
Theodore E. Burton ...Ohio	Carroll S. Page ......Vermont
Moses E. Clapp...Minnesota	Miles Poindexter...Washington
Albert B. Cummins ....Iowa	Elihu Root ....New York
Charles Curtis ....Kansas	Newell Sanders ....Tennessee
Shelby M. Cullom ...Illinois	Wm. Alden Smith ...Michigan
Coe I. Crawford, South Dakota	George Sutherland ......Utah
Joseph M. Dixon ...Montana	Charles E. Townsend Michigan
Albert B. Fall ....New Mexico	John D. Works.....California

DEMOCRATS

Henry F. Ashurst ...Arizona	James A. O'Gorman New York
Augustus O. Bacon...Georgia	Lee S. Overman.. N. Carolina
N. P. Bryan ....Florida	Atlee Pomerene ....Ohio
G. E. Chamberlain ...Oregon	Isidor Rayner ......Maryland
James P. Clarke ...Arkansas	James A. Reed ......Missouri
Obediah Gardner .....Maine	B. F. Shively ......Indiana
Thomas P. Gore ...Oklahoma	F. M. Simmons.... N. Carolina
G. M. Hitchcock ...Nebraska	Marcus A. Smith ....Arizona
C. F. Johnson ......Maine	Hoke Smith ....Georgia
John W. Kern ......Indiana	E. D. Smith ..... S. Carolina
Luke Lea ....Tennessee	William J. Stone...Missouri
Thomas S. Martin... Virginia	Claude A. Swanson .. Virginia
James E. Martine ..New Jersey	C. W. Watson ..... W. Virginia
Henry L. Myers .....Montana	John S. Williams..Mississippi
Francis G. Newlands ..Nevada	

FOR LORIMER: 28.

REPUBLICANS

William O. Bradley, Kentucky	Wesley L. Jones : Washington
F. B. Brandegee ..Connecticut	H. F. Lippitt ....Rhode Island
H.E.Burnham .New Hampshire	P. J. McCumber....N. Dakota
Thos. B. Catron ..New Mexico	Geo. T. Oliver....Pennsylvania
Clarence D. Clark...Wyoming	Boies Penrose ..Pennsylvania
W. Murray Crane ....Mass.	Geo. C. Perkins...California
W. P. Dillingham ...Vermont	H. A. Richardson..Delaware
J.H.Gallinger .New Hampshire	Reed Smoot ....Utah
R. J. Gamble ...S. Dakota	Isaac Stephenson ..Wisconsin
Simon Guggenheim..Colorado	G. P. Wetmore..Rhode Island

DEMOCRATS

Joseph W. Bailey ....Texas	Thos. H. Paynter...Kentucky
O. U. Fletcher .....Florida	J. W. Smith ......Maryland
M. J. Foster .....Louisiana	John R. Thornton ...Louisiana
J. F. Johnston .....Alabama	B. R. Tillman... S. Carolina

PAIRED—AGAINST LORIMER.

W. E. Chilton, D. W.Virginia	Jeff Davis, D. ....Arkansas
C. A. Culberson, D. ....Texas	R L. Owen, D. ....Oklahoma

PAIRED—FAVORING LORIMER.

J. H. Bankhead, D...Alabama	W. B. Heyburn, R......Idaho
H. A. DuPont, R. ...Delaware	E. F. Warren, R....Wyoming
William Lorimer (Illinois)....	....Did Not Vote

against Lorimer would have been exactly the jackpot but for their votes for Lorimer.

That Thomas and John Bradstock committed perjury when they denied bribing the men named.

That Robert P. Wilson was the corrupt agent of Lee O'Neill Browne.

On that occasion Lorimer was saved by ten men who had been defeated for reelection—Bradley, Crawford, Richardson, Stewart, Michigan; Depew, New York; Dick, Ohio; Carter, Montana; Flint, California; Hale, Maine; Kean, New Jersey; Piles of Washington, and Scott of West Virginia. When the new senate came in with men fresh from the people and anxious only to represent the people, men of higher ideals and believers in the preservation of the institutions of the government, it was possible to secure an unbiased judgment.

NEW SENATORS OPPOSE LORIMER.

The vote today was significant in the one respect—every man who succeeded the "lame ducks" voted against Lorimer. Of all the new senators only two, Catron of New Mexico and Lippitt of Rhode Island, supported Lorimer. Five members of the senate who voted for Lorimer more than a year ago voted to oust him this time.

These include Briggs of New Jersey, Cullom of Illinois, Curtis of Kansas, Simmons of North Carolina, and Watson of West Virginia.

The change of Senator Cullom was based upon the conclusive character of the evidence as gathered upon the second investigation. His careful consideration of the facts before him as chairman of the committee induced him to determine its case his vote against Lorimer this time.

PROGRESSIVES OUT IN FORCE.

Senators Briggs, Curtis, Simmons, and Watson gotten the same consideration as the witness stood in denying the Republican party for the election this fall.

All the progressives opposed Lorimer to-day as they opposed him during the winter of 1911. It was on them that Lorimer threw the brunt of his attack in the speeches he has made—on Borah, Crawford...

Chicago *Tribune*, July 14, 1912

THE CHIEF MOURNER.

[Copyrighted: 1912: By John T. McCutcheon.]

"POOR LORIMER!" HE NEVER FAILED ME WHEN I NEEDED HIS VOTE."

bers of the Legislature . . . I could not do otherwise than to vote against him." And yet, added Cullom, he had done so "reluctantly," and "had come to feel that it was a great pity that he had to be turned out of the Senate." [31]

As for Roosevelt and Taft, each had a comment to make, one private, the other public. Speaking to the press, Roosevelt boasted that it "was my fight and it is my victory. The whole thing began when I refused to dine with him at the Hamilton Club dinner." [32] President Taft was not so sure. He wrote to his wife, "It will be a good thing to get Lorimer out of the Senate. He is a man of some taking qualities, but he is utterly despised in Illinois. . . ." But he added in an enigmatic phrase, *"I think he has not been fairly treated. . . ."* [33] What these words meant, Taft never explained.

Most of the nation's press had no doubts. The fight against Lorimer was largely a newspaper fight, and Lorimer had not spared harsh words in rebutting their attack. Now the press gloated that Lorimer's ouster was a "victory for public decency" and an "extraordinary triumph of public opinion." For the *Tribune* it was a great climax to a long campaign, and it boasted that "truth wins; justice is done." [34] There were some doubters, but these were among the stalwart papers of the country. The New York *Sun* commented that Lorimer did not have a "fair trial," while the Philadelphia *Inquirer* suggested that the "evidence" pointed to a different decision. Most critical of all, as expected, was the *Inter-Ocean,* which warned that other heads would fall under "the guillotine of the mob" stirred up by "the forces of unscrupulous wealth armed with a venal press and the direct primary. . . ." In contemplation of such a future, it asked all Americans to pray, "God help the United States and its people." [35]

Whether Lorimer's election was dependent on bribery or whether he was involved in the corruption will probably never be answered. The evidence does, however, reveal a legislative "jackpot" in the Illinois General Assembly.[36] More pertinent is why the Senate, after

[31] Cullom to Dr. A. W. Foreman, July 23, 1912, Cullom Papers.

[32] For Roosevelt's comment see *Tribune,* July 14, 1912.

[33] Taft to Helen H. Taft, July 13, 1912, Taft Papers; Pringle, *Taft,* II, 618–619.

[34] *Tribune,* July 15, 1912.

[35] For a survey of newspaper opinion see "Lorimer Out," *The Literary Digest* (July 27, 1912), XLV, 134–135. See also *The Broadax,* July 20, 1912. *The Broadax* was a Chicago Negro newspaper.

[36] Two matters involving legislative corruption, in addition to the Lorimer case, were investigated by State's Attorney Edmund Burke of Sangamon County. The first involved kickbacks paid by a furniture dealer to members of the General

voting to retain Lorimer, reversed its decision. Analysis and comparison of the 1911 and 1912 roll calls suggest some of the reasons. While the Republicans controlled the upper house in the Sixty-second Congress as they had in the Sixty-first, the Senate's composition had changed since 1911 and the Lorimer vote reflected this change. In 1911 eighteen Democrats and twenty-two Republicans voted to expel Lorimer. In 1912 twenty-nine Democrats and twenty-six Republicans voted to unseat. In 1911 ten Democrats and thirty-six Republicans voted for Lorimer. In 1912 only eight Democrats and twenty Republicans voted this way.[37]

Most significant in 1912 was that twenty-one of the twenty-three freshman senators who cast a ballot voted against Lorimer. Of the new Republicans, six voted yea and two nay, while all fifteen freshman Democrats voted for expulsion.[38] Of the sixty senators who had voted on both the 1911 Beveridge resolution and the 1912 Lea resolution, thirteen altered their votes, and nine of these represented a change from votes to retain to votes to expel or no vote.[39] The Democrats voted with a high degree of unity on the case, while the Re-

---

Assembly in return for contracts to supply furniture for the House and Senate chambers, while the second concerned money paid by Illinois fishermen to prevent the passage of legislation inimical to their interests. Illinois Senator Holstlaw confessed to Burke that he had been promised $1,500 by a furniture dealer in return for a state contract, while several fishermen told Burke that they annually contributed to a fund that was used to affect legislation in the General Assembly. The Sangamon County grand jury eventually brought indictments against Holstlaw, Stanton C. Pemberton, and Joseph S. Clark of the General Assembly for conspiracy to commit bribery and against Archibald B. Johnston for bribery in the furniture case, and against Louis D. Herscheimer and Frank J. Traut for conspiracy to commit bribery in the fish case. No convictions, however, were obtained. For discussion of these aspects of the "jackpot," see the testimony of State's Attorney Burke in *Dillingham Committee Hearings*, V, 4622–4703; *Tribune*, May 20, June 1, 4–8, 25, 26, Oct. 30, 1910. For a discussion of corruption in a more recent Illinois legislature, see Paul Simon and Alfred Balk, "The Illinois Legislature: A Study in Corruption," *Harper's Magazine* (Sept., 1964), CCXXIX, 74–78.

[37] In percentage terms, in 1911 64 percent of the Democrats and 37 percent of the Republicans voting voted to expel; in 1912 78 percent of the Democrats and 57 percent of the Republicans voted to expel.

[38] The new Democrats voting yea were Ashurst, Bryan, Gardner, Hitchcock, Johnson, Kern, Lea, Martin, Myers, O'Gorman, Pomerene, Reed, Smith (Arizona), Smith (Georgia), and Williams; the Republicans were Fall, Kenyon, Poindexter, Sanders, Townsend, and Works. The two Republicans voting nay were Catron and Lippitt. Chilton (Democrat) and McLean (Republican) cast no vote.

[39] Among the Republicans, Jones changed from yea to nay, Briggs, Cullom, and Curtis from nay to yea, and Dupont, Heyburn, and Dupont from nay to no vote. Among the Democrats, Simmons and Watson changed from nay to yea, Bankhead from nay to no vote, and Davis, Owen, and Perry from yea to no vote.

publicans sharply split, reflecting the factionalism within the GOP during the Taft congresses. Democratic unity and Republican disunity was a key element in Lorimer's expulsion.[40]

Knowledge of the Senate divisions, however, does not explain the vote of individual senators. Many of the new men who opposed Lorimer were more attuned to the political morality of the progressive period than were their predecessors. Some, like Kern, Kenyon, and Lea, were "drys," and suspicious of the part that the liquor interests played in Lorimer's election.[41] Others were hostile to political bosses and believed them synonymous with corruption of the political process. Through their votes they struck at what Senator Kern called "the system which undertakes by corrupt methods to thwart the popular will." And fear of public reprisal may have influenced the shift of nine 1911 pro-Lorimer votes.[42]

Toward the end of the nineteenth century, and well into the twentieth, crises caused by rapid technological and industrial change, massive immigration, unprecedented social mobility, and major political transformations wracked America and shook the established institutional and societal structure. The city proved the critical testing ground; here tensions rose and innovations proliferated.

William Lorimer's career reflected many of the main problems confronting the city. Chicago's political and social fragmentation helped him rise from a poor immigrant boy to an acknowledged wielder of real power. Through his machine and his alliances with downstate politicians, he consolidated political power in Illinois and helped overcome Chicago's formal political decentralization with an informal centralization focusing on himself as boss. He represented

[40] Jerome M. Clubb and Howard W. Allen, "Party Loyalty in the Progressive Years: The Senate, 1909–1915," *Journal of Politics* (Aug., 1967), XXIX, 567–584. Among the Republicans, a vote to expel Lorimer correlated with a pro-reform record, but no such relationship existed among the Democrats. The vote also had geographical dimensions. Ten of the Republicans who voted to retain Lorimer came from states east of the Mississippi, while nineteen of the Republicans who voted to expel came from states west of the Mississippi; the eight Democrats who voted for Lorimer were all southerners. See Allen, "Geography and Politics," 219–227, and Clubb, "Congressional Opponents of Reform," 281–286.

[41] Timberlake, *Prohibition and the Progressive Movement*, 162–163; Bowers, *Kern*, 6, 12, 432–433; Isaac, *Prohibition and Politics*, 182, 195–196.

[42] Twelve senators who had voted for Lorimer's retention in 1911 were candidates for re-election in 1912. The *Tribune* observed that if the Lorimer vote had been held over until after the fall elections, the twelve would probably have supported Lorimer. See *Tribune*, Apr. 12, May 20, 1912.

within the councils of the Republican party the attitudes and opinions of a mass of ethnic and working-class voters customarily overlooked in that party; his organization supplied to them services not available through normal governmental channels and enabled them to cope better with the vicissitudes of urban life. His organization also aided business interests in obtaining the franchises and favors, both legal and illegal, that they sought from government. In short, whether for good or for ill, Lorimer filled a political and governmental vacuum that existed in Chicago.

Lorimer's activities stimulated within the Chicago GOP a conflict between machine politicians and political reformers. This conflict mirrored similar contests in other urban areas. While outwardly the struggle appeared to be between "honest" reformers and "corrupt" professional politicians, there were deep-seated cultural questions involved. Lorimer's supporters came from ethnic groups whose ritualistic religious perspective caused them to look with distrust upon reform crusades. They were concerned with preserving their cultural norms and in protecting "personal liberty." They favored a loose arrangement of society which conserved local and ethnic life-styles and tolerated considerable disorder and political "corruption."

The critics of Lorimer and his machine, in contrast to his supporters, were often native Americans who derived from pietistic religious backgrounds. Their religious perspective helped make "reform" congenial to them. They opposed the cultural norms of Lorimer's backers ("the cheap and nasty elements of the community") as bitterly as they fought his political views. Many of the reformers were also members of a cosmopolitan and professionally trained upper class who advocated urban centralization and the application of corporate organizational methods stressing efficiency and expertise to municipal government. They used democratic rhetoric in making their proposals for governmental change, but their prime interest was in giving decision-making power to men with backgrounds and philosophies similar to their own.

Lorimer's domination of the Chicago Republican party cost it the local support of many native Americans who voted Republican on the national level. Conversely, many ethnics who approved the stance of the local Democratic party in favor of personal liberty would not endorse the national Democratic party under the leadership of the pietistic crusader William Jennings Bryan. They found the culturally neutral leadership of Republicans William McKinley and Theodore Roosevelt far more to their liking.[43] From 1896 to 1908, Chicago voted Republican in presidential elections but only elected one Republican mayor (who was a German), as ethnocultural groups moved from party to party seeking a political home hospitable to their value systems.

The Senate's expulsion of William Lorimer involved some of the same types of conflict evident in Chicago politics. While all who voted to oust Lorimer were not advocates of the doctrine of efficiency and expertise, many shared a distrust of those areas of city life that Lorimer represented. In addition, the ethos of the progressive period, with its emphasis on democratic reforms such as the direct primary and the popular election of senators, intensified distrust of political bosses and of those who appeared to hold power without responsibility. The irony of Lorimer's expulsion is that a crusade supposedly devoted to honest and responsible government claimed a victim in a case where there was no evidence that he had broken the law. But Lorimer had become a symbol to his most avid Senate antagonists, and in ejecting him they struck at boss politics, immigrant-based political machines, the liquor evil, and legislative corruption. Their vision of American society had no room for these elements.

[43] Morgan, "William McKinley as a Political Leader," 421; Blum, *The Republican Roosevelt,* 37.

Epilogue

Lᴏʀɪᴍᴇʀ ʀᴇᴛᴜʀɴᴇᴅ to Chicago from Washington on July 23 and met a reception fit for a hero rather than an unseated U.S. senator. Lorimer lieutenants "Poor Fred" Lundin and "Big Bill" Thompson had organized the festivities. From Union Station Lorimer led an automobile caravan to Orchestra Hall, where 2,500 cheering followers greeted him. After the Rev. Archibald J. Carey of the Abyssinian Baptist Church read the invocation, Thompson introduced Lorimer as a "martyr"—"a living example . . . that a trust press controls this city and nation, and that a man who will not bend his knee to its dictates can be driven from political or public life."

Lorimer spoke draped with an American flag, and largely repeated his Senate speech. He called his ouster the "crime of the United States Senate," and promised to seek vindication and to campaign "to free this country from the stifling grasp of the monster, the trust press." Father John O'Callaghan, who followed Lorimer, charged that the *Tribune* was "the greatest criminal in Illinois, a moral leper." The meeting concluded with the audience approving a resolution extolling Lorimer: "That in this type of man and in such a character lies the hope of the future of the nation." [1]

Although he had threatened to tour the state and tell the truth about his case, Lorimer never kept his promise, and during the next two years he stayed out of the public eye. He still had some political influence, however, and in 1913 helped elect Lawrence Y. Sherman rather than a progressive to fill the unexpired years of his Senate term.[2] There were indications during 1913 and 1914 that Lorimer

[1] *Tribune*, July 18, 24, 1912; Wendt and Kogan, *Big Bill*, 77–79.
[2] Sherman wrote Frank O. Lowden that "the kindly manner in which Lorimer has interested himself in my behalf, unexpected as it is, is none the less appreciated." Feb. 19, 1913, Sherman Papers. The same session of the General Assembly elected a Democrat, James Hamilton Lewis, to the full Senate term. Edward J.

was regrouping his political forces for a comeback, but a financial disaster in the late spring of 1914 blocked his plans.[3]

On June 12, 1914, Lorimer's bank, the La Salle Street Trust and Savings Company, and three other affiliated banks, failed. Investigation into the bank's history revealed a sorry story of mismanagement, unlawful use of funds, and political involvement. Lorimer and his partner Charles B. Munday had opened their bank with a national charter in 1910, just after the *Tribune* published White's bribery confession. Because Lorimer was a senator, the Comptroller of the Currency had not conducted the customary investigation into his charter application.[4] Among the bank's stockholders were a number of politicians, and Lorimer and Munday expected to secure public deposits.

The La Salle Street bank's troubles began on the day it opened. The Lorimer senatorial scandal caused a large deposit withdrawal and forced Lorimer and Munday to cancel plans for a state trust company.[5] Considering the bad publicity surrounding Lorimer, it is surprising that his bank opened at all. National bank examiner Edwin F. Rorebeck wrote in his first report: "The future of this bank cannot be predicted. Handicapped as it was at its birth by the notoriety attendant to certain disclosures reflecting on its President, it is not to be expected that it could be immediately successful. It is surprising that it has secured any business at all and it must be said that the line of deposits carried indicates that the management has a considerable following." Rorebeck added that "sooner or later, however, it will have to sell out or get out of business." [6]

Brundage wrote Sherman that Lorimer "hates the Bull Moose crowd most cordially." Feb. 12, 1913, Sherman Papers. See also Sherman to Brundage, Sept. 21, Nov. 19, Dec. 14, 19, 21, 1912, Feb. 17, 1913, Brundage to Sherman, Nov. 14, Dec. 13, 16, 20, 1912, Feb. 5, 12, 1913, *ibid.;* Sherman to Charles G. Dawes, Jan. 20, Feb. 5, 1913, Dawes Papers; Lowden to Harry B. Ward, Feb. 14, 1913, Lowden Papers; Theodore Roosevelt to Ruth Hanna McCormick, Dec. 4, 1912, *Roosevelt Letters,* VII, 661. Cullom wrote that he would rather see Lorimer elected than either Sherman or James Hamilton Lewis. See Cullom to John C. Ames, Dec. 29, 1912, Cullom Papers.

[3] Lawrence Y. Sherman to W. W. Rosenfield, Sept. 11, 1913, Jan. 5, 1914, Sherman Papers; Lorimer to Frank O. Lowden, Nov. 6, 1914, Harry B. Ward to Lowden, Aug. 18, 1913, Lowden Papers; Lorimer to ———, June 23, 30, 1913, to William E. Nye, Aug. 11, 1913, Small Papers.

[4] Note signed E. F. Quinn, Feb. 4, 1910, in the La Salle Street National Bank file, Records of the Office of the Comptroller of the Currency (Record Group 101), National Archives, hereafter referred to as Comptroller's Records.

[5] *Tribune,* Apr. 14, 1916.

[6] Rorebeck to Murray, May 9, 20, 1910, and Examiner's Report, Sept. 22, 1910 [Edwin F. Rorebeck, examiner], Comptroller's Records. In 1910 the La Salle Street bank had a $50,000 loan to the Alonzo Curtis Brick Company and a $30,000 loan

Those who knew of the La Salle Street bank's affairs believed that Lorimer's partner Munday caused its downfall. The downstate businessman made unsecured loans to his own enterprises, "kited" funds to his southern Illinois banks, and lied to the national bank examiners.[7] The La Salle Street National had applied for membership in the Chicago Clearing House Association, but at the end of its one-year probationary period the Clearing House committee denied the application. Chairman James R. Forgan maintained that the bank had an excess of poorly secured loans to firms in which Munday and Lorimer were interested. Forgan wrote Comptroller Murray that the management of the bank was "inefficient," and that unless it secured better direction, the bank would "become a 'black sheep' in the fold of the Chicago banking fraternity." [8]

Comptroller Murray sought improvements in the bank's affairs, but Munday and Lorimer did not cooperate. Bank examiner Owen T. Reeves reported early in 1912 that the bank was "a hopeless derelict," and that there existed "no good excuse for . . . [its] doing business." Reeves wrote Comptroller Murray that Munday admitted he knew nothing of banking and that Lorimer was too occupied with his Senate case to pay attention to business.[9] Murray's demands for a reformation of the bank's procedures would have necessitated a complete overhaul of the bank's direction; rather than agree to this, Lorimer and Munday applied for a state charter. The state auditor accepted their application and in October, 1912, the La Salle Street National Bank became the La Salle Street Trust and Savings Company.[10]

Although Lorimer devoted full attention to the state bank, its

---

to Edward C. Curtis. Curtis was a state senator and a political ally of Len Small, as well as a banker. In 1907 he forfeited his national bank charter because of unsecured loans to his own brick company; he then secured a state charter. In 1921 he and Small were sued for loaning state funds, deposited in Curtis' bank by Small, at exorbitant interest rates. See Wooddy, *Case of Frank L. Smith*, 156–157, 160–161.

[7] T. P. Kane [acting comptroller of the currency] to Board of Directors, La Salle Street National Bank, Mar. 3, 1911, Examiner's Report [Owen T. Reeves, examiner], Mar. 14, 1911, Owen T. Reeves to Lawrence O. Murray, Jan. 22, Apr. 5, 1912, Comptroller's Records.

[8] Forgan to Murray, Feb. 8, May 26, 31, 1911, Comptroller's Records.

[9] Reeves to Murray, Jan. 22, 1912, Examiner's Reports, Jan. 27, Mar. 3, 1912 [Reeves, examiner], Murray to Board of Directors, La Salle Street National Bank, Comptroller's Records.

[10] Reeves to Murray, Aug. 30, Oct. 7, 1912, Comptroller's Records. Reeves wrote Murray that he had done nothing to hamper the new organization.

business practices did not improve. Loans to Lorimer and Munday firms and the kiting of funds to Munday's downstate banks continued.[11] Many of Lorimer's political friends received loans on poor security, possibly in return for securing public funds for the La Salle Street bank. At the time of its failure, public funds composed 26 percent of its total deposits. Munday's downstate banks also held large public deposits.[12] To avoid strict regulation by the state auditor's office, Lorimer and Munday hired several state bank examiners at high salaries. J. K. Seagrave, head state examiner, was a Munday business associate and a stockholder in the La Salle Street bank; he was appointed to the auditor's office through Lorimer's influence. As the *Tribune* commented, the La Salle Street bank "was a political bank and its capitalization was political influence." [13]

In spite of their political connections, Lorimer's and Munday's inefficient and improper methods predetermined the bank's failure. When the La Salle Street Trust and Savings Company collapsed, three allied Chicago state banks and a number of Munday's downstate institutions accompanied it.[14] In the late summer and fall of 1914, the Cook County grand jury and a federal grand jury returned indictments against Lorimer, Munday, and other of their bank officials for misappropriation of funds and conspiracy to defraud. The State's Attorney had discovered that the La Salle Street bank accepted deposits after its managers knew of its insolvency. The government did not act on the federal charges, but the state brought Lorimer and Munday to trial.[15]

In March of 1916, the Lorimer-Munday trial began before Judge William E. Dever. As in the Lorimer Senate investigation, the testimony was voluminous, and, also as in the Senate case, Lorimer maintained that there was a conspiracy against him. In his opening statement, Lorimer's lawyer, Albert Fink, claimed that James R. Forgan and the Clearing House committee had refused the La Salle Street

[11] *Tribune*, June 13, 18, 1914; "Lorimer Banks Fail," *Chicago Economist*, June 13, 1914.

[12] *Tribune*, June 25, 27, 1914.

[13] *Ibid.*, June 13, 19, 23, 1914; James, *Growth of Chicago Banks*, II, 836. Examiner Reeves wrote Comptroller Murray that Munday had offered him a salary of $25,000 a year to join the La Salle Street bank staff. Reeves to Murray, Apr. 5, 1912, Comptroller's Records.

[14] *Tribune*, June 13, 19, 28, 29, 1914; "Lorimer Banks Fail"; James, *Growth of Chicago Banks*, II, 835.

[15] *Tribune*, June 20, 21, 27, July 3, 12, 1914.

National Bank admission to the Clearing House Association because of fear of competition. Forgan, however, denied the charge and held that he had advised Lorimer to liquidate his bank because of its many unsecured loans.[16]

Charles G. Dawes, now president of the Central Trust Company, also testified. In 1912 Dawes had made it possible for Lorimer to meet the state auditor's cash reserve requirements by cashing Lorimer's bank check for $1,250,000. Dawes now agreed that Forgan correctly refused the La Salle Street National admission to the Clearing House and that he had erred in cashing Lorimer's check.[17]

On April 13, and for several days after, Lorimer testified about the circumstances of his bank's failure. He named the Chicago press, bankers Forgan, Dawes, and James B. McDougal of the Federal Reserve Bank, and federal bank examiners Owen T. Reeves, Charles H. Meyer, and Daniel V. Harkin as conspirators against him. Lorimer also attacked his partner Munday for juggling bank records, and his secretary Charles E. Ward for involving the bank in Ward's business difficulties. Most of his friends, however, said Lorimer, were honest: "When the bank opened, I don't believe five percent of the depositors were not my warm personal friends." [18] Here lay most of Lorimer's difficulties. He attempted to run his bank on the same personal basis as he did his politics. Lorimer admitted lending money to people regardless of security if he thought they needed it. Those Lorimer considered his friends defrauded him, and as a result, as Senator Lawrence Y. Sherman observed, the bank went "the same way . . . [Lorimer's] politics went." [19]

The prosecution, directed by Assistant District Attorney William H. Holly, would not accept Lorimer's ignorance plea. Lorimer knew, said Holly, of his bank's condition, and noted that he had used bad checks to pay up the capital stock of the William Lorimer Lumber Company.[20] Albert Fink, however, characterized Lorimer as "one of the finest, sweetest, most loveable personal characters" he had ever met. This innocent man, said Fink, had been victimized by his un-

16 *Ibid.*, Mar. 21, 25, Apr. 14, 1916; James, *Growth of Chicago Banks*, II, 832–835. A number of character witnesses, including "Hinky Dink" Kenna, Congressman James McAndrews, and Lorimer's Sunday School teacher, testified of his reputation for "truth, integrity, and moral courage."
17 James, *Growth of Chicago Banks*, II, 832–835; *Tribune*, Mar. 25, 1916.
18 *Tribune*, Apr. 15, 16, 18, 20, 21, 30, 1916.
19 Sherman to Homer Tice, June 19, 1914, Sherman Papers.
20 *Tribune*, Mar. 15, Apr. 23, May 4, 5, 1916.

scrupulous partner and by a conspiracy led by James R. Forgan. After six hours of deliberation, the jury acquitted Lorimer but found Munday guilty of the charges. Lorimer's friends, who packed the courtroom, gave a resounding cheer, and Lorimer shook the jurors' hands and promised he would reimburse those who had lost in his bank's failure. He also announced that he would run for Congress that fall.[21]

Lorimer had actually "never been out of politics." In November of 1914 he had written to Frank O. Lowden and asked Lowden to run for governor. "We can win two years from now," said Lorimer, "granted that we can perfect an organization and have a leader to rally around." But, he added, "men cannot be organized on generalities," and he urged Lowden to furnish his followers " 'definite issues' to fight for." Lowden, commented the ex-boss, had "stood for the historical principles of the party 'while the nation has been on a political drunk' "; now was the time to act because "there is a tide in the affairs of men which if taken at the flood, leads on to fortune." [22]

But while Lowden ran for governor and won in 1916, Lorimer was not active in his campaign; neither did he benefit or attempt to benefit from his old friend's election. Professor William T. Hutchinson, Lowden's biographer, notes that in the whole "vast mass" of Lowden patronage correspondence there is only one Lorimer letter.[23] More important for Lorimer was "Big Bill" Thompson's election as Chicago mayor in April of 1915. Thompson's organization rested on Lorimer's old framework, but he mobilized the voters, pulling from both Republicans and Democrats, in a way that Lorimer's mayoralty candidates never had. While Thompson's Democratic opponent, Robert M. Sweitzer, charged that Thompson was an "errand boy for the discredited Billy Lorimer," "Poor Fred" Lundin, another Lorimer protégé, was the real power behind "Big Bill." [24]

Although he had gained much from his Lorimer association, Lundin determined to be Thompson's sole adviser. He shut Lorimer out of city hall, and when Lorimer attempted to win the Sixth District con-

---

[21] *Ibid.,* May 4, 5, 1916.
[22] Lorimer to Lowden, Nov. 6, 1914, Lowden Papers.
[23] Hutchinson, *Lowden,* I, 308n27.
[24] Wendt and Kogan, *Big Bill,* 103. "Thompson is entirely under the control of Lundin. His policy and political ideas are unfathomable." See Edward J. Brundage to Lawrence Y. Sherman, May 8, 1915, Mar. 23, 1918, Sherman Papers.

gressional nomination in 1916, the Lundin candidate overwhelmed him.[25] After Thompson's second victory in 1919, however, Lundin relented, and Lorimer gained some influence in the administration. In 1921 the Municipal Voters' League exaggeratedly charged that Lorimer was the "real works" in the Thompson machine.[26]

During the first half of the 1920's Lorimer mainly worked to rebuild his fortune and pay his financial debts rather than regain political power. His activities ranged from searching for railroad and lumber concessions in South America to dealing and investing in Insull Utility Company stock.[27] By 1926 Lorimer had supposedly accumulated over $100,000 to repay his former bank depositors, and he again involved himself fully in politics.

In 1923 scandals had wracked the Thompson administration, many of them involving Fred Lundin. The unfavorable publicity forced Thompson to withdraw as a candidate for a third term and "Big Bill" held Lundin responsible for his difficulties. Thompson broke with his "Warwick," but the wily Swede moved to Springfield where another old Lorimerite, Len Small of Kankakee, was in his second term as governor.[28] In 1926, when Thompson again sought the mayoralty, Lorimer appeared as the "Thompson general." According to William H. Stuart, political editor of the Chicago *American* and "Big Bill's" close friend, Thompson "knew Lorimer's great mind and the great things he had done, and could do." [29] Lorimer became Thompson's chief tactician and helped direct the campaign which brought Thompson back to office in 1927.[30]

Proving that he could still weld political alliances between metropolitan and downstate forces, Lorimer restored amicable relationships

[25] *Tribune,* July 11, Aug. 4, Sept. 14, 1916.

[26] *Ibid.,* Mar. 14, 1919, Apr. 8, 1920, Apr. 3, 1921.

[27] *Ibid.,* July 18, 28, 1922, May 25, 1924, Jan. 27, 1925; *News,* Sept. 20, Oct. 20, 1926, Oct. 11, 1932; McDonald, *Insull,* 311–312. Lorimer was on a list of "insiders" who were allowed to purchase Insull Utility Investments common stock at a reduced price. On Aug. 24, 1964, Samuel Insull, Jr., told the author that his father had a "sentimental feeling for Lorimer."

[28] Wendt and Kogan, *Big Bill,* 206–216; Wooddy, *Case of Frank L. Smith,* 180–181.

[29] William H. Stuart, *The Twenty Incredible Years* (Chicago, 1935), 203.

[30] Thompson attacked the press and reformers in a manner similar to that used by Lorimer in the past. One writer blames the disorder and corruption of Chicago politics in the 1920's on "the persisting influence of this evil [Lorimer] tradition." See Wooddy, *Case of Frank L. Smith,* 153–155, 164. In his thorough study of Chicago ethnic voting in the 1920's, John M. Allswang notes that the key to Thomp-

between Thompson and Small and soon had replaced Lundin in Springfield as well as Chicago.[31] In 1927 Lorimer, Thompson, and Small toured the Mississippi Valley agitating for Lorimer's old project, the Lakes-to-the-Gulf deep waterway, probably attempting to use the project to divert attention from the corruption that marked the Small administration. But "the revival of the close association between Thompson, Small, and Lorimer proved a little too much for the electorate to swallow," and in 1928 Secretary of State L. L. Emmerson defeated Small for the Republican gubernatorial nomination.[32]

Small's defeat was followed, in the 1931 mayoralty election, by Anton J. Cermak's victory over Thompson, and Lorimer was again without a political home. During 1931 and 1932 he toured the state speaking for Small's renomination and attacking his old nemesis, "the coward-breeding direct primary," but it was his last political campaign.[33] In 1932 the Insull Utility empire, in which the Lorimer family had invested its capital, collapsed, wiping out the savings of thousands of Chicagoans. The crash nearly bankrupted Lorimer, but, typically loyal to his friends, when an impoverished Insull returned from Greece in May, 1934, to stand trial for using the mails to defraud, Lorimer greeted him with an envelope containing $500.[34]

During much of 1933 heart trouble confined Lorimer to his home. By the summer of 1934 his doctors believed him recovered, but on September 3, in the Chicago and Northwestern Railroad Station, the Blond Boss died from a heart attack. His funeral was held at the Saint Catherine of Siena Church in suburban Oak Park, which he had attended during the latter years of his life. An overflow crowd of friends and foes came to bid him farewell. Charles S. Deneen, Roy O. West, Len Small, Frank L. Smith, John Broderick, Samuel Insull, and many others heard Father John S. Bowen pay tribute to Lorimer

son's strength was "a socio-economic, or class, rather than ethnic attraction to the socio-economically lowest among virtually all ethnic groups." See "The Political Behavior of Chicago's Ethnic Groups," 257.

[31] *News*, Aug. 31, 1927; Wendt and Kogan, *Big Bill*, 279; Wooddy, *Case of Frank L. Smith*, 153, 164.

[32] Wooddy, *Case of Frank L. Smith*, 153–154, 164; Stuart, *Twenty Incredible Years*, 205, 208, 336–338; Wendt and Kogan, *Big Bill*, 278–279; *News*, Nov. 8, 1927. In 1928 Lorimer had breakfast at the White House with President Coolidge.

[33] *News*, May 20, Oct. 2, 1931.

[34] Linn, *James Keeley*, 117–118; McDonald, *Insull*, 305–319.

as "the father of a family and a churchman." Politics was absent from the eulogy, but not from the talk in the crowd. Lorimer, the mourners said time and again, never forgot his friends.[35]

[35] *Tribune,* Sept. 14, 18, 1934; New York *Times,* Mar. 24, Sept. 14, 16, 18, 1934. A different sort of epitaph was written earlier on Lorimer by Lawrence Y. Sherman: "The experiences of all who come in contact with Lorimer are ultimately the same. I hope he may recover from his misdeeds. I cannot however keep down the thought how everyone who has come in contact with him has suffered. . . . I do not say that he intentionally hurts his friends, but the injury results even without intention. . . . I hope he may get upon his feet financially. . . . I do not look for him to do so, however, Great men have done so." Sherman to Charles G. Dawes, Apr. 28, 1917, Sherman Papers. Lorimer's estate consisted of 1,000 shares of La Salle Street bank stock.

A Note on the Analysis of Chicago Voting Behavior

THE INTERPRETATIONS of voting behavior in this work rest mainly upon a statistical analysis of Chicago election and demographic data. Election returns were obtained from the *Chicago Daily News Almanac,* and from manuscript sources in the Chicago Municipal Reference Library and the office of the Chicago Board of Election Commissioners.

The principal sources for determining the ethnic composition of Chicago wards were the school censuses printed in the *Annual Reports* of the Chicago Board of Education for 1894, 1904, 1906, and 1908; the "Composition of Chicago's Vote—1892," a chart printed in the *Chicago Daily News Almanac for 1894,* 318 (totals corrected for errors), giving the nationality of Chicago's electorate in 1892; and the population schedules for Chicago given in the eleventh, twelfth, and thirteenth U.S. censuses.

Information pertaining to the class character of wards was obtained from school attendance figures in the *Annual Reports* of the Chicago Board of Education for 1894, 1904, 1906, and 1908; from mortality rates in the "Vital Statistics" volumes of the eleventh, twelfth, and thirteenth U.S. censuses; from a qualitative description of each Chicago ward in *Vital Statistics: Cities of 100,000 and Upwards, U.S. Eleventh Census,* IV, Pt. 2, 161–181; and from illiteracy and school attendance figures for Chicago in the thirteenth U.S. census.

Securing information concerning the religious composition of Chicago wards was most difficult. Sources for the 1890–1900 period were supplied to the author by Paul J. Kleppner, who had determined the religious character of Chicago wards for his doctoral dissertation, "The Politics of Change in the Midwest: The 1890's in Historical and Behavorial Perspective" (University of Pittsburgh, 1967). For the 1900–1912 period, estimates were made based upon the ethnic composition of wards; the location of churches within wards; the U.S. Bureau of the Census, Special Reports, *Religious Bodies: 1906* (2 vols., Washington, 1910); and from information in various secondary works.

The election and demographic data were fed into an IBM 360 computer. The program rank-ordered Chicago wards according to the political or demographic variable involved. (A rank order consists of listing a number of units [wards] from highest to lowest according to some common quality.) Spearman rank-order correlations were then run between the sets of political data, between the political data and the demographic data, and between the demographic data itself. A series of correlation coefficients were thus obtained which ranged from −1 to +1, with the extreme values representing either a perfect agreement or a perfect disagreement between the rankings. The Spearman rank-order correlation technique supplied insight into the relationships between large masses of quantitative data.[1]

There were, however, several pitfalls in the Spearman method, especially in regard to demographic data. This material was only available on a ward basis and wards were not demographically homogeneous. Oftentimes correlation coefficients furnished a confusing picture of relationships between political and demographic variables, and interpretations were therefore based upon a combination of the correlation coefficients and empirical data. In addition, totals in the election and demographic sources were often inexact, and one can only speculate on the possible additional errors made by the compiler. Because of the inexact nature of the sources, the interpretations derived from them are intended to serve as a *relative* estimate of the behavior of Chicago voting groups.

[1] For a more detailed explanation of the theory behind rank-ordering and rank-order correlations see Maurice G. Kendall, *Rank Correlation Methods* (2nd rev. ed., New York, 1955).

Chicago Major and Minor Party Percentages, 1892–1912 (over 2% of the vote)

	1892 President	1892 Governor	1893 Mayor (April)	1893 Mayor (December)
Republican	41.7	42.3	44.0	49.1
Democratic	56.4	55.9	54.0	49.7
Populist				
Other				

	1898 State Treasurer	1899 Mayor	1900 President	1900 Governor
Republican	47.9	35.3	49.6	46.5
Democratic	49.8	48.8	47.6	50.9
Socialist				
Other		15.5 (J. P. Altgeld, Munic. Owner.)		

	1905 Mayor	1906 State Treasurer	1907 Mayor	1908 President
Republican	42.2	54.9	48.6	54.5
Democratic	49.3	31.3	45.7	38.0
Socialist	7.0	11.2	3.9	4.6
Progressive				

1894 State Treasurer	1895 Mayor	1896 President	1896 Governor	1897 Mayor
51.5	55.0	57.3	53.1	20.0
35.3	39.5	41.3	44.8	50.2
12.0	4.9			23.5 (J. M. Harlan)
				5.2 (W. Hesing)

1901 Mayor	1902 State Treasurer	1903 Mayor	1904 President	1904 Governor
43.1	48.3	44.7	57.3	59.3
52.7	43.1	47.2	27.1	27.8
	4.83	3.6	12.6	10.4
	2.3 (Soc. Labor)	3.2 (Ind. Labor)		

1908 Governor	1910 State Treasurer	1911 Mayor	1912 President	1912 Governor
45.3	41.3	43.8	17.7	23.9
47.2	47.9	48.5	31.4	39.3
4.3	9.0	6.8	13.0	12.1
			37.7	24.0

Intra- and Inter-Party Correlations, 1908 Republican Primary and 1908 Election

Table 1 Intra-Party Correlations: 1908 Republican Primary

	Deneen	Yates	Healy	Wayman	Hopkins	Foss	Mason
Governor							
Deneen		−.999	+.760	−.759	−.323	+.462	−.015
Yates			−.766	+.763	+.327	−.478	+.023
State's Attorney							
Healy				−.820	−.451	+.536	−.041
Wayman					+.433	−.353	−.134
U.S. Senator							
Hopkins						−.820	−.286
Foss							−.049

Table 2 Intra-Party Correlations: 1908 Republican Primary with 1908 Election

1908 ELECTION	1908 PRIMARIES			
	Deneen	Yates	Healy	Wayman
Deneen	+.662	−.661	+.754	−.641
Wayman	+.376	−.381	+.536	−.353
Taft	+.463	−.470	+.720	−.538

Table 3   Inter-Party Correlations: 1908 Republican Primary with Republican and Democratic Vote; 1904 Presidential Election; 1905 Mayoralty Election; 1907 Mayoralty Election

	1904		1905		1907	
	Rep.	**Dem.**	**Rep.**	**Dem.**	**Rep.**	**Dem.**
Governor						
Deneen	+.340	−.499	+.528	−.579	+.381	−.446
Yates	−.347	+.504	−.535	+.586	−.394	+.457
State's Attorney						
Healy	+.681	−.643	+.706	−.718	+.622	−.665
Wayman	−.429	+.618	−.586	+.602	−.398	+.456
U.S. Senator						
Hopkins	−.549	+.483	−.722	+.597	−.695	+.661
Foss	+.583	−.504	+.741	−.684	+.755	−.746
Mason	+.072	−.288	+.198	−.098	+.003	+.012

Table 4   Inter- and Intra-Party Correlations: 1908 Election

REP.	**REP.**		**DEM.**			**PROHIB.**
						W. Street
	Wayman	**Taft**	**Stevenson**	**J. J. Kern**	**Bryan**	**(St. Attor.)**
Deneen	+.703	+.830	−.947	−.836	−.790	+.676
Wayman		+.873	−.931	−.844	−.931	+.591
Taft			−.790	−.931	−.970	+.844

Nationality of Chicago Registered Voters, 1892 [1]

Ward	Native American	Naturalized	Canadian	German	Irish	English	Scotch	Swedish
1	4,791	1,840	143	477	382	138	61	44
2	5,147	1,619	180	488	450	195	44	77
3	5,275	1,914	169	751	371	164	64	133
4	5,950	2,153	196	716	492	260	90	109
5	3,679	4,599	167	1,859	1,166	186	66	521
6	2,863	5,805	196	2,371	2,298	290	73	205
7	1,732	4,365	68	1,542	623	70	20	35
8	1,661	4,142	136	839	816	63	22	26
9	2,178	5,103	143	1,639	762	136	29	71
10	3,542	5,538	201	2,385	839	201	72	306
11	5,785	2,672	309	413	653	331	137	133
12	10,511	3,860	652	793	862	745	281	88
13	5,967	3,378	307	891	936	417	145	174
14	2,298	6,162	77	3,676	211	97	55	393
15	2,651	6,248	112	3,054	575	290	92	599
16	1,364	7,229	46	2,450	218	65	25	312
17	1,718	3,177	89	679	523	85	50	248
18	5,319	2,547	282	674	738	320	133	45
19	4,232	4,828	436	721	1,635	285	99	39
20	2,310	2,802	82	2,111	217	101	27	112
21	2,360	3,278	91	2,445	182	120	27	139
22	2,805	3,677	56	2,577	210	92	22	385
23	2,275	4,443	108	682	1,044	104	48	2,121
24	6,035	2,395	251	853	583	225	58	155
25	3,421	2,882	159	1,291	231	198	54	682
26	2,666	4,581	100	3,370	199	213	49	358
27	1,422	1,443	64	750	79	125	36	167
28	1,396	1,453	164	289	370	142	49	158
29	3,294	4,121	238	978	2,174	240	58	81
30	6,811	6,573	406	2,170	1,563	410	152	974
31	4,869	2,381	258	708	425	292	87	247
32	7,076	2,132	329	406	504	416	130	145
33	2,022	3,788	131	1,003	608	325	59	725
34	5,010	4,506	346	994	639	503	141	831
Total	130,435	127,634	6,692	47,005	23,578	7,844	2,555	10,838

[1] Published in the *Chicago Daily News Almanac for 1894* (Chicago, 1894), 318; totals have been corrected where necessary.

Norwegian	Danish	Bohemian	Austrian	Polish	Russian	Italian	French	Other	Total
19	20	5	35	44	80	137	29	226	6,631
9	37	3	30	23	34	9	25	55	6,766
25	28	12	59	7	19	25	21	66	7,189
24	100	13	51	12	20	7	26	37	8,103
38	24	185	162	6	40	18	29	132	8,278
24	19	46	119	45	39	5	13	62	8,668
22	14	325	297	20	1,230	11	6	79	6,097
17	5	1,705	225	39	166	4	8	71	5,803
32	14	1,512	103	402	40	1	15	204	7,281
41	34	723	345	246	21	6	16	102	9,080
382	87	10	69	7	40	15	15	71	8,457
78	35	15	103	15	34	41	34	84	14,371
195	97	8	33	4	17	21	21	112	9,345
745	411	15	214	16	114	11	20	107	8,460
624	292	35	101	298	41	12	29	94	8,899
859	204	86	180	2,631	79	5	15	54	8,593
818	204	1	83	74	39	208	16	60	4,895
34	38	3	63	23	78	32	28	56	7,866
18	14	468	189	38	477	278	35	96	9,060
25	16	6	45	4	7	2	10	37	5,112
30	21	11	84	3	9	9	22	85	5,638
34	32	6	86	5	21	16	20	115	6,482
69	35	2	35	14	59	58	17	47	6,718
22	38	7	51	6	14	11	17	104	8,430
66	63	8	40	3	9	3	14	61	6,303
66	40	4	69	4	13	8	10	78	7,247
69	38	29	37	2	9	3	5	30	2,865
127	37	63	9	—	4	2	5	34	2,849
22	36	98	42	40	30	9	14	61	7,415
71	44	264	111	159	42	12	31	164	13,384
26	36	22	52	8	11	22	13	174	7,250
26	41	6	42	4	9	2	23	49	9,208
63	83	13	37	645	25	4	15	52	5,810
112	96	12	79	18	33	25	23	654	9,516
4,832	2,333	5,271	3,280	4,865	2,903	1,032	643	3,513	258,069

Composition of the Population of Chicago, 1910 [1]

		WARDS		
1910	City	1	2	3
Total Population	2,185,283	29,528	42,801	46,135
Male	1,125,764	19,087	21,196	22,538
Female	1,059,519	10,441	21,605	23,597
Native-born of native parents	445,139	9,797	11,642	12,865
Native-born of foreign or mixed parents	912,701	6,734	11,225	13,124
Foreign-born white	781,217	9,840	9,118	8,974
Negro	44,103	2,603	10,709	11,081
Other	2,123	554	107	91
Males of Voting Age	700,590	16,100	16,205	16,467
Native-born of native parents	125,703	6,529	4,071	4,282
Foreign-born or native-born of foreign or mixed parents	555,247	7,757	7,399	7,536
Naturalized	190,693	2,126	2,376	2,501
Negro	17,845	1,350	4,646	4,575

	WARDS		
1910	10	11	12
Total Population	51,707	57,664	91,521
Male	27,069	30,167	48,582
Female	24,638	27,497	42,939
Native-born of native parents	1,841	3,730	8,318
Native-born of foreign or mixed parents	20,980	26,189	44,221
Foreign-born white	28,863	27,728	38,774
Negro	12	13	176
Other	11	4	32
Males of Voting Age	14,603	16,705	27,587
Native-born of native parents	226	498	1,693
Foreign-born or native-born of foreign or mixed parents	14,361	16,196	25,761
Naturalized	4,135	5,344	8,995
Negro	6	7	103

[1] All figures are compiled from U.S., *Thirteenth Census, 1910,* "Population," II, 512–514.

WARDS

4	5	6	7	8	9
49,650	57,131	75,121	90,423	65,810	44,801
26,280	30,451	33,328	42,485	37,188	24,862
23,370	26,680	41,793	47,938	28,622	19,939
6,676	7,417	29,354	39,764	9,572	1,701
23,492	28,021	25,751	29,862	28,086	15,915
19,310	21,646	17,935	18,710	28,020	27,149
167	38	1,962	1,903	95	19
5	9	119	184	37	17
14,995	17,026	24,587	29,984	22,463	14,552
1,084	1,273	9,370	12,817	2,609	229
13,843	15,735	14,377	16,292	19,785	14,295
4,333	5,167	4,487	5,287	5,518	3,668
63	12	733	723	38	11

WARDS

13	14	15	16	17	18
58,721	52,770	60,438	65,223	70,099	26,137
28,344	26,963	30,323	34,110	37,954	16,930
30,377	25,807	30,115	31,113	32,145	9,207
20,952	14,073	5,686	2,555	3,034	9,094
24,688	21,381	28,216	31,691	27,193	7,868
12,797	14,875	26,487	30,941	39,814	8,347
212	2,409	23	18	49	798
72	32	26	18	9	30
18,839	16,938	18,054	18,181	22,688	13,900
5,690	3,624	1,044	304	469	4,716
13,012	12,359	16,981	17,854	22,193	8,818
4,195	3,966	7,049	6,127	5,558	2,787
76	932	6	5	18	344

Composition of the Population of Chicago, 1910   (cont.)

	WARDS		
1910	**19**	**20**	**21**
Total Population	58,023	61,708	47,906
Male	31,834	31,544	26,226
Female	26,189	30,164	21,680
Native-born of native parents	3,573	19,372	17,779
Native-born of foreign or mixed parents	22,118	22,526	14,393
Foreign-born white	32,252	19,327	14,929
Negro	62	369	721
Other	18	114	84
Males of Voting Age	18,477	21,991	21,314
Native-born of native parents	929	6,826	8,036
Foreign-born or native-born of foreign or mixed parents	17,503	14,888	12,877
Naturalized	4,955	4,995	3,657
Negro	29	175	329

	WARDS		
1910	**28**	**29**	**30**
Total Population	68,183	81,985	51,308
Male	34,329	44,667	26,571
Female	33,854	37,318	24,737
Native-born of native parents	8,691	6,365	8,278
Native-born of foreign or mixed parents	33,847	37,823	21,659
Foreign-born white	25,600	37,654	14,887
Negro	26	124	6,431
Other	19	19	53
Males of Voting Age	20,016	25,270	16,104
Native-born of native parents	1,717	1,055	1,904
Foreign-born or native-born of foreign or mixed parents	18,271	24,152	11,924
Naturalized	8,180	7,452	4,542
Negro	10	44	2,241

WARDS

22	23	24	25	26	27
49,324	44,320	52,428	99,696	74,793	112,793
26,359	21,881	26,963	46,261	36,958	56,829
22,965	22,439	25,465	53,435	37,835	55,964
4,807	9,128	8,052	33,650	17,791	19,504
20,039	19,164	25,324	38,386	35,265	56,874
23,949	15,858	19,024	27,156	21,625	36,223
524	141	20	419	77	167
5	29	8	85	35	25
16,022	14,359	16,028	32,109	22,073	30,978
1,068	2,187	1,634	9,603	3,815	3,683
14,746	12,104	14,377	22,292	18,205	27,238
5,053	4,400	5,405	8,082	7,310	11,860
204	50	9	146	24	42

WARDS

31	32	33	34	35
78,571	70,408	70,841	67,769	59,547
39,446	34,877	39,674	33,644	29,844
39,125	35,531	31,167	34,125	29,703
20,174	26,304	12,123	15,036	16,441
34,923	27,497	28,040	33,864	26,322
21,587	16,003	30,543	18,757	16,515
1,806	514	101	72	242
81	90	34	40	27
22,949	21,397	24,546	19,467	17,616
4,874	7,263	3,235	3,352	3,994
17,446	13,873	21,233	16,044	13,520
7,278	5,231	6,810	6,452	5,412
560	178	49	31	76

Chicago Population, 1910: Foreign-Born and Native-Born of Foreign-Born Parents Combined [1]

	City	**WARDS**					
		1	**2**	**3**	**4**	**5**	**6**
Austrian	217,267	1,336	585	542	6,303	6,202	1,434
⌐Lithuanian⌐	87,089	58	166	263	2,126	487	295
Bohemian	7,593	—	3	—	640	2,007	—
⌊Polish ⌋	129,733	528	152	194	6,214	4,460	307
Belgian	2,665	27	31	17	98	38	80
Canad.–French	9,140	100	201	175	148	708	223
Canad.–Other	30,820	481	1,014	1,050	447	724	2,266
Danish	18,504	110	280	467	107	48	745
English	42,750	602	1,056	1,237	483	792	2,485
French	4,875	253	231	166	117	45	327
German	426,466	2,052	4,186	4,334	12,717	14,696	9,945
Greek	6,564	327	215	80	51	82	76
Dutch	17,702	34	89	80	103	114	212
Hungarian	37,224	247	154	238	576	274	848
Irish	165,309	2,119	3,347	4,028	5,718	10,090	6,965
Italian	72,906	4,898	577	359	3,134	188	198
Norwegian	42,342	119	222	176	134	139	420
Romanian	3,344	13	26	33	16	25	38
Russian	180,203	955	1,111	1,236	4,981	6,821	2,230
Scottish	16,582	213	402	511	314	247	786
Swedish	109,626	394	1,805	1,516	1,053	1,075	2,585
Swiss	5,526	94	136	113	153	76	187
Turkish	1,886	239	31	24	8	12	29
Welsh	3,285	36	46	61	10	147	136
Other	68,825	647	1,295	1,416	1,525	1,702	2,635

[1] Figures are derived from U.S., *Thirteenth Census, 1910,* "Population," 512–514, except those for the Bohemian, Lithuanian, and Polish groups, which were not listed separately in the U.S. census. Figures for Bohemians, Lithuanians, and Poles were obtained from the 1908 school census in Chicago, Board of Education, *Annual Report* (Chicago, 1908), 12–19. In the U.S. census, Bohemians were included under Austria, Lithuanians under Russia, and Poles under Austria, Germany, or Russia, depending on birthplace. See U.S., *Thirteenth Census, 1910,* "Population," 879.

WARDS

	7	8	9	10	11	12	13
Austrian	958	8,184	6,752	23,290	16,631	36,803	712
⌐Bohemian ⌐	225	172	3,745	19,391	7,498	27,127	325
Lithuanian |	—	537	1,381	10	267	584	4
⌊Polish ⌋	220	16,118	1,134	838	11,109	8,953	90
Belgian	80	48	40	186	53	37	46
Canad.–French	330	178	14	81	213	272	646
Canad.–Other	3,160	724	78	131	247	504	2,021
Danish	691	445	11	6	16	105	237
English	3,318	1,404	353	413	429	702	2,217
French	265	93	28	25	54	84	132
German	8,582	14,031	3,935	2,501	13,845	16,208	5,699
Greek	167	56	150	97	72	145	86
Dutch	207	102	62	571	1,280	326	242
Hungarian	636	1,342	3,622	1,286	996	1,481	150
Irish	7,883	3,617	1,260	1,494	2,550	4,140	9,971
Italian	243	932	559	85	150	1,161	560
Norwegian	661	373	21	27	175	306	548
Romanian	23	13	735	751	206	70	10
Russian	1,381	10,289	22,999	15,818	11,472	9,014	1,267
Scottish	1,183	415	27	33	57	229	1,142
Swedish	4,170	5,770	45	59	446	2,430	617
Swiss	185	105	45	14	40	134	76
Turkish	45	58	111	29	2	82	17
Welsh	243	306	4	3	5	25	456
Other	3,204	2,075	853	910	1,314	1,895	2,286

Chicago Population, 1910 (cont.)

	WARDS						
	14	15	16	17	18	19	20
Austrian	1,182	4,382	7,690	26,796	523	3,742	1,277
⎡Bohemian ⎤	151	808	247	177	96	911	294
⎢Lithuanian ⎢	—	—	171	4	—	—	7
⎣Polish ⎦	562	1,300	32,790	17,059	158	1,216	339
Belgian	75	161	57	50	39	37	31
Canad.–French	246	67	13	32	227	774	705
Canad.–Other	1,043	346	85	196	646	420	1,851
Danish	525	1,731	102	565	187	44	344
English	1,510	567	258	199	959	580	2,101
French	116	76	48	98	135	178	196
German	7,114	18,288	30,935	11,394	3,199	1,681	5,200
Greek	94	82	54	292	456	1,069	329
Dutch	370	171	50	84	62	19	211
Hungarian	1,360	1,992	867	2,880	279	619	590
Irish	5,875	1,172	1,154	1,202	3,036	5,118	5,457
Italian	3,054	281	214	8,503	751	23,406	854
Norwegian	1,458	5,040	314	3,351	338	58	593
Romanian	17	107	65	19	18	636	291
Russian	1,241	10,504	15,460	5,731	1,097	11,619	11,556
Scottish	585	256	38	109	370	165	784
Swedish	1,112	2,117	246	1,117	433	97	744
Swiss	171	152	54	83	100	68	113
Turkish	76	16	3	86	283	135	72
Welsh	99	54	5	12	67	41	151
Other	1,928	2,088	1,478	1,470	1,004	1,351	2,330

WARDS

	21	22	23	24	25	26	27
Austrian	692	1,853	1,646	2,050	1,088	908	5,262
⌐Bohemian ⌐	41	120	114	110	184	163	1,753
Lithuanian	3	—	19	1	—	—	3
⌐Polish ⌐	90	768	98	635	126	75	3,199
Belgian	55	77	44	322	159	110	163
Canad.–French	173	43	79	51	196	146	288
Canad.–Other	1,378	292	471	456	2,353	964	1,074
Danish	250	127	138	165	655	455	2,514
English	1,463	239	665	546	2,392	1,433	1,883
French	307	111	132	120	277	166	251
German	7,252	9,943	18,009	24,578	17,793	25,182	36,187
Greek	575	195	130	101	158	53	68
Dutch	105	64	93	70	203	111	457
Hungarian	357	1,523	2,126	1,989	525	623	786
Irish	4,837	4,093	1,791	2,694	4,973	2,418	3,179
Italian	663	12,780	192	335	285	215	604
Norwegian	486	287	258	239	1,276	574	9,707
Romanian	29	12	14	15	8	3	22
Russian	695	853	575	952	782	344	1,539
Scottish	523	145	163	172	708	408	705
Swedish	2,855	6,351	1,550	1,749	15,129	9,540	8,807
Swiss	275	182	357	219	429	342	419
Turkish	122	37	12	9	40	30	15
Welsh	67	23	29	24	153	42	97
Other	1,871	1,344	1,307	1,649	3,920	2,761	4,464

Chicago Population, 1910 (cont.)

	28	29	30	31	32	33	34	35
Austrian	2,578	19,233	587	1,274	931	5,077	16,247	1,517
Bohemian	370	6,727	127	478	328	743	10,805	464
Lithuanian	4	1,623	10	26	50	239	—	—
Polish	8,054	9,358	121	105	165	2,248	555	397
Belgian	234	57	27	24	26	34	21	81
Canad.– French	142	553	160	295	296	839	334	236
Canad.– Other	506	547	706	1,675	2,053	1,118	1,243	1,247
Danish	3,244	126	307	1,251	426	756	164	1,522
English	892	671	973	2,211	2,189	1,921	1,427	1,990
French	125	85	71	131	122	121	110	101
German	22,472	21,078	6,791	11,060	9,190	7,513	10,196	8,680
Greek	95	79	218	93	378	301	61	79
Dutch	193	194	88	1,519	2,637	6,558	575	446
Hungarian	457	2,707	1,265	251	150	3,224	352	449
Irish	1,904	8,260	13,880	9,471	6,709	3,669	7,492	3,743
Italian	310	230	848	1,275	411	4,054	215	382
Norwegian	7,761	58	251	509	321	844	351	4,877
Romanian	51	28	13	9	9	8	5	6
Russian	2,659	12,268	1,044	1,552	1,114	5,430	1,102	502
Scottish	443	471	337	1,226	1,233	629	770	784
Swedish	4,743	496	2,031	10,420	3,487	7,920	1,028	5,419
Swiss	165	125	101	175	216	178	119	125
Turkish	10	18	64	17	2	145	3	4
Welsh	42	42	104	176	119	168	149	153
Other	2,940	2,050	1,500	2,751	2,432	1,881	1,992	2,557

Bibliography

THE IMPORTANT SOURCES for this study fall into the following categories: personal papers and unpublished records; newspapers and contemporary periodical articles; government publications; reports and pamphlets; unpublished theses and papers; autobiographies, memoirs, and published letters; secondary books and articles; interviews.

I. Personal Papers and Unpublished Records

THE FOLLOWING COLLECTIONS WERE MOST VALUABLE FOR THIS STUDY.

Beveridge, Albert J. Papers. Library of Congress. Useful for the fight over meat-inspection legislation and the Lorimer Senate case. Also contain correspondence between Beveridge and John C. Shaffer, publisher of the Chicago *Evening Post,* and A. C. Bartlett, an important Chicago businessman.

Cannon, Joseph G. Papers. Illinois State Historical Library. Springfield.

Cullom, Shelby M. Papers. Illinois State Historical Library. Springfield.

Dawes, Charles G. Papers. Northwestern University Library. Evanston. An immensely valuable collection for Illinois politics in the 1895–1908 period.

Fisher, Walter L. Papers. Library of Congress.

Kent, William. Papers. Yale University Library. New Haven.

Lawson, Victor. Papers. Newberry Library. Chicago. Mostly letterbooks. Useful for reform and the press.

Lowden, Frank O. Papers. University of Chicago. A valuable collection, especially useful for the Lorimer Senate election in 1909.

McKinley, William. Papers. Library of Congress.

Manuscript Election Returns, Second Illinois Congressional District, 1894–1900, and Sixth Illinois Congressional District, 1902–10. Board of Election Commissioners. Chicago.

Merriam, Charles E. Papers. Harper Library. University of Chicago.

Oglesby, John G. Papers. Illinois State Historical Library. Springfield.

Primary Election Returns, Cook County, 1904–12. Municipal Reference Library. Chicago City Hall.

Records of the Office of the Comptroller of the Currency. Record Group 101.

335

National Archives. Examiner's reports and correspondence concerning the John R. Walsh banks and Lorimer's bank.

Roosevelt, Theodore. Papers. Library of Congress.

Sherman, Lawrence Y. Papers. Illinois State Historical Library. Springfield. A very rich collection for Illinois political history, 1897–1912.

Small, Lennington. Papers. Illinois State Historical Library. Springfield. Useful for the Lincoln League and the 1912 Illinois primary fight. Contains a number of Lorimer letters.

Taft, William Howard. Papers. Library of Congress.

THE FOLLOWING COLLECTIONS WERE USEFUL FOR A MORE LIMITED RANGE OF TOPICS.

Addams, Jane. Papers. Chicago Historical Society (microfilm).

Aldrich, J. Frank. Papers. Chicago Historical Society; Chicago Union League Club Civic and Arts Foundation; and in possession of C. Knight Aldrich, Chicago. Letters and unpublished memoirs.

Aldrich, Nelson. Papers. Library of Congress.

Allison, William B. Papers. Iowa State Department of History and Archives. Des Moines. Useful for the 1896 presidential nomination.

Carter, Thomas H. Papers. Library of Congress.

Chandler, William E. Papers. Library of Congress. Useful for the Senate and the coming of the Spanish-American War.

Citizen's Association Minute Book. Citizen's Association Office. Chicago.

Copley, Ira C. Papers. Copley Residence. Aurora.

Crane, Charles R. Papers. Institute of Current World Affairs. New York.

Deneen, Charles S. Papers. Illinois State Archives. Springfield. Official governor's correspondence.

Dennis, Charles H. Papers. Newberry Library. Chicago. Useful for the struggle for postal savings bank legislation in 1897.

Devers, William E. Papers. Chicago Historical Society. Devers was the judge in the Lorimer bank trial and mayor of Chicago from 1923 to 1927.

Eastman, Sidney C. Papers. Chicago Historical Society. Useful for the 1897 traction and gas legislation.

Fifer, Joseph W. Papers. Illinois State Historical Library. Springfield. Useful for Illinois politics before 1896.

Forgan, James B. Papers. Library of the First National Bank of Chicago.

Harrison, Carter H. Papers. Newberry Library. Chicago. Harrison thoroughly sifted his papers, leaving few useful items.

Hilles, Charles D. Papers. Yale University Library. New Haven. Useful for the 1912 presidential primary fight.

Hitt, Robert R. Papers. Library of Congress.

Humphrey, J. Otis. Papers. Illinois State Historical Library. Springfield.

Index to Contracts Listed in the Proceedings of the Chicago Sanitary District, 1892–1914. Chicago Historical Society.

Keeley, James. Papers. Chicago Historical Society.

Kohlsaat, Herman H. Papers. Illinois State Historical Library. Springfield. All incoming letters, some on the Lorimer case.

Lloyd, Henry Demerest. Papers. Wisconsin State Historical Library. Madison.

Newlands, Francis G. Papers. Yale University Library. New Haven. Useful for waterway matters.

Oglesby, Richard J. Papers. Illinois State Historical Library. Springfield. Valuable letters on intra-party Republican struggles in 1907–09.

Perkins, George W. Papers. Columbia University Library. New York.

Post, Louis F. Papers. Library of Congress.

Rainey, Henry T. Papers. Library of Congress.

Robins, Raymond. Papers. State Historical Society of Wisconsin. Madison.

Root, Elihu. Papers. Library of Congress. Material on the Lorimer Senate case.

Springer, William McKendree. Papers. Chicago Historical Society.

Stringer, Lawrence B. Papers. Illinois State Historical Library. Springfield.

Tanner, John R. Papers. Illinois State Archives. Springfield. Official governor's correspondence. Contains Lorimer letters on patronage.

———. Papers. Illinois State Historical Library. Springfield. Few useful items.

Taylor, Graham. Papers. Newberry Library. Chicago.

Tree, Lambert. Papers. Newberry Library. Chicago.

White, William Allen. Papers. Library of Congress.

Yates, Richard. Papers. Illinois State Archives. Springfield. Official governor's correspondence. Contains Lorimer letters on patronage and meat inspection.

———. Papers. Illinois State Historical Library. Springfield.

II. Newspapers, Newspaper Scrapbooks, and Contemporary Periodical Articles

A. NEWSPAPERS, ENGLISH-LANGUAGE (CHICAGO UNLESS OTHERWISE NOTED)

American. 1904–12.

The Broadax. 1909–12.

Chronicle. 1892–1906.

Citizen. 1895–1910. Irish. Weekly.

Daily News. 1884–1934.

Evening Journal. 1890–1909.

Evening Post. 1893–1912.

Examiner. 1901–12.

Herald. 1884–95.

Inter-Ocean. 1887–1912.

Record. 1892–1900.

Record-Herald. 1901–12.

Times. 1884–95.

Times-Herald. 1895–1900.

Tribune. 1884–1934.

The Western Catholic. 1912.
New York *Times.* 1898–1916.
New York *Tribune.* 1898–1901.

B. NEWSPAPERS, FOREIGN-LANGUAGE, FROM THE CHICAGO FOREIGN
LANGUAGE PRESS SURVEY (CHICAGO UNLESS OTHERWISE NOTED)

Bohemian: *Denni Hlasatel.* 1901–18, 1920–22.
             Svornost. 1878–85, 1890–92, 1896–1900.
German: *Die Abendpost.* 1889–1911, 1914–15, 1918–19, 1923–35.
             Illinois Staats-Zeitung. 1861–81, 1885–93, 1899–1901, 1914–18.
Jewish: *Daily Courier.* 1906–28.
             Daily Forward. 1919–32.
Norwegian: *Skandinaven.* 1896–1912.
Polish: *Dziennik Chicagoski.* 1890–97, 1903–08.
             Dziennik Zwiazkowy Zgoda. 1908–18.
             Narod Polski. 1897–1902, 1904–20.
Swedish: *Svenska Amerikanaren.* 1907–09.
             Svenska Tribunen. 1878–1906.
             Svenska Tribunen-Nyheter. 1906–16.

C. NEWSPAPER SCRAPBOOKS

Civic Association Scrapbooks (John C. Ambler, comp.). Chicago Historical
Society. A collection of 87 volumes of newspaper clippings on various phases
of Chicago civic affairs from 1887 to 1909.
Charles G. Dawes Scrapbooks. Northwestern University Library. Evanston.
Charles S. Deneen Scrapbooks. Illinois State Historical Library. Springfield. A
collection of 214 scrapbooks of newspaper clippings and campaign materials
covering government and politics from 1904 to 1930.
William Kent Scrapbooks. Yale University Library. New Haven.
Frank O. Lowden Scrapbooks. University of Chicago.

D. CONTEMPORARY PERIODICAL ARTICLES

"Another Lorimer Vindication." *The Literary Digest* (June 1, 1912), LXIV,
1147–48.
Baker, Ray Stannard. "The Civic Federation of Chicago." *The Outlook* (July
27, 1895), LII, 132–133.
"Chicago's Graft Inquiry." *The Outlook* (Mar. 5, 1910), XCIV, 509–511.
"Chicago's Sunday Closing Crusade." *The Outlook* (Dec. 21, 1907), LXXXVII,
835.
"Chicago's Sunday Closing Fight." *The Outlook* (Mar. 7, 1908), LXXXVIII,
524.
"Clean Meat in Sight." *Collier's* (June 30, 1906), XXXVII, 9–10.
"Commercial and Industrial Aspects of the Chicago Drainage Canal." *Dry
Goods Reporter* (Jan. 1, 1898), XXXVIII, 27–28.
Cruice, Daniel L. "Direct Legislation in Illinois: A Story of Triumph for

Popular Government." *The Arena* (June, 1904), XXXI, 561–568.

"The Fight for Clean Meat." *Collier's* (June 16, 1906), XXXVII, 9–10.

"For Clean Meat." *The Outlook* (June 9, 1906), LXXXIII, 299–300.

Foreman, Milton J. "Chicago New Charter Movement—Its Relation to Municipal Ownership." *Annals of the American Academy of Political and Social Science* (May, 1908), XXXI, 639–648.

"The Government and the Packers." *The World Today* (June, 1906), XI, 675–676.

Halsey, Edward A. "The Possibilities of the Lakes-to-the-Gulf Deep Waterway." *The World Today* (Oct., 1910), XIX, 1249–53.

Hard, William. "Robert Rutherford McCormick: A Matter-of-Fact Young Man in Politics." *The World Today* (Jan., 1908), XIV, 87–91.

Harvey, Charles M. "The Lakes-to-the-Gulf Deep Waterway Association." *The World Today* (Jan., 1907), XII, 39–41.

Hotchkiss, Willard E. "Chicago Traction: A Study in Political Evolution." *Annals of the American Academy of Political and Social Science* (Nov., 1906), XXVIII, 385–404.

"Important Municipal Elections." *The World Today* (May, 1903), IV, 577.

Jackson, J. C. "The Work of the Anti-Saloon League." *Annals of the American Academy of Political and Social Science* (1908), XXXII, 482–496.

Jones, Walter Clyde. "The Direct Primary in Illinois." *Proceedings of the American Political Science Association* (1910), VII, 138–150.

Judson, Harry Pratt. "Against the Machine or in the Machine?" *The World Today* (Jan., 1904), VI, 103–107.

King, Hoyt. "Commercial Importance of the Sanitary Canal and Gulf Waterway." *The World Today* (Sept., 1907), XIII, 897–901.

————. "The Reform Movement in Chicago." *Annals of the American Academy of Political and Social Science* (Mar., 1905), XXV, 235–247.

Long, Theodore K. "The Lakes-to-the-Gulf Deep Waterway." *The World Today* (Dec., 1909), XVII, 1265–68.

"Lorimer Banks Fail." *Chicago Economist,* June 13, 1914.

"Lorimer Case Open Again." *The Literary Digest* (Apr. 22, 1911), XLII, 769–770.

"Lorimer Out." *The Literary Digest* (July 27, 1912), XLV, 134–135.

"Lorimer Plucked from the Burning." *The Literary Digest* (Mar. 11, 1911), XLII, 443–445.

"Lorimer's Suspended Vindication." *The Literary Digest* (Jan. 7, 1911), XLII, 2–3.

Lowry, Edward G. "Lorimer: The Career and Qualities of the Much-Discussed Junior Senator from Illinois." *Harper's Weekly* (Jan. 7, 1911), LV, 20.

Mann, James R. "Political Reform in Congressional Districts." *The World Today* (Aug., 1906), XI, 788–789.

"Mayor Busse and the Future." *The World Today* (May, 1907), XII, 467.

"Meaning of the Illinois Primary." *The Literary Digest* (Apr. 20, 1912), XLIV, 792–795.

Merriam, Charles E. "Investigations as a Means of Securing Administrative Efficiency." *Annals of the American Academy of Political and Social Science* (May, 1912), XLI, 281–303.

"The New Senator from Illinois." *The Outlook* (June 5, 1909), XCII, 301–302.

Parker, Francis W. "The Machine or A Machine." *The World Today* (Mar., 1904), VI, 371–375.

———. "Municipal Ownership and Graft." *The World Today* (July, 1905), IX, 721–724.

"The President and the Bosses." *The Nation* (Jan. 18, 1906), LXXXII, 45–46.

"President Taft's Denunciation of Mr. Roosevelt." *The Literary Digest* (May 4, 1912), XLIV, 922–923.

Raymond, C. S. "The Lorimer Scandal: Turning on the Light in Illinois." *The American Magazine* (Sept., 1910), LXX, 571–584.

"Report of the Pure Food Committee." *Annals of the American Academy of Political and Social Science* (Sept., 1906), XXVIII, 296–301.

"Revolt against Boss Rule." *The World Today* (June, 1903), IV, 714–715.

"The Revolt of the Illinois Legislature." *The World Today* (Feb., 1909), XVI, 130–132.

"The Re-election of Mayor Harrison." *The American Monthly Review of Reviews* (May, 1899), XIX, 516–517.

Russell, Charles Edward. "The Man the Interests Wanted." *Cosmopolitan Magazine* (Oct., 1910), XLIX, 592–601.

———. "Where Did You Get It Gentlemen?" *Everybody's Magazine* (Sept., 1907), XVII, 348–360.

"Saloon License Made $1,000 in Chicago." *The Outlook* (Mar. 17, 1906), LXXXII, 587–588.

"Senator Lorimer: A Veritable 'Ragged Dick' Hero." *Current Literature* (July, 1910), XLIX, 33–37.

Sikes, George C. "The Liquor Question and Municipal Reform." *National Municipal Review* (July, 1916), V, 411–418.

Sullivan, Mark. "Lorimer and Lumber." *Collier's* (Apr. 22, 1911), XLVII, 20.

Tarbell, Ida M. "How Chicago Is Finding Herself." *The American Magazine* (Nov., 1908), LXVII, 29–41.

Tinker, Jackson. "Who Killed the Pure Food Bill?" *Public Opinion* (Apr. 15, 1905), XXXVIII, 572–573, 590.

III. Government Publications

CHICAGO

Board of Education. *Annual Reports, 1894, 1904, 1906, 1908.* Chicago, 1894, 1904, 1906, 1908.

City Council. *Proceedings, 1889–1912.* Chicago, 1889–1912.

———. "Report of Finance Committee on Split-Interest." *Council Journal, 1914–15,* I, 1941–52.

Department of Public Works. *Sixteenth Annual Report.* Chicago, 1892.
Sanitary District. *Proceedings of the Board of Trustees, 1895–1908.* Chicago, 1896–1909.
South Park Commissioners. *Annual Reports, 1884–1909.* Chicago, 1885–1910.
West Park Commissioners. *Annual Reports, 1889–1909.* Chicago, 1890–1910.

ILLINOIS

Blue Book of the State of Illinois 1933–34. Springfield, 1934.
Internal Improvement Commission. *Report.* Springfield, 1907.
Journal of the House of Representatives of the . . . General Assembly, 1892–1912. Springfield, 1893–1913.
Journal of the Senate of the . . . General Assembly, 1892–1912. Springfield, 1893–1913.
Rose, James A., comp. *Blue Book of the State of Illinois 1909.* Danville, 1909.

UNITED STATES

Biographical Directory of the American Congress 1774–1949. Washington, 1950.
Bureau of the Census. *Eleventh Census . . . 1890* to *Thirteenth Census . . . 1910.* Washington, 1892–1913.
———. *Historical Statistics of the United States.* Washington, 1961.
———. Special Reports. *Religious Bodies: 1906.* 2 vols. Washington, 1910.
Congressional Record, 1895–1912. Washington, 1895–1912.
House of Representatives. *Hearings before the Committee on Agriculture . . . on the so-called "Beveridge Amendment."* Washington, 1906.
———. *House Doc. 263.* 59th Cong., 1st Sess. Washington, 1905–06.
Senate. *Compilation of Senate Election Cases from 1789 to 1913. Senate Doc. 1036.* 62nd Cong., 3rd Sess. Washington, 1913.
———. *Election of Isaac Stephenson. . . . Senate Doc. 312.* 62nd Cong., 2nd Sess. 2 vols. Washington, 1912.
———. *Election of William Lorimer. . . . A Copy of the Report of the Special Investigating Committee of the Illinois Senate, Douglas W. Helm, Chairman, in Regard to the Election of William Lorimer as United States Senator. Senate Doc. 45.* 62nd Cong., 1st Sess. Washington, 1912.
———. *Election of William Lorimer: Hearings before a Committee of the Senate Pursuant to Senate Resolution No. 60 Directing a Committee of the Senate to Investigate Whether Corrupt Methods and Practices Were Used or Employed in the Election of William Lorimer as a Senator of the United States from the State of Illinois. Senate Doc. 484.* 62nd Cong., 2nd Sess. 9 vols. Washington, 1912.
———. *Senate Doc. 769.* 2 parts. 62nd Cong., 1st Sess. Washington, 1912.
———. *Senate Report 942* [Burrows Committee hearings]. 4 parts. 61st Cong., 3rd Sess. Washington, 1911.

IV. Reports and Pamphlets

Adams, Frederick Upham. *The Story of Edward Hines Who Is Falsely Accused of Having Secured by Bribery the Election of William Lorimer to the Senate of the United States.* Chicago, n.d.
————. *The Plot That Failed.* N.p., n.d.
Chicago Bureau of Public Efficiency. *The City Manager Plan for Chicago.* Chicago, 1917.
————. *The Office of County Treasurer of Cook County.* Chicago, 1913.
Chicago Commercial Association. *From the Great Lakes to the Gulf of Mexico.* Chicago, 1906.
The Chicago Foreign Press Survey: A General Description of Its Contents. Chicago, 1942.
Citizen's Association of Chicago. *Annual Reports.* Chicago, 1900–1909.
————. *Bulletins.* Chicago, 1900–1909.
Cooley, Lyman E. *The Lakes and Gulf Waterway: A Brief.* Chicago, 1888.
————. *The Lakes and Gulf Waterway as Related to the Chicago Sanitary Problem: A Preliminary Report.* Chicago, 1891.
Hines, Edward. *Edward Hines to the Union League Club.* N.p., n.d.
Lakes-to-the-Gulf Deep Waterway Association. *Minutes of the First . . .* through *Sixth Annual Conventions.* St. Louis, 1906–12.
Legislative Voters' League. *Biennial Reports.* Chicago, 1902–12.
————. *The Illinois Legislature: Its Organization and Methods.* Chicago, 1903.
Merriam, Charles E. *Report on the Municipal Revenues of Chicago.* Chicago, 1906.
Municipal Voters' League. *Reports.* Chicago, 1897–1909.
The Truth about Governor Deneen and His Political Partner and Manager Roy O. West. N.p., n.d.

V. Unpublished Theses and Papers

Allswang, John M. "The Political Behavior of Chicago's Ethnic Groups, 1918–1932." Ph.D. dissertation, University of Pittsburgh, 1967.
Barfield, Claude E., Jr. "The Democratic Party in Congress, 1909–1913." Ph.D. dissertation, Northwestern University, 1965.
Beckman, Ellen J. "The Relationship of the Government of the City of Chicago to Cook County from 1893 to 1916." M.A. thesis, University of Chicago, 1940.
Blair, George Simms. "Cumulative Voting in Illinois." Ph.D. dissertation, Northwestern University, 1951.
Clubb, Jerome M. "Congressional Opponents of Reform, 1901–1913." Ph.D. dissertation, University of Washington, 1963.
Eisenstein, Sophie J. "The Election of 1912 in Chicago." M.A. thesis, University of Chicago, 1947.

Ellis, Lewis Ethan. "A History of the Chicago Delegation in Congress, 1843–1925." Ph.D. dissertation, University of Chicago, 1927.

Flynt, James Warne. "Duncan Upshaw Fletcher: Florida's Reluctant Progressive." Ph.D. dissertation, Florida State University, 1965.

Formisano, Ronald. "The Social Bases of American Voting Behavior, Wayne County, Michigan, 1837–1852, as a Test Case." Ph.D. dissertation, Wayne State University, 1966.

Forth, William Stuart. "Wesley L. Jones: A Political Biography." 2 vols. Ph.D. dissertation, University of Washington, 1962.

Forthal, Sonya. "Six Hundred Precinct Captains in the Chicago Party System 1926–1928." Ph.D. dissertation, American University, 1938.

Fulkerson, Stephen V. "History of the Democratic Party in Chicago, 1893–1895." M.A. thesis, University of Chicago, 1947.

Harlan, Homer Charles. "The Chicago Street Railway Franchise Struggle, 1897–1898." M.A. thesis, University of Chicago, 1948.

Hemdahl, Reuel Gustav. "The Swedes in Illinois Politics: An Immigrant Group in an American Political Setting." Ph.D. dissertation, Northwestern University, 1932.

Hoffman, George C. "Big Bill Thompson: His Mayoral Campaigns and Voting Strength." M.A. thesis, University of Chicago, 1956.

Hoing, Willard L. "James Wilson as Secretary of Agriculture, 1897–1913." Ph.D. dissertation, University of Wisconsin, 1964.

Jensen, Richard. "The Historical Roots of Party Identification." Mimeographed. Paper delivered at the American Political Science Association Convention, 1968.

―――. "The Winning of the Midwest: A Social History of Midwestern Elections, 1888–1896." Ph.D. dissertation, Yale University, 1967.

Kent, Elizabeth. "William Kent, Independent." Typewritten manuscript, University of Chicago, 1950.

Key, V. O., Jr. "The Techniques of Political Graft in the United States." Ph.D. dissertation, University of Chicago, 1934.

Kingsbury, Joseph Bush. "Municipal Personnel Policy in Chicago, 1895–1915." Ph.D. dissertation, University of Chicago, 1923.

Kleppner, Paul J. "The Political Revolution of the 1890's: A Behavioral Interpretation." Mimeographed. Paper delivered at the Midwest Political Science Association Convention, 1968.

―――. "The Politics of Change in the Midwest: The 1890's in Historical and Behavioral Perspective." Ph.D. dissertation, University of Pittsburgh, 1967.

Logsdon, Joseph A. "The Rev. Archibald J. Carey and the Negro in Chicago Politics." M.A. thesis, University of Chicago, 1961.

McSeveney, Samuel T. "The Political Realignment of the 1890's: Observations on the Northeast." Mimeographed. Paper delivered at the American Political Behavior—New Approaches Conference, State University of New York at Cortland, 1968.

―――. "The Politics of Depression: Voting Behavior in Connecticut, New

York, and New Jersey, 1893–1896." Ph.D. dissertation, University of Iowa, 1965.

————. "Voting in the Northeastern States during the Late Nineteenth Century." Mimeographed. Paper delivered at the University of Wisconsin Political and Social History Conference, 1968.

Marcus, Robert D. "Republican National Party Organization, 1880–1896." Ph.D. dissertation, Northwestern University, 1967.

Miller, Joan S. "The Politics of Municipal Reform in Chicago during the Progressive Era: The Municipal Voters' League as a Test Case, 1896–1920." M.A. thesis, Roosevelt University, 1966.

Mitchell, Rena. "The Congressional Career of James R. Mann." M.A. thesis, University of Chicago, 1938.

Philip, William Booth. "Chicago and the Down State: A Study of Their Conflicts, 1870–1934." Ph.D. dissertation, University of Chicago, 1940.

Pixton, John E., Jr. "The Early Career of Charles G. Dawes." Ph.D. dissertation, University of Chicago, 1952.

Roberts, Sidney I. "Businessmen in Revolt: Chicago 1874–1900." Ph.D. dissertion, Northwestern University, 1960.

Schmidt, Royal J. "The Chicago *Daily News* and Illinois Politics, 1876–1923." Ph.D. dissertation, University of Chicago, 1954.

Straetz, Ralph A. "The Progressive Movement in Illinois, 1910–1916." Ph.D. dissertation, University of Illinois, 1951.

Tarr, Joel A. "William Lorimer of Illinois: A Study in Boss Politics." Ph.D. dissertation, Northwestern University, 1963.

Tingley, Ralph. "Chicago Politics from Carter Harrison to Fred Busse, 1897–1907." Ph.D. dissertation, University of Chicago, 1952.

Tree, Robert L. "Victor Fremont Lawson and His Newspapers, 1890–1900: A Study of the Chicago *Daily News* and the Chicago *Record*." Ph.D. dissertation, Northwestern University, 1959.

Waller, Robert A. "Congressman Henry T. Rainey of Illinois: His Rise to the Speakership, 1903–1934." Ph.D. dissertation, University of Illinois, 1963.

Wish, Harvey. "The Administration of Governor John Peter Altgeld of Illinois, 1893–1897." Ph.D. dissertation, Northwestern University, 1936.

Wooddy, Carroll Hill. "The Direct Primary in Chicago." Ph.D. dissertation, University of Chicago, 1926.

VI. Autobiographies, Memoirs, and Published Letters

Addams, Jane. *Twenty Years at Hull House.* New York, 1910.

Busby, L. White, ed. *Uncle Joe Cannon: The Story of a Pioneer American.* New York, 1927.

Butt, Archie. *Taft and Roosevelt: The Intimate Letters of Archie Butt.* 2 vols. New York, 1930.

Clark, Champ. *My Quarter Century of American Politics.* 2 vols. New York, 1920.

Collins, Lorin C., Jr. *Autobiography.* Chicago, 1934.

Correspondencia Diplomática de la Delegación Cubana en Nueva York durante la Guerra de Independencia de 1895 a 1898. Publicaciones del Archivo Nacional de Cuba, Vol. V. Havana, 1946.

Coyne, Frederick E. *In Reminiscence: Highlights of Men and Events in the Life of Chicago.* Chicago, 1941.

Cullom, Shelby M. *Fifty Years of Public Service.* Chicago, 1911.

Dawes, Charles G. *A Journal of the McKinley Years, 1893–1913.* Ed. Bascom N. Timmons. Chicago. 1950.

Dunn, Arthur. *From Harrison to Harding: A Personal Narrative, Covering a Third of a Century, 1888–1921.* 2 vols. New York, 1922.

Foraker, Joseph Benson. *Notes on a Busy Life.* 2 vols. Cincinnati, 1916.

Harrison, Carter H. *Growing up with Chicago: Sequel to "Stormy Years."* Chicago, 1944.

————. *Stormy Years: The Autobiography of Carter H. Harrison, Five Times Mayor of Chicago.* Indianapolis, 1935.

Hermann, Charles H. *Recollections of Life and Doings in Chicago: From the Haymarket Riot to the End of World War I.* Chicago, 1945.

Ickes, Harold L. *The Autobiography of a Curmudgeon.* New York, 1943.

Kohlsaat, Herman H. *From McKinley to Harding: Personal Recollections of Our Presidents.* New York, 1923.

Kraus, Adolf. *Reminiscences and Comments.* Chicago, 1925.

Krenkel, John H., ed. *Serving the Republic—Richard Yates: An Autobiography.* Danville, 1968.

Morison, Elting E., ed. *The Letters of Theodore Roosevelt.* 8 vols. Cambridge, 1951–54.

Pinchot, Gifford. *Breaking New Ground.* New York, 1947.

Richberg, Donald. *My Hero: The Indiscreet Memoirs of an Eventful but Unheroic Life.* New York, 1954.

————. *Tents of the Mighty.* New York, 1930.

Steffens, Lincoln. *Autobiography.* New York, 1931.

Stephenson, Isaac. *Recollections of a Long Life 1829–1915.* Chicago, 1915.

Stuart, William H. *The Twenty Incredible Years.* Chicago, 1935.

Sullivan, William L., comp. *Dunne: Judge, Mayor, Governor.* Chicago, 1916.

Watson, James E. *As I Knew Them.* New York, 1936.

Wiley, Harvey. *An Autobiography.* Indianapolis, 1930.

Williams, H. Beaumont, ed. *A Many-Colored Toga: The Diary of Henry Fountain Ashurst.* Tucson, 1962.

VII. Secondary Books and Articles

A. BOOKS

Abbott, Edith. *The Tenements of Chicago 1908–1935.* Chicago, 1936.

Abrams, Richard M. *Conservatism in a Progressive Era: Massachusetts Politics 1900–1912.* Cambridge, 1964.

Acheson, Sam Hanna. *Joe Bailey, the Last Democrat.* New York, 1932.

Adams, William Forbes. *Ireland and Irish Emigration to the New World from 1815 to the Famine.* New Haven, 1932.

Addams, Jane, comp. *Hull House Maps and Papers: A Presentation of Nationalities and Wages in a Congested District of Chicago.* New York, 1895.

Allswang, John M. *A House for All Peoples: Ethnic Politics in Chicago, 1890–1936.* Lexington, 1971.

Anderson, Oscar E., Jr. *The Health of a Nation: Harvey W. Wiley and the Fight for Pure Food.* Chicago, 1958.

Andrews, Wayne. *Battle for Chicago.* New York, 1946.

Banfield, Edward C. *Political Influence.* New York, 1961.

———, and James Q. Wilson. *City Politics.* Cambridge, 1963; Vintage ed., New York, 1966.

Barnard, Harry. *"Eagle Forgotten": The Life of John Peter Altgeld.* New York, 1938.

Barron, Milton L., ed. *American Minorities.* New York, 1957.

Bean, Walton. *Boss Ruef's San Francisco.* Los Angeles, 1952.

Beer, Thomas. *Hanna, Crane, and the Mauve Decade.* New York, 1929, 1941.

Benson, Lee. *The Concept of Jacksonian Democracy: New York as a Test Case.* Atheneum ed., New York, 1964.

Bernheimer, Charles S., ed. *The Russian Jew in the United States.* Philadelphia, 1905.

Berthoff, Rowland T. *British Immigrants in Industrial America.* Cambridge, 1953.

Blum, John Morton. *The Republican Roosevelt.* Cambridge, 1954.

Bogart, Ernest Ludlow, and John Mabry Mathews. *The Modern Commonwealth: 1893–1918. The Centennial History of Illinois,* ed. Clarence W. Alvord, Vol. V. Springfield, 1920.

Bolles, Blair. *Tyrant from Illinois: Uncle Joe Cannon's Experiment with Personal Power.* New York, 1951.

Bowers, Claude G. *Beveridge and the Progressive Era.* Cambridge, 1932.

———. *The Life of John Worth Kern.* Indianapolis, 1918.

Bowers, David F., ed. *Foreign Influences in American Life.* Princeton, 1944.

Brent, Edgar W. *Martin B. Madden: Public Servant.* Chicago, 1901.

Brown, Thomas N. *Irish-American Nationalism 1870–1890.* Philadelphia, 1966.

Bryce, James. *The American Commonwealth.* 2 vols. New York, 1893.

Burner, David. *The Politics of Provincialism: The Democratic Party in Transition, 1918–1932.* New York, 1968.

Callow, Alexander B., Jr. *The Tweed Ring.* New York, 1966.

Church, Charles A. *History of the Republican Party in Illinois 1854–1912.* Rockford, 1912.

Clark, Norman H. *The Dry Years: Prohibition and Social Change in Washington.* Seattle, 1965.

Coletta, Paolo E. *William Jennings Bryan I. Political Evangelist, 1860–1908.* Lincoln, 1964.

Crissey, Forest. *Theodore E. Burton, American Statesman.* Cleveland, 1956.

Dahl, Robert A. *Who Governs? Democracy and Power in an American City.* New Haven, 1961.

Daily News Almanac and Political Register for 1892–1912. Chicago, 1893–1913.

David, Henry. *The History of the Haymarket Affair.* New York, 1936, 1958.

Davis, Allen F. *Spearheads for Reform: The Social Settlements and the Progressive Movement 1890–1914.* New York, 1967.

Davis, J. McCan. *The Breaking of the Deadlock.* Springfield, 1904.

Dennis, Charles H. *Victor Lawson: His Time and His Work.* Chicago, 1935.

Destler, Chester McArthur. *American Radicalism, 1865–1901.* Quadrangle ed., Chicago, 1966.

————. *Henry Demarest Lloyd and the Empire of Reform.* Philadelphia, 1963.

Dorsett, Lyle W. *The Pendergast Machine.* New York, 1968.

Dreier, Mary E. *Margaret Dreier Robins: Her Life, Letters, and Work.* New York, 1950.

Dunne, Edward F. *Illinois, the Heart of the Nation.* 5 vols. Chicago, 1933.

Eldersveld, Samuel J. *Political Parties: A Behavioral Analysis.* Chicago, 1964.

Ellis, Elmer. *Mr. Dooley's America: A Life of Finley Peter Dunne.* New York, 1941.

Ellis, L. Ethan. *Newsprint: Producers, Publishers, and Political Pressures.* New Brunswick, 1960.

————. *Reciprocity 1911.* New Haven, 1939.

Faulkner, Harold U. *Politics, Reform and Expansion, 1890–1900.* New York, 1959.

Froman, Lewis A., Jr. *Congressmen and Their Constituencies.* Chicago, 1963.

Fuchs, Lawrence H., ed. *American Ethnic Politics.* New York, 1968.

Gans, Herbert J. *The Urban Villagers.* Glencoe, 1962.

Garraty, John A. *Henry Cabot Lodge: A Biography.* New York, 1953.

————. *Right-Hand Man: The Life of George W. Perkins.* New York, 1960.

Gerson, Louis L. *The Hyphenate in Recent American Politics and Diplomacy.* Lawrence, 1964.

Ginger, Ray. *Altgeld's America: The Lincoln Ideal versus Changing Realities.* New York, 1958; Quadrangle ed., Chicago, 1965.

Glad, Paul W. *McKinley, Bryan, and the People.* New York, 1964.

Glazer, Nathan. *American Judaism.* Chicago, 1957.

————, and Daniel Patrick Moynihan. *Beyond the Melting Pot: The Negroes, Puerto Ricans, Jews, Italians, and Irish of New York City.* Cambridge, 1963.

Goodspeed, Weston A., and Daniel D. Healy. *History of Cook County, Illinois.* 2 vols. Chicago, 1909, 1935.

Gosnell, Harold F. *Machine Politics: Chicago Model.* Chicago. 1937.

————. *Negro Politicians: The Rise of Negro Politics in Chicago.* Chicago, 1935.

Gottfried, Alex. *Boss Cermak of Chicago: A Study in Political Leadership.* Seattle, 1962.

Grant, Bruce. *Fight for a City: The Story of the Union League Club of Chicago and Its Times, 1880–1955.* Chicago, 1956.

Grantham, Dewey W., Jr. *Hoke Smith and the Politics of the New South.* Baton Rouge, 1958; paperback ed., 1967.

Griffin, Clifford S. *Their Brothers' Keepers: Moral Stewardship in the United States, 1800–1865.* New Brunswick, 1960.

Gusfield, Joseph R. *Symbolic Crusade: Status Politics and the American Temperance Movement.* Urbana, 1963.

Gwinn, William Rea. *Uncle Joe Cannon: Arch Foe of Insurgency.* New York, 1957.

Haber, Samuel. *Efficiency and Uplift: Scientific Management in the Progressive Era, 1890–1920.* Chicago, 1964.

Handlin, Oscar. *The Uprooted.* New York, 1951.

Harbaugh, William Henry. *Power & Responsibility: The Life and Times of Theodore Roosevelt.* New York, 1961.

Haynes, George H. *The Senate of the United States: Its History and Practice.* 2 vols. Boston, 1938.

Hays, Samuel P. *Conservation and the Gospel of Efficiency: The Progressive Conservation Movement, 1890–1920.* Cambridge, 1959.

———. *The Response to Industrialism, 1885–1914.* Chicago, 1958.

Hechler, Kenneth W. *Insurgency: Personalities and Politics of the Taft Era.* New York, 1940.

Hidy, Ralph W., Frank Ernest Hill, and Allan Nevins. *Timber and Men: The Weyerhaeuser Story.* New York, 1963.

Higham, John. *Strangers in the Land: Patterns of American Nativism, 1860–1925.* New Brunswick, 1955.

Hofstadter, Richard. *The Age of Reform from Bryan to F.D.R.* New York, 1955.

Holli, Melvin G. *Reform in Detroit: Hazen S. Pingree and Urban Politics.* New York, 1969.

Holt, James. *Congressional Insurgents and the Party System, 1909–1916.* Cambridge, 1968.

Howe, Frederic C. *The City: The Hope of Democracy.* New York, 1905.

———. *The Modern City and Its Problems.* New York, 1915.

Hoyt, Homer. *One Hundred Years of Land Values in Chicago.* Chicago, 1933.

Hudson, Winthrop S. *Religion in America.* New York, 1965.

Hull, Denison Bingham. *The Legislative Life of Morton Denison Hull.* Chicago, 1948.

Hutchinson, William T. *Lowden of Illinois.* 2 vols. Chicago, 1957.

Huthmacher, J. Joseph. *Massachusetts People and Politics 1919–1933.* Cambridge, 1959.

Inter-Ocean. *A History of the City of Chicago.* Chicago, 1901.

Isaac, Paul E. *Prohibition and Politics: Turbulent Decades in Tennessee 1885–1920.* Knoxville, 1965.

James, F. Cyril. *The Growth of Chicago Banks.* 2 vols. New York, 1938.

Jessup, Philip C. *Elihu Root.* 2 vols. New York, 1938.

Jeter, Helen R. *Trends of Population in the Region of Chicago.* Chicago, 1927.

Johnson, Claudius O. *Carter Henry Harrison I: Political Leader.* Chicago, 1928.

Jones, Maldwyn Allen. *American Immigration*. Chicago, 1960.

Jones, Stanley L. *The Presidential Election of 1896*. Madison, 1964.

Key, V. O., Jr. *American State Politics: An Introduction*. New York, 1956.

———. *Politics, Parties, and Pressure Groups*. 4th ed. New York, 1958.

King, Hoyt. *Citizen Cole of Chicago*. Chicago, 1931.

Kinsley, Philip. *The Chicago Tribune: Its First Hundred Years*. 3 vols. Chicago, 1943–46.

Kirkland, Edward C. *Industry Comes of Age: Business, Labor, and Public Policy 1860–1897. The Economic History of the United States*, Vol. VI. New York, 1961.

Kleppner, Paul J. *The Cross of Culture: A Social Analysis of Midwestern Politics, 1850–1900*. New York, 1970.

Kolko, Gabriel. *The Triumph of Conservatism: A Reinterpretation of American History 1900–1916*. Glencoe, 1963.

LaFeber, Walter. *The New Empire: An Interpretation of American Expansion 1860–1898*. Ithaca, 1963.

La Follette, Belle Case and Fola. *Robert M. La Follette*. 2 vols. New York, 1953.

Lane, Robert E. *Political Life: Why People Get Involved in Politics*. Chicago, 1959.

Leech, Margaret. *In the Days of McKinley*. New York, 1959.

Lenski, Gerhard. *The Religious Factor: A Sociologist's Inquiry*. Anchor ed., Garden City, 1961.

Leopold, Richard W. *Elihu Root and the Conservative Tradition*. Boston, 1954.

Levine, Edward M. *The Irish and Irish Politicians*. Notre Dame, 1966.

Lewis, Lloyd, and Henry J. Smith. *Chicago: The History of Its Reputation*. New York, 1929.

Lindsey, Almont. *The Pullman Strike*. Chicago, 1942.

Link, Arthur S. *Wilson: Road to the White House*. Princeton, 1947.

———. *Woodrow Wilson and the Progressive Era*. New York, 1954.

Linn, James Weber. *James Keeley: Newspaperman*. New York, 1937.

Lipset, Seymour Martin. *Political Man: The Social Bases of Politics*. Garden City, 1960.

Luebke, Frederick C. *Immigrants and Politics: The Germans of Nebraska, 1880–1900*. Lincoln, 1969.

McDonald, Forrest. *Insull*. Chicago, 1962.

McKelvey, Blake. *The Urbanization of America 1860–1915*. New Brunswick, 1963.

McKenna, Marian C. *Borah*. Ann Arbor, 1961.

Mandelbaum, Seymour J. *Boss Tweed's New York*. New York, 1965.

Mann, Arthur. *La Guardia: A Fighter against His Times 1882–1933*. New York, 1959.

Marcus, Robert D. *Grand Old Party: Political Structure in the Gilded Age, 1880–1896*. New York, 1971.

Marquis, Albert N., comp. *The Book of Chicagoans*. Chicago, 1905, 1911.

———, ed. *Who's Who in Chicago, 1926*. Chicago, 1926.

Martin, Edward M. *The Role of the Bar in Electing the Bench in Chicago.* Chicago, 1936.

Masters, Edgar Lee. *The Tale of Chicago.* New York, 1933.

Matthews, Donald R. *U.S. Senators and Their World.* New York, 1960.

May, Ernest R. *American Imperialism.* New York, 1968.

————. *Imperial Democracy: The Emergence of America as a Great Power.* New York, 1961.

May, Henry. *The End of American Innocence: A Study of the First Years of Our Own Time 1912–1917.* New York, 1959.

Merriam, Charles E. *Chicago: A More Intimate View of Urban Politics.* New York, 1929.

————, Spencer D. Parratt, and Albert Lepawsky. *The Government of the Metropolitan Region of Chicago.* Chicago, 1933.

Merton, Robert K. *Social Theory and Social Structure.* Rev. ed. Glencoe, 1957.

Miller, William D. *Boss Crump of Memphis.* Baton Rouge, 1964.

Miller, Zane L. *Boss Cox's Cincinnati: Urban Politics in the Progressive Era.* New York, 1968.

Moore, Blaine F. *The History of Cumulative Voting and Minority Representation in Illinois, 1870–1919.* Urbana, 1919.

Morgan, H. Wayne. *William McKinley and His America.* Syracuse, 1963.

————, ed. *The Gilded Age: A Reappraisal.* Syracuse, 1963.

Mowry, George E. *The Era of Theodore Roosevelt, 1900–1912.* New York, 1958.

————. *Theodore Roosevelt and the Progressive Movement.* New York, 1946.

Munro, William Bennett. *The Government of American Cities.* 3rd ed. New York, 1920.

Neilson, James W. *Shelby M. Cullom: Prairie State Republican.* Urbana, 1962.

Nelli, Humbert S. *Italians in Chicago 1880–1930.* New York, 1970.

Nevins, Allan. *Grover Cleveland: A Study in Courage.* New York, 1932.

Norton, Samuel Wilber. *Chicago Traction: A History, Legislative and Political.* Chicago, 1907.

Nye, Russell B. *Midwestern Progressive Politics: A Historical Study of Its Origins and Development 1870–1958.* Harper Torchbook ed., New York, 1965.

Orcutt, William Dana. *Burrows of Michigan and the Republican Party.* 2 vols. New York, 1917.

Ostrander, Gilman M. *The Prohibition Movement in California, 1848–1933.* Berkeley, 1957.

Ostrogorski, M. *Democracy and the Organization of Political Parties.* Ed. and abr. Seymour Martin Lipset. 2 vols. Garden City, 1964.

Overacker, Louise. *Money in Elections.* New York, 1932.

Peterson, Virgil W. *Barbarians in Our Midst: A History of Chicago Crime and Politics.* Boston, 1952.

Pierce, Bessie Louise. *A History of Chicago.* 3 vols. Chicago, 1937–57.

————, ed. *As Others See Chicago: Impressions of Visitors 1673–1933.* Chicago, 1933.

Phillips, Clifton J. *Indiana in Transition: The Emergence of an Industrial Commonwealth, 1880–1920.* Indianapolis, 1968.

Poole, Ernest. *Giants Gone: Men Who Made Chicago.* New York, 1943.

Pratt, Julius W. *Expansionists of 1898.* Baltimore, 1936; Quadrangle ed., Chicago, 1964.

Pringle, Henry F. *The Life and Times of William Howard Taft.* 2 vols. New York, 1939.

Rapport, George C. *The Statesman and the Boss: A Study of American Political Leadership Exemplified by Woodrow Wilson and Frank Hague.* New York, 1961.

Raum, Green B. *History of Illinois Republicanism.* Chicago, 1900.

Richardson, Leon B. *William E. Chandler, Republican.* New York, 1940.

Riordan, William L. *Plunkitt of Tammany Hall.* New York, 1948.

Rischin, Moses. *The Promised City: New York's Jews, 1870–1914.* Cambridge, 1962; New York, 1964.

Robinson, Edgar Eugene. *The Presidential Vote 1896–1932.* Stanford, 1947.

Robinson, William A. *Thomas B. Reed: Parliamentarian.* New York, 1930.

Ross, Thomas R. *Jonathan Prentiss Dolliver: A Study in Political Integrity and Independence.* Iowa City, 1958.

Rothman, David J. *Politics and Power: The United States Senate, 1869–1901.* Cambridge, 1966.

Sage, Leland L. *William Boyd Allison: A Study in Practical Politics.* Iowa City, 1956.

Salter, J. T. *Boss Rule: Portraits in City Politics.* New York, 1935.

Schrier, Arnold. *Ireland and the American Emigration 1850–1900.* Minneapolis, 1958.

Shannon, William V. *The American Irish.* New York, 1963.

Shaughnessy, Gerald. *Has the Immigrant Kept the Faith?* New York, 1969.

Sinclair, Upton. *The Jungle.* New York, 1906.

Smith, Edwin Burritt. *Essays and Addresses.* Chicago, 1909.

Smith, Timothy L. *Revivalism & Social Reform: American Protestantism on the Eve of the Civil War.* New York, 1957.

Sparling, Samuel E. *Municipal History and Present Organization of the City of Chicago.* Madison, 1898.

Spear, Allan H. *Black Chicago: The Making of a Negro Ghetto 1890–1920.* Chicago, 1967.

Stead, William T. *If Christ Came to Chicago!* Chicago, 1894.

Steffens, Lincoln. *The Shame of the Cities.* New York, 1904, 1960.

———. *The Struggle for Self-Government.* New York, 1906.

Steiner, Gilbert, and Samuel K. Gove. *Legislative Politics in Illinois.* Urbana, 1960.

Stephenson, George M. *The Religious Aspects of Swedish Immigration: A Study of Immigrant Churches.* Minneapolis, 1932.

Strickland, Arvarh. *History of the Chicago Urban League.* Urbana, 1966.

Tebbel, John. *An American Dynasty: The Story of the McCormicks, Medills, and Pattersons.* Garden City, 1947.

Thrasher, Frederic M. *The Gang: A Study of 1,313 Gangs in Chicago.* Chicago, 1936; Phoenix abr. ed., Chicago, 1963.

Timberlake, James H. *Prohibition and the Progressive Movement 1900–1920.* Cambridge, 1963.

Townsend, Andrew J. *The Germans of Chicago.* Chicago, 1927.

Townsend, Walter A. *Illinois Democracy.* Springfield, 1935.

Truman, David B., ed. *The Congress and America's Future.* Englewood Cliffs, 1965.

Wade, Louise C. *Graham Taylor: Pioneer for Social Justice, 1851–1938.* Chicago, 1964.

Waldrop, Frank C. *McCormick of Chicago: An Unconventional Portrait of a Controversial Figure.* Englewood Cliffs, 1966.

Walters, Everett. *Joseph Benson Foraker, an Uncompromising Republican.* Columbus, 1948.

Warner, Sam B., Jr. *The Private City: Philadelphia in Three Periods of Its Growth.* Philadelphia, 1968.

———. *Streetcar Suburbs: The Process of Growth in Boston, 1870–1900.* Cambridge, 1962.

Waterman, A. N. *Historical Review of Chicago and Cook County.* Chicago, 1908.

Weber, Harry P. *Outline History of Chicago Traction.* N.p., n.d.

Weiss, Nancy Joan. *Charles Francis Murphy, 1858–1924: Respectability and Responsibility in Tammany Politics.* Northampton, 1968.

Wendt, Lloyd, and Herman Kogan. *Bet a Million! The Story of John W. Gates.* New York, 1948.

———, and Herman Kogan. *Big Bill of Chicago.* Indianapolis, 1953.

———, and Herman Kogan. *Lords of the Levee: The Story of Bathhouse John and Hinky Dink.* New York, 1943.

White, William S. *Citadel: The Story of the U.S. Senate.* New York, 1956.

Whyte, William F. *Street Corner Society: The Social Structure of an Italian Slum.* Chicago, 1943, 1955.

Wiebe, Robert H. *Businessmen and Reform: A Study of the Progressive Movement.* Cambridge, 1962.

———. *The Search for Order 1877–1920.* New York, 1967.

Wilensky, Norman M. *Conservatives in the Progressive Era: The Taft Republicans of 1912.* Gainesville, 1965.

Wirth, Louis. *The Ghetto.* Chicago, 1928; Phoenix ed., Chicago, 1956.

Wooddy, Carroll Hill. *The Case of Frank L. Smith: A Study in Representative Government.* Chicago, 1931.

———. *The Chicago Primary of 1926: A Study in Election Methods.* Chicago, 1926.

Young, James Harvey. *The Toadstool Millionaires: A Social History of Patent Medicines in America before Federal Regulation.* Princeton, 1961.

Zink, Harold. *City Bosses in the United States.* Durham, 1930.

Zueblin, Charles. *American Municipal Progress.* New York, 1916.

B. ARTICLES

Allen, Howard W. "Geography and Politics: Voting on Reform Issues in the United States Senate, 1911–1916." *Journal of Southern History* (May, 1961), XXVII, 216–228.

Auxier, George W. "The Propaganda Activities of the Cuban *Junta* in Precipitating the Spanish-American War, 1895–1898." *The Hispanic American Review* (Aug., 1939), XXIX, 286–305.

Barnes, James A. "Illinois and the Gold-Silver Controversy, 1890–1896." *Transactions of the Illinois State Historical Society* (Springfield, 1931), XXXII, 35–59.

Bell, Daniel. "Crime as an American Way of Life." In *The End of Ideology* (rev. ed., New York, 1961), 127–150.

Benson, Lee. "Research Problems in American Political Historiography." In *Common Frontiers of the Social Sciences,* ed. Mirra Komarovsky (Glencoe, 1957), 113–183.

Benton, Elbert J. "George Wheeler Hinman." In *Dictionary of American Biography,* ed. Dumas Malone (New York, 1933), IX, 65.

Bonsard, Stephen. "William James Calhoun." In *Dictionary of American Biography,* ed. Dumas Malone (New York, 1933), III, 420.

Bradley, Donald S., and Mayer N. Zald. "From Commercial Elite to Political Administrator: The Recruitment of the Mayors of Chicago." *American Journal of Sociology* (Sept., 1965), LXXI, 153–167.

Braeman, John. "The Square Deal in Action: A Case Study in the Growth of the 'National Police Power.'" In *Change and Continuity in Twentieth-Century America,* ed. John Braeman, Robert H. Bremner, and Everett Walters (Columbus, 1964), 35–80; Harper Colophon ed. (New York, 1966), 35–80.

Buenker, John D. "Edward F. Dunne: The Urban New Stock Democrat as Progressive." *Mid-America* (Jan., 1968), L, 3–21.

————. "Urban Immigrant Lawmakers and Progressive Reform in Illinois." In *Essays in Illinois History in Honor of Glen Huron Seymour,* ed. Donald F. Tingley (Carbondale, 1968), 52–74.

Burnham, John C. "New Perspectives on the Prohibition 'Experiment' of the 1920's." *Journal of Social History* (Fall, 1968), II, 51–68.

Burnham, Walter Dean. "The Changing Shape of the American Political Universe." *American Political Science Review* (Mar., 1965), LIX, 7–28.

Clubb, Jerome M., and Howard W. Allen. "Party Loyalty in the Progressive Years: The Senate, 1909–1915." *Journal of Politics* (Aug., 1967), XXIX, 567–584.

Cornwell, Elmer E., Jr. "Bosses, Machines, and Ethnic Groups." In "City Bosses and Political Machines," ed. Lee S. Greene. *Annals of the American Academy of Political and Social Science* (May, 1964), CCCLIII, 27–39.

Davis, Allen F. "Jane Addams vs. the Ward Boss." *Journal of the Illinois State Historical Society* (Summer, 1960), LIII, 247–265.

Davis, Allen F. "Raymond Robins: The Settlement Worker as Municipal Reformer." *Social Service Review* (June, 1959), XXXIII, 131–141.

———. "Settlement Workers in Politics, 1890–1914." *Review of Politics* (Oct., 1964), XXVI, 505–517.

Degler, Carl N. "American Political Parties and the Rise of the Cities: An Interpretation." *Journal of American History* (June, 1964), LI, 41–59.

Diamond, William. "Urban and Rural Voting in 1896." *American Historical Review* (Jan., 1941), XLVI, 281–305.

Dozer, Donald M. "Benjamin Harrison and the Presidential Campaign of 1892." *American Historical Review* (Oct., 1948), LIV, 49–69.

Ellis, Lewis Ethan. "A History of the Chicago Delegation in Congress, 1843–1925." *Transactions of the Illinois State Historical Society* (Springfield, 1930), XXXVII, 52–149.

———. "Martin Barnaby Madden." In *Dictionary of American Biography,* ed. Dumas Malone (New York, 1933), XII, 180–181.

———. "William Ernest Mason." In *Dictionary of American Biography,* ed. Dumas Malone (New York, 1933), XII, 379.

Ford, Henry Jones. "Municipal Corruption." *Political Science Quarterly* (1904), XIX, 676–686.

Formisano, Ronald. "Analyzing American Voting, 1830–1860: Methods." *Historical Methods Newsletter* (Mar., 1969), II, 2–11.

Greene, Victor R. "For God and Country: The Origins of Slavic Catholic Self-Consciousness in America." *Church History* (Dec., 1966), XXXV, 1–15.

Greenstein, Fred I. "The Changing Pattern of Urban Party Politics." In "City Bosses and Political Machines," ed. Lee S. Greene. *Annals of the American Academy of Political and Social Science* (May, 1964), CCCLIII, 1–13.

Greer, Scott. "Catholic Voters and the Democratic Party." *Public Opinion Quarterly* (Winter, 1961), XXV, 611–625.

Harvard, William C. "From Bossism to Cosmopolitanism: Changes in the Relationship of Urban Leadership to State Politics." In "City Bosses and Political Machines," ed. Lee S. Greene. *Annals of the American Academy of Political and Social Science* (May, 1964), CCCLIII, 84–94.

Hays, Samuel P. "Political Parties and the Community-Society Continuum." In *The American Party Systems: Stages of Political Development,* ed. William Nisbet Chambers and Walter Dean Burnham (New York, 1967), 152–181.

———. "The Politics of Reform in Municipal Government in the Progressive Era." *Pacific Northwest Quarterly* (Oct., 1964), LV, 157–169.

———. "The Social Analysis of American Political History, 1880–1920." *Political Science Quarterly* (Sept., 1965), LXXX, 373–394.

Hoffman, Charles. "The Depression of the Nineties." *Journal of Economic History* (June, 1956), XVI, 137–164.

Holbo, Paul S. "The Convergence of Moods and the Cuban-Bond 'Conspiracy' of 1898." *Journal of American History* (June, 1968), LV, 54–72.

————. "Presidential Leadership in Foreign Affairs: William McKinley and the Turpie-Foraker Amendment." *American Historical Review* (July, 1967), LXXII, 1321–35.

Huthmacher, J. Joseph. "Urban Liberalism and the Age of Reform." *Mississippi Valley Historical Review* (Sept., 1962), XLIX, 231–241.

Key, V. O., Jr. "A Theory of Critical Elections." *Journal of Politics* (Feb., 1955), XVII, 3–18.

Kleppner, Paul J. "Lincoln and the Immigrant Vote: A Case of Religious Polarization." *Mid-America* (July, 1966), XLVIII, 176–195.

Lerner, Max. "John W. Gates." In *Dictionary of American Biography,* ed. Dumas Malone (New York, 1933), VII, 188–190.

————, and Mary F. Holter. "Charles Tyson Yerkes." In *Dictionary of American Biography,* ed. Dumas Malone (New York, 1933), XX, 609–611.

Luebke, Frederick C. "German Immigrants and Churches in Nebraska, 1889–1915." *Mid-America* (April, 1968), L, 116–130.

McKitrick, Eric L. "The Study of Corruption." *Political Science Quarterly* (Dec., 1957), LXXII, 502–514.

Macrae, Duncan, Jr., and James A. Neldrum. "Critical Elections in Illinois: 1888–1958." *American Political Science Review* (Sept., 1960), LIV, 669–683.

Marshall, George. "Charles Tyson Yerkes." In *Encyclopaedia of the Social Sciences,* ed. Edwin R. A. Seligman (New York, 1934), XV, 513–514.

Miller, Warren E., and Donald E. Stokes. "Constituency Influence in Congress." In *Elections and the Political Order,* ed. Angus Campbell *et al.* (New York, 1966), 351–372.

Morgan, H. Wayne. "William McKinley as a Political Leader." *Review of Politics* (Oct., 1966), XXVIII, 417–432.

Paxson, Frederick L. "Herman Henry Kohlsaat." In *Dictionary of American Biography,* ed. Dumas Malone (New York, 1933), X, 489–490.

Regier, C. C. "The Struggle for Federal Food and Drug Legislation." *Law and Contemporary Problems* (Dec., 1933), I, 3–15.

Riedel, James A. "Boss and Faction." In "City Bosses and Political Machines," ed. Lee S. Greene. *Annals of the American Academy of Political and Social Science* (May, 1964), CCCLIII, 14–26.

Roberts, Sidney I. "The Municipal Voters' League and Chicago's Boodlers." *Journal of the Illinois State Historical Society* (Summer, 1960), LIII, 117–148.

————. "Portrait of a Robber Baron: Charles T. Yerkes." *Business History Review* (Autumn, 1961), XXXV, 344–371.

Ross, Edward A. "Immigrants in Politics." In *Immigration: An American Dilemma,* ed. Benjamin M. Ziegler (Boston, 1953), 71–77.

Simon, Paul, and Alfred Balk. "The Illinois Legislature: A Study in Corruption." *Harper's Magazine* (Sept., 1964), CCXXIX, 74–78.

Solvick, Stanley D. "William Howard Taft and the Payne-Aldrich Tariff." *Mississippi Valley Historical Review* (Dec., 1963), L, 430.

Stone, Ralph A. "Two Illinois Senators among the Irreconcilables." *Mississippi Valley Historical Review* (Dec., 1963), L, 445.

Strevey, Tracy E. "Joseph Medill." In *Dictionary of American Biography,* ed. Dumas Malone (New York, 1933), XII, 491–492.

Tarr, Joel A. "John R. Walsh of Chicago: A Case Study in Banking and Politics, 1881–1905." *Business History Review* (Winter, 1966), XL, 451–466.

———. "President Theodore Roosevelt and Illinois Politics, 1901–1904." *Journal of the Illinois State Historical Society* (Autumn, 1965), LVIII, 245–264.

———. "The Urban Politician as Entrepreneur." *Mid-America* (Jan., 1967), XLIX, 55–67.

———. "William Kent to Lincoln Steffens: Origins of Progressive Reform in Chicago." *Mid-America* (Jan., 1965), XLVII, 48–57.

Taylor, George Rogers. "The Beginnings of Mass Transportation in Urban America, Parts I & II." *Smithsonian Journal of History* (Summer, Autumn, 1966), I, no. 2, 35–50; no. 3, 31–54.

Thernstrom, Stephan. "Urbanization, Migration, and Social Mobility in Late Nineteenth-Century America." In *Towards a New Past: Dissenting Essays in American History,* ed. Barton J. Bernstein (New York, 1967), 158–175.

Thomas, R. G. "Bank Failures in Chicago before 1925." *Journal of the Illinois State Historical Society* (Oct., 1935), XXVIII, 188–203.

Wade, Richard C. "The City in History—Some American Perspectives." In *Urban Life and Form,* ed. Werner Z. Hirsch (New York, 1963), 59–80.

———. "Urbanization." In *The Comparative Approach to American History,* ed. C. Vann Woodward (New York, 1968), 197–199.

Weinstein, James. "Organized Business and the City Commission and Manager Movements." *Journal of Southern History* (May, 1962), XXVIII, 166–182.

West, Roy O., and William C. Walton. "Charles S. Deneen, 1863–1940." *Journal of the Illinois State Historical Society* (Mar., 1941), XXXIV, 12–27.

Wilson, James Q. "The Political Economy of Patronage." *Journal of Political Economy* (Aug., 1961), LIX, 369–380.

Wish, Harvey. "John Peter Altgeld and the Election of 1896." *Journal of the Illinois State Historical Society* (Oct., 1937), XXX, 353–384.

Wolfinger, Raymond E. "The Development and Persistence of Ethnic Voting." *American Political Science Review* (Dec., 1965), LIX, 896–908.

VIII. Interviews

Blaisdell, Fred W. June 27, 1960. Chicago.
Dienhart, John. Oct. 31, 1960. Chicago.
Insull, Samuel, Jr. Aug. 24, 1964. Chicago.
Kucharski, Felix. Feb. 8, Aug. 2, 1960. Chicago.
Lorimer, Walter L. M. Apr. 23, 1964. Beverly Hills.
Lorimer, Mrs. William Healy. Aug. 20, 1964. Chicago.
Lyle, Judge John H. Dec. 26, 1961. Chicago.

O'Brien, Congressman Thomas J. Nov. 15, 1960. Chicago.
O'Hara, Congressman Barrat. Nov. 14, 1960. Chicago.
Southerland, Douglas. Feb. 21, 1961. Chicago.
Stuart, William. July 4, 1960. Chicago.

Index

★　★　★　★　★　★　★　★　★　★　★

DATE DUE

APR 7

APR 2 5 72

MAY 1 1 1973

GAYLORD

PRINTED IN U.S.A.

E
748
L87
T19

Tarr, Joel Arthur.
    A study in boss politics: William Lorimer of Chicago.
Urbana, University of Illinois Press ₁1971₁

    xi, 376 p. illus., facsim., map, ports. 24 cm. $12.50
    Bibliography: p. 335–357.

241735

    1. Lorimer, William, 1861–1934. 2. Illinois—Politics and govern-
ment—1865–1950.   I. Title.

E748.L892T3   328.73′0924 [B]   72–133945
ISBN 0-252-00139-7   MARC

Library of Congress   71 ₁4₁